Mathematical Models of Perception and Cognition Volume I

In this two-volume Festschrift, contributors explore the theoretical developments (Volume I) and applications (Volume II) in traditional cognitive psychology domains and model other areas of human performance that benefit from rigorous mathematical approaches. It brings together former classmates, students, and colleagues of Dr. James T. Townsend, a pioneering researcher in the field since the early 1960s, to provide a current overview of mathematical modeling in psychology. Townsend's research critically emphasized a need for rigor in the practice of cognitive modeling and for providing mathematical definition and structure to ill-defined psychological topics. The research captured demonstrates how the interplay of theory and application, bridged by rigorous mathematics, can move cognitive modeling forward.

Joseph W. Houpt is Assistant Professor of Psychology, Wright State University, USA.

Leslie M. Blaha is Engineering Research Psychologist, United States Air Force Research Laboratory, USA.

Scientific Psychology

SERIES EDITORS: James T. Townsend, Indiana University Bloomington, USA, and Stephen Link, University of California San Diego, USA

For a full list of titles in this series, please visit www.routledge.com

16 **Psychophysics Beyond Sensation**
   Laws and Invariants of Human Cognition
   Edited by Christian Kaernbach, Erich Schr"ger, Hermann Miller, Hermann Muller, and Erich Schroger

17 **Measurement and Representation of Sensations**
   Edited by Hans Colonius and Ehtibar N. Dzhafarov

18 **Introduction to the Theories of Measurement and Meaningfulness and the Use of Symmetry in Science**
   Louis Narens

19 **Unified Social Cognition**
   Norman Anderson

20 **Information-Processing Channels in the Tactile Sensory System**
   A Psychophysical and Physiological Analysis
   George A. Gescheider, John H. Wright, and Ronald T. Verrillo

21 **Measurement With Persons**
   Theory, Methods, and Implementation Areas
   Edited by Birgitta Berglund, Giovanni B. Rossi, James T. Townsend, and Leslie R. Pendrill

22 **Mathematical Principles of Human Conceptual Behavior**
   The Structural Nature of Conceptual Representation and Processing
   Ronaldo Vigo

23 **Mathematical Models of Perception and Cognition Volume I**
   A Festschrift for James T. Townsend
   Edited by Joseph M. Houpt and Leslie W. Blaha

Mathematical Models of Perception and Cognition Volume I

Edited by Joseph W. Houpt and Leslie M. Blaha

NEW YORK AND LONDON

First published 2016
by Routledge
711 Third Avenue, New York, NY 10017

and by Routledge
2 Park Square, Milton Park, Abingdon, Oxon OX14 4RN

First issued in paperback 2018

Routledge is an imprint of the Taylor & Francis Group, an informa business

© 2016 Taylor & Francis

The right of Joseph Houpt and Leslie Blaha to be identified as editors of this work has been asserted by them in accordance with sections 77 and 78 of the Copyright, Designs and Patents Act 1988.

All rights reserved. No part of this book may be reprinted or reproduced or utilised in any form or by any electronic, mechanical, or other means, now known or hereafter invented, including photocopying and recording, or in any information storage or retrieval system, without permission in writing from the publishers.

Trademark Notice: Product or corporate names may be trademarks or registered trademarks, and are used only for identification and explanation without intent to infringe.

Library of Congress Cataloguing-in-Publication Data
Names: Houpt, Joseph W., Author. | Blaha, Leslie M., Author.
Title: Mathematical models of perception and cognition / by Joseph W. Houpt and Leslie M. Blaha.
1 Edition. | New York : Routledge, 2016- | Series: Scientific psychology ; 24 | Includes bibliographical references and index.
Identifiers: LCCN 2015049077 | ISBN 9781138125766
Subjects: LCSH: Psychology–Mathematical models. | Cognitive psychology.
Classification: LCC BF39 .H688 2016 | DDC 153.01/51–dc23
LC record available at https://lccn.loc.gov/2015049077

A catalog record for this book has been requested

ISBN 13: 978-1-138-60026-3 (pbk)
ISBN 13: 978-1-138-12576-6 (hbk)

Typeset in Sabon
by Apex CoVantage, LLC

These volumes are dedicated to Distinguished Rudy Professor James Tarlton Townsend in recognition of his many contributions to Mathematical Psychology, cognitive modeling and generally to the scientific study of human perception and cognition. He has influenced these areas through research, mentorship, professional service and collegiality.

Contents

Figures and Tables xi

1 **Introduction** 1
LESLIE M. BLAHA AND JOSEPH W. HOUPT
   1.1 *A Brief Biography of James Townsend 3*

2 **High-Probability Logic and Inheritance** 13
DONALD BAMBER, I. R. GOODMAN, AND HUNG T. NGUYEN
   2.1 *Reasoning With Imperfect Rules 13*
   2.2 *High-Probability Logics 18*
   2.3 *Weak Versus Strong Association 26*
   2.4 *Extending High-Probability Logics 29*
   2.5 *Relevance of High-Probability Logics to the Study of Human Reasoning 32*
   2.6 *Summary and Conclusion 33*

3 **Stochastic Orders of Variability** 37
HANS COLONIUS
   3.1 *Introduction: Some Variability Orders 37*
   3.2 *The Quantile Spread 40*
   3.3 *The Quantile Spread Order 42*
   3.4 *The Quantile Spread Order for the Kumaraswamy Distribution 43*

4 **Subset System: Mathematical Abstraction of Object and Context** 47
JUN ZHANG AND YITONG SUN
   4.1 *Introduction 47*
   4.2 *Mathematical Preliminaries 50*
   4.3 *Pre-order and Tolerance on V Induced from (V, E) 53*
   4.4 *Discussion 63*

viii Contents

5 Uniqueness of a Multinomial Processing Tree Constructed by
   Knowing Which Pairs of Processes Are Ordered   65
   RICHARD SCHWEICKERT AND HYE JOO HAN

   5.1 Combining Information About Different Pairs
        of Processes 68
   5.2 When Is a Tree Possible? 70
   5.3 When Is Only One Tree Possible? 73
   5.4 Conclusion 74

6 Simple Factorial Tweezers for Detecting Delicate Serial
   and Parallel Processes   77
   MARIO FIFIĆ

   6.1 The Theoretical Breakthrough 79
   6.2 Pure Stretching Method 80
   6.3 Single Factor Manipulation: Stretching One Process 80
   6.4 Double Factorial Manipulation: Stretching
        Two Processes 81
   6.5 SFT Statistical Tests for Two-Process
        Mental Networks (N = 2): MIC and SIC 82
   6.6 SFT Statistical Tests for 2-Process
        Mental Networks (N = 2): The Principle Limitations 87
   6.7 N-Factorial SIC for Homogeneous Systems:
        Advances to Higher Factorials 87
   6.8 Statistical Tests, the SIC General Form 88
   6.9 Limitations 89
   6.10 Simple Factorial SIC Functions for
        Homogenous Systems 90
   6.11 Limitations 92
   6.12 N-Factorial SIC for Non-homogenous Networks 94
   6.13 Statistical Tests and Subnetwork Decomposability 95
   6.14 Findings 96
   6.15 Limitations 97
   6.16 Putting It All Together: Homogeneous and
        Non-homogeneous Subnetworks N = 2 97
   6.17 Discussion 100

7 Identifying Spatiotemporal Information   107
   JOSEPH S. LAPPIN

   7.1 Introduction: From Stimulation to Information 108
   7.2 Visual Representations of Spatiotemporal Variation 117
   7.3 Empirical Criteria: Resolution and Invariance 130
   7.4 Conclusion 144

Contents ix

8 Models of Intertemporal Choice   152
JUNYI DAI AND JEROME R. BUSEMEYER

- 8.1 Probabilistic Models of Intertemporal Choice 154
- 8.2 Results of Model Fitting and Comparisons 163
- 8.3 Mental Architecture and Stopping Rules of Intertemporal Choice 165
- 8.4 Equivalence Between Intertemporal Choice Models 166
- 8.5 Concluding Comments 168

9 Variations on the Theme of Independence: Tasks and Effects of Stroop, Garner, and Townsend   171
DANIEL ALGOM

- 9.1 Selective Attention and Perceptual Independence: A Bit of History 172
- 9.2 General Recognition Theory and the Selectivity of Attention 175
- 9.3 The Stroop Effect and Perceptual Separability 181
- 9.4 Garnerian Separable Dimensions and GRT Perceptual Separability 186
- 9.5 Conclusion 191
- 9.6 Epilogue: The Marriage of Selectivity and Independence Gets Personal 192

10 Modeling Interactive Dimensions in a Component Comparison Task Using General Recognition Theory   197
ROBIN D. THOMAS, NOAH H. SILBERT,
EMILY GROSSMAN, AND SHAWN ELL

- 10.1 Introduction 197
- 10.2 GRT and the Same-Different Task 198
- 10.3 Perceptual Interactions and Component Comparisons 206
- 10.4 Conclusions 219

11 Symmetry Provides a Turing-Type Test for 3D Vision   223
ZYGMUNT PIZLO

- 11.1 Introduction 223
- 11.2 How Physicists Explain Natural Phenomena 224
- 11.3 Importing the Least-Action Principle Into Perception 226
- 11.4 Bringing Symmetry into Theories of Perception 228
- 11.5 Veridicality of 3D Shape Perception Seen as a Conservation Law 230
- 11.6 Empirical Tests Verifying that Čapek Sees as We Do 234
- 11.7 Generality and Implications of Our Test 236

12 Cognitive Psychometrics — 245
WILLIAM H. BATCHELDER

12.1 Introduction 245
12.2 Mathematics and Statistics in Psychology 247
12.3 Behavioral Learning Theory and Cognitive Modeling 248
12.4 Comparing Cognitive Modeling and Psychometric Test Theory 252
12.5 Examples of Cognitive Psychometric Models 257
12.6 Conclusion 262

Index 267

Figures and Tables

Figures

3.1 Two Weibull distributions with $\alpha = 2$ and $\alpha = 6$, and $\beta = 2$. The horizontal arrows indicate their quantile spread at $p = 0.8$. The order $\leq_{QS}$ is defined in the next section.   41

5.1 A multinomial processing tree. The arc directed from vertex x to vertex y indicates that the process represented by x precedes the process represented by y. Vertices x and y are ordered. Interpretation of other arcs is analogous. Each arc occurs with a certain probability. Probabilities are not illustrated.   66

5.2 The comparability graph corresponding to the multinomial processing tree in Figure 5.1. An edge between two vertices indicates that the two processes represented by the vertices are ordered, but it does not indicate which precedes which. Arrow heads can be drawn on the edges to indicate precedence.   71

5.3 In the comparability graph of Figure 5.2, suppose x is arbitrarily selected to precede a. Then x is forced to precede y, b, and c. Directions of no other edges are forced.   71

5.4 All the oriented edges, arbitrarily selected or forced, are removed from the graph. A new arbitrary orientation will be made, and the procedure will continue.   72

6.1 (a) The showcase of the distinct diagnostic predictions of MIC and SIC patterns for each mental network (rows) of a size up to four processes (columns) for fullfactorial research designs (top row). For the serial-exhaustive mental network, the circles emphasize the intersection points of the SIC function and x-axis. (b) The bottom row indicates the type of simple interaction factorial test, derived from the 4-way full-factorial design. Each column indicates 2-way simple,

xii *Figures and Tables*

        3-way simple, and 4-way full-factorial designs and corresponding diagnostic predictions of MIC and SIC patterns. Note that all six 2-way simple interaction designs predict equivalent SICs and MICs for different mental networks. The same holds for the four 3-way simple interaction designs. Both (A) and (B) predicted MIC and SIC results are only relevant for the homogeneous mental networks (see the text for more details).   85

6.2 The simple interaction SIC test for the three-factorial research design. The research design, starting with the full-factorial design, are displayed in the first column, crossed with the different types of mental networks. Although the full-factorial SIC cannot distinguish between parallel minimum-time and parallel exhaustive models (the first row, SICs of the models are in a box), the simple 2-way factorial SIC (the second row, boxed) can distinguish between the two.   92

6.3 SIC function predictions for the serial and parallel subnetworks, crossed with the minimum-time stopping rule (OR) and exhaustive stopping rule (AND). The factorially manipulated processes (indicated by the arrows in the first row), are embedded in the serial-parallel network. The SIC shape expectations are not exact, because they are the result of not-so-strict inequalities (Dzhafarov et al., 2004; Schweickert et al., 2000). The unknown properties are indicated by the question signs.   93

6.4 The simulation results of the serial-parallel network depicted in the first column for two different stopping rules (AND and OR). The subnetwork of interest is made of two serial processes and one in parallel with the first two. Across columns, the duration of the third parallel process is manipulated, such that the process is shortened, whereas the two processes in serial are of fixed parameter value time duration. In the simulation model, each processing time completion was determined by a simple random walk process with two bounds and probability p stepping to one of the bounds. Ten thousand trials were conducted per factorial condition.   94

7.1 Schematic illustrations of deformations of 2-D second-order image structure produced by rotation of a surface around a central vertical axis. Before the rotation, each of these image patches was circular. The central point in each diagram is a central reference point that does not move. The deformation involves relative horizontal displacements of the surrounding image points. As may be seen, the five surface

Figures and Tables xiii

shapes, from left to right, are a plane, horizontal cylinder, vertical cylinder, ellipsoid, and saddle. The shapes are defined by the relative surface curvatures in the two principal coordinate directions, direction of minimum and maximum curvature, which are horizontal and vertical in this illustration for purposes of simplicity. Thus planes have zero curvature in both directions; cylinders (parabolic patches) have zero curvature in one axis, ellipsoids (elliptic patches) have the same sign of curvature in both axes, and saddle shapes (hyperbolic patches) have opposite signs of curvature in the principal directions. These second-order deformations are invariant under transformations of lower-order structure, such as image translations, 2-D rotation, dilation, and shear (produced by surface slant). (Copyright ©2000 by the American Psychological Association. Reproduced with permission.) The official citation that should be used in referencing this material is Lappin and Craft (2000, Fig. 3, p. 14). The use of APA information does not imply endorsement by APA.) 122

7.2 Koenderink & van Doorn's shape index, S, and curvedness index, C, describe a two-dimensional space. The angular measure represents shape, and the radius represents curvedness. (Copyright ©1996 by the American Psychological Association. Reproduced with permission.) The official citation that should be used in referencing this material is Phillips and Todd (1996, Fig. 5, p. 933). (The use of APA information does not imply endorsement by APA.) 123

7.3 A famous drawing by Pablo Picasso, *Fragment de corps de femme,* elegantly illustrates correspondence between the curvature of 2-D boundary contours and 3-D surface shape. 124

9.1 Panel A: The Baseline (two blocks of trials) and the Filtering conditions of the Garner paradigm. The asterisk indicates that dimension A is the relevant dimension for responding. Panel B: Two general patterns of the results. Performance in Baseline and Filtering is comparable in the left-hand graph, indicating separable dimensions. Performance is worse in Filtering than at Baseline in the right-hand graph, the difference—Garner interference—indicating integral dimensions. 187

10.1 Basic GRT configuration with RT-distance hypothesis illustrated. 199

xiv *Figures and Tables*

10.2	Subclassification GRT model of same-different judgments. When applied to the selective-attention component task, only one of the decision criteria is relevant.	202
10.3	Component same-different judgment on A according to distance-based DS.	203
10.4	a) Mean-shift integrality on both dimensions. b) Separability with positive perceptual correlation.	207
10.5		211
10.6		212
10.7		213
10.8		214
10.9		215
10.10		216
10.11		217
10.12		218
10.13	PS with positive correlation and partition induced by optimal responding in a "same-on-A" judgment task.	219
11.1	N is our natural law for mapping a 3D mirror-symmetrical object, u, to its mental representation. M is a 3D reflection.	229
11.2	Top-left: A 3D indoor scene as seen from Čapek's point of view. Bottom: The top-view (floor plan) as perceived by Čapek. Black quadrilaterals show the ground truth. Grey rectangles represent Čapek's percept of individual objects. Top-right: The corresponding regions in Čapeks's 2D camera image. Individual grey polygons indicate where in the image Čapek detected objects.	235
11.3	Each edge of the cube is a 1Ω resistor. Find the equivalent resistance between corners A and B.	238

Tables

9.1	Summary of Shared and Different Features of STROOP, GARNER, and TOWNSEND (GRT) Measures	190
10.1	Configuration Parameters for RT Simulations	209

1 Introduction

Leslie M. Blaha and Joseph W. Houpt

These volumes are compiled in honor of Distinguished Rudy Professor James (Jim) Tarlton Townsend. Jim is a major contributor to both theoretical developments in mathematical psychology and in applications of mathematical models to studying human perception and cognition. The contributed chapters to this Festschrift represent the breadth of these contributions, ranging from work that would not be out of place in mathematical or statistical journals to work with direct implications for the treatment of clinical psychological disorders. Among the diversity of the contributions, a common theme runs throughout both volumes, a theme that drove Jim's work throughout his career: Formal psychological theory should drive empirical methodology rather than empirical innovation driving theory. In his own words, there is a definite role for "mathematical structures to serve as theories of psychology, when the proper correlative definitions are drawn between the mathematical and empirical terms" (Townsend & Kadlec, 1990, pg. 226).

The first volume is dedicated to theoretical developments. The first chapters contribute to work in formal statistics, mathematics, and logic. In Chapter 2, Drs. Donald Bamber, I. R. Goodman, and Hung Nguyen propose a particular type of logic as a model of psychological representation of categorical structures. Dr. Hans Colonius builds on previous collaborative work with Jim by exploring different ways to measure the variability of a random variable and their connections to psychological mechanisms in Chapter 3. Drs. Jun Zhang and Yitong Sun present the formal framework of subset systems as representing the relational structure of objects, features, and their contexts in Chapter 4. "Subset System: Mathematical Abstraction of Object and Context." The next set of contributions further theory addressing questions of mental organization and representation. In Chapter 5, Drs. Richard Schweickert and Hye Joo Han examine ordering of processes captured in multinomial processing trees. In Chapter 6, Dr. Mario Fifić offers new proofs of theories and elucidates connection among theories regarding the temporal organization of psychological processes, and Dr. Joseph Lappin explores the formal concept of information and its transmission in psychological contexts in Chapter 7. In Chapter 8, Drs. Junyi Dai and Jerome Busemeyer offer an overview of current probabilistic, dynamic models of intertemporal choice. In Chapter 9, Dr. Daniel Algom highlights the parallels among formal notions of independence proposed by James T. Townsend, John Ridley Stroop, and Wendell R. Garner. In Chapter 10, Drs. Robin Thomas, Noah Silbert, Emily Grossman, and Shawn Ell follow by extending General Recognition Theory to novel same-different judgment paradigms, including deriving novel predictions for empirical work. Dr. Zygmunt Pizlo argues for perceptual invariants, particularly in 3D shape perception as a fundamental indicator of cognition in Chapter 11. Ending Volume I, Dr. William Batchelder argues that one of the primary utilities of cognitive models is the study of individual variation.

The second volume is dedicated to the empirical application of mathematical modeling. The volume opens with contributors connecting neural processes to formal theories of cognition. In Chapter 2, Dr. Søren Kyllingsbæk reviews Bundeson's Theory of Visual Attention and connects the theory with neural mechanisms. In the first Chapter, Drs. F. Gregory Ashby and Fabian Soto examine the neural evidence for General Recognition Theory. Dr. Ronaldo Vigo and Derek Zeigler demonstrate the use of Vigo's Generalized Invariance Structure Model for studying subjective temporal estimations in Chapter 3. Drs. Peter Cassey and Ami Eidels revisit empirical data from early in Jim's career on letter confusion with modern approaches to modeling spatial relations in Chapter 4. In Chapter 5, Dr. Stephen Link builds on a theory based on an ideal referent for comparative judgment and demonstrates the implications for numerical interval judgments and face perception. Jim's influence in multi-modal perceptual applications inspired the contribution of Dr. Nicholas Altieri, who proposes parallel, interactive models to explain a well-studied phenomenon in crossmodal letter perception in Chapter 6. Drs. Jennifer Lentz, Yuan He, Dr. Joseph Houpt, Dr. Julia Delong, and Jim explore the perceptual combination monaural pure tones in Chapter 7. The next set of chapters build on formal theories of information processing. Dr. Michael Wenger and Stephanie Rhoten survey the use of the capacity coefficient, a measure developed by Jim, including their recent work in measuring the cognitive effects of iron deficiency in Chapter 8. In Chapter 9, Dr. Richard W. J. Neufeld further leverages notions of capacity for modeling stress effects on coping-related cognition. Dr. Cheng-Ta Yang uses a framework developed mainly by Jim, Systems Factorial Technology, to study change detection in Chapter 10. In the final chapter, we (Drs. Blaha and Houpt), we discuss the use of statistical learning techniques for discovering regularities in the individual differences of workload capacity in various clinical populations and over the course of perceptual learning.

For the remainder of this introduction, we give a brief overview of Jim's career, interweaving details of his personal and professional connections with the contributors represented herein.

1.1 A Brief Biography of James Townsend

Jim's story is a quintessentially American tale, from humble roots, to the first graduate program in the burgeoning field of mathematical psychology, and now to distinguished professor status. His dedication to technical rigor and meticulous, deep thinking enabled him to produce a set of scientific contributions that not only have stood the test of time, but continue to inspire his colleagues and students. Jim also exemplifies the spirit of collaboration, both through long-running discussions in numerous areas of interest and joint efforts resulting in papers in both theory and application. Both by his research and by his mentorship, Jim has influenced numerous researchers over the past 50 years.

Jim was born in Amarillo, Texas, on July 9, 1939, to Tarlton Byrd Townsend and Virginia Leona Townsend (née McAllister). While Jim was a young child, the Townsends moved west to California to resume careers that had been waylaid by the Great Depression. Both of Jim's parents were school teachers in California and instilled the importance of education and learning in him from a very young age. Long-time colleague Dr. Batchelder observed that of all the people he'd worked with, Jim was most adamant about pursuing advanced education, well beyond the completion of his Ph.D.

1.1.1 Professional Development

In 1957, Jim matriculated at Fresno State College, where he majored in psychology and minored in mathematics. Although Fresno State was not recognized as a hub for formal methods in psychology, the famous psychometrician Dr. Lee Cronbach had been a faculty member there prior to Jim's arrival.

Following the completion of his bachelor's degree in 1961, Jim taught mainly sixth and seventh grade mathematics in Fresno. While working as a teacher, he applied to the physiological psychology program at the University of Iowa and the just-forming graduate program in mathematical psychology founded by Richard Atkinson, Patrick Suppes, and William K. Estes at Stanford University, which had begun with support from a grant from the National Defense Education Act.

Despite the offer of a full fellowship from Iowa, the appeal of mathematical psychology drew Jim to Stanford, which had offered only a teaching assistantship. In a move that would set the bold tone for his career, Jim phoned Professor Atkinson at home on the weekend for a better offer.

Luckily, Jim was successful and joined the inaugural class of the mathematical psychology graduate program in 1962. His class included Dr. William Batchelder (Volume I, Chapter 12), Dr. Robert Bjork, Dr. Jack Yellott, Dr. Michael Levine, Dr. Alan Ruskin, and Dr. Joseph Young. Later classes included many other future luminaries, including Dr. Stephen Link (Volume II, Chapter 5), Dr. Donald Bamber (Volume I, Chapter 2), Dr. Geoffrey Loftus, Dr. Elizabeth Loftus, Dr. Richard Shiffrin, Dr. George Wolford, Dr. Peter Shaw, Dr. John Anderson, Dr. David Rumelhart, Dr. Roberta Klatzky, Dr. Douglas Hintzman, Dr. Frank Norman, Dr. Guy Groen, and many others. Together with program founders, Dr. Atkinson, Dr. Gordon Bower, Dr. William Estes and Dr. Patrick Suppes, and the students who later entered the program, this stellar group of researchers launched the fields of mathematical psychology and cognitive modeling.

After completing graduate school in 1966, Jim accepted a faculty position at the University of Hawaii; however, he did not stay long. With the help of Drs. Ruskin who was an Assistant Professor at Purdue at the time, Jim moved to Purdue University in 1968, where he remained for 21 years. During his transition, Jim traveled to Germany to develop new connections. On that trip, he had the opportunity to develop relationships with Drs. Dirk Vorberg, Hans Christoph Micko, Dietrich Albert, and Hans Colonius (Volume I, Chapter 3) among others. After returning to Purdue, Jim was able to persuade Dr. Colonius to join him there. Purdue's then-department head, Dr. James Naylor, promoted an environment in which Jim was able to spend the time learning new mathematical theory and developing deep theoretical work. During his years at Purdue, Jim had the opportunity to develop productive relationships with Dr. Schweickert (Volume I, Chapter 5) and Dr. Busemeyer (Volume I, Chapter 8), in addition to Dr. Colonius and the late Dr. Peter Schönemann.

Jim took advantage of two sabbaticals while at Purdue to further his collaborations, first with Dr. Estes at Rockefeller University in 1972, and second, in 1976–1977, at the Institut für Psychologie, Technische Universität, Braunschweig, Germany. Visiting scholar awards enabled him to visit Dr. Batchelder and collaborators at the University of California, Irvine, in 1982, and to return to Stanford as a visiting professor in 1986. A hallmark of his relationships is their longevity and, true to form, Jim has maintained connections with his colleagues at Purdue, including members of the department with whom he did not overlap, particularly Dr. Pizlo (Volume I, Chapter 11) who joined the department as Jim was leaving.

In 1989, Jim accepted the Rudy Professorship of Psychology at Indiana University during the establishment of its Cognitive Science Program. At that time, the Department of Psychology (now the Department of Psychological and Brain Sciences) grew to include some strong mathematical modelers, including Dr. Shiffrin (one of Jim's Stanford peers), Dr. Robert Nosofsky,

Dr. David Pisoni, and Dr. Robert Goldstone. Soon after, Dr. Busemeyer (whom Jim encouraged to move from Purdue), Dr. John Kruschke (who arrived contemporaneously with Jim), and Dr. Thomas Busey joined the department.

During his sabbaticals from Indiana University, he continued developing strong international collaborations by spending time during the 1992–1993 academic year working with Dr. Vicki Bruce at Stirling University, Scotland, with Dr. Ana Garriga at Comportaminento U.N.E.D Ciudad Universitaria, Madrid, with Dr. Ashby at the University of California–Santa Barbara, as well as spending time at the World Congress of Psychology in Brussels. A more recent sabbatical in 2000–2001 allowed him to continue work with Dr. Colonius as a senior scientist at the Hanse Institute for Advanced Study, Oldenburg Institute for Psychology Research. Jim was named Distinguished Professor of Psychological and Brain Sciences in 2008, where he continues to head the Mathematical Psychology Laboratory.

1.1.2 Professional Service and Honors

Following the successful establishment of the *Journal of Mathematical Psychology* in 1964, the first symposium dedicated to mathematical psychology gathered at Stanford University in 1968. It was there that Jim presented his first talk on the parallel-serial identifiability problem. The Society for Mathematical Psychology was formally established in 1977. Jim would serve as the president of the society from 1985 to 1986 and again from 2004 to 2005. More recently, he was a co-founder of the Configural Processing Consortium in 2006, serving as its first president as well. For his dedication to rigorous mathematical and experimental psychology work and service to supporting societies, Jim has been named a fellow of both the American Psychological Society (1998) and the American Psychological Association (2004). He was elected to the Society for Experimental Psychology in 1993 and was awarded their Norman Anderson Lifetime Achievement Award in 2003.

1.1.3 Intellectual Contributions

Jim is interested in hard problems. He explored various formalisms for both rigorously defining open questions and detailing the potential solution spaces to those questions. His two main areas of interest are processing system organization and perceptual/cognitive representation. This first area of emphasis was modeling the fundamental characteristics of human information processing, including questions of architecture, stochastic dependencies, and processing capacity. Such models emphasized the processes underlying various tasks or decisions, primarily using response-time as the dependent measure. The goal of this line of work was the development of the strongest tools for identifying the possible systems, producing observable response dynamics based on systematic manipulation of the input variables. One of Jim's critical (and signature) insights in this domain is that information processing systems can mimic each other in many ways, and robust solutions are challenged to overcome non-identifiability.

The first paper on parallel-serial mimicry was not easily published. True to form, Jim persevered for two years to find a journal that would entertain the possibility of publication. What was eventually published as "A Note on the Identifiability of Parallel and Serial Processes" in *Perception & Psychophysics* (1971, volume 10, pp. 161–163) was initially rejected, with no invitation for resubmission, from three of the major theoretical journals in psychology. The first editor indicated that the paper was interesting and worthy of publication, but not in that journal due to its mathematical content. One of the reviewers suggested removing the math for submission to another top journal. Jim followed this suggestion. Of course, the editor for the second submission, having garnered reviewer feedback, concluded that without the supporting mathematics, it couldn't be adjudicated and might be better suited to a journal with different emphases. The third editor rejected the paper and suggested submission to one of the first two journals. Jim did not give up. Following a personal appeal to a senior colleague who had done some work on model mimicry in another field, Jim was invited to submit a short theoretical note to a top perception journal. Thus, some two-and-a-half years following initial review, the short note was published. As of August 2015, this note has been cited 269 times, more than the related technical work in both "Some Results Concerning the Identifiability of Parallel and Serial Processes" (*British Journal of Mathematical and Statistical Psychology, 25*, 168–199; 231 citations) and "Issues and Models Concerning the Processing of a Finite Number of Inputs" (In B. H. Kantowitz (Ed.), *Human Information Processing: Tutorials in Performance and Cognition* (pp. 133–168). Hillsdale, NJ: Erlbaum Press; 261 citations). Jim defined identifiability as a challenging problem not just within but *between* classes of models/systems. This was a call to action within the field to increase the rigor and attention paid to these questions and to pursue the development of methodologies that would allow for solutions.

Following this start, Jim proved himself to be a consistently productive, steadfast champion of rigorous theory conjoined with theoretically driven empirical methods. As of midyear 2015, he has authored or coauthored 125 peer-reviewed journal articles and book chapters, with numerous conference presentations and proceedings. With Dr. Ashby, he published the touchstone book in mathematical psychology, *The Stochastic Modeling of Elementary Psychological Processes* (1983, Cambridge University Press). He co-edits the Scientific Psychology Series (Taylor & Francis) with longtime colleague Dr. Stephen Link. He served as the editor of the *Journal of*

Mathematical Psychology from 1985, where he is currently an editor emeritus. He also serves as consulting editor for multiple journals, including *Psychonomic Bulletin & Review* and *Psychological Review*.

Some of Jim's most noteworthy contributions in process modeling include Systems Factorial Technology for the assessment of information processing characteristics, including parallel/serial architectures (Townsend & Nozawa, 1995; Townsend & Wenger, 2004) and Decision Field Theory for assessing the dynamics of choice preference (Busemeyer & Townsend, 1993). Both represent the pairing of strong mathematical modeling with theoretically grounded experimental methodologies. These works also illustrate the need for the use of multiple areas of mathematical theory to be unified in meaningful ways in order to make inferences about psychological processes. For example, Systems Factorial Technology originated with probability theory to define the problem space and derive candidate system models. It was expanded to incorporate linear dynamic systems models to simulate models' associated predictions. The combination of tools provide tests applicable to empirical data for determining model viability and applicability. In a problem space as complex as human cognition, Jim's work illustrates that finding the right combinations of tools can lead to fruitful insights and that sticking with only one model or, indeed, only one area of mathematics is not likely to tell the complete story.

To pull such various threads together, one must reach out to others with diverse areas of expertise, and Jim's work exemplifies successful collaborations. For example, in modeling of processing architectures, he had long-running discussions with Dr. Schweickert (Volume I, Chapter 5). A long relationship with Dr. Ehitbar Dzhafarov similarly served the theoretical advances on the related topic of selective influence. In terms of developing stochastic tools for studying response times, collaborations with Dr. Colonius (Volume I, Chapter 3), Dr. Trisha Van Zandt, Dr. Thomas (Volume I, Chapter 10), Dr. Wenger (Volume II, Chapter 8), and ourselves (Volume II, Chapter 11), among numerous other mathematical psychologists.

Applications and extensions of Systems Factorial Technology appear many times in these volumes, including chapters from Dr. Fifić (Chapter 6) in Volume I and, in Volume II, Dr. Alitieri (Chapter 6), Dr. Lentz and colleagues (Chapter 7), Dr. Yang (Chapter 10), Dr. Wenger and Ms. Rhoten (Chapter 8), and our own chapter (Chapter 11). Closely related, Drs. Dai and Busemeyer (Volume I, Chapter 8) address connections between and extension of Decision Field Theory and issues addressed within Systems Factorial Technology.

Jim's second area of emphasis is on models of perceptual representation spaces, from both probabilistic and geometric perspectives. This work emphasized choice frequency as the fundamental dependent variable. Jim pursued research exploring the psychological implications of geometric frameworks varying in their complexity. This range includes straightforward, multidimensional scaling with low-dimensional Euclidean embedding spaces (e.g., Townsend, 1971a, 1971b) and advances in infinite dimensional Riemannian manifolds as theoretical tools for psychological representation, particularly for faces (Townsend, Solomon, Wenger, and Spencer-Smith, 2001). This work was developed through extensive collaboration Bruce Solomon, a Mathematics professor at Indiana University. Long-running discussions with Dr. Zhang (Volume I, Chapter 4) in the area of differential geometry, and Dr. Lappin (Volume I, Chapter 7) on feature representations served to advance Jim's own thinking in this area.

One of Jim's critical contributions in perceptual representation is General Recognition Theory (GRT), developed in collaboration with former graduate student Dr. Ashby (Ashby & Townsend, 1986). GRT was the result of another diligent effort that began in the late 1970s as one idea for Dr. Ashby's dissertation, and which Dr. Ashby did pursue in his postdoctoral research supported by the National Science Foundation and Dr. Estes at Harvard. Initial progress was presented at the 1982 meeting of the Society for Mathematical Psychology; GRT was formally named that year in a series of conversations between Jim and Greg on a sailing trip. That concentrated, extended discussion really pushed the ideas forward. But GRT wasn't published until 1986 in "Varieties of Perceptual Independence" (*Psychological Review, 93*, 154–179) after a long review process. General Recognition Theory extends traditional signal detection to multiple dimensions, allowing deeper examinations of the ways perceptual factors and decisional biases play into and against each other. The ideas evolved in the late 1970s to early 1980s as Jim's thinking progressed from models assuming feature knowledge toward stochastic perspectives on testing feature representations. Together, Jim and Greg formulated the theoretical tenets of GRT and other aspects of independence based on a tight coupling of theory and experiments, with many of the early experiments published in Ashby and Gott (1988) and Ashby and Perrin (1988). Like Systems Factorial Technology, General Recognition Theory appears throughout this Festschrift, in chapters by Dr. Algom (Chapter 9) and Dr. Thomas and colleagues (Chapter 10) in Volume I and Drs. Ashby and Soto (Chapter 1) in Volume II.

As we mentioned, a distinction in Jim's work is that he not only pursues technically precise theories, but he ties those theories to empirical paradigms. When experiments are designed according to such paradigms, the investigators have the critical conditions needed to apply the modeling tools and make meaningful inferences. With Systems Factorial Technology, he proposed the Double Factorial Paradigm for the systematic, factorial manipulation of subprocesses in a system. With General Recognition Theory, he championed the complete identification task on factorial manipulated feature/decision spaces. But even more than providing sets of tools, Jim's consistent efforts in theory-driven methodologies provides ways for non-modelers to use the strong theoretical tools.

It is in the application of his models, particularly through his theory-driven methodologies, that the breadth of Jim's collaborations really stand out. In his early days, he worked with Dr. Link on tactile perception. Dr. Neufeld (Volume II, Chapter 9) sought Jim out in the 1980s to work on modeling aspects of psychological stress. Jim's clinical collaborations grew to include collaborations with Dr. Richard McFall in clinical assessment. Jim collaborated with Dr. Coreen Farris, applying General Recognition Theory to perceptions in sexual aggression, with Dr. Julie Stout, applying Decision Field Theory to questions of motivation, and with Dr. Shannon Johnson, applying Systems Factorial Technology to autism spectrum disorders. Jim's work on Gestalt perception involved collaborations with Dr. Algom (Volume II, Chapter 9) and the other founders of the Configural Processing Consortium, Drs. James Pomerantz, Ruth Kimchi, and Mary Peterson. This included collaborative work on face perception with Drs. Alice O'Toole, Wenger, Nicholas Donnelly, together with his former students Drs. Jesse Spencer-Smith, Fifić (Volume I, Chapter 6), and Dr. Blaha (Volume I, Chapter 1; Volume II, Chapter 11). Jim continues to form new collaborations including Dr. Kyllingsbæk (Volume II, Chapter 2), Dr. Yang (Volume II, Chapter 10), and Dr. Vigo (Volume II, Chapter 3) in areas as diverse as memory, perception, and categorization, respectively.

Jim also collaborates with Dr. Silbert (Volume I, Chapter 10), Dr. Altieri (Volume II, Chapter 6), and Dr. Lentz (Volume II, Chapter 7) in areas of auditory perception and speech processing. Recently, he worked with researchers at the Air Force Research Laboratory on stretching applications into military-relevant problem solving, such as improving cockpit symbology and audio-visual cuing in dynamic environments, working with Dr. Daniel Repperger, and continuing to work with former student Dr. Blaha.

1.1.4 Dedicated Teacher and Mentor

Among his personal influences, Jim recalls the confluence of strong researchers at Stanford in the 1960s as providing a rich and stimulating environment for developing new lines of mathematical theory. In particular, the clean, logical thinking of Dr. Suppes and the deep thinking of Dr. Estes were some of the most impactful on his own approach to research, together with the rigorous training received under Drs. Atkinson and Bower. But in the nearly 50 years, since completing his doctoral degree, Jim has been the influencing factor in the lives of over 20 graduate students and postdoctoral researchers. Some continued into academia, whereas some departed for civil service in government agencies and research laboratories and others apply their training in industry.

Jim is a dedicated teacher as well as researcher, training not only the aforementioned students in his own lab, but both graduate and undergraduate courses. This is evidenced by the many successful careers that began in Jim's lab and the quality of work of his students, many of whom have contributed to this Festschrift. The graduate students and postdoctoral researchers for whom Jim was their major advisor and mentor include:

F. Gregory Ashby	Graduate Student (Ph.D. 1980)	Volume II, Chapter 1
Douglas E. Landon	Graduate Student (Ph.D. 1983)	
Trisha van Zandt	Undergraduate / Graduate Student (1983–1988)	
G. Gary Hu	Graduate Student (Ph.D. 1984)	
Ronald J. Evans	Graduate Student (Ph.D. 1989)	
Helena Kadlec	Graduate Student (Ph.D. 1991)	
Thomas G. Fikes	Postdoc (1993–1994)	
Robin D. Thomas	Graduate Student (Ph.D. 1995)	Volume I, Chapter 10
Michael J. Wenger	Postdoc (1995–1997)	Volume II, Chapter 8
Jesse Spencer-Smith	Graduate Student (Ph.D. 2001)	
Åse Innes-Ker	Graduate Student / Postdoc (1995–2003)	
Ami Eidels	Postdoc (2004–2008)	Volume II, Chapter 4
Mario Fifić	Graduate Student (Ph.D. 2005)	Volume I, Chapter 6
Noah H. Silbert	Postdoc (2009–2010)	Volume I, Chapter 10
Nicholas Altieri	Graduate Student (Ph.D. 2010)	Volume II, Chapter 6
Leslie M. Blaha	Graduate Student (Ph.D. 2010)	Volume II, Chapter 11
Joseph W. Houpt	Graduate Student (Ph.D. 2012)	Volume II, Chapter 11
Devin M. Burns	Graduate Student (Ph.D. 2014)	
Mohammad Abdolvahab	Postdoc (2014–Present)	

In addition to individual mentoring and formal lecturing, Jim was a key mentor and investigator for training grants in both cognitive modeling and clinical science training with rigorous theoretical foundations. In this way, he impacted the training of students across the Department of Psychological and Brain Sciences in the cognitive, developmental, and clinical specialty areas. His students recall him with admiration, using terms such as generous, unselfish, appreciative, and compassionate to capture their memories of working with him during their graduate studies. Indeed, he currently maintains an active laboratory with five graduate students (as of mid-2015): Haiyuan Yang, Arash Khodadadi, Brett Jefferson, Yanjun Liu, Mikaela Arkenius, and Freddie Shi.

Reflecting on the early challenges in his career pursuing hard theoretical problems before a literature in those areas was established, Jim offers a few key lessons for future researchers.

1. Write the best paper of which you are capable.
2. If your first effort is rejected but you are allowed to resubmit, pay the greatest respect and attention to the comments and do your utmost to address the objections.
3. If your paper is rejected, put it aside for a minimum of a week before deciding on an action.
4. If you honestly believe that the reviewers have made mistakes in their assessment or that they, perhaps due to theoretical bias, have not been completely fair, consider an appeal and a request that the editor collect more reviews.
5. It rarely happens, but if an editor is biased or otherwise acting in a non-scientific or unethical manner, the author should consider appeal to the scientific board responsible for publishing the journal (e.g., an editorial advisory board, the executive board of the journal's associated society). This would be a drastic step, perhaps having consequences for the entire career of the writer and should only be undertaken if said writer has substantive proof of misbehavior.

It is because of researchers like Jim that journals in the behavioral science today are more amenable to theoretical and mathematical content than was previously the case. In his career, Jim never backed away from the hard problems, demonstrating that following your own instincts about theory-driven research can be more than worth the effort.

Acknowledgments

We have many people to thank for bringing this book together, including all the contributing authors. We would especially like to thank all our reviewers for the content of the book. In addition to many contributing authors who offered reviews, we appreciate the hard work by Dr. Jennifer Bittner, Dr. Scott Brown, Dr. Devin Burns, Dr. Chris Fisher, Ms. Mary Frame, Dr. Assaf Harel, Mr. Brett Jefferson, Dr. Daniel Little, Dr. Megan Morris, Dr. Robert Patterson, Dr. Patrick Simen, Dr. Trisha van Zandt, and Dr. Rik Warren. We thank Ms. Katie Voiles for her assistance with proofreading the copy.

This book began with a conference honoring the career of Jim Townsend held in April 2013 at Indiana University. We are indebted to our conference co-organizers, Drs. Ashby and Busemeyer, for their efforts in planning the conference and helping initiate this book as a follow-on compilation. We are also grateful to Drs. Ashby and Batchelder for sharing stories for the introduction material. We thank Dr. Michael Wenger for contributing feedback on early drafts of Jim's biography.

Leslie M. Blaha
Joseph W. Houpt
October 2015

References

Ashby, F. G., & Gott, R. E. (1988). Decision rules in the perception and categorization of multidimensional stimuli. *Journal of Experimental Psychology: Learning, Memory, and Cognition, 14*, 33–53.

Ashby, F. G., & Perrin, N. A. (1988). Toward a unified theory of similarity and recognition. *Psychological Review, 95*(1), 124–150.

Ashby, F. G., & Townsend, J. T. (1986). Varieties of perceptual independence. *Psychological Review, 93*, 154–179.

Busemeyer, J. R., & Townsend, J. T. (1993). Decision field theory: A dynamic-cognitive approach to decision making in an uncertain environment. *Psychological Review, 100*, 432–459.

Townsend, J. T. (1971a). Alphabetic confusion: A test of models for individuals. *Perception & Psychophysics, 9*, 449–454.

Townsend, J. T. (1971b). Theoretical analysis of an alphabetic confusion matrix. *Perception & Psychophysics, 9*, 40–50.

Townsend, J. T., & Kadlec, H. (1990). Psychology and mathematics. In R. E. Mickens (Ed.), *Mathematics and science* (pp. 223–248). Singapore: World Scientific.

Townsend, J. T., & Nozawa, G. (1995). Spatio-temporal properties of elementary perception: An investigation of parallel, serial, and coactive theories. *Journal of Mathematical Psychology, 39*, 321–359.

Townsend, J. T., Solomon, B., Wenger, M. J., & Spencer-Smith, J. S. (2001). The perfect Gestalt: Infinite dimensional Riemannian face space and other aspects of face cognition. In M. J. Wenger & J. T. Townsend (Eds.), *Computational, geometric, and process issues in facial cognition* (pp. 39–82). Mahwah, NJ: Lawrence Erlbaum Associates.

Townsend, J. T., & Wenger, M. J. (2004). A theory of interactive parallel processing: New capacity measures and predictions for a response-time inequality series. *Psychological Review, 111*, 1003–1035.

2 High-Probability Logic and Inheritance

Donald Bamber, I. R. Goodman, and Hung T. Nguyen

2.1 Reasoning With Imperfect Rules

We know how to reason with generalizations that have no exceptions: We simply apply classical logic. But many useful generalizations have occasional exceptions. An example is the generalization:

Birds fly. (2.1)

From now on, let us refer to generalizations as *rules*, and let us say that rules with no exceptions are *perfect* and that rules with occasional exceptions are *imperfect*.

How should we reason with imperfect rules? We might pretend that imperfect rules are perfect and then apply classical logic. But that doesn't work. Consider, for example, the two rules:

Birds fly.
Penguins are nonflying birds. (2.2)

If we pretend that the first rule doesn't have exceptions, it follows that nonflying birds such as penguins don't exist and, since there aren't any penguins, all of them are green. Thus, we conclude:

Penguins are green. (2.3)

We see here an important limitation of classical logic: It doesn't work when applied to imperfect rules. Even though classical logic is one of the great achievements of the human mind and is virtually indispensable for reasoning with complex mathematical expressions, when it is applied to imperfect rules, it leads to errors that a schoolchild wouldn't make.

Thus we want a non-classical logic for reasoning with imperfect rules. Just as humans don't make the error of inferring the conclusion (2.3) from the two rules (2.2), we want a logic that doesn't make that error either.

14 *Donald Bamber et al.*

In fact, numerous non-classical logics have been invented for reasoning both with imperfect rules and with syntactically more complex expressions (Antoniou, 1997; Ginsberg, 1987).

2.1.1 Reasoning Outside of Classical Logic

More generally, outside of classical logic, there has been a broad study of reasoning as performed by people, ideal reasoners, and artificial intelligence programs. Some instances of this study of reasoning include the following: (*a*) the discipline of artificial intelligence has developed non-classical logics to aid in the goal of building programs with humanlike reasoning capabilities; (*b*) the discipline of informal logic has examined everyday human reasoning as carried out in natural language (Walton, 1989); (*c*) there is an educational movement whose goal is to teach critical thinking skills (Moore & Parke, 2004); this involves teaching, not just logic but also the nonprobative value of arguments that appeal to emotion; (*d*) it has been shown that nonmonotonic logic is used in a wide variety of fields (Pelletier & Elio, 2005); and (*e*) empirical studies of human nonmonotonic reasoning have been done (Strasser & Antonelli, 2015, Section 4).

2.1.2 The Inheritance Controversy

Multiple logics have been invented for reasoning with imperfect rules (Antoniou, 1997; Ginsberg, 1987). Because competing logics of imperfect rules have been developed, there are, of course, controversies. Perhaps the most important controversy concerns how "inheritance" should operate.

This paper examines the inheritance controversy from the viewpoint of high-probability logics (Adams, 1966, 1975, 1986, 1998; Bamber, 2000; Bamber, Goodman, & Nguyen, 2004, 2005) and shows how to extend high-probability logics so as to resolve the inheritance controversy. The inheritance controversy concerns whether an exceptional subclass within a larger class should "inherit" properties possessed by the larger "parent" class.

Before describing this controversy in greater detail, we need to say more about rules. Rules, whether perfect or imperfect, are statements about the properties possessed by entities. Specifically, rules have the form:

Entities having property α have property β. (2.4)

The abbreviated form of the aforementioned rule is:

α's are β's.[1] (2.5)

The inheritance controversy is over the issue of whether or not an exceptional subclass within a "parent" class should "inherit" properties of the parent class. More specifically, the issue is whether, given the two rules

(2.6), one should infer the rule (2.7).

$$\begin{aligned} &\alpha\text{'s are } \beta\text{'s.} \\ &\alpha\text{'s are } \gamma\text{'s.} \end{aligned} \qquad (2.6)$$

$$\alpha\text{'s that are not } \beta\text{'s are } \gamma\text{'s.} \qquad (2.7)$$

In this example, the parent class consists of entities having property α. The two rules (2.6) indicate that typical members of the parent class have properties β and γ. Thus entities having property α but not β are atypical members of the parent class because they have not "inherited" the property β from the parent class. The key question in the controversy is over whether members of the parent class that are atypical in one respect, i.e., not having inherited property β, may be assumed typical in a different respect, i.e., inheriting property γ. In other words, should we expect an entity that is atypical in one respect to be typical or atypical in other respects?

Different logics treat this matter differently; in some logics, (2.7) is inferred from (2.6) and in some it is not. For a discussion of the issue, see Bacchus, Grove, Halpern, and Koller (1996, Section 3.3).

2.1.3 Opposing Examples

In this section, we will present two examples. In one example, it seems intuitively reasonable for the exceptional subclass to inherit a property from the parent class; in the other example, such inheritance does not seem reasonable. We will then analyze the two examples to determine what the key difference between them is that makes exceptional-subclass inheritance reasonable in one example and unreasonable in the other.

Example 2.1.1. Positive example. *Suppose that the adult inhabitants of the Island of Gort are called "Gortians." And suppose that we are given two imperfect rules concerning Gortians:*

$$\begin{aligned} &\textit{Gortians are tall.} \\ &\textit{Gortians are literate.} \end{aligned} \qquad (2.8)$$

It would seem sensible to infer:

$$\textit{Gortians who are not tall are literate.} \qquad (2.9)$$

The reason this inference seems sensible is that the causes of an adult being tall and an adult being literate are largely different and, so we expect the properties of tallness and literateness to be roughly independent. There may be some association between tallness and literateness, but that association is weak. Knowing that someone is not tall provides little, if any,

16   Donald Bamber et al.

information about whether they are literate. But knowing that someone is a Gortian provides strong evidence that they are literate. Therefore it is sensible to infer (2.9) from (2.8).

Example 2.1.2. Negative example. *Suppose we are given these two rules:*

> Gortians are tall.
> Gortians are long-legged. (2.10)

In this case, it seems doubtful whether one should infer:

> Gortians who are not tall are long-legged. (2.11)

The reason it seems dubious to infer (2.11) from (2.10) is that the property of being tall and the property of being long-legged are far from independent; they are strongly associated. Knowing that someone is not tall provides substantial evidence that they are not long-legged. This counteracts the evidence, based on their being Gortian, that they are long-legged. Given two opposing pieces of evidence, it is prudent not to make any inference. And, thus, we should not infer (2.11) from (2.10).

But, what if we are agnostic as regards whether tallness and long-leggedness are strongly associated? If we don't have an opinion on this issue, that means we are unwilling to rule out the possibility that tallness and long-leggedness are strongly associated. Thus it would be unsafe to assume that tallness and long-leggedness are only weakly associated. Therefore, it would not be prudent to infer (2.11) from (2.10).

Analysis. We have just seen two examples where we were given two premises of the form:

> α's are β's.
> α's are γ's. (2.12)

In one case, it seems reasonable to infer the conclusion:

> α's that are not β's are γ's. (2.13)

And, in the other case, it does not seem reasonable to infer that conclusion. What explains this difference?

The key difference between the two examples is this. In the first example, there is good reason to think that β and γ are, to a loose approximation, conditionally independent given α. Given this rough conditional independence, it is reasonable to infer (2.13) from (2.12). But, in the second example, there is no good reason to think that β and γ are approximately conditionally independent given α. As a consequence, in the second example, it is not reasonable to infer (2.13) from (2.12).

Thus the difference between the two examples is that the first example employs an unexpressed premise, namely that β and γ are approximately

High-Probability Logic and Inheritance 17

conditionally independent given α. And the second example does not employ that premise. In other words, the first example is an enthymeme. In logic, an *enthymeme* is an argument in which one of the premises is not explicitly stated, but is instead implicitly assumed.[2]

2.1.4 Eschewal of Enthymemes

We should avoid enthymemes. All premises in an argument should be explicit rather than implicit. This leads to the following desiderata for logics of imperfect rules.

Desideratum 2.1.1. *The two premises*

$$\alpha\text{'s are } \beta\text{'s.} \qquad \qquad (2.14)$$
$$\alpha\text{'s are } \gamma\text{'s.}$$

should not *imply the conclusion*

$$\alpha\text{'s that are not } \beta\text{'s are } \gamma\text{'s.} \qquad (2.15)$$

Desideratum 2.1.2. *The three premises*

$$\alpha\text{'s are } \beta\text{'s.}$$
$$\alpha\text{'s are } \gamma\text{'s.} \qquad \qquad (2.16)$$
$$\beta \text{ and } \gamma \text{ are approximately conditionally independent given } \alpha.$$

should imply the conclusion (2.15).

Remark. It has been argued (Bacchus et al., 1996, Section 3.3) that Desideratum 2.1.1 is actually an *anti*-desideratum and that, contrary to Desideratum 2.1.1, the premises (2.14) *should* entail the conclusion (2.15). The difficulty with this position is that it implies in Example 2.1.2 that, contrary to intuition, Gortians who are not tall are long-legged.

2.1.5 Inheritance in High-Probability Logic

High-probability logics satisfy Desideratum 2.1.1. But, until now, they have not satisfied Desideratum 2.1.2, for the simple reason that the syntax of these logics does not allow statements of approximate conditional independence and thus (2.16) is not a legal set of premises.

The next section will describe high-probability logics in detail. Later sections will show how these logics can be extended by allowing premises to be of two different types: (*a*) rules and (*b*) statements of approximate conditional independence. The goal of adding statements of conditional independence is to enable these logics to satisfy Desideratum 2.1.2.

Remark. There are logics that incorporate a concept of conditional independence, but not with the goal of satisfying Desideratum 2.1.2. First,

Ivanovska and Giese (2011) take an existing logic for reasoning about probability (Halpern, 2003, Section 7.3) and add *conditional independence formulas* in order to enhance the logic's ability to reason about probabilities. Second, a concept of *logical* conditional independence (as distinguished from *probabilistic* conditional independence) has been developed (Darwiche, 1997; Lang, Liberatore, & Marquis, 2002) with the goal of using this concept to reduce the computation needed to make inferences from propositional-logic databases.

2.2 High-Probability Logics

Currently there are two basic approaches to high-probability logic: Adams's Logic of conditionals (Adams, 1966, 1975, 1986, 1998) and second-order probability logic (SOPL; Bamber, 2000; Bamber et al., 2004, 2005).

Why use high-probability logics? The reviewer of this paper asked us what the attraction of high-probability logics is. After all, there are a number of alternative, reasonably successful approaches to reasoning with rules (Antoniou, 1997; Ginsberg, 1987). Why not use one of them? In particular, why not use fuzzy logic?

While we have high regard for fuzzy logic (Nguyen & Walker, 2006), we nonetheless have manifold reasons for liking high-probability logic. First, the interpretation of imperfect rules in terms of high conditional probability seems apposite. Second, high-probability logics have a simple syntax and simple deductive procedures. Third, and most important, SOPL implements a powerful method of reasoning: Bayesian analysis. (Although Adams's Logic is not Bayesian, it is an intellectual ancestor of SOPL and shares semantic concepts with SOPL.)

2.2.1 Preliminaries

In order to explain high-probability logics, we begin with some preliminary concepts.

Operations on properties. Concepts from propositional calculus can be usefully applied to properties. Thus the operations of *negation, conjunction, disjunction*, and *material conditional* may be applied to properties. Suppose that α and β are properties. Then an entity has property α', called the *negation* of α, if and only if it does not have the property α. An entity has the property $\alpha \wedge \beta$ (often abbreviated $\alpha\beta$), called the *conjunction* of α and β, if and only if it has both the property α and the property β. An entity has the property $\alpha \vee \beta$, called the *disjunction* of α and β, if and only if it has either the property α or the property β. And, an entity has the *material conditional* property $\alpha \to \beta$ if and only either it does not have the property α or it does have the property β.

High-Probability Logic and Inheritance

A relation between properties. Some properties are broader than others. The notation $\alpha \vdash \beta$ means that the property β is at least as broad as the property α in the sense that β can be deduced from α in propositional calculus. For example, $\kappa \vdash (\kappa \vee \lambda)$. In addition, if A is a finite set of properties $\{\alpha_1, \ldots, \alpha_m\}$, then $A \vdash \beta$ means that $\alpha_1 \wedge \ldots \wedge \alpha_m \vdash \beta$. And $A \nvdash \beta$ means that it is not the case that $A \vdash \beta$. If $\alpha \vdash \beta$ and $\beta \vdash \alpha$, then α and β are said to be *equivalent*.

Primitive and atomic properties. We begin with a finite number k of *primitive* properties: $\sigma_1, \ldots, \sigma_k$. From these primitive properties, other properties are constructed via the operations of negation, conjunction, and disjunction. Thus an *atomic* property is any property expressible as the k-fold conjunction $\xi_1 \wedge \xi_2 \wedge \ldots \wedge \xi_k$, where each ξ_i is either the primitive property σ_i or its negation σ_i'. There are a total of 2^k atomic properties. Every property is equivalent to the disjunction of some set of atomic properties.

Universal and null properties. It will be convenient to have a special symbol $\top$ for the *universal property* which, of necessity, is possessed by every entity. This is the property expressible as the disjunction of all 2^k atomic properties. We call the negation of the universal property the *null property* and denote it $\bot$; it may be regarded as the disjunction of zero atomic properties. Thus, for every property α, it is the case that $\bot \vdash \alpha$ and $\alpha \vdash \top$.

Probability measures. A probability measure π over properties is analogous to a probability measure over events. Thus $\pi(\bot) = 0$ and $\pi(\top) = 1$. For all properties α, $\pi(\alpha) \geq 0$. And for all α and β, if the conjunction of α and β is equivalent to the null property, then $\pi(\alpha \vee \beta) = \pi(\alpha) + \pi(\beta)$. Finally, for all α and β that are equivalent, $\pi(\alpha) = \pi(\beta)$.

To specify a probability measure π, it suffices to specify the probability of each of the 2^k atomic properties. Let us index the atomic properties with the integers 1 through 2^k. Having done so, we may identify each probability measure π with a point in 2^k-dimensional space having the form

$$(x_1, x_2, \ldots, x_{2^k}) \text{ with all } x_i \geq 0 \text{ and } \sum_{i=1}^{2^k} x_i = 1.$$

The set of all points having the aforementioned form constitute a simplex, which we will denote Π. Thus each probability measure may be identified with a point in Π and vice versa.

Conditional probabilities. In this chapter, we use statements about conditional probabilities as convenient abbreviations for longer statements about unconditional probabilities. To achieve our goal of brevity of expression, we adopt the convention that

$$\mathbf{Pr}(\beta | \alpha) = 1 \text{ if } \mathbf{Pr}(\alpha) = 0.{}^3$$

In other words, regardless of whether $\Pr(\alpha)$ is positive or zero,

$$\mathbf{Pr}(\beta | \alpha) = \max\{t \in [0,1] : \mathbf{Pr}(\alpha\beta) = t\,\mathbf{Pr}(\alpha)\}.$$

As a result of using this convention, "$\Pr(\beta \mid \alpha) = 1$" becomes an abbreviation for "$\Pr(\alpha\beta) = \Pr(\alpha)$." And "$\Pr(\beta \mid \alpha)$ is close to one" becomes an abbreviation for "$\Pr(\alpha\beta) = t\Pr(\alpha)$ for some $t \in [0,1]$ that is close to one."

We call this convention the *null-unity convention* for conditional probabilities, and we adopt it for use in this paper. In so doing, we follow previous practice of Adams (Adams, 1966, 1986, 1998), but not Adams (1975), and of ourselves (Bamber, 2000; Bamber et al., 2004, 2005).

Syntax and semantics of imperfect rules. High-probability logics deal with imperfect rules whose exceptions are *rare*; that is, they have low probability of occurrence. An imperfect rule may be expressed either in symbols or in words. When expressed in symbols, an imperfect rule has the form

$$\alpha \triangleright \beta. \tag{2.17}$$

Nearly everything having property α has property β, \hfill (2.18)

where α and β are both properties. Equivalent ways of expressing the rule (2.17) in words rather than symbols are:

Nearly all α's are β's. \hfill (2.19)

The conditional probability of β given α is close to one. \hfill (2.20)

Note: The assertion that a conditional probability is close to one does not exclude the possibility that it might be exactly one.

Syntax and semantics of perfect rules. A *perfect rule* is a statement with syntactic form $\alpha \blacktriangleright \beta$, and which means that the conditional probability of β given α is exactly one, rather than merely close to one. Now, note that $\Pr(\beta \mid \alpha) = 1$ iff $\Pr(\alpha\beta') = 0$ iff $\Pr(\bot \mid \alpha\beta') = 1$ iff $\Pr(\bot \mid \alpha\beta') \approx 1$. Thus the *perfect* rule $\alpha \blacktriangleright \beta$ is equivalent to the *imperfect* rule $\alpha\beta' \triangleright \bot$.

This implies that, although high-probability logics were developed for reasoning with imperfect rules, they can be applied to perfect rules. Because if we have a premise set containing one or more perfect rules, we can replace each perfect rule with the equivalent imperfect rule and then apply a high-probability logic.

2.2.2 Entailment in Adams's Logic of Conditionals

Ernest W. Adams[4] defined a high-probability logic that, although designed to be a logic of conditional statements (Adams, 1966, 1975, 1998), can also be used as a logic of imperfect rules (Adams, 1986).

Roughly speaking, in Adams's Logic, a set of premises entails a conclusion if and only if the premise probabilities all being close to one *guarantee* that the conclusion probability will be close to one. Let us now be precise.

Suppose that $\alpha \triangleright \beta$ is an imperfect rule and that $\delta > 0$. Define

$$\begin{aligned}\Pi_\delta(\alpha \triangleright \beta) &= \{\pi \in \Pi : \pi(\beta|\alpha) \geq 1 - \delta\} \\ &= \{\pi \in \Pi : \pi(\alpha\beta) \geq (1-\delta)\pi(\alpha)\}.\end{aligned} \qquad (2.21)$$

Given a finite set of imperfect rules

$$\Theta_{\text{ir}} = \{\mu_1 \triangleright \nu_1, ..., \mu_n \triangleright \nu_n\}, \qquad (2.22)$$

let

$$\Pi_\delta(\Theta_{\text{ir}}) = \begin{cases} \bigcap_{i=1}^n \Pi_\delta(\mu_i \triangleright \nu_i) & \text{if } n \geq 1, \\ \Pi & \text{if } n = 0. \end{cases} \qquad (2.23)$$

Definition 1. In Adams's Logic, a collection of premises Θ_{ir} *entails with surety* a conclusion $\kappa \triangleright \lambda$ if and only if, for every $\varepsilon > 0$, there exists a $\delta > 0$ such that

$$\Pi_\delta(\Theta_{\text{ir}}) \subseteq \Pi_\varepsilon(\kappa \triangleright \lambda). \qquad (2.24)$$

Remark. We call this entailment with *surety* for the following reason. Let π_{true} denote the "true" probability measure.[5] All we know about π_{true} is that, for $i = 1, ..., n$, $\pi_{\text{true}}(\nu_i \mid \mu_i) \geq 1 - \delta$, where δ is small. In other words, for some small δ, $\pi_{\text{true}} \in \Pi_\delta(\Theta_{\text{ir}})$. What we want to infer about π_{true} is whether $\pi_{\text{true}}(\lambda \mid \kappa) \geq 1 - \varepsilon$ or, in other words, whether $\pi_{\text{true}} \in \Pi_\varepsilon(\kappa \triangleright \lambda)$. From (2.24), we can be *sure* that this is the case if δ is sufficiently small.

Notation 2.1 The notation

$$\Theta_{\text{ir}} \vDash_s \kappa \triangleright \lambda$$

means that the premises Θ_{ir} entail the conclusion $\kappa \triangleright \lambda$ with surety. And the notation

$$\Theta_{\text{ir}} \nvDash_s \kappa \triangleright \lambda$$

means that Θ_{ir} does *not* entail $\kappa \triangleright \lambda$ with surety.

2.2.2.1 Deduction in Adams's Logic

The difference between entailment and deduction. Given a collection of premises and a potential conclusion, a logic's *entailment relation* specifies whether the conclusion is a consequence of the premises. An entailment relation is defined in terms of the logic's semantics. (Definition 1 is an example of such a definition.) In contrast, a *deductive procedure* is a method that ignores semantics and examines only the syntax of premises and a conclusion to corroborate whether the conclusion is entailed by the premises. A deductive procedure is *sound* if it does not corroborate any incorrect entailment; it is *complete* if it corroborates every correct entailment.

Notation 2.2 If a rule $\alpha \triangleright \beta$ is applicable to an entity (meaning that the entity has property α), then the entity would *normally* have the property $\alpha\beta$ and would only *abnormally* have the property $\alpha\beta'$. This motivates the following notation:

$$\text{normal}(\alpha \triangleright \beta) = \alpha\beta \text{ and } \text{abnormal}(\alpha \triangleright \beta) = \alpha\beta'. \tag{2.25}$$

Adams formulated rules of inference[6] (Adams 1966, Definition 6) for his logic. The following rules of inference can be shown to be equivalent to, but simpler than, the Concise Rules of Inference of Bamber (2000, Definition 2.10) which, in turn, are equivalent to Adams's rules of inference.

Definition 2. Simplified Rules of Inference.
S1 For any α, it is permissible to infer $\alpha \triangleright \alpha$.
S2 Given $\alpha \triangleright \beta$, it is permissible to infer $\kappa \triangleright \lambda$ provided that

$$\text{normal}(\alpha \triangleright \beta) \vdash \text{normal}(\kappa \triangleright \lambda) \text{ and} \tag{2.26}$$

$$\text{abnormal}(\kappa \triangleright \lambda) \vdash \text{abnormal}(\alpha \triangleright \beta) \tag{2.27}$$

S3 Given $\alpha \triangleright \beta$ and $\alpha \triangleright \gamma$, it is permissible to infer $\alpha \triangleright \beta\gamma$.

Remark. If $\pi(\alpha)$ and $\pi(\kappa)$ are positive and if $\alpha\beta \not\vdash \bot$ and $\kappa \not\vdash \lambda$, then (2.26) and (2.27) jointly constitute a necessary and sufficient condition for $\pi(\lambda \mid \kappa) \geq \pi(\beta \mid \alpha)$ (Goodman, Nguyen & Walker, 1991, Chapter 2, Lemma 2).

Definition 3. Suppose that Θ_{ir} is a finite collection of imperfect rules and that $\kappa \triangleright \lambda$ is an imperfect rule. A *proof*[7] of the conclusion $\kappa \triangleright \lambda$ from the premises Θ_{ir} is a finite sequence of imperfect rules having the following characteristics:

- Each imperfect rule in the sequence is either (*a*) a premise or (*b*) is inferable from earlier imperfect rules in the sequence via a rule of inference.
- The last imperfect rule in the sequence is $\kappa \triangleright \lambda$.

Adams (1966, Theorem 7) showed that his rules of inference were sound and complete. That is: $\Theta_{\text{ir}} \vDash_s \kappa \triangleright \lambda$ if and only if there exists a proof of $\kappa \triangleright \lambda$ from Θ_{ir}.

Subsequently, Adams (1983, 1986) developed an algorithm[8] for obtaining a yes-no answer to the question of whether $\Theta_{\text{ir}} \vDash_s \kappa \triangleright \lambda$. Later Bamber (1994) developed a computationally more efficient algorithm.

Example. Derivation of Bamber (2000, Definition 2.10, **C3**). Suppose that $\beta_1 \vdash \alpha_1$ and $\beta_2 \vdash \alpha_2$. Show that, from the premise set $\{\alpha_1 \triangleright \beta'_1, \alpha_2 \triangleright \beta'_2\}$, the conclusion $(\alpha_1 \vee \alpha_2) \triangleright (\beta_1 \vee \beta_2)'$ is entailed with surety. The following is a proof.

(1) $\alpha_1 \triangleright \beta_1'$ Premise;

(2) $\alpha_2 \triangleright \beta_2'$ Premise;

(3) $(\alpha_1 \vee \alpha_2) \triangleright \beta_1'$ Inferred from (1) via **S2**;

(4) $(\alpha_1 \vee \alpha_2) \triangleright \beta_2'$ Inferred from (2) via **S2**;

(5) $(\alpha_1 \vee \alpha_2) \triangleright (\beta_1' \wedge \beta_2')$ Inferred from (3) & (4) via **S3**;

(6) $(\alpha_1 \vee \alpha_2) \triangleright (\beta_1 \vee \beta_2)'$ Inferred from (5) via **S2**.

System P. Subsequent to Adams's Logic (Adams, 1966), Kraus, Lehmann, and Magidor (1990) developed a logic called *System P*, which, although it has a very different semantics from Adams's Logic, nevertheless has a syntactically equivalent entailment relation.

2.2.3 Entailment in SOPL

Roughly speaking, second-order probability logic (SOPL; Bamber, 2000; Bamber et al., 2004, 2005)[9] is a Bayesian form of high-probability logic in which an entailed conclusion's probability is *nearly sure* to be close to one (rather than guaranteed to be close to one as in Adams's Logic) whenever the premise probabilities are all close to one. Let us now be precise.

Recall that we identify each probability measure over properties with a point in the simplex Π. Let $\mathbb{P}$ denote the *uniform* probability measure over the points of Π. Then we may say that $\mathbb{P}$ is a *second-order* probability measure.

In the following definition, recall that the meanings of the notations Θ_{ir}, $\Pi_\delta(\Theta_{ir})$, and $\Pi_\varepsilon(\kappa \triangleright \lambda)$ are given by (2.21), (2.22), and (2.23).[10]

Definition 4. In SOPL, a set of premises Θ_{ir} *entails with near surety* a conclusion $\kappa \triangleright \lambda$ if and only if, for every $\varepsilon > 0$,

$$\lim_{\delta \downarrow 0} \mathbb{P}[\Pi_\varepsilon(\kappa \triangleright \lambda) \mid \Pi_\delta(\Theta_{ir})] = 1. \qquad (2.28)$$

Here is an equivalent definition: The premises Θ_{ir} *entail with near surety* the conclusion $\kappa \triangleright \lambda$ if and only if, for every $\varepsilon > 0$ and every $\eta > 0$, there exists a $\delta^*(\varepsilon, \eta) > 0$ such that, for all positive δ less than $\delta^*(\varepsilon, \eta)$,

$$\mathbb{P}[\Pi_\varepsilon(\kappa \triangleright \lambda) \mid \Pi_\delta(\Theta_{ir})] \geq 1 - \eta. \qquad (2.29)$$

Remark. We call this entailment with near surety for the following reason. We treat the unknown "true" probability measure as a random point in the simplex Π and denote it π_{true}. We take $\mathbb{P}$ to be the prior distribution of π_{true}.[11] We want to know whether $\pi_{\text{true}} \in \Pi_\varepsilon(\kappa \triangleright \lambda)$. We are given "evidence" about π_{true}, namely that $\pi_{\text{true}} \in \Pi_\delta(\Theta_{ir})$. Conditioning on the "evidence," the posterior probability that $\pi_{\text{true}} \in \Pi_\varepsilon(\kappa \triangleright \lambda)$ is given by the left side of (2.29). For any $\eta > 0$, if δ is sufficiently small, then the left side of (2.29) will be at least $1 - \eta$. So for sufficiently small δ, we can be *nearly sure* that $\pi_{\text{true}} \in \Pi_\varepsilon(\kappa \triangleright \lambda)$.

Notation 2.2.2 The notation

$$\Theta_{\text{ir}} \vDash_{\text{ns}} \kappa \triangleright \lambda$$

means that the premises Θ_{ir} entail the conclusion $\kappa \triangleright \lambda$ with near surety. And the notation

$$\Theta_{\text{ir}} \nvDash_{\text{ns}} \kappa \triangleright \lambda$$

means that Θ_{ir} does *not* entail $\kappa \triangleright \lambda$ with near surety.

2.2.3.1 Deduction in SOPL

A general method for deducing whether or not a collection of premises entails a conclusion with near surety is given by Theorems 3.17 and 3.15 of Bamber (2000). An equivalent method is presented in Bamber, et al. (2005, Section 10.2.1).

Definition 5. Suppose that Γ is a finite collection of imperfect rules:

$$\Gamma = \{\alpha_1 \triangleright \beta_1, ..., \alpha_m \triangleright \beta_m\}.$$

Then define $\Gamma^\rightarrow$ to be the finite collection of properties given by

$$\Gamma^\rightarrow = \{\alpha_1 \rightarrow \beta_1, ..., \alpha_m \rightarrow \beta_m\}.$$

Also, define

$$\text{EX}(\Gamma) = \{\alpha_i \triangleright \beta_i \in \Gamma : \Gamma^\rightarrow \vdash \alpha_i \rightarrow \beta_i'\}.$$

If Θ_{ir} is a finite set of imperfect rules, define its *exclusion sequence* to be a sequence of its subsets

$$\Theta_{\text{ir}}[1], \ \Theta_{\text{ir}}[2], \ \Theta_{\text{ir}}[3], \ ...$$

constructed as follows. Let $\Theta_{\text{ir}}[1] = \Theta_{\text{ir}}$ and, for $j \geq 1$, let $\Theta_{\text{ir}}[j+1] = \text{EX}(\Theta_{\text{ir}}[j])$.

Note that $\Theta_{\text{ir}}[j+1]$ is a proper subset of $\Theta_{\text{ir}}[j]$, unless the two sets are equal, in which case $\Theta_{\text{ir}}[k] = \Theta_{\text{ir}}[j]$ for all $k > j$.

Theorem 1. (Bamber et al., 2005, Theorem 10.5)) Suppose that Θ_{ir} is a finite collection of imperfect rules and that $\kappa \triangleright \lambda$ is a potential conclusion. Then $\Theta_{\text{ir}} \vDash_{\text{ns}} \kappa \triangleright \lambda$ if and only if one or both of the following conditions holds:

1. For some $j \geq 1$, $\Theta_{\text{ir}}[j]^\rightarrow \vdash \kappa \rightarrow \lambda$ but $\Theta_{\text{ir}}[j]^\rightarrow \nvdash \kappa \rightarrow \lambda'$.
2. For all $j \geq 1$, $\Theta_{\text{ir}}[j]^\rightarrow \vdash \kappa \rightarrow \lambda$.

Example. Suppose that α, β, and γ are primitive properties. Let $\Theta_{ir} = \{\alpha \triangleright \beta, \beta \triangleright \gamma, \alpha \triangleright \gamma'\}$. Use Theorem 1 to show that $\Theta_{ir} \vDash_{ns} \gamma \triangleright \alpha'$. The exclusion sequence for Θ_{ir} is

$$\Theta_{ir}[1] = \Theta_{ir}, \quad \Theta_{ir}[2] = \{\alpha \triangleright \beta, \alpha \triangleright \gamma'\}, \text{ and } \Theta_{ir}[j] = \emptyset \text{ for all } j \geq 3.$$

Furthermore, $\Theta_{ir}[2]^{\rightarrow} \vdash \gamma \rightarrow \alpha'$ but $\Theta_{ir}[2]^{\rightarrow} \nvdash \gamma \rightarrow \alpha''$. Therefore, $\Theta_{ir} \vDash_{ns} \gamma \triangleright \alpha'$.

2.2.4 Comparison of Adams's Logic and SOPL

Comparing the definition of entailment with surety (2.24) with the definition of entailment with near surety (2.28), it is evident that entailment with surety is a sufficient condition for entailment with near surety. That is, if

$$\Theta_{ir} \vDash_s \kappa \triangleright \lambda \tag{2.30}$$

then

$$\Theta_{ir} \vDash_{ns} \kappa \triangleright \lambda. \tag{2.31}$$

The converse does not hold, however. For example, suppose α, β, and γ are jointly compatible properties (i.e., $\alpha\beta\gamma \nvdash \bot$). Then

$$\{\alpha \triangleright \beta, \beta \triangleright \gamma\} \vDash_{ns} \alpha \triangleright \gamma, \tag{2.32}$$

but

$$\{\alpha \triangleright \beta, \beta \triangleright \gamma\} \nvDash_s \alpha \triangleright \gamma. \tag{2.33}$$

The reason for the non-entailment (2.33) in Adams's Logic is that there exist probability measures π such that

$$\pi(\beta|\alpha) \approx 1 \text{ and } \pi(\gamma|\beta) \approx 1 \text{ but } \pi(\gamma|\beta) \not\approx 1. \tag{2.34}$$

In fact, given any $s, t, u \in (0, 1)$, there exists probability measures π such that $\pi(\beta \mid \alpha) = s$, $\pi(\gamma \mid \beta) = t$, and $\pi(\gamma \mid \alpha) = u$ (Bamber, et al., 2004, Example 1.1).

In contrast, the reason for the entailment (2.32) in SOPL is that, even though probability measures π exist such that Equation 2.34 is true, such probability measures are *rare* (as measured by $\mathbb{P}$).

Adams's Logic is *monotonic*, meaning that, given finite sets of premises Θ_{ir} and Θ_{ir}^*,

if $\Theta_{ir} \vDash_s \kappa \triangleright \lambda$ and $\Theta_{ir} \subseteq \Theta_{ir}^*$ then $\Theta_{ir}^* \vDash_s \kappa \triangleright \lambda$. (2.35)

On the other hand, SOPL is *nonmonotonic*. This nonmonotonicity results from a basic feature of Bayesian analysis. In (2.29), changing the "evidence" from $\Pi_\delta(\Theta_{ir})$ to $\Pi_\delta(\Theta_{ir}^*)$ may cause the posterior probability of $\Pi_\varepsilon(\kappa \triangleright \lambda)$ to move from near one to far from one. As an example of nonmonotonicity, suppose that α, β, and γ are properties such that neither $\alpha\beta\gamma$ nor $\alpha\beta\gamma'$ is equivalent to $\perp$. Then

$$\{\alpha \triangleright \gamma\} \vDash_{ns} \alpha\beta \triangleright \gamma \text{ but } \{\alpha \triangleright \gamma, \beta \triangleright \gamma'\} \nvDash_{ns} \alpha\beta \triangleright \gamma. \tag{2.36}$$

Thus, in this case, the acquisition of a new premise leads to the retraction of a conclusion.

In summary, Adams's Logic entails fewer conclusions than does SOPL. But we can have greater confidence in the conclusions from Adams's Logic because they can never be retracted as a result of acquiring new premises.

2.2.5 Logics With Syntactically Equivalent Entailment

One of the surprising facts about logics of imperfect rules is that logics that have different semantics and that define entailment differently can, nevertheless, have entailment relations that are syntactically equivalent. Given syntactically equivalent premises, syntactically equivalent conclusions follow even though semantically the logics look entirely different from each other and appear unrelated. We have already seen an instance of this with Adams's Logic (Adams, 1966) and System P (Kraus, Lehmann & Magidor, 1990).

It turns out that entailment with near surety is syntactically equivalent or nearly so to reasoning in a number of other systems: rational closure (Lehmann & Magidor, 1992), System Z (Pearl, 1990), least specific possibilistic consequence (Benferhat, Dubois, & Prade, 1997), least-commitment consequence based on ε-belief functions (Benferhat, Saffiotti, & Smets, 2000), and a certain kind of maximum-entropy closure (Hill & Paris, 2003). In addition, on the basis of informal analysis, it *appears* that the preceding list should also include the random-structures method of Bacchus, Grove, Halpern, and Koller (Bacchus Grove, Halpern, & Koller, 1992; Grove, Halpern, & Koller, 1996).

This set of (near) equivalences of entailment is encouraging. It shows that, as a method of reasoning, SOPL's deduction procedure can be justified from a variety of perspectives.

2.3 Weak Versus Strong Association

In this section, we will define what it means for β and γ to be weakly associated (i.e., approximately conditionally independent) given α.

Let us say that a probability measure π satisfies the *positivity condition* if $\pi(\alpha) > 0$ and if each of the conditional probabilities in the following 2 × 2 contingency table is positive.

	γ	γ'
β	$\pi(\beta\gamma\|\alpha)$	$\pi(\beta\gamma'\|\alpha)$
β'	$\pi(\beta'\gamma\|\alpha)$	$\pi(\beta'\gamma'\|\alpha)$

(2.37)

In the following, it is assumed that positivity holds.

Consider the (β, γ) cell of the contingency table and consider the quantity

$$r_\alpha^{\beta,\gamma}(\pi) = \frac{\pi(\beta\gamma|\alpha)}{\pi(\beta|\alpha)\,\pi(\gamma|\alpha)}. \tag{2.38}$$

If $r_\alpha^{\beta,\gamma}(\pi) = 1$, then β and γ are conditionally independent given α. If $r_\alpha^{\beta,\gamma}(\pi) > 1$, then the ($\beta$, γ) cell has "surplus" probability relative to conditional independence. And if $r_\alpha^{\beta,\gamma}(\pi) < 1$, then the ($\beta$, γ) cell is "deficient" in probability relative to conditional independence. For the other three cells of the contingency table, we define the analogous quantities $r_\alpha^{\beta,\gamma'}(\pi)$, $r_\alpha^{\beta',\gamma}(\pi)$, and $r_\alpha^{\beta',\gamma'}(\pi)$.

Only certain patterns of "surplus" and "deficit" are possible across the cells of the contingency table. Thus if any cell has a surplus, then the two adjacent cells must have deficits, and the diagonally opposite cell must have a surplus. As a result, the quantities

$$r_\alpha^{\beta,\gamma}(\pi),\ \frac{1}{r_\alpha^{\beta,\gamma'}(\pi)},\ \frac{1}{r_\alpha^{\beta',\gamma}(\pi)},\ r_\alpha^{\beta',\gamma'}(\pi) \tag{2.39}$$

are either (a) all equal to one, (b) all greater than one, or (c) all less than one. This motivates the following definition.

Definition 6.

$$R_\alpha^{\beta,\gamma}(\pi) = r_\alpha^{\beta,\gamma}(\pi) \cdot \frac{1}{r_\alpha^{\beta,\gamma'}(\pi)} \cdot \frac{1}{r_\alpha^{\beta',\gamma}(\pi)} \cdot r_\alpha^{\beta',\gamma'}(\pi) \tag{2.40}$$

$$= \frac{\pi(\beta\gamma|\alpha)\,\pi(\beta'\gamma'|\alpha)}{\pi(\beta\gamma'|\alpha)\,\pi(\beta'\gamma|\alpha)}. \tag{2.41}$$

Remark. $R_\alpha^{\beta,\gamma}(\pi)$ can be expressed as a ratio of odds in two different ways. Thus

$$R_\alpha^{\beta,\gamma}(\pi) = \frac{\pi(\gamma|\alpha\beta)/\pi(\gamma'|\alpha\beta)}{\pi(\gamma|\alpha\beta')/\pi(\gamma'|\alpha\beta')} = \frac{\pi(\beta|\alpha\gamma)/\pi(\beta'|\alpha\gamma)}{\pi(\beta|\alpha\gamma')/\pi(\beta'|\alpha\gamma')}. \tag{2.42}$$

Assuming that π satisfies the positivity condition, the logarithm of $R_\alpha^{\beta,\gamma}(\pi)$ is defined and may be used as a measure of both the strength and direction of conditional association between β and γ given α. Its value may be zero, or any positive number, or any negative number. If $\log R_\alpha^{\beta,\gamma}(\pi)$ is zero, then β and γ are conditionally independent given α. If $\log R_\alpha^{\beta,\gamma}(\pi)$ is positive, then we say that β and γ are positively associated given α. And, if $\log R_\alpha^{\beta,\gamma}(\pi)$ is negative, then we say that β and γ are negatively associated given α.

Note that β and γ are negatively associated given α if and only if β and γ' are positively associated given α. Thus

$$\log R_\alpha^{\beta,\gamma'}(\pi) = -\log R_\alpha^{\beta,\gamma}(\pi). \tag{2.43}$$

Remark. Consider the case where α is the universal property $\top$. Then probabilities conditioned on $\alpha = \top$ in (2.41) are unconditional probabilities. The quantity $R_\top^{\beta,\gamma}(\pi)$ is used in the log-linear analysis of 2×2 contingency tables; it is known as the *cross-product ratio* and as the *odds ratio*, and its logarithm is a measure of row-column interaction (Bishop, Fienberg, & Holland 1975, pp. 13–18).

How should we define whether the conditional association between β and γ given α is strong or weak? If the positivity condition holds so that $\log R_\alpha^{\beta,\gamma}(\pi)$ is defined, a sensible strategy is to choose some positive real number τ—the choice being arbitrary—and use it as a threshold to separate strong from weak association. Then, bearing in mind the symmetry of (2.43), we may define the conditional association to be weak if

$$|\log R_\alpha^{\beta,\gamma}(\pi)| \leq \tau. \tag{2.44}$$

Although the choice for the threshold τ is arbitrary, once it has been made, it will be held fixed and not varied.

What if the positivity condition does not hold? We want a definition of weak association that can be applied both when the positivity condition holds and when it does not hold. Note that, given positivity, (2.44) is true if and only if the following double inequality is true:

$$e^{-\tau}\pi(\beta\gamma'|\alpha)\,\pi(\beta'\gamma'|\alpha) \leq \pi(\beta\gamma|\alpha)\,\pi(\beta'\gamma'|\alpha) \leq e^{\tau}\pi(\beta\gamma'|\alpha)\,\pi(\beta'\gamma|\alpha). \tag{2.45}$$

Also note that all the quantities in (2.45) are always defined, no matter whether positivity holds or not. This motivates the following definition.

Definition 7. β and γ are *weakly associated* given α if Eq. 2.45 is true; otherwise, they are *strongly associated*.

As mentioned, the choice of a value for $\tau>0$ is arbitrary. The smaller the value we choose, the stricter will be our definition of weak association; and the larger the τ, the looser the definition. We want to choose τ so that our formal definition of weak association agrees fairly well with our intuitive notion of weak association. A good choice might be $\tau = \log 2$ so that $e^{-\tau} = 1/2$ and $e^{\tau} = 2$ in Equation 2.45.

2.3.1 A Consequence of Weak Association

If β and γ are only weakly associated given α, then as $\pi(\gamma|\alpha)$ gets close to one, so does $\pi(\gamma|\alpha\beta')$. This will now be demonstrated.

Proposition 1. *Let π be any probability measure such that β and γ are only weakly associated given α. Then*

$$\pi(\gamma|\alpha\beta') \geq \frac{\pi(\gamma|\alpha)}{\pi(\gamma|\alpha) + e^\tau [1 - \pi(\gamma|\alpha)]}. \tag{2.46}$$

Proof. Case 1. $\pi(\alpha\beta')=0$.
Then $\pi(\gamma|\alpha\beta')=1$, which satisfies (2.46).
Case 2. $\pi(\alpha\beta')>0$.

Note that $\pi(\alpha\beta')$ being positive implies that $\pi(\alpha)$ is also. Because β and γ are only weakly associated given α, the double inequality (2.45) holds. Of these two inequalities, we use only the second one:

$$\pi(\beta\gamma|\alpha)\,\pi(\beta'\gamma'|\alpha) \leq e^\tau\,\pi(\beta\gamma'|\alpha)\,\pi(\beta'\gamma|\alpha). \tag{2.47}$$

The next equation follows because the right side equals the left side multiplied by e^τ, which is greater than one.

$$\pi(\beta'\gamma|\alpha)\,\pi(\beta'\gamma'|\alpha) \leq e^\tau\,\pi(\beta'\gamma|\alpha)\,\pi(\beta'\gamma'|\alpha). \tag{2.48}$$

Adding first the left sides of (2.47) and (2.48) and then the right sides yields

$$\pi(\gamma|\alpha)\,\pi(\beta'\gamma'|\alpha) \leq e^\tau\,\pi(\gamma'|\alpha)\,\pi(\beta'\gamma|\alpha).$$

Dividing both sides by $\pi(\beta'|\alpha)$ yields

$$\pi(\gamma|\alpha)\,\pi(\gamma'|\alpha\beta') \leq e^\tau\,\pi(\gamma'|\alpha)\,\pi(\gamma|\alpha\beta').$$

Hence

$$\pi(\gamma|\alpha)\,[1 - \pi(\gamma|\alpha\beta')] \leq e^\tau\,[1 - \pi(\gamma|\alpha)]\,\pi(\gamma|\alpha\beta'),$$

which implies (2.46).

2.4 Extending High-Probability Logics

We wish now to extend high-probability logics so that they can not only "reason" with rules but also weak-association statements. By a *statement of weak association* it is meant a statement of the form

$$\beta \text{ and } \gamma \text{ are only weakly associated given } \alpha, \tag{2.49}$$

which will be written symbolically as either

$$\beta \perp\!\!\!\perp \gamma | \; \alpha \; \text{ or } \; (\beta \perp\!\!\!\perp \gamma | \; \alpha). \tag{2.50}$$

30 Donald Bamber et al.

This notation is patterned after the commonly used notation $\beta \perp\!\!\!\perp \gamma \mid \alpha$ that indicates that β and γ are conditionally independent given α (Dawid, 1979).

Suppose that $\beta \not\!\perp\!\!\!\perp \gamma \mid \alpha$ is a statement of weak association. Having chosen a threshold τ to separate strong from weak association, we define

$$\Pi_\tau(\beta \not\!\perp\!\!\!\perp \gamma \mid \alpha) = \{\pi \in \Pi : \text{Equation 2.45 is true}\}. \tag{2.51}$$

Given a finite set of weak-association statements

$$\Theta_{\text{wa}} = \{(\chi_1 \not\!\perp\!\!\!\perp \psi_1 \mid \rho_1), \ldots, (\chi_m \not\!\perp\!\!\!\perp \psi_m \mid \rho_m)\}, \tag{2.52}$$

let

$$\Pi_\tau(\Theta_{\text{wa}}) = \begin{cases} \bigcap_{i=1}^m \Pi_\tau(\chi_i \not\!\perp\!\!\!\perp \psi_i \mid \rho_i) & \text{if } m \geq 1, \\ \Pi & \text{if } m = 0. \end{cases} \tag{2.53}$$

In both *Extended Adams's Logic* and *Extended SOPL*, premises may be imperfect rules and/or statements of weak association. We now define entailment in these two logics. In this definition, the premises are $\Theta_{\text{ir}} \cup \Theta_{\text{wa}}$, where Θ_{ir} is a finite collection of imperfect rules and Θ_{wa} is a finite collection of weak-association statements; the potential conclusion is $\kappa \triangleright \lambda$. Recall that meaning of the notations $\Pi_\delta(\Theta_{ir})$ and $\Pi_\varepsilon(\kappa \triangleright \lambda)$ is given by (2.21), (2.22), and (2.23).

Definition 8. (a) In Extended Adams's Logic, $\Theta_{\text{ir}} \cup \Theta_{\text{wa}}$ *entails with surety* a conclusion $\kappa \triangleright \lambda$ if and only if, for every $\tau > 0$ *and every* $\varepsilon > 0$, there exists a $\delta > 0$ such that

$$\Pi_\delta(\Theta_{\text{ir}}) \cap \Pi_\tau(\Theta_{\text{wa}}) \subseteq \Pi_\varepsilon(\kappa \triangleright \lambda). \tag{2.54}$$

(b) In Extended SOPL, a set of premises $\Theta_{\text{ir}} \cup \Theta_{\text{wa}}$ *entails with near surety* a conclusion $\kappa \triangleright \lambda$ if and only if, for every $\tau > 0$ and every $\varepsilon > 0$,

$$\lim_{\delta \downarrow 0} \mathbb{P}[\Pi_\varepsilon(\kappa \triangleright \lambda) \mid \Pi_\delta(\Theta_{\text{ir}}) \cap \Pi_\tau(\Theta_{\text{wa}})] = 1. \tag{2.55}$$

Thus, as in SOPL, entailment in Extended SOPL is Bayesian.

Remark. Although we have suggested setting the strong-versus-weak association threshold τ equal to $\log 2$, we do not want our definition of entailment to depend upon any particular value of τ. Therefore, the aforementioned definition requires that (2.54) and (2.55) hold for all values of $\tau > 0$.

Just as before, (a) entailment with surety in Extended Adams's Logic implies entailment with near surety in Extended SOPL, (b) Entailment with surety is monotonic, and (c) Entailment with near surety is nonmonotonic.

Notation. As before, the symbols $\models_s$ and $\not\models_s$ will denote entailment with surety and its negation. And the symbols $\models_{ns}$ and $\not\models_{ns}$ will denote entailment with near surety and its negation.

2.4.1 Inheritance to Exceptional Subclasses Revisited

We will now examine how Extended Adams's Logic and Extended SOPL handle inheritance from a parent class to an exceptional subclass. In the following, we will assume that none of the properties $\alpha\beta\gamma$, $\alpha\beta\gamma'$, $\alpha\beta'\gamma$, and $\alpha\beta'\gamma'$ are equivalent to $\bot$.

First, we examine Extended Adams's Logic.

Theorem 2. (a) *Extended Adams's Logic satisfies Desideratum 2.1.1. Thus, without weak association, we have*

$$\{\alpha \triangleright \beta, \alpha \triangleright \gamma\} \not\models_s \alpha\beta' \triangleright \gamma. \tag{2.56}$$

(b) *Extended Adams's Logic satisfies Desideratum 2.1.2. Thus, with weak association, we have*

$$\{\alpha \triangleright \beta, \alpha \triangleright \gamma, (\beta \perp\!\!\!\perp \gamma | \alpha)\} \models_s \alpha\beta' \triangleright \gamma. \tag{2.57}$$

Proof. (a) Because entailment with surety implies entailment with near surety, the nonentailment (2.60) proved in Theorem 3 implies the nonentailment (2.56).

(b) To demonstrate the entailment (2.57), what must be shown is: Given any $\tau > 0$ and any $\varepsilon \in (0, 1)$, there exists a $\delta(\tau, \varepsilon) \in (0,1)$ such that

$$\Pi_{\delta(\tau,\varepsilon)}(\alpha \triangleright \beta) \cap \Pi_{\delta(\tau,\varepsilon)}(\alpha \triangleright \gamma) \cap \Pi_\tau(\beta \perp\!\!\!\perp \gamma \mid \alpha) \subseteq \Pi_\varepsilon(\alpha\beta' \triangleright \gamma). \tag{2.58}$$

We proceed as follows: Given any $\tau > 0$ and any $\varepsilon \in (0,1)$, set

$$\delta(\tau, \varepsilon) = \frac{\varepsilon}{\varepsilon + e^\tau(1 - \varepsilon)}. \tag{2.59}$$

Consider any probability measure π that is a member of the set on the left side of (2.58). Then, for this π, $\pi(\gamma|\alpha) \geq 1 - \delta(\tau,\varepsilon)$ and β and γ are only weakly associated given α. Applying Proposition 1, we see that $\pi(\gamma \mid \alpha\beta') \geq 1-\varepsilon$. This demonstrates (2.58) and, thus, the entailment (2.57).

Next, we examine Extended SOPL.

Theorem 3. (a) *Extended SOPL satisfies Desideratum 2.1.1. Thus, without weak association, we have*

$$\{\alpha \triangleright \beta, \alpha \triangleright \gamma\} \not\models_{ns} \alpha\beta' \triangleright \gamma. \tag{2.60}$$

(b) *Extended SOPL satisfies Desideratum 2.1.2. Thus, with weak association, we have*

$$\{\alpha \triangleright \beta, \alpha \triangleright \gamma, (\beta \perp\!\!\!\perp \gamma | \alpha)\} \models_{ns} \alpha\beta' \triangleright \gamma. \tag{2.61}$$

Proof. (a) Apply Theorem 1. Let $\Theta_{ir} = \{\alpha \triangleright \beta, \alpha \triangleright \gamma\}$. Its exclusion sequence is:

$$\Theta_{ir}[1] = \Theta_{ir} \text{ and } \Theta_{ir}[j] = \emptyset \text{ for all } j \geq 2.$$

Furthermore,

$$\Theta_{ir}[1]^{\neg} \vdash \alpha\beta' \to \gamma.$$
$$\Theta_{ir}[1]^{\neg} \vdash \alpha\beta' \to \gamma'.$$
$$\Theta_{ir}[2]^{\neg} \nvdash \alpha\beta' \to \gamma.$$

Therefore, (2.60) holds.

(*b*) Because entailment with surety implies entailment with near surety, the entailment (2.61) follows from the corresponding entailment (2.57) of Theorem 2.

Thus we have achieved our goal. We have succeeded in extending both Adams's Logic and SOPL by allowing statements of weak association to be included among premise sets and, furthermore, we have done this in such a way that Desiderata 2.1.1 and 2.1.2 are satisfied.

2.4.2 Future Work

We have reached the goal that we set out to achieve earlier in this paper. However, we do not yet have a deduction procedure for either Extended Adams's Logic or Extended SOPL. The goal of our future work is to develop sound and complete deduction procedures for both logics.

2.5 Relevance of High-Probability Logics to the Study of Human Reasoning

Human reasoning is commonly considered to be a guide to how nonmonotonic logics should be constructed (Pelletier & Elio, 2005). Often the proposer(s) of a nonmontonic logic will present a reasoning problem, claim that a particular answer to that problem is intuitively correct, and then state that their logic is constructed so as to give the intuitively correct answer. Indeed, we did just that when we presented Examples 2.1.1 and 2.1.2 to motivate Desiderata 2.1.1 and 2.1.2 and then stated that we would develop high-probability logics that would satisfy those desiderata.

In everyday life, to avoid inferential paralysis, humans constantly need to reach conclusions that are not certain to be correct given the available information. Thus, although there is a need to reach conclusions that are not certain, it would be undesirable if those conclusions were wrong very often. Thus (Extended) SOPL would seem to fit the needs of human reasoners because it delivers conclusions that have high probability of being correct. But, of course, the seeming suitability of a logic is no guarantee that people use it.

Furthermore, no logic can fully explain human reasoning. First, humans make errors. Second, there are individual differences in reasoning (Stanovich, 2008). Third, logics do not provide a process model for reasoning; for example, they don't predict reaction times.

And it has been argued that human reasoners don't use logic but, rather, reason in a Bayesian fashion (Oaksford & Chater, 2009). Of course, our work with (Extended) SOPL has shown that reasoning can be simultaneously Bayesian and conform to a logic.

What do empirical studies of human reasoning reveal? To date, most studies of the conformance of human reason to logic have centered on classical logic. However, a few studies have focused on nonmonotonic logics (Strasser & Antonelli (2015, Section 4).

A study relevant to the question of whether human reasoning conforms to SOPL was performed by Benferhat, Bonnefon, and da Silva Neves (2005). They examined whether research participants' reasoning conformed better to Lexicographical Closure or to Minimum Specificity Principle (MSP) Closure. Both these logics are nonmonotonic and the latter has an entailment relation that is nearly equivalent to that of SOPL. They found that participants' inferences agreed with Lexicographical Closure more often than with MSP Closure; nevertheless, a substantial portion of participants' inferences agreed with MSP Closure. Clearly, then, human reasoners make their inferences in conformance with SOPL only some of the time at most. But, given that different people sometimes make different inferences, there isn't any logic that can predict people's inferences with complete accuracy.

Logics alone cannot explain the variability in people's inferences. Some additional mechanism(s) must be invoked to explain that variability. Perhaps different people encode the premises in reasoning problems differently. Perhaps people do attempt to follow some deduction procedure, such as that of SOPL, but have some probability of making an error at each step.

It remains to be seen then whether logics will have a useful role in explaining human inferences.

2.6 Summary and Conclusion

In the study of logics of imperfect rules, perhaps the most important controversy has concerned whether an exceptional subclass should inherit properties from its parent class. Some logics have this feature, some do not.

We have shown that high-probability logics can have their cake and eat it too. Specifically, we have extended both Adams's Logic and SOPL so that premise sets can include statements of weak association, not just rules. And we have shown that in these extended high-probability logics, inheritance to an exceptional subclass occurs if and only if an appropriate statement of weak association is included among the premises.

Notes

1. Rules can be paraphrased in terms of sets. Thus if A and B respectively denote the set of entities having property α and the set of entities having property β, then the rule (2.5) can be paraphrased as stating, with exceptions possible, that the members of A are members of B.
2. Ernest W. Adams (1983) studied certain intuitive arguments, which he suggested were enthymematic. However, those arguments did not involve inheritance to exceptional subclasses.
3. This is the probabilistic analogue of $A \subseteq B$ if $A = \emptyset$.
4. Ernest W. Adams (1926–2009) was a philosopher at the University of California, Berkeley, where he and Alfred Tarski founded the Group in Logic and Methodology of Science. Previously, Adams had been Patrick Suppes's first graduate student. Early in his career, he collaborated with R. Duncan Luce. A substantial portion of Adams's writings are relevant to mathematical psychology. Adams's work up to 1994 was summarized by Suppes in (Suppes, 1994), which appeared in the Adams Festschrift (Eells & Skyrms, 1994).
5. We may think of this as being the probability measure that governs the real world.
6. Rules of inference are not to be confused with either perfect or imperfect rules.
7. A proof is an example of a deductive procedure.
8. Such an algorithm is another kind of deductive procedure, different from a proof.
9. Multiple versions of SOPL are presented in these papers. We describe here the simplest version, i.e., the version where premises and conclusions are "unscaled."
10. To simplify exposition, it will be assumed from hereon that the premise set Θ_{ir} is consistent as defined by Pearl (1990) in his System Z. For further details, see Section 9 of Bamber et al. (2005).
11. It is not essential that the prior be uniform. Any quasi-uniform prior will work equally well (Bamber, 2000, p. 22–23)).

References

Adams, E. W. (1966). Probability and the logic of conditionals. In J. Hintikka & P. Suppes (Eds.), *Aspects of inductive logic* (pp. 265–316). Amsterdam: North Holland Publishing.
Adams, E. W. (1975). *The logic of conditionals*. Dordrecht: D. Reidel.
Adams, E. W. (1983). Probabilistic enthymemes. *Journal of Pragmatics, 7*, 283–295.
Adams, E. W. (1986). On the logic of high probability. *Journal of Philosophical Logic, 15*, 255–279.
Adams, E. W. (1998). *A primer of probability logic*. Stanford, CA: CSLI Publications, Center for the Study of Language and Information.
Antoniou, G. (1997). *Nonmonotonic reasoning*. Cambridge, MA: MIT Press.
Bacchus, F., Grove, A. J., Halpern, J. Y., & Koller, D. (1992). From statistics to degrees of belief. In *Proceedings of AAAI-92 (tenth national conference on artificial intelligence)* (pp. 602–608).

Bacchus, F., Grove, A. J., Halpern, J. Y., & Koller, D. (1996). From statistical knowledge bases to degrees of belief. *Artificial Intelligence, 87*, 75–143.
Bamber, D. (1994). Probabilistic entailment of conditionals by conditionals. *IEEE Transactions on Systems, Man, and Cybernetics, 24*, 1714–1723.
Bamber, D. (2000). Entailment with near surety of scaled assertions of high conditional probability. *Journal of Philosophical Logic, 29*, 1–74.
Bamber, D., Goodman, I. R., & Nguyen, H. T. (2004). Deduction from conditional knowledge. *Soft Computing, 8*, 247–255.
Bamber, D., Goodman, I. R., & Nguyen, H. T. (2005). Robust reasoning with rules that have exceptions: From second-order probability to argumentation via upper envelopes of probability and possibility plus directed graphs. *Annals of Mathematics and Artificial Intelligence, 45*, 83–171.
Benferhat, S., Bonnefon, J. F., & da Silva Neves, R. (2005). An overview of possibilistic handling of default reasoning, with experimental studies. *Synthese, 146*, 53–70.
Benferhat, S., Dubois, D., & Prade, H. (1997). Nonmonotonic reasoning, conditional objects and possibility theory. *Artificial Intelligence, 92*, 259–276.
Benferhat, S., Saffiotti, A., & Smets, P. (2000). Belief functions and default reasoning. *Artificial Intelligence, 122*, 1–69.
Bishop, Y. M. M., Fienberg, S. E., & Holland, P. W. (1975). *Discrete multivariate analysis: Theory and practice*. Cambridge, MA: MIT Press.
Darwiche, A. (1997). A logical notion of conditional independence: Properties and applications. *Artificial Intelligence, 97*, 45–82.
Dawid, A. P. (1979). Conditional independence in statistical theory. *Journal of the Royal Statistical Society, Series B (Methodological), 41*, 1–31.
Eells, E., & Skyrms, B. (Eds.). (1994). *Probability and conditionals: Belief revision and rational decision*. Cambridge, UK: Cambridge University Press.
Ginsberg, M. L. (Ed.). (1987). *Readings in nonmonotonic reasoning*. Los Altos, CA: Morgan Kaufmann.
Goodman, I. R., Nguyen, H. T., & Walker, E. A. (1991). *Conditional inference and logic for intelligent systems: A theory of measure-free conditioning*. North-Holland.
Grove, A. J., Halpern, J. Y., & Koller, D. (1996). Asymptotic conditional probabilities. *SIAM Journal on Computing, 25*, 1–51.
Halpern, J. Y. (2003). *Reasoning about uncertainty*. Cambridge, MA: MIT Press.
Hill, L. C., & Paris, J. B. (2003). When maximizing entropy gives the rational closure. *Journal of Logic and Computation, 13*, 51–68.
Ivanovska, M., & Giese, M. (2011). Probabilistic logic with conditional independence formulae. In T. Ågnotes (Ed.), *Fifth starting AI researchers' symposium, STAIRS 2010* (pp. 127–139). Amsterdam: IOS Press.
Kraus, S., Lehmann, D., & Magidor, M. (1990). Nonmonotonic reasoning, preferential models and cumulative logics. *Artificial Intelligence, 44*, 167–207.
Lang, J., Liberatore, P., & Marquis, P. (2002). Conditional independence in propositional logic. *Artificial Intelligence, 141*, 79–121.
Lehmann, D., & Magidor, M. (1992). What does a conditional knowledge base entail? *Artificial Intelligence, 55*, 1–60.
Moore, B. N., & Parke, R. (2004). *Critical thinking* (7th ed.). New York: McGraw-Hill.
Nguyen, H. T., & Walker, E. A. (2006). *A first course in fuzzy logic* (3rd ed.). Boca Raton, FL: Chapman & Hall/CRC.
Oaksford, M., & Chater, N. (2009). Précis of Bayesian rationality: The probabilistic approach to human reasoning (with discussion). *Behavioral and Brain Sciences, 32*, 69–120.

Pearl, J. (1990). System Z: A natural ordering of defaults with tractable applications to nonmonotonic reasoning. In R. Parikh (Ed.), *Theoretical Aspects of Reasoning about Knowledge. Proceedings of the Third Conference. (TARK 1990)* (pp. 121–135). San Mateo, CA: Morgan Kaufmann.

Pelletier, F. J., & Elio, R. (2005). The case for psychologism in default and inheritance reasoning. *Synthese, 146*, 7–35.

Stanovich, K. E. (2008). Individual differences in reasoning and the algorithmic/intentional level distinction in cognitive science. In J. E. Adler & L. J. Rips (Eds.), *Reasoning: Studies of human inference and its foundations* (pp. 414–438). Cambridge, UK: Cambridge University Press.

Strasser, C., & Antonelli, G. A. (2015). Non-monotonic logic. In E. N. Zalta (Ed.), *Stanford encyclopedia of philosophy (fall 2015 edition)*, http://plato.stanford.edu/archives/fall2015/entries/logic-nonmonotonic/

Suppes, P. (1994). A brief survey of Adams' contributions to philosophy. In E. Eells & B. Skyrms (Eds.), *Probability and Conditionals: Belief Revision and Rational Decision* (pp. 201–204). Cambridge, UK: Cambridge University Press.

Walton, W. N. (1989). *Informal logic: A handbook for critical argumentation.* Cambridge UK: Cambridge University Press.

3 Stochastic Orders of Variability

Hans Colonius

3.1 Introduction: Some Variability Orders

The fact that the response to one and the same stimulus, under seemingly identical conditions, varies from one instance to the next is a fundamental observation of reaction time (RT) research and, arguably, of behavioral science in general. Moreover, recent neurophysiological modeling approaches seek to identify the sources of variability at the neuronal level (e.g., Goris, Movshon, & Simoncelli, 2014; Lin, Okun, Carandini, & Harris, 2015; van den Berg, Shin, Chou, George, & Ma, 2012) and often try relate them to trial-to-trial variability in behavior. In psychology, the recognition that the complete distribution function of RTs may contain critical information about the underlying stochastic mechanism not accessible by only considering their mean, has led to the development of many RT models predicting specific distribution functions, e.g., race, counter, and diffusion models (Luce, 1986). However, these models are often testable only if one takes specific distributional assumptions for granted, even if these assumptions are not part of the models' core assumptions (for a recent discussion, see Jones & Dzhafarov, 2014).

Much of Townsend's work is in a different tradition, however (e.g., Townsend & Eidels, 2011; Townsend & Nozawa, 1995; Townsend & Wenger, 2004). Order relations between RT distributions that compare the "location" or the "magnitude" of random variables—such as stochastic order, hazard rate order, or likelihood order—have played an important role in his work (e.g., Townsend, 1990). More recently, we addressed the issue of comparing RT distributions with respect to measures of variability (Townsend & Colonius, 2005). In this chapter, I recollect some results of the latter paper and relate them to some recent developments in statistics.

While specific distributions are typically described by certain moments (mean and variance) and transforms thereof, in particular skewness and kurtosis, this approach has certain shortcomings. For example, the variance may not be finite. Several notions of variability, weaker and stronger than the variance, have been investigated in the statistical literature (cf., Shaked & Shanthikumar, 2007).[1] The first variability order considered here requires the definition of a *convex function* $\phi:\Re\to\Re$, i.e.,

$$\phi(\alpha x + (1-\alpha)y) \leq \alpha\phi(x) + (1-\alpha)\phi(y),$$

for all $x, y \in \Re$ and $\alpha \in [0,1]$.

Definition 9 (Convex order).[2] *Let X and Y be two random variables, such that*

$$E\phi(X) \leq E\phi(Y) \text{ for all convex functions } \phi : \Re \to \Re,$$

provided the expectations exist. Then X is said to be smaller than Y in the convex order denoted as

$$X \leq_{cx} Y.$$

Roughly speaking, convex functions take on their (relatively) larger values over regions of the form $(-\infty,a)\cup(b,+\infty)$ for $a<b$. Therefore, when the condition in the earlier definition holds, Y is more likely to take on "extreme" values than X; that is, Y is "more variable" than X.[3]

The convex order has some strong implications. Using the convexity of functions $\phi(x)=x, \phi(x)=-x$ and $\phi(x)=x_2$, it is can be shown that

$$X \leq_{cx} Y \text{ implies } EX = EY \text{ and } \operatorname{Var} X \leq \operatorname{Var} Y.$$

Moreover, when $EX = EY$, then a condition equivalent to $X \leq_{cx} Y$ is

$$E[\max(X,a)] \leq E[\max(Y,a)] \text{ for all } a \in \Re.$$

The convex order only compares random variables that have the same means. One way to drop this requirement is to introduce a so-called *dilation order* by order

Definition 10 (Dilation order).

$$X \leq_{dil} Y, \text{ if } [X - EX] \leq_{cx} [Y - EY].$$

For nonnegative random variables X and Y with finite means, one can alternatively define the *Lorenz order* by

$$X \leq_{Lorenz} Y, \text{ if } \frac{X}{EX} \leq_{cx} \frac{Y}{EY},$$

which can be used to order random variables with respect to the *Lorenz curve* used, e.g., in economics to measure the inequality of incomes.

For the next order type, we need the concept of a *quantile function*, closely related to that of a distribution function.

Definition 11 (Quantile function). *Let X be a real-valued random variable with distribution function F(x). Then the quantile function of X is* *defined as*

$$Q(u) = F^{-1}(u) = \inf\{x \mid F(x) \geq u\}, \quad 0 \leq u \leq 1. \tag{3.1}$$

For every $-\infty < x < +\infty$ and $0 < u < 1$, we have

$$F(x) \geq u \quad \text{if, and only if,} \quad Q(u) \leq x.$$

Thus if there exists x with $F(x) = u$, then $F(Q(u)) = u$ and $Q(u)$ is the smallest value of x satisfying $F(x) = u$. If $F(x)$ is continuous and strictly increasing, $Q(u)$ is the unique value x such that $F(x) = u$.

The specification of a distribution through its quantile function takes away the need to describe a distribution through its moments. Alternative measures in terms of quantiles are available, e.g., the median as a measure of location, defined as $md(X)=Q(0.5)$, or the interquartile range as a measure of dispersion, defined as $IQR=Q(.75)-Q(.25)$.

The following order is based on comparing difference between quantiles of the distribution functions.

Definition 12 (Dispersive order). *Let X and Y be random variables with quantile functions F^{-1} and G^{-1}, respectively. If*

$$F^{-1}(\beta) - F^{-1}(\alpha) \leq G^{-1}(\beta) - G^{-1}(\alpha), \quad \text{whenever} \quad 0 < \alpha \leq \beta < 1,$$

then X is said to be smaller than Y in the dispersive order denoted by $X \leq_{disp} Y$.

In contrast to the convex order, the dispersive order is clearly *location free*:

$$X \leq_{disp} Y \Leftrightarrow X + c \leq_{disp} Y, \quad \text{for any real } c.$$

The dispersive order is also *dilative*, i.e., $X \leq_{\text{disp}} aX$ whenever $a \geq 1$ and, moreover,

$$X \leq_{disp} Y \Leftrightarrow -X \leq_{disp} -Y.$$

However, it is not closed under convolutions. Its characterization requires two more definitions.

First, a random variable Z is called *dispersive* if $X + Z \leq_{disp} Y + Z$ whenever $X \leq_{disp} Y$ and Z is independent of X and Y. Second, a density (more general, any nonnegative function) g is called *logconcave* if $\log g$ is concave, or, equivalently,

$$g[\alpha x + (1-\alpha)y] \geq [g(x)]^{\alpha} [g(y)]^{1-\alpha}.$$

Proposition 2. *The random variable X is dispersive if, and only if, X has a logconcave density.*[4]

It can be shown that the dispersion order implies the dilation order, that is, for random variables with finite means,

$$X \leq_{disp} Y \Rightarrow X \leq_{dil} Y,$$

from which it immediately follows that also $\operatorname{Var} X \leq \operatorname{Var} Y$.

3.2 The Quantile Spread

All variability orders considered so far are strong enough to imply a corresponding ordering of the variances. Moreover, if X and Y have the same finite support and satisfy $X \leq_{disp} Y$, then they must have the same distribution. Hence a weaker concept is desirable. In Townsend and Colonius (2005), we developed such a weaker concept of variability order in an attempt to describe the effect of sample size on the shape of the distribution of the extreme order statistics $X_{1:n}$ (minimum) and $X_{n:n}$ (maximum). It is based on the notion of *quantile spread*.

Definition 13. *The quantile spread of random variable X with distribution F is*

$$QS_X(p) = F^{-1}(p) - F^{-1}(1-p),$$

for $0.5 < p < 1$.

With $S = 1 - F$ (the survival function), $F^{-1}(p) = S^{-1}(1-p)$ implies

$$QS_X(p) = S^{-1}(1-p) - S^{-1}(p).$$

It turns out that the concept of a *spread function*, as already defined by Balanda and MacGillivray (1990), is equivalent to the quantile spread. The quantile spread of a distribution describes how the probability mass is placed symmetrically about its median and hence can be used to formalize concepts such as peakedness and tailweight traditionally associated with kurtosis. This way, it allows us to separate concepts of kurtosis and peakedness for asymmetric distributions.

Example 3.2.1 (Weibull). *For the Weibull distribution (see Figure 3.1) defined by*

$$F(x) = 1 - \exp(-\beta x^\alpha) \text{ with } \alpha, \beta > 0,$$

the quantile spread is

$$QS_X(p) = \beta^{-1/\alpha} \left[\left(\ln \frac{1}{1-p} \right)^{1/\alpha} - \ln \left(\frac{1}{p} \right)^{1/\alpha} \right]$$

for $0.5 < p < 1$.

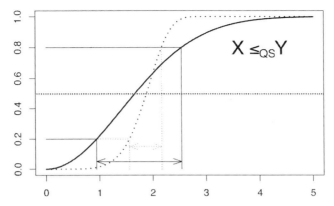

Figure 3.1 Two Weibull distributions with $\alpha = 2$ and $\alpha = 6$ and $\beta = 2$. The horizontal arrows indicate their quantile spread at $p = 0.8$. The order $\leq_{QS}$ is defined in the next section.

For $\alpha = 1$ (exponential distribution with parameter β), one gets

$$QS_X(p) = (1/\beta) \ln \frac{p}{1-p}.$$

For $\beta = 1/2$, this equals the quantile spread function for the (standard) *logistic distribution*

$$F(x) = \frac{1}{1 + \exp(-x)}, \quad -\infty < x < +\infty.$$

Note: This shows that the quantile spread does not uniquely characterize the distribution function from which it has been generated.

Example 3.2.2 (Cauchy distribution). *The Cauchy distribution with density*

$$f(x) = \frac{\gamma}{\pi(x^2 + \gamma^2)}, \quad \gamma > 0,$$

has no finite variance; the quantile function is

$$F^{-1}(p) = \gamma \tan[\pi(p - 0.5)],$$

yielding the quantile spread

$$F^{-1}(p) - F^{-1}(1-p) = \gamma\{\tan[\pi(p - 0.5)] - \tan[\pi(0.5 - p)]\}$$

for $0.5 < p < 1$.

Example 3.2.3 (Extreme order statistics). *For the extreme order statistics, one gets simple expressions for the quantile spread, making it easy* to describe their behavior as a function of sample size n:

$$QS_{min}(p) = S^{-1}[(1-p)^{1/n}] - S^{-1}(p^{1/n})$$

and

$$QS_{max}(p) = F^{-1}(p^{1/n}) - F^{-1}[(1-p)^{1/n}].$$

Not surprisingly, the case of a symmetric parent distribution leads to a simplification with respect to the order statistics.

Proposition 3. *For a symmetric parent distribution, the quantile spread for the maximum is identical to the quantile spread for the minimum.*

Proof. For a proof assuming symmetry around zero, see Townsend and Colonius (2005, p. 765). The general case follows similarly.

3.3 The Quantile Spread Order

Definition 14. *Let X and Y be random variables with quantile spreads QS_X and QS_Y, respectively. Then X is called smaller than Y in quantile spread order, denoted as $X \leq_{QS} Y$, if*

$$QS_X(p) \leq QS_Y(p) \text{ for all } p \in (0.5, 1).$$

The following properties of the quantile spread order can be determined:

1. The order $\leq_{QS}$ is *location-free*, i.e.,

    $X \leq_{QS} Y$ iff $X + c \leq_{QS} Y$ for any real c

2. The order $\leq_{QS}$ is *dilative*, i.e, $X \leq_{QS} aX$ whenever $a \geq 1$.
3. $X \leq_{QS} Y$ if, and only if $-X \leq_{QS} -Y$.
4. Assume F_X and F_Y are symmetric, then

    $X \leq_{QS} Y$ if, and only if, $F_X^{-1}(p) \leq F_Y^{-1}(p)$ for $p \in (0.5, 1)$.

5. $\leq_{QS}$ implies ordering of the *mean absolute deviation around the median*, MAD,

    $$MAD(X) = E[|X - md(X)|]$$

    (md the median), i.e.,

    $X \leq_{QS} Y$ implies $MAD(X) \leq MAD(Y)$.

The last point follows from writing

$$\text{MAD}(X) = \int_{0.5}^{1} [F^{-1}(p) - F^{-1}(1-p)] \, dp.$$

For the Cauchy distribution with quantile spread

$$QS(p) = \gamma \{ \tan [\pi(p - 0.5)] - \tan [\pi(0.5 - p)] \},$$

it is obvious that parameter γ clearly defines the QS order for this distribution.

The next example demonstrates how the QS order can be used to describe the effect of sample size on the minimum order statistic.

Example 3.3.1. *The quantile spread for the Weibull minimum (cf. Example 3.2.1) is*

$$QS_{min}(p;n) = (n\lambda)^{-1/\alpha} \left[\left(\ln \frac{1}{1-p} \right)^{1/\alpha} - \left(\ln \frac{1}{p} \right)^{1/\alpha} \right].$$

For $p \in (0.5, 1)$, this is decreasing in n. Thus

$$X_{1:n} \leq_{QS} X_{1:n-1},$$

i.e., the quantile spread for the Weibull minimum decreases as a function of sample size n.

The next section illustrates a recent application of the quantile spread order to define the dispersive properties of a not yet well-known distribution.

3.4 The Quantile Spread Order for the Kumaraswamy Distribution

The density for the Beta distribution, frequently used in modeling, is

$$f(x) = \frac{\Gamma(\alpha + \beta)}{\Gamma(\alpha)\Gamma(\beta)} x^{\alpha-1} (1-x)^{\beta-1}, \quad 0 < x < 1,$$

where Γ is the gamma function, $\alpha > 0$, and $\beta > 0$. It is flexible and has simple closed-form expressions for the moments. However, it has no closed-form solution for its quantile function $F^{-1}(p)$, which is often a drawback in simulation and estimation studies.

An alternative distribution is the *Kumaraswamy distribution*, which is, in many respects, very similar to the Beta distribution. Its dispersion properties have recently been studied by Mitnik and Baek (2013). The distribution function is

$$F(x) = 1 - \left[1 - \left(\frac{x-c}{b-c}\right)^p\right]^q,$$

where $c < x < b$ and p, q are shape parameters with $p < 0, q < 0$ (Kumaraswamy, 1980). Let us denote this general form of the distribution by $K(p, q, c, b)$. In contrast to the Beta distribution, it has no closed-form expressions for the mean and variance, but a simple quantile function:

$$x = Q(u) = c + (b-c)\left[1 - (1-u)^{\frac{1}{q}}\right]^{1/p}$$

for $0 < u < 1$. One question addressed in Mitnik and Baek (2013) was how to reparametrize the distribution so that members of its distribution family can be compared with respect to their variability. From the quantile function, one obtains for the median

$$\text{md}(x) = c + (b-c)\left(1 - 0.5^{\frac{1}{q}}\right)^{1/p}.$$

From this, the authors derived two reparametrizations of the distribution $K_p(\omega, d_p, c, b)$ and $K_q(\omega, d_q, c, b)$, where $d_p = p^{-1}$, $d_q = q^{-1}$ and $\omega = \text{md}(x)$ (For details see Mitnik and Baek, 2013, p. 181). They went on to show that d_p and d_q are in fact dispersion parameters with reference to a well-defined dispersion order. Note that this order cannot be the dispersive order $\leq_{disp}$ (cf. Definition 12): The Kumaraswamy distribution has a finite support, so any two distributions with the same b and c parameters ordered by $\leq_{disp}$ would be identical (see Shaked & Shanthikumar, 2007, Theorem 3. B.14). This argument, however, does not rule out the dilation order that is derived from the convex order (see Definition 10). In an additional study (see supplement to Mitnik & Baek, 2013), they showed, via numerical computations, that the dilation order is not an order consistent with values of parameters d_p and d_q, but that the quantile spread order is. They proved the following:

Proposition 4. Let X be distributed as $K_r(\omega, d_{rx}, c, b)$ and Y as $K_r(\omega, d_{ry}, c, b)$; then $X \leq_{QS} Y$ if, and only if, $d_{rx} \leq d_{ry}$ with $r = p, q$.

Trivially the interquartile range, defined as $QS_X(.75)$, is consistent with values of the parameters d_p and d_q. Finally, it also follows from the aforementioned that

if $d_{rx} \leq d_{ry}$, then $\text{MAD}(X) \leq \text{MAD}(Y)$,

for $r = p, q$.

Thus Mitnik and Baek (2013) concluded that the only known variability order that is appropriate for the Kumaraswamy distribution is the quantile spread order defined in Townsend and Colonius (2005) (see also p. 151, Shaked & Shanthikumar, 2007).

Acknowledgment

This chapter is dedicated to my friend and former colleague, Jim Townsend, at the occasion of a conference held in his honor at Indiana University, Bloomington, in April 2013. Comments by Trisha van Zandt and Joe Houpt on an earlier version, improving readability and correcting errors, are gratefully acknowledged.

Notes

1. If not indicated otherwise, proofs of all statements made here can be found in this referenced monograph.
2. Definitions, examples, and propositions are numbered jointly and consecutively.
3. Clearly, it is sufficient to consider only functions ϕ that are convex on the union of the supports of X and Y rather than over the whole real line.
4. Note that a logconcave density follows from its distribution function G being *strongly unimodal*, i.e., if the convolution $G * F$ is unimodal for every unimodal F.

References

Balanda, K. P., & MacGillivray, H. L. (1990). Kurtosis and spread. *The Canadian Journal of Statistics, 18*(1), 17-30.

Goris, R. L. T., Movshon, J. A., & Simoncelli, E. P. (2014). Partitioning neuronal variability. *Nature Neuroscience, 17*(6), 858–865.

Jones, M., & Dzhafarov, E. N. (2014). Unfalsifiability and mutual translatability of major modeling schemes for choice reaction time. *Psychological Review, 121*, 1–32.

Kumaraswamy, P. (1980). A generalized probability density function for double-bounded random processes. *Journal of Hydrology, 46*, 79–88.

Lin, I.-C., Okun, M., Carandini, M., & Harris, K. D. (2015). The nature of shared cortical variability. *Neuron, 87*, 644–656.

Luce, R. D. (1986). *Response times: Their role in inferring elementary mental organization.* New York: Oxford University Press.

Mitnik, P. A., & Baek, S. (2013). The Kumaraswamy distribution: Median-dispersion re-parameterizations for regression modeling and simulation-based estimation. *Statistical Papers, 54*, 177–192.

Shaked, M., & Shanthikumar, J. G. (2007). *Stochastic orders.* New York: Springer Science & Business Media.

Townsend, J. T. (1990). Truth and consequences of ordinal differences in statistical distributions: Toward a theory of hierarchical inference. *Psychological Bulletin, 108*, 551–567.

Townsend, J. T., & Colonius, H. (2005). Variability of the max and min statistic: a theory of the quantile spread as a function of sample size. *Psychometrika, 70*(4), 759–772.

Townsend, J. T., & Eidels, A. (2011). Workload capacity spaces: A unified methodology for response-time measures of efficiency as workload is varied. *Psychonomic Bulletin & Review*, *18*, 659–681.

Townsend, J. T., & Nozawa, G. (1995). Spatio-temporal properties of elementary perception: An investigation of parallel, serial, and coactive theories. *Journal of Mathematical Psychology*, *39*(4), 321–359.

Townsend, J. T., & Wenger, M. J. (2004). A theory of interactive parallel processing: New capacity measures and predictions for a response-time inequality series. *Psychological Review*, *111*, 1003–1035.

van den Berg, R., Shin, H., Chou, W.-C., George, R., & Ma, W. J. (2012). Variability in encoding precision accounts for visual short-term memory limitations. *Proceedings of the National Academy of Sciences of the United States of America*, *109*(22), 8780–8785.

4 Subset System
Mathematical Abstraction of Object and Context

Jun Zhang and Yitong Sun

4.1 Introduction

Set theory is a universal language for modeling mathematical objects. Modern set theory, initiated by Cantor and Dedekind in the 1870s and amended by Zermelo-Fraenkel axioms, is held by mainstream mathematicians as providing a solid foundation for all branches of mathematics and has enjoyed great success in providing a universal language to construct necessary tools for handling physical and engineering systems. To explore the potential power of mathematics as applied to social, behavioral, cognitive, and information systems, there is a need to identify set-theoretic primitives for modeling relational structures that are prevalent in these systems yet distinct from physical applications. In this chapter, we offer an initial attempt at mathematical primitives for modeling relational structures based on naïve set theory. Our theory is based on a mathematical concept that we call "subset system" here, which is naturally equipped with *two* pairs of relations, namely "pre-order" and "tolerance," that would allow us to model, in a most abstract fashion, objects, features, contexts, etc.

A *subset system* is a pair of sets (V, E), where V is a set called ground-set and E is a collection of subsets on V. So a subset system is a set (the V-part of the definition) along with a family of its subsets (the E-part of the definition). Denote $\mathscr{P}(V) \equiv 2^V$ as the power-set of V. E itself can be viewed as a subset $E \subseteq \mathscr{P}(V)$ (and hence a point of $\mathscr{P}\mathscr{P}(V)$, the power of the power-set). To alleviate confusion, we will use the word *"element"* $v \in V$ when referring to the ground-set V, and the word *"member"* $e \in E$ when referring to the subset collection E.

In the graph-theoretic literature, a subset system (V, E) is also called a "hypergraph," where each element $v \in V$ is called a vertex, and each member e (which is a subset of V) of E is called a "hyperedge" (i.e., an "edge" connecting multiple vertices) or, with an abuse of terminology, "face." We used the term subset system in this chapter because of our much broader perspective than the graph-theoretic approach. A subset system can also be viewed as defining a binary relation R between a set V and another set E such that vRe if and only if $v \in e$. Under this viewpoint, a subset system is a special case of the so-called cross-table $V \times E$, the data structure that lists the co-occurrences of elements of a pair of sets (here E is treated, a priori, as a set in the same way as V is), as used in the so-called *Formal Concept Analysis* (Ganter & Wille, 2012). As a concrete example, think about the coauthorship network in the study of patterns of scientific collaborations. Here V is a list of authors, and E is the list of papers some of these authors have collaboratively written—single-authored papers are included, but multiple publications by the same collaborators are condensed and counted as single occurrence.

A subset system is an abstraction of many algebraic and topological structures that lie at the core of modern mathematics. The notion is quite generic, as it does not impose, a priori, any requirement about the inclusion/exclusion of particular members in the collection of subsets that make up the subset system. Examples of subset systems abound as familiar mathematical objects:

- *Topped $\cap$ system*: The subset system is required to be closed with respect to the set-intersection operation and must also contain the full set V. In this case, the system becomes a complete lattice ordered by the set-inclusion relation.
- *Topology*: The subset system is required to be closed with respect to arbitrary (countably many) unions and finite intersections. In this case, the system becomes a bounded distributive lattice. To "topologize" a subset system, that is, using the subset system as a (topological) sub-base to make it a topology, amounts to adding more members to the collection so that the collection is closed under the two operations mentioned earlier.
- *Alexandrov topology*: The system of subsets needs to satisfy a stronger condition than that of a topology, i.e., arbitrary intersection needs to be closed within the system. In this case, the system becomes a complete distributive lattice. To "Alexandrovize" a topology, that is, making a topology an Alexandrov topology, will require more members to be added to the collection (and hence the collection is larger).
- *Lattice of sets*: The subset system is such that for any two members, there exists a member that includes both and also a member that is included by both. The system forms a lattice ordered by inclusion of subsets.
- *Ring of sets*: The subset system is required to be closed under union and under intersection (or set-theoretic difference). The system forms a distributive lattice.
- *Field of sets*: The subset system, in addition to being a ring of sets, needs also to satisfy closure with respect to the complementation operation. The system forms a Boolean lattice.

- *Borel sets with σ-algebra*: The subset system is required to be closed under complementation and under countably many union and intersection. They form the starting point of modern measure theory.

From its definition, a subset system has two natural binary relations imposed upon members of E—two members e_1, e_2 of E (which are subsets of V) are said to have a

(i) pre-order $\leqslant$ relation, denoted as $e_1 \leqslant e_2$, iff $e_1 \subseteq e_2$ as subsets of V;
(ii) tolerance $\simeq$ relation, denoted as $e_1 \simeq e_2$, iff $e_1 \cap e_2 \neq \emptyset$ as subsets of V.

These two binary relations $\leqslant$ and $\simeq$ for members of the collection E are inherited from the set-inclusion relation and non-empty set-intersection relationships among subsets of V. That is, both $\leqslant$ and $\simeq$ characterize relations among members of the power-set $\mathscr{P}(V)$. What we are going to study are two *new* relations among elements of the ground-set V. We will show that, by virtue of the makeup of E, the particular *collection* of subsets, there can be a pre-order relation (denoted P) and a tolerance relation (denoted T) induced on V. This makes elements of the ground-set V in various relations with one another. This is the main contribution of our present work. Our chapter will show that defining these binary relations is "natural," if we want the collection of subsets to provide a "context" for elements of the ground-set. Our theoretical framework (which is still in its infancy) aims to provide a universal modeling language drawn from order theory (including lattice), topology, measure, and other well-studied algebraic structures, but applicable in weaker contexts than each of the traditional tools.

The relaxation offered by our theory, that is, the consideration of the subset system without any a priori assumptions on the collection of subsets, has practical convenience. In social-cognitive-behavioral settings, when objects are modeled as elements of a ground-set, the co-appearance (co-occurrence) of objects can be modeled as a subset. A collection of subsets, therefore, provides contextual information about objects and their relations. We will show that, without making any assumptions about this collection, we can uncover two types of information about the collection of objects by simply using input data in this format. The first is a pre-order relation, which gives information about whether one object is more generic/special than another object. Here generic (special) is in the sense of appearing in more (less) occasions in the input data. The second is a tolerance relation, which gives information about whether two objects are similar (or its opposite, dissimilar) or not. Pre-order and tolerance are two important relations. Mathematically, they provide two ways of falling short of an equivalence class, by violating either symmetry or transitivity. Our framework thus proposes an algorithmic analysis of input data that mimics two rational and complementary styles of cognitive processing—similarity judgment in perception (enforcing symmetry) and preference judgment in decision (enforcing transitivity).

The plan of this chapter is as follows. Section 2 reviews the mathematical background of binary relations, in particular, pre-order and tolerance relations. Specifically, the close relationship between Alexandrov topology and pre-order is reviewed. Section 3 investigates the pre-order and tolerance structures induced on the ground-set of an arbitrary subset system. Independence and information completeness of the two induced relations are studied. Two transformations of subset systems are discussed: complementation and closure with respect to the induced tolerance. A familiar example, biorder, is revisited as a special kind of subset system, one that is "chained." Finally, Section 4 discusses various ways to modify the structure of a subset system, bringing in the possibility of learning and dynamics into our theoretical framework.

4.2 Mathematical Preliminaries

4.2.1 Binary Relations

Recall the notions of binary relation, pre-order, and equivalence. The basic description of a binary relation is a collection of ordered binary pairs. Specifically, a binary relation (X, R) is a collection $\mathscr{C}$ of subsets of $X \times X$. Two elements $x, y \in X$ are said to be in relation R, denoted as xRy, when $(x, y) \in \mathscr{C}$.

There are three basic essential aspects of a binary relation:

1. *reflexivity*: for all x, xRx holds;
2. *symmetry*: for all x, y, xRy implies yRx;
3. *transitivity*: for any $x, y, z \in X$, xRy and yRz implies that xRz.

A binary relation (X, R) is called an

1. *equivalence*: if R is reflexive, symmetric, and transitive.
2. *pre-order*: if R is reflexive and transitive.
3. *tolerance*: if R is reflexive and symmetric.

So pre-order and tolerance are short of an equivalence relation, as they do not enforce symmetry and transitivity, respectively.

For any binary relation R on the set X, there are two induced binary relations on X, denoted as I and $\simeq$ (we could have used a subscript $_R$ to indicate the induced nature of these relations):

1. Indifference relation I: xIy iff $\neg(xRy)$ and $\neg(yRx)$;
2. Indistinguishable relation $\simeq$: $x \simeq y$ iff for any $z \in X$, zRx and zRy mutually imply each other, and xRz and yRz mutually imply each other.

Regardless of the properties (or lack thereof) of R, it can be easily seen that the two induced relations are always symmetric. The binary relation $\simeq$ describes a relation of two elements with respect to all other elements of the set. It is always reflexive, always transitive, and hence is always an equivalence relation. On the other hand, I is reflexive iff R is irreflexive (i.e., $\neg(aRa)$, $\forall a$), and I may still be intransitive despite of transitivity in R). The importance of intransitivity of I for behavioral science was first recognized in the invention of the semi-order (Luce, 1956).

For a binary relation (X, R), we can define the upsets and downsets of X, as members of $\mathscr{P}(X)$, the power set of X. An upset is any set $U \in \mathscr{P}(X)$ such that if $x \in U$, then $y \in U$ for any y that satisfies xRy; a downset is any set $D \in \mathscr{P}(X)$ such that if $x \in D$, then $y \in D$ for any y that satisfies yRx. For a given X, we denote all upsets as $U(X)$ (called "upset system") and all downsets as $D(X)$ (called "downset system"). They are examples of subset systems.

Upsets and downsets enjoy the following well-known property:

Lemma 1. *Arbitrary union and/or intersection of upsets is an upset. Arbitrary union and/or intersection of downsets is a downset.*

Hence, for any binary relation R, the associated upset system $U(X)$ forms a complete lattice, with $\wedge$ implemented as set-intersection ($\cap$) and $\vee$ as set-union ($\cup$) operations on elements of power-set $\mathscr{P}(X)$; that is, $\forall u_1, u_2 \in U(X)$:

1. $\wedge$-operation: $u_1 \wedge u_2 = \{x \in X \mid x \in u_1 \text{ and } x \in u_2\}$;
2. $\vee$-operation: $u_1 \vee u_2 = \{x \in X \mid x \in u_1 \text{ and } x \in u_2\}$.

Hence $U(X)$ provides a "model" of the original binary relation (X, R): On the one hand, they are isomorphic with R prescribed on X and used to construct $U(X)$ in the first place (see next Proposition); on the other hand, $(U(X), \wedge, \vee)$ forms a lattice, whereas (X, R) is generally not a lattice. The earlier discussions apply to downset system $D(X)$ as well.

Now let us consider the following sets:

$$U(x) = \{y \in X \mid xRy\}$$
$$D(x) = \{y \in X \mid yRx\}.$$

They are used as equivalent definitions of the binary relation R:

$$xRy \Leftrightarrow y \in U(x) \Leftrightarrow x \in D(y).$$

It is obvious that R is reflexive iff x is contained within $U(x)$: $x \in U(x)$.

Proposition 5. *With respect to a binary relation (X, R), let $U(x)$ and $D(x)$ be defined as aforementioned. Consider the following three statements:*

(i) xRy;
(ii) $U(y) \subseteq U(x)$;
(iii) $D(x) \subseteq D(y)$.

Then

1. *When R is transitive, then (i) implies (ii) and (iii);*
2. *When R is reflexive, then (ii) or (iii) implies (i);*
3. *When R is a pre-order, then (i), (ii), and (iii) are equivalent.*
4. *When R is symmetric, then $U(x) = D(x)$ for all $x \in X$.*

When R is transitive, then $U(x)$ are upsets and $D(x)$ are downsets themselves. The mapping $x \mapsto U(x)$, when viewed as a map from X to $\mathscr{P}(X)$, preserves the order relation of elements in X; the same holds for the mapping $x \mapsto D(x)$. Furthermore, $U(x)$ (or $D(x)$) are always join-irreducible nodes of the lattice $U(X)$ (or the lattice $D(X)$), for all $x \in X$.

4.2.2 Alexandrov Topology and Pre-order

Because of the important status of Alexandrov topology (a subset system itself) with respect to a generic subset system, we review background materials relating pre-order to Alexandrov topology; in particular, we review the notion of "specialization order."

Definition 15. *A topology $\mathscr{F}$ is an Alexandrov topology if an arbitrary intersection of open sets is open.*

A set-theoretic complement of an open set is called a closed set. In Alexandrov topology, by definition, open sets and closed sets have "symmetrical" standing.

A topological space $(X, \mathscr{F})$, i.e., a set X equipped with a topology $\mathscr{F}$, has a well-defined *topological closure* operation on any subset A of X: $\bar{A}$ is the intersection of all closed sets that contain A; it is the smallest closed set that contains A. Using this topological closure operation, we can define a binary relation $\lesssim$ on X:

$$x \lesssim y \text{ iff } \overline{\{x\}} \subseteq \overline{\{y\}}.$$

It can be shown that this definition is equivalent to saying that, $x \lesssim y$ iff for any open set U, $x \in U$ implies that $y \in U$. So open set here plays the role of upset for the introduced order $x \lesssim y$.

Because the binary relation $\lesssim$ on X is defined by a set-inclusion relationship, $(X, \lesssim)$ is a pre-order, called the *specialization pre-order* on X, induced from the topology $\mathscr{F}$ on the same set X.

As a consequence of Lemma 1, the set $U(X)$ of all upsets of binary relation (X, R) form an Alexandrov topology on the set X, which is called the Alexandrov upset topology $\mathscr{F}_R$ of the relation (X, R). Under this topology, open sets are identified with upsets, and the downsets can be shown to be equivalent to the closed sets. In particular, assuming R is transitive, the lower holdings $D[x] = D(x) \cup \{x\}$ equals the closure of the singleton set $\{x\}$: $D[x] = \overline{\{x\}}$. Furthermore, $\{U[x] : x \in X\}$ is the topological base of

$\mathscr{F}_R$ because $U[x]$ is the smallest open neighborhood of x. For any x, $U(x)$ is the deleted open neighborhood of x if R is irreflexive. The existence of the smallest neighborhood makes the verification of the accumulation point much easier. It can be shown that under $\mathscr{F}_R$, x is the accumulation point of a set A iff $(U(x)\setminus\{x\})\cap A \neq \emptyset$.

It is a well-known result that any Alexandrov topology is in one-to-one correspondence with pre-order:

Lemma 2 (Correspondence between Alexandrov topology and pre-order). *Let X be a set, with P denoting a pre-order on X and $\mathscr{F}$ denoting an Alexandrov topology on X.*

1. *Start from any pre-order (X, P), with its Alexandrov upset topology denoted by $(X, \mathscr{F}_P)$. Then the specialization pre-order $\precsim$ of $\mathscr{F}_P$ is the same as P.*
2. *Start from any Alexandrov topology $(X, \mathscr{F})$, with its specialization pre-order denoted by $(X, \precsim)$. Then the Alexandrov upset topology $\mathscr{F}_{\precsim}$ with respect to $\precsim$ (i.e., constructed by treating upsets of $\precsim$ as open sets) is the same as $\mathscr{F}$.*

Proof. For part 1, we only need to show that $x \precsim y$ implies that xPy. Notice that $U[x]$ is an upper set. Then $y \in U[x]$ implies that xPy. For part 2, first we show that $\mathscr{F} \subseteq \mathscr{F}_P$. Assume $A \in \mathscr{F}$. Then for any $x \in A$, xPy implies that $y \in A$. Hence A is an upper set with respect to P. Then we show that $\mathscr{F}_P \subseteq \mathscr{F}$. We only need to show that $U[x] \in \mathscr{F}$. Assume $A \in \mathscr{F}$ and $x \in A$. For any $y \in U[x]$, we have $y \in A$. Hence $U[x]$ is the intersection of all open neighborhoods of x, which is still open by the property of Alexandrov topology.

It is also known that Alexandrov topology is the finest topology that enjoys this one-to-one correspondence to a given pre-order.

4.3 Pre-Order and Tolerance on V Induced From (V, E)

In this section, we start from a general subset system (V, E) and derive its properties. To simplify our discussion, we assume that in a subset system (V, E), E is a simple set and every element v in V appears in some e in E. No other assumptions about the makeup of E is assumed other than that it is a collection of subsets of V.

Recall from the "Introduction" that a subset system (V, E) has a natural pre-order $\preccurlyeq$ among its members (subsets of V) using the set-inclusion relation

$$e_1 \preccurlyeq e_2 \text{ (as members of } E) \leftrightarrow e_1 \subseteq e_2 \text{ (as subsets of } V).$$

This is the order among members of E. Likewise, (V, E) also has a natural tolerance $\simeq$ among its members (that is, members of E) using the set-intersection relation

$$e_1 \asymp e_2 \text{ (as members of } E) \leftrightarrow e_1 \cap e_2 \neq \emptyset \text{ (as subsets of } V).$$

Both $\leqslant$ and $\asymp$ *defined on members of E* are inherited from the natural pre-order and tolerance on the power-set $\mathscr{P}(V)$. The remainder of this section will discuss two new relations, a pre-order P and a tolerance T, *defined on elements of* V as induced from the subset system (V, E).

4.3.1 Neighborhood and Distinguishability

Each member of $e \in E$ for which $v \in e$ is called a *neighbor* of v. Denote the collection of members of E (each of which is a subset of V) containing the element v by $E(v)$. For every v, $E(v)$ is a subcollection of E, called the *neighborhood system* of v. Denote $\mathscr{PP}(V)$ as the power-set of $\mathscr{P}(V)$, then $E : V \to \mathscr{PP}(V)$ in fact defines a mapping, such that (E, ε), where

$$\varepsilon = \{E(v) \mid v \in V\},$$

is a subset system on E (i.e., with members of E as base set).

With the notion of neighbor, we may define various degrees of pairwise separability (distinguishability) for elements in V. Two points v_1, v_2 are called S-*indistinguishable* iff all neighbors of v_1 are neighbors of v_2, and vice versa. In other words, v_1 and v_2 are S-indistinguishable iff there is no subset e in E that contains one but not the other. When two elements v_1, v_2 are not S-indistinguishable, then they are said to be S-distinguishable. S-indistinguishability can be shown to be an equivalence relation.

Given two elements v_1, v_2, if v_1 has a neighbor that does not contain v_2, and vice versa for v_2, then v_1, v_2 are said to be S_1-distinguishable. Otherwise, when no such neighbor exists, these two elements are S_1-indistinguishable. S_1-distinguishability can be shown to be symmetric but not reflexive. S_1-indistinguishability is a tolerance relation.

Given two elements v_1, v_2, if there exists a neighbor e_1 of v_1 and a neighbor e_2 of v_2 such that e_1 does not contain v_2, e_2 does not contain v_1, and $e_1 \cap e_2 = \emptyset$, then v_1, v_2 are said to be S_2-distinguishable. Otherwise, when no such pair of neighbors exist, these two elements are S_2-indistinguishable. S_2-distinguishability can be shown to be a tolerance relation.

Formally, these definitions are written as follows:

1. S-indistinguishable: $E(v_1) = E(v_2)$;
2. S-distinguishable: $E(v_1) \neq E(v_2)$;
3. S_1-distinguishable: There exist $e_1 \in E(v_1)$, $e_2 \in E(v_2)$ such that $v_2 \notin e_1$, $v_1 \notin e_2$, $e_1 \cap e_2 \neq \emptyset$;
4. S_2-distinguishable: There exist $e_1 \in E(v_1)$, $e_2 \in E(v_2)$ such that $v_2 \notin e_1$, $v_1 \notin e_2$, $e_1 \cap e_2 = \emptyset$;

4.3.2 Induced Pre-order on V

Given (V, E), we can define a pre-order P among elements of V, called *specialization order*, as follows.

Definition 16. *vPu if and only if $E(v) \subseteq E(u)$.*

It is easy to show that P is transitive and reflexive, and hence is a pre-order. We call P a specialization pre-order because it is a generalization of the terminology used in the setting of a topology: When the subset system is a topology of V, then P is just the specialization pre-order with respect to the topology. See Section 2.2.

One immediate application of this pre-order P is its relationship to the various degrees of distinguishability we introduced earlier.

Theorem 4. *Given a subset system (V, E), we have the following statements:*

1. *vPu and uPv if and only if $E(v) = E(u)$, i.e., they are S-indistinguishable;*
2. *vPu and $\neg(uPv)$ if and only if $E(v) \subset E(u)$, i.e., v and u are S-distinguishable, but not S_1-distinguishable;*
3. *$\neg(vPu)$ and $\neg(uPv)$ if and only if $E(v) \not\subseteq E(u)$ and $E(u) \not\subseteq E(v)$, i.e., v and u are S_1-distinguishable.*

Also notice that $\subseteq$ is a pre-order on E, and it plays the same role as P on V.

From the P induced from (V, E), we can construct the set of upsets $U(V)$ and the set of downsets $D(V)$, which are subset systems themselves. Note the differences of U and D from E, all of which are subset systems, that is, distinct points of $\mathscr{P}\mathscr{P}(V)$. As sets, U and D have equal cardinality, which is equal to the cardinality of V. On the other hand, E as a set may have larger or smaller cardinality.

Recall (Section 2.1) upset $U(v)$ (and downset $D(v)$) of any element $v \in V$. The proposition that follows gives a precise relationship between $U(v)$ and $E(v)$.

Proposition 6. *$U(v) = \cap E(v)$.*

Proof. First we show that $U(v) \subseteq e$ for every $e \in E(v)$. For any $u \in U(v)$, $E(v) \subseteq E(u)$. So $u \in e$ for any $e \in E(v)$, i.e., $u \in \cap E(v)$. On the other hand, we want to show that $\cap E(v) \subseteq U(v)$. For any $u \in \cap E(v)$, every member in $E(v)$ contains u, hence $E(u) \supseteq E(v)$, that is, vPu. So $u \in U(v)$.

With respect to the Alexandrov upset topology of (V, P), each $e \in E(v)$ is a neighborhood (in a topological sense) of v and is open.

Proposition 7. *Every e in E is an open set with respect to the Alexandrov upset topology determined by P.*

Proof. For every $v \in e$, $U(v) \subseteq e$ by Proposition 6. Hence e must be an upset with respect to P.

When the subset system (V, E) forms an Alexandrov topology, $E = U(V)$, then $\{U(v) \mid v \in V\}$ forms the collection of the local basis of the Alexandrov upset topology $U(V)$.

4.3.3 Clique, Block, Circuit, and Atom

With respect to a tolerance relation T on X, a *clique* is a subset of elements of X such that they are all pairwise in tolerance relations; this subset of elements forms an equivalence class. A *block* is a maximal clique; that is, no additional element can be added to still make the subset a clique (i.e., all pairwise in tolerance relations). A *circuit* is a subset of X that is not a clique and is minimally so; that is, removing any of its elements turns it into a block.

Lemma 3. *Any subset of a clique is a clique ("hereditary property"). The set of all cliques, which is a subset system, is closed under set-wise intersection operation.*

Note that the union of two cliques is, in general, no longer a clique.

Denote $T(x) = \{y \mid xTy\}$, the set of elements that are in tolerance relation T with x; we call it an *adjacent set*. $T(x)$ has a simple graph-theoretic interpretation: It is the set of neighboring (adjacent) vertices connected to vertex x. Any clique involving $x \in X$ must be a subset of $T(x)$. Stated differently, for any x, if the set $T(x)$ forms a clique, then it must be a block.

For a tolerance relation, some blocks have special elements that are called "atoms." We denote $B(x)$ as those elements of X that may participate in a specific block B containing the element x. Note that given x, $B(x)$ as a subset of X may not be unique. Clearly, $B(x) \subseteq T(x)$. If, for certain a, we have $B(a) = T(a)$, then a is called an "atom," or generic point, of the block $B = T(a)$.

Definition 17. *For a block B under tolerance T, any element $a \in B$ such that $T(a) = B$ is called an atom of B.*

It can be shown that any atom can only belong to one block. We have the following characterization for the "atomic" property of an element.

Proposition 8. *An element a in X is an atom of some block $B = T(a)$ with respect to the tolerance T if and only if $\cap T(T(a)) = T(a)$. Here $T(A)$ is defined as follows for any subset A of X:*

$$T(A) = \{T(a) \mid a \in A\}.$$

A tolerance T on X is called *connected* if for any elements $x, y \in X$ there exist elements $a_1, \ldots, a_n \in X$ such that $xTa_1Ta_2 \ldots Ta_nTy$; in this case, X is called *T-connected*.

Recall that a covering C on a set X is a collection of subsets of X whose union is X:

$$\bigcup_{e \in C} e = X.$$

As is easily shown, the collection of all blocks of a tolerance T on a set X form a covering of X if X is T-connected. Conversely, given a covering C as a subset system of X, we define a tolerance relation T by declaring xTy iff there is a member $e \in C$ such that $x \in e$, $y \in e$. Then T is necessarily connected on X. If C is a non-redundant cover, meaning that the removal of any $e \in C$ will destroy the "covering" property, and then each member of C is a block with respect to the induced T. Hence each member of a non-redundant cover contains some atoms.

4.3.4 Induced Tolerance on V

With respect to any subset system (V, E), we now construct a tolerance relation T on V. Recall that $E(v)$ denotes the subcollection of E, which contains the element v.

Definition 18. *vTu if and only if $E(v) \cap E(u) \neq \emptyset$.*

This definition is equivalent to the statement: vTu if and only if there exists $e \in E$ such that $v \in e$ and $u \in e$.

In hypergraph language, what we have done is to construct a new (regular) graph on the original set of nodes, such that two nodes are (undirectedly) connected if in the original hypergraph there is at least one hyperedge connecting then. Comparing their respective definitions, Definition 16 and Definition 18, we easily have:

Proposition 9. *vPu implies that vTu.*

Lemma 4. *For subset system (V, E), every $e \in E$ is a clique with respect to the induced tolerance relation T given by Definition 18.*

Furthermore, we can verify the following:

Proposition 10. *$T(v) = \cup E(v)$.*

The following theorem gives a sufficient condition for $e \in E$ to be a block.

Theorem 5. *For $e \in E$, if $e \cap e' \neq \emptyset$ implies that $e' \subseteq e$ for any $e' \in E$, then e is a block.*

Proof. To show that e is a block, we only need to show that if there is any $v \in V$ that vTu for any $u \in e$, then $v \in e$. If there is such v, then we have $e \subseteq T(v)$. If $e \in E(v)$, then we have $v \in e$. If $e \notin E(v)$, then for any $u \in e$ there must be some $e' \in E(v)$ such that $u \in e'$, which implies that $e' \subseteq e$. But notice that $v \in e'$, so we get $v \in e$.

When a set of non-redundant blocks covers V, then each block contains at least one atom. Using the pre-order P induced from the same subset system, every element can be put into an ordered set, with atoms at the bottom.

4.3.5 Subset Systems as Captured by P and T

The main results of the previous two sections can be summarized as:

Theorem 6. *Let (V, E) be a subset system, with neighborhood function $E(v)$ for any $v \in V$. Denote $U(v)$ as the upset and $T(v)$ as the adjacent set, corresponding to the induced pre-order P and tolerance T, respectively. Then*

1. $U(v) = \cap E(v)$;
2. $T(v) = \cup E(v)$.

Defining P and T on the ground-set V of a subset system (V, E) is "natural" if we want the collection of subsets to provide a "context" for elements of V. Let us treat each member of E as a context, as defined by the co-occurrence of certain elements of V. Then the relationship P gives information about whether one element is more generic/special than another element, as determined by the set of contexts each element appears in. On the other hand, the relationship T gives information about whether two elements share a same context or not. Given these interpretations, it is natural to ask:

1. Independence of P and T: Are P and T two *independent* relations induced from the same subset system?
2. Information Completeness of P and T: Do P and T encode complete information about (V, E) so that (V, E) can be recovered by them?

Next we give negative answers to both of these questions.

Regarding (1), the following are examples of subset systems sharing the same specialization pre-order P, but with different tolerance T, or vice versa.

Example 4.3.1. *(Same P with different T).*
For $V = \{a, b, c\}$, take $E_1 = \{\{a\}, \{b\}, \{c\}\}$ and $E_2 = \{\{a, b\}, \{b, c\}, \{a, c\}\}$. (V, E_1) and (V, E_2) induce the same pre-order (a trivial one) with different tolerance.

Example 4.3.2. *(Same T with different P).*
For $V = \{a, b, c\}$, take $E_1 = \{\{a, b, c\}\}$ and $E_2 = \{\{a\}, \{a, b, c\}\}$. (V, E_1) and (V, E_2) induce the same tolerance with different pre-orders.

Regarding (2), the following is an example of different subset systems with the same pre-order (V, P) and the same tolerance (V, T).

Example 4.3.3. *(Same P and T, but different subset systems).*
For $V = \{a, b, c, d\}$, take $E_1 = \{\{a, b\}, \{a, c\}, \{a, d\}, \{b, c\}, \{b, d\}, \{c, d\}\}$ and $E_2 = \{\{a, b, c\}, \{b, c, d\}, \{a, c, d\}, \{a, b, d\}\}$. (V, E_1) and (V, E_2) induce the same tolerance and specialization pre-order on V.

To conclude, P and T are two independent relations induced from the same subset system. By independence we mean there exists subset systems sharing the same specialization pre-order P, but with different tolerance T, or vice versa. Furthermore, different subset systems, say (V, E) and (V, E'), can induce the same pre-order P on V.

4.3.6 Galois Connection Between V and E

Given any subset system (V, E), we can define two operations as follows:

$$A^{\triangleright} = \{e \in E \mid A \subseteq e\}$$

$$F^{\triangleleft} = \left\{v \in V \mid \bigcap_{e \in F} e\right\}$$

Then $\triangleright : \mathscr{P}(V) \to \mathscr{P}(E)$ and $\triangleleft : \mathscr{P}(E) \to \mathscr{P}(V)$ form a pair of order-reversing maps between $\mathscr{P}(V)$ and $\mathscr{P}(E)$; that is, the following holds for any $A \subseteq V, F \subseteq E$:

$$A^\triangleright \supseteq F \leftrightarrow A \subset F^\triangleleft.$$

The pair of maps $\triangleright$ and $\triangleright$ are called (antitone version of) a *Galois connection*; they enjoy nice properties:

1. $A_1 \subseteq A_2 \to A_1^\triangleright \supseteq A_2^\triangleright$ and $F_1 \subseteq F_2 \to F_1^\triangleleft \supseteq F_2^\triangleleft$;
2. $A^\triangleright = A^{\triangleright\triangleleft\triangleright}$ and $F^\triangleleft = F^{\triangleleft\triangleright\triangleleft}$;
3. $A \subseteq A^{\triangleright\triangleleft}$ and $F \subseteq F^{\triangleleft\triangleright}$.

The pair of maps are adjoints of each other (exchanging the domain and target spaces). Each of $\triangleright$ and $\triangleleft$ uniquely determines the other via the formulae

$$A^\triangleright = \inf\{F \subseteq E \mid A \supseteq F^\triangleleft\}$$
$$F^\triangleleft = \inf\{A \subseteq V \mid A^\triangleright \subseteq F\}$$

The statement "$\triangleright$ is a surjective map" is equivalent to "$\triangleleft$ is an injective map," which is equivalent to $\triangleright\triangleleft = \text{Id}$. An analogous set of equivalent statements can be obtained by switching $\triangleright$ and $\triangleleft$ in the aforementioned statements.

The compositions $\text{Cl}_V \equiv \triangleright\triangleleft$ and $\text{Cl}_E \equiv \triangleleft\triangleright$ are monotonic and idempotent maps on $\mathscr{P}(V)$ and on $\mathscr{P}(E)$, respectively:

1. Monotonicity: $\text{Cl}_V(A_1) \subseteq \text{Cl}_V(A_2), \forall A_1 \subseteq A_2 \subseteq V$ and $\text{Cl}_E(F_1) \subseteq \text{Cl}_E(F_2), \forall F_1 \subseteq F_2 \subseteq E$;
2. Idempotency: $\text{Cl}_V(\text{Cl}_V(A)) = \text{Cl}_V(A)$ and $\text{Cl}_E(\text{Cl}_E(F)) = \text{Cl}_E(F)$.

Together with the noncontraction property (3) Cl_V and Cl_E are, by definition, closure operators on $\mathscr{P}(V)$ and on $\mathscr{P}(E)$. The fixed points of these operators form the so-called concept lattices (Ganter & Wille, 2012). In such lattices, $\triangleright$ preserves existing joins and $\triangleleft$ preserves existing meets.

Dual to the closure operator Cl is the interior operator Int, which is also monotonic and idempotent. Denote $A^c = X \backslash A$ for any $A \subset X$. Then $\text{Int}(A) = (\text{Cl}(A^c))^c$ and $\text{Cl}(A) = (\text{Int}(A^c))^c$. Unlike the noncontracting property of Cl, Int is nonexpanding.

4.3.7 Upper and Lower Approximations on V

The two induced relations P and T on the ground-set V allow us to define rough approximations of any subsets of V.

Let R be any binary relation on V, with $U(v) = \{w \in V : vRw\}$ for any $v \in V$. For any subset A, the lower approximation $\blacktriangledown : \mathscr{P}(V) \to \mathscr{P}(V)$ and upper approximation ▲ : $\mathscr{P}(V) \to \mathscr{P}(V)$ of A with respect to the binary relation R:

$$A^{\blacktriangledown} = \{v \in V \mid U(v) \subseteq A\},$$
$$A^{\blacktriangle} = \{v \in V \mid U(v) \cap A \neq \emptyset\}.$$

The operation ▲ preserves $\cup$, whereas ▼ preserves $\cap$. They are both order-preserving; that is, $X \subseteq Y$ implies $X^{\blacktriangledown} \subseteq Y^{\blacktriangledown}$ and $X^{\blacktriangle} \subseteq Y^{\blacktriangle}$.

Let A^c denote the complement $V \backslash A$ of A. Then

$$A^{\blacktriangle c} = A^{c\blacktriangledown}, \quad A^{\blacktriangledown c} = A^{c\blacktriangle}.$$

This means, ▲ and ▼ are dual.

The properties of the binary relation R leads to the following properties of lower and upper approximations (where $A \subseteq V$, i.e., $A \in \mathscr{P}(V)$):

- when R is reflexive: $A^{\blacktriangledown} \subseteq A \subseteq A^{\blacktriangle}$;
- when R is symmetric: $A^{\blacktriangledown \blacktriangle} \subseteq A \subseteq A^{\blacktriangle \blacktriangledown}$;
- when R is transitive: $A^{\blacktriangle \blacktriangle} \subseteq A^{\blacktriangle}$ and $A^{\blacktriangledown} \subseteq A^{\blacktriangledown \blacktriangledown}$;
- when R is left-total: $A^{\blacktriangledown} \subseteq A^{\blacktriangle}$.

We may also determine rough set approximations using the downset system $D(v)$:

$$A^{\triangledown} = \{v \in V : D(v) \subseteq A\},$$
$$A^{\triangle} = \{v \in V : D(v) \cap A \neq \emptyset\}.$$

The pair (▲, $\triangledown$) and the pair (▼, $\triangle$) are both order-preserving Galois connections on $\mathscr{P}(V)$.

When R is a pre-order, then for $A \subseteq V$,

$$A^{\blacktriangle \blacktriangle} = A^{\blacktriangle}, \quad A^{\blacktriangledown \blacktriangledown} = A^{\blacktriangledown}, \quad A^{\triangle \triangle} = A^{\triangle}, \quad A^{\triangledown \triangledown} = A^{\triangledown}.$$

This is to say, ▲ and $\triangle$ are closure operators, and ▼ and $\triangledown$ are interior operators. Moreover,

$$A^{\blacktriangle \triangledown} = A^{\blacktriangle}, \quad A^{\triangle \blacktriangledown} = A^{\triangle}, \quad A^{\blacktriangledown \triangle} = A^{\blacktriangledown}, \quad A^{\triangledown \blacktriangle} = A^{\triangledown}.$$

These two approximations determine two Alexandrov topologies on V:

$$\mathscr{T}^{\uparrow} = \{A^{\blacktriangle} : A \subseteq V\} = \{A^{\triangledown} : A \subseteq V\}$$

and

$$\mathscr{T}^{\downarrow} = \{A^{\blacktriangledown} : A \subseteq V\} = \{A^{\triangle} : A \subseteq V\}$$

These topologies are dual; that is,

- $A \in \mathscr{T}^\uparrow \Leftrightarrow A^c \in \mathscr{T}^\downarrow$;
- Under $\mathscr{T}^\uparrow$, $\triangle$ is the closure operator and $\triangledown$ is the interior operator; $\blacktriangle$ is the smallest neighborhood operator, and the set $\{\{v\}^\blacktriangle : v \in V\} = \{U(v) : v \in V\}$ is the smallest base;
- Under $\mathscr{T}^\downarrow$, $\blacktriangle$ is the closure operator and $\blacktriangledown$ is the interior operator; $\triangle$ is the smallest neighborhood operator, and the set $\{\{v\}^\triangle : v \in V\} = \{D(v) : v \in V\}$ is the smallest base;
- We have

$$\{v\}^\blacktriangledown = \emptyset, \quad \{v\}^\triangledown = \emptyset,$$

$$\{v\}^\blacktriangle = D(v), \quad \{v\}^\triangle = U(v).$$

When R is tolerance, $\blacktriangle = \triangle$ and $\blacktriangledown = \triangledown$, so

$$A^\blacktriangle = A^\triangle, \quad A^\blacktriangledown = A^\triangledown$$

for any $A \subseteq V$. In this case, $\blacktriangle : \mathscr{P}(V) \to \mathscr{P}(V)$ is a monotone Galois connection on $\mathscr{P}(V)$. The map $A \mapsto A^{\blacktriangle\blacktriangledown}$ is a closure operator, with the set $\{A^\blacktriangledown \mid A \subseteq V\}$ as fixed points. The map $A \mapsto A^{\blacktriangledown\blacktriangle}$ is the interior operator, with the set $\{A^\blacktriangle \mid A \subseteq V\}$ as fixed points. We have

$$\{v\}^\blacktriangledown = \{v\}^\triangledown = \emptyset,$$

$$\{v\}^\blacktriangle = \{v\}^\triangle = T(v).$$

4.3.8 Complement of Subset System

Given a subset system (V, E), we can also consider the complement system (V, E^{co}), where $E^{co} = \{V \backslash e \mid e \in E\}$. It is called a complement system because if we denote the relation defined by (V, E) as R, then the relation R^c can be defined as $vR^c e$ if and only if $v \in V \backslash e$. Here we need another assumption that $\cap E = \emptyset$ so that every v is contained in some member of E^{co}. The system (V, E^{co}) also gives a pre-order and a tolerance on V, denoted by P^{co} and T^{co}, respectively. As we defined earlier, $v_1 P v_2$ if and only if $E(v_1) \subseteq E(v_2)$. And this is equivalent to $E^{co}(v_1) \supseteq E^{co}(v_2)$, which is further equivalent to $v_2 P^{co} v_1$. Therefore, we have the following proposition:

Proposition 11. *vPu if and only if $uP^{co}v$.*

Different from the relation between P and P^{co}, T and T^{co} encode non-redundant information of the system. Neither one of them implies the other, because $v_1 T v_2$ if and only if there is an $e \in E$ such that $v_1 \in e$, $v_2 \in e$, and $v_1 T^{co} v_2$ if and only if there is an $e \in E$ such that $v_1 \notin e$, $v_2 \notin e$. It is possible that $v_1 T v_2$ and $v_1 T^{co} v_2$ both hold. Therefore, Proposition 9 can be strengthened as follows:

Proposition 12. *vPu implies both vTu and $vT^{co}u$.*

4.3.9 Chained Subset System

We call a subset system (V, E) "chained" if $\{E(v), v \in V\}$, when properly arranged, forms an increasing (or decreasing) sequence of sets. When a subset system (V, E) is chained, then the corresponding cross-table can be shown to be a "biorder" (Guttman scale). In particular, both (V, P) and $(E, \preccurlyeq)$ are weak orders; they are linearly ordered by inclusion relation. This leads to the following two propositions characterizing a chained subset system:

Proposition 13. *Let I denote the indifference relation with respect to the specialization pre-order P induced by (V, E); that is, vIu iff neither vPu nor uPv. Then we have the conclusion: I is empty if and only if the subset system (V, E) is chained.*

Using the well-known characterization of biorders (Doignon, Ducamp, & Falmagne, 1984), we have:

Proposition 14. *A subset system (V, E) is a chained system iff the following holds for all $v_1, v_2 \in V$ and $e_1, e_2 \in E$:*

If $v_1 \in e_1, v_2 \in e_2$, then either $v_1 \in e_2$ or $v_2 \in e_1$.

4.3.10 Subset Systems with Same P

We already see that $\preccurlyeq$ and P are two different pre-orders, on E and on V, respectively, associated with any subset system (V, E). Whereas $\preccurlyeq$ is naturally endowed, P depends on the collection E of subsets. We now investigate various subset systems that will yield the same specialization pre-order P.

First, recall Lemma 2 stating that a given pre-order P uniquely corresponds with an Alexandrov topology, which is a subset system itself. This means that if the subset system (V, E) we started with is already an Alexandrov topology (i.e., E is already closed under arbitrary union and arbitrary intersection), then we cannot add more members to E without perturbing (V, P) as a pre-order.

For any subset system (V, E), when fixing V, we perform two incremental steps of closure to E to turn (V, E) into (1) topped $\cap$ system and then into (2) Alexandrov topology. During each step, the induced pre-order on V remains unchanged.

In the first step, we supply more members to E to turn E from a pre-ordered set (when E is viewed as a point in $\mathscr{P}\mathscr{P}(V)$) into a complete lattice E' of sets (where each member of E' is a subset of V). These additional member e's are of the form $e = \cap e_i$, where each e_i is a member of E. Through this operation, we make $\wedge$ operation on elements of E identical with $\cap$, the set-wise intersection operation on subsets of V. The resulting E' forms a complete lattice (because any topped intersection system is a complete lattice; see Davey & Priestley, 2002).

In the second step, we supply more members to E' to turn E' from a complete lattice into a complete distributive lattice E'' of sets. The additional members e' are of the form $e = \cup\, e'_i$, where each e'_i is a member of $E' \supseteq E$. Through this operation, we make $\vee$ operation on members of E identical with $\cup$, the set-wise union operation on subsets of V. The subset system (V, E'') is an Alexandrov topology $\mathcal{T}_F$, whereby each member $e \in E''$ is its open set of $\mathcal{T}_F$. In particular, each $e \in E$ is an open set (Proposition 7 proved earlier). Once in E'', its specialization pre-order P is the specialization pre-order $\lesssim$ of the Alexandrov topology, as given by Lemma 2.

$$(V, E) \quad \rightarrow \quad (V, E') \quad \rightarrow \quad (V, E'') \equiv (V, U(V)).$$
Subset System → Topped ∩ System → Alexandrov topology.

4.4 Discussion

In this chapter, we proposed the notion of *subset system* (V, E) as a set-theoretic foundation of relational structure. This conceptualization merely stipulates that whenever a set V is specified, one needs to also specify the collection of subsets E. These two aspects are inalienably linked in order for elements of V, as well as for members of E, to be in various relations with each other. So our conceptualization for binary relations refocuses from *set* to *systems of subsets*.

We showed that any subset system (V, E) comes with

1. two natural relations on the set E:

    - pre-order $\leqslant$
    - tolerance $\asymp$

2. two induced relations on the set V:

    - pre-order P
    - tolerance T

Therefore, subset system (V, E) provides the concise mathematical language to describe the "context" (modeled by E) for relationships between objects (modeled by V). This framework, thus, may provide rigorous yet rich vocabulary for defining part-whole relations, context, and configural/Gestalt processes as investigated by the honoree of this book, Prof. J. T. Townsend (e.g., Eidels, Townsend, & Pomerantz, 2008; Wenger & Townsend, 2001).

Readers familiar with elementary point-set topology (e.g., Pervin, 1964) will notice that the notions introduced in this chapter for neighborhood, (various levels of) distinguishability, and the induced order P mirror corresponding notions in topology (topological neighborhood, topological distinguishability, and separability specialization pre-order). Our analysis shows that these concepts can be defined independently of the closure requirement of the subset system discussed in Section 4.3.10

Finally, we discuss briefly how to modify subset systems and introduce dynamics through learning. Given V, the binary relations P and T on its elements are completely specified whenever E is specified. There are two operations that can be implemented to modify a subset system: One is to enlarge E to E'; this is what we discussed in Section 4.3.10. Another is to enlarge V to V' without changing the specialization pre-order among elements in V. These two operations correspond to the operations of adding attributes and adding objects into a cross-table. Future research will be devoted to understanding mechanisms through which subset systems can be "evolved" with both V and E changing.

Acknowledgments

This work is supported by ARO grant W911NF-12-1-0163 (PI: Jun Zhang).

References

Davey, B. A., & Priestley, H. A. (2002). *Introduction to lattices and order*. Cambridge: Cambridge University Press.

Doignon, J.-P., Ducamp, A., & Falmagne, J.-C. (1984). On realizable biorders and the biorder dimension of a relation. *Journal of Mathematical Psychology, 28*(1), 73–109.

Eidels, A., Townsend, J. T., & Pomerantz, J. R. (2008). Where similarity beats redundancy: The importance of context, higher order similarity, and response assignment. *Journal of Experimental Psychology: Human Perception and Performance, 34*(6), 1441–1463.

Ganter, B., & Wille, R. (2012). *Formal concept analysis: Mathematical foundations*. Berlin: Springer Science & Business Media.

Luce, R. D. (1956). Semiorders and a theory of utility discrimination. *Econometrica: Journal of the Econometric Society, 24*, 178–191.

Pervin, W. J. (1964). *Foundations of general topology*. New York: Academic Press.

Wenger, M. J., & Townsend, J. T. (2001). *Computational, geometric, and process perspectives on facial cognition: Contexts and challenges*. Mahwah, NJ: Lawrence Erlbaum Associates.

5 Uniqueness of a Multinomial Processing Tree Constructed by Knowing Which Pairs of Processes Are Ordered

Richard Schweickert and Hye Joo Han

Suppose we could figure out which mental processes are executed one after another and which are not. What would we learn about the overall arrangement of the processes? Here we consider the implications for learning the structure of a multinomial processing tree underlying a task. We learn a lot: whether a tree is possible, if so, its form, and whether more than one tree is possible.

The importance of the problem of distinguishing serial and parallel processes is indicated by the continual attention James T. Townsend has devoted to it, from early work criticizing methods popular but unsound (e.g., Townsend, 1972) to recent work presenting methods sophisticated and sound (Yang, Fifić, & Townsend, 2014). There has been much progress through the work of Jim and others. There are far too many papers to mention; for surveys, see Townsend and Ashby (1983), Townsend and Wenger (2004), Logan (2002), and Schweickert, Fisher, and Sung (2012). The story is still unfolding.

Multinomial processing trees have been successfully used to model processes in many tasks, including perception (e.g., Ashby, Prinzmetal, Ivry, & Maddox, 1996), memory (e.g., Batchelder & Riefer, 1986; Chechile & Meyer, 1976), and social cognition (e.g., Klauer & Wegener, 1998). They are useful when each mental process involved in a task has mutually exclusive outcomes. In a memory task, for example, it may be reasonable to assume a retrieval attempt is successful or not. If not, the participant guesses, and a guess is either correct or incorrect. The tree in Figure 5.1 represents these processes. The retrieval attempt is at x. If retrieval is successful, the outcome is a. If retrieval is unsuccessful, a guess is made, represented at y. The possible outcomes of the guess are represented at b and c. Using intuition, an investigator can often rather quickly sketch a plausible multinomial tree model for a task, and statistical tests are often easily conducted (e.g., Stahl & Klauer, 2007). For selection of a tree based on minimum description length, see Wu, Myung, and Batchelder (2010). For reviews, see Batchelder and Riefer (1999), and Erdfelder et al. (2009).

In such a tree, processes are represented by vertices (see Figure 5.1). Processing begins at the *source*, a vertex preceded by no other vertex. The

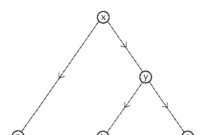

Figure 5.1 A multinomial processing tree. The arc directed from vertex x to vertex y indicates that the process represented by x precedes the process represented by y. Vertices x and y are ordered. Interpretation of other arcs is analogous. Each arc occurs with a certain probability. Probabilities are not illustrated.

source typically represents the presentation of a stimulus. An arc directed from a given vertex to a second vertex indicates that the second vertex represents a possible outcome of the process represented by the given vertex. At each outcome vertex, either a further process starts, with its own possible outcomes, or a response is made at a *terminal vertex*, a vertex followed by no other vertices. Each arc has associated with it the probability that the outcome it leads to will occur. Vertices at which responses are made are partitioned into response classes, say, correct and incorrect. The probability that a particular path is taken is the product of the probabilities on arcs of the path. The probability that a response in a particular class is made is the sum of the probabilities of the paths leading to that class from the source.

In Figure 5.1, processing starts at x and can produce outcome y. Processing at y can in turn produce outcome c. We say processes x and y are ordered, as are y and c, and x and c. But there is no way processing at y can lead to processing at a or vice versa. We say y and a are unordered. We can find out experimentally which pairs of processes in a multinomial processing tree are ordered and which are unordered through the technique of selectively influencing processes.

The technique was pioneered by Sternberg (1969), although he was not writing about multinomial processing trees. Suppose, to carry out a task, a participant executes a set of processes in order, one beginning after its predecessor has finished. The processes are *serial*. It is natural to assume that the time to complete the task, the reaction time, is the sum of the durations of the individual processes. In this situation, an experimental factor, such as the brightness of a stimulus, is said to selectively influence a process if it changes the duration of that process, leaving all else invariant. Sternberg (1969) pointed out that if each of two experimental factors selectively influences a different process in a series of processes, the combined effect of the factors on reaction time would be the sum of their separate effects. This is the basis of his additive factor method. Two processes are in *parallel* if they are executed simultaneously. Suppose, to carry out a task, a participant executes two parallel processes. Suppose they start at the same time, but need not end at the same time, and when both are finished, a response is made. The reaction time is the maximum of the durations of the two individual processes. Sternberg (1969) noted that if each of two factors selectively influences a different process in a set of parallel processes, the factors' combined effect will be the maximum of their separate effects, not the sum. An experimenter selectively influencing processes can discover whether they are serial or parallel, because the effects will differ.

Development of use of selective influence includes work by Townsend and Ashby (1983), Townsend (1984), Townsend and Schweickert (1989), Schweickert and Townsend (1989), Sternberg (2001), Dzhafarov (2003), and Dzhafarov, Schweickert, and Sung (2004). Work on critical path networks was done by Schweickert (1978). Work on multinomial processing trees was done by Jacoby (1991) and Hu (2001). Further applications were to evoked potentials (Kounios & Holcomb, 1992) and rates of responding (S. Roberts, 1987). See Dzhafarov and Kujala (2014) for discussion of recent work on connections to quantum mechanics.

Processes in series are executed in order; the first process precedes the second, which precedes the third and so on. Processes in parallel are not executed in an order; not one of them precedes another. Distinguishing serial and parallel processes is analogous to distinguishing ordered and unordered processes in a multinomial processing tree. Consider a task performed by executing processes in a multinomial processing tree. Suppose an experiment is done in which changing the level of a factor, e.g., changing proactive interference, changes probabilities associated with arcs that leave from one and only one vertex, all else remaining invariant. The factor is said to *selectively influence* the process represented by the vertex. If each of two factors selectively influences a different process, whether the two processes are ordered or unordered is indicated by patterns in the probabilities of the response types and reaction times (Schweickert & Chen, 2008; Schweickert & Han, 2014; Schweickert & Xi, 2011). For example, suppose there are two categories of response, correct and incorrect. If the processes are unordered, the pattern is simple: The factors will have additive effects on the probability of a correct response and additive effects on reaction times. Patterns for ordered processes are more complicated, but they are easily checked; for details, see the papers mentioned.

If the patterns do not appear, no multinomial processing tree exists in which the two factors each selectively influence a different process. An investigator need not wonder whether with enough ingenuity a suitable multinomial processing tree could be found; it's time to consider something different. If the patterns do appear, the data determine the form of a multinomial processing tree that represents the two processes and probabilities associated with the arcs can be estimated.

Here are two examples from immediate serial recall tasks in which a participant is shown a short list of words and immediately attempts to recall them in order. First, in an experiment by Poirier and Saint-Aubin (1995), some lists had words all in the same semantic category, and other lists had words each in a different semantic category. For the probability of correct recall, the effect of a same-or-different semantic category was the same at every serial position; i.e., the factors had additive effects. With additivity, the conclusion is that the two factors selectively influence unordered processes in a multinomial processing tree. Second, in an experiment by Poirier, Schweickert, and Oliver (2005), serial position and list length had interactive effects on the probability of a correct response. The interaction is of the form predicted by the multinomial processing tree in Figure 5.1, with serial position selectively influencing process x and list length selectively influencing process y. The conclusion is that these two factors selectively influence ordered processes in a multinomial processing tree. See Schweickert et al. (2012) for details and more examples.

In these examples, serial position and semantic category selectively influence unordered processes, while serial position and list length selectively influence ordered processes. Suppose we accumulate information about many such pairs. How will we figure out how all the processes fit together?

5.1 Combining Information About Different Pairs of Processes

A typical cognitive task requires execution of more than two processes. In principle, one could carry out a multifactor experiment with one factor intended to selectively influence each process, but this is not practical. Fortunately, there is a procedure, the *Transitive Orientation Algorithm*, for constructing a partial order from only the knowledge of which pairs of elements are ordered and which are unordered; see Golumbic (1980) for an introduction. The algorithm can make a single tree by combining results of separate experiments, each establishing whether a particular pair of processes is ordered or unordered.

A problem may arise in practice. A response is made at a terminal vertex, but there may be no experimental factor available to selectively influence the vertex. The problem does not arise if every terminal vertex leads to a response of a different category. If selectively influencing a given vertex changes the probability of responses in that category, then the given vertex must precede the corresponding terminal vertex. But if more than one terminal vertex leads to the same response category, it may not be possible to determine which vertices are comparable to a particular terminal vertex. In such a case, one can remove the terminal vertices from consideration and construct a tree for the others.

A multinomial processing tree has a probability associated with each arc. Although these probabilities may have been estimated in each separate experiment, they are ignored by the Transitive Orientation Algorithm. Probabilities for the tree that result from the algorithm would have to be estimated by some other procedure. In practice, with different subjects and laboratories, it is unlikely that probability estimates from different experiments could be satisfactorily combined, and it is fortunate that the Transitive Orientation Algorithm does not require probability estimates as inputs.

To continue, we need to make precise some notions informally introduced earlier and to introduce further definitions.

A *graph* G is a finite nonempty set of vertices V together with a set E of edges, which are unordered pairs of distinct vertices, with no more than one edge for a given pair of vertices. In an illustration of a graph, vertices are drawn as points and edges as undirected lines between points.

Let G be a graph. A *chain* is an alternating sequence $v_1, e_1, v_2, \ldots, e_n, v_{n+1}$ of vertices, at least one, and edges, in which edge e_i is incident with vertices v_i and v_{i+1}. Note that a chain may consist of a single point and have no edges.

A chain is a *simple chain* if all vertices in it are distinct, except possibly $v_1 = v_{n+1}$.

A simple chain is a *circuit* if v_1 and v_{i+1} are the same vertex and $n > 3$.

G is *connected* if between every pair of distinct vertices there is a simple chain.

A *tree* is a connected graph with no circuit.

A *directed graph* D is a finite nonempty set of vertices V together with a set A of arcs, which are ordered pairs of distinct vertices, such that there is no more than one arc for a given ordered pair of vertices. In an illustration of a directed graph, vertices are drawn as points and arcs as lines directed (with an arrow) from one point to another.

Let D be a directed graph. A *semipath* is an alternating sequence $v_1, a_1, v_2, \ldots, a_n, v_{n+1}$ of vertices, at least one, and arcs, in which arc a_i is incident with vertices v_i and v_{i+1}. Such a semipath is a *path* v_1 to v_{n+1} if each arc a_i is directed from v_i to v_{i+1}.

Such a semipath or path is *simple* if all vertices are distinct, except possibly $v_1 = v_{n+1}$.

Such a simple path is a *cycle* if v_1 and v_{n+1} are the same vertex and $n > 3$.

A directed graph is *acyclic* if it has no cycles.

A directed graph is *weakly connected* if every pair of vertices is joined by a semipath.

A directed graph is a *directed tree* if whenever every arc is replaced by an edge, the resulting graph is a tree. Note that a directed tree is weakly connected.

A directed tree will often be called a tree if the meaning is clear from context.

Note that a directed tree is acyclic, but not every directed acyclic graph is a directed tree.

Also note that in a directed graph, if there is a path from vertex u to vertex v, then there is a simple path from vertex u to vertex v (e.g., Roberts, 1976, Theorem 2.1).

A pair of distinct vertices in a multinomial processing tree is related in one of two ways. If there is a path directed from one to the other, the vertices and the processes they represent are called *ordered* or *comparable*. If there is no such path, the vertices and processes are called *unordered* or *incomparable*. A single vertex is considered incomparable with itself; that is, order is *irreflexive*. If a pair of processes is ordered, there is at least one way to perform the task in which one of the processes is executed before the other. If a pair is unordered, there is no way to perform the task in which one of the processes is executed before the other. If a path is directed from a vertex x to a vertex y, then x *precedes* y. Note that the order of distinct vertices on a path is *transitive*: If a precedes b and b precedes c, then a precedes c. The set of all processes in a multinomial processing tree is *partially ordered*; that is, the relation of precedence between two processes is irreflexive and transitive.

5.2 When Is a Tree Possible?

Suppose we know for every pair of processes whether they are ordered or unordered. But suppose for each a pair of ordered processes we do not know which comes first. The Transitive Orientation Algorithm can be used to arrange the processes in a multinomial processing tree, if such a tree is possible.

The Transitive Orientation Algorithm is based on a graph in which each process is represented by a vertex, and there is an edge (undirected) between two vertices if and only if the two corresponding processes are ordered. If the edges can be oriented (i.e., directed) in such a way that the vertices are partially ordered, the orientation is called a *transitive orientation*, and the graph is called a *comparability graph*. For example, Figure 5.2 shows the comparability graph for the tree in Figure 5.1. The first step in the algorithm is to orient one edge, arbitrarily, from a vertex, u, to another, v, to indicate that u precedes v. This orientation may force the orientations of further edges.

For example, in Figure 5.2, suppose the edge joining x and a is arbitrarily oriented to indicate that x precedes a. This orientation is shown in Figure 5.3. The edge joining x and b is now forced to be oriented from x to b. Otherwise, with the opposite orientation, by transitivity the orientations would indicate b precedes a, impossible because there is no edge joining a and y. Likewise, after making the arbitrary selection that x precedes a, x is forced to precede y and c. After all forced orientations are made, the oriented edges

Uniqueness of a Multinomial Processing Tree Constructed 71

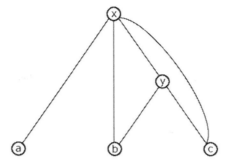

Figure 5.2 The comparability graph corresponding to the multinomial processing tree in Figure 5.1. An edge between two vertices indicates that the two processes represented by the vertices are ordered, but it does not indicate which precedes which. Arrow heads can be drawn on the edges to indicate precedence.

are removed and the procedure begins again; see Figures 5.3 and 5.4. If at some step a single edge is forced to become oriented in both directions, no partial order is possible. The graph was not a comparability graph after all. If the procedure continues until all edges are oriented, the resulting orientations form a partial order. Not only will the Transitive Orientation Algorithm produce a partial order, if one is possible, but by running it systematically, it will produce all possible partial orders. See Golumbic (1980) for further information.

The directed acyclic graph that is produced will ordinarily not be a tree. One reason is that not all partial orders can be represented by trees. Another is that there may be redundant paths, which make circuits not allowed in a tree. Suppose u is immediately followed by v, which is immediately followed by w. The directed acyclic graph will have an arc

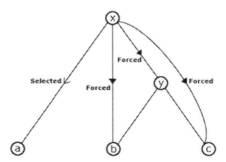

Figure 5.3 In the comparability graph of Figure 5.2, suppose x is arbitrarily selected to precede a. Then x is forced to precede y, b, and c. Directions of no other edges are forced.

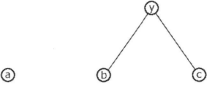

Figure 5.4 All the oriented edges, arbitrarily selected or forced, are removed from the graph. A new arbitrary orientation will be made, and the procedure will continue.

from u to w. This arc makes a redundant path from u to w and can be removed. The directed acyclic graph that results from removing all arcs that make redundant paths is called a *Hasse diagram*. It may be a directed tree but need not be. If it is not, one would need to consider whether the processes are partially ordered in some more complicated arrangement, such as a critical path network. Comparability graphs for critical path networks are beyond the scope of this paper, but they are discussed in Schweickert (1992).

Sometimes a model has two separate multinomial processing trees, say one for recall, the other for recognition. In what follows, we assume there is a single tree, so the corresponding comparability graph is connected. An *arborescence* is a directed tree with a single source o. Note that because a directed tree is weakly connected, in an arborescence T. there is exactly one simple path from o to each vertex v of T. A single multinomial processing tree is an arborescence.

Suppose our hypothesis is that a certain task is performed by executing processes in a multinomial processing tree, and we have results, perhaps from several experiments, indicating for each pair of processes whether they are ordered or unordered. The alleged order information is represented in a graph. There is a simple test for whether the graph is the comparability graph of an arborescence (Wolk, 1962). A path with four vertices, a joined by an edge to b, b joined by an edge to c, and c joined by an edge to d, is denoted $P4$. A cycle with four vertices, a joined by an edge to b, b joined by an edge to c, c joined by an edge to d, and d joined by an edge to a, is denoted $C4$. The subgraph of an undirected graph G *induced by a set of vertices* consists of those vertices together with all edges connecting those vertices in G. A graph is a comparability graph whose Hasse diagram is an arborescence if and only if the graph has no induced subgraph of $P4$ or $C4$ (see Golumbic, 1980, p. 142).

5.3 When Is Only One Tree Possible?

There may be more than one way the comparability graph for an arborescence can be oriented to produce an arborescence. When is the resulting arborescence unique? Note that if the direction of every arc in an arborescence is reversed, the result is a transitively oriented tree. But the resulting tree may have more than one source and, thus, may not be an arborescence. The following theorem specifies when the resulting tree is unique. We need a definition for the term series when speaking of an arborescence.

Let T be an arborescence. A subset of vertices of T is *in series* if every simple path from the source of T to a terminal vertex of T containing one of the vertices contains all of them. The following theorem shows that whether a comparability graph has a unique orientation whose Hasse diagram is an arborescence depends on whether there are vertices in series in the arborescence.

Theorem. *A comparability graph G with a transitive orientation whose Hasse diagram is an arborescence has only one such orientation iff the arborescence has no nonsingleton set of vertices in series.*

Proof. i). Suppose comparability graph G has a transitive orientation whose Hasse diagram is an arborescence, and suppose this arborescence has two (or more) vertices in series. The order of two vertices in series can be reversed without changing the comparability relations. Hence G has more than one transitive orientation whose Hasse diagram is an arborescence.

ii). Suppose comparability graph G has a transitive orientation whose Hasse diagram is an arborescence, and suppose this arborescence has no nonsingleton set of vertices in series.

Suppose there are two vertices x and y. In one transitive orientation of G whose Hasse diagram is an arborescence, x precedes y, and in another such transitive orientation of G, y precedes x. Consider the transitive orientation in which x precedes y. By assumption, x and y are not in series. Thus there is a simple path from the source to a terminal vertex t containing x that does not contain y.

If every vertex other than y on the simple path containing x from the source to t is comparable to y, then y is on that simple path. Hence some vertex z on this simple path does not precede or follow y. If z precedes x, then z would precede y, so z follows x.

Now consider the transitive orientation in which y precedes x. The comparability relations are the same, so in this transitive orientation, z must be comparable to x but not comparable to y. If z follows x, then z would follow y. Hence z precedes x in this transitive orientation. Then there is a simple path from the source of the arborescence to z, and this simple path can be continued to x. But there already is a simple path from the source of the arborescence to y, and this simple path can be continued to

x. Then there are two simple paths from the source to x, contradicting the assumption that the Hasse diagram of the transitive orientation is a tree.

Hence G has only one transitive orientation whose Hasse diagram is an arborescence.

5.4 Conclusion

The directed graph of a multinomial processing tree can be constructed from knowledge of which pairs of processes are ordered and which are unordered. Construction does not require estimates of the probabilities on the arcs, nor does it produce estimates of these probabilities. The directed graph is unique if and only if two or more vertices are not in series. Nonuniqueness is not a practical problem at this time, because so far, to our knowledge, no multinomial processing tree for a cognitive task has been proposed with vertices in series.

Townsend's tenacity in working on the problem of distinguishing serial and parallel processing is well known, as is his insistence on methods that are sound. Cognitive psychology would benefit from more such care that inferences are secure. A prevalent attitude is that because the system is so complicated, there is no point in wasting time working out details. But a complex conceptual structure is a house of cards if the details are not secure. We illustrate here that a collection of details can be assembled into a complex structure. If the details are secure, the structure is secure.

References

Ashby, F. G., Prinzmetal, W., Ivry, R., & Maddox, W. T. (1996). A formal theory of feature binding in object perception. *Psychological Review, 103*, 165–192.

Batchelder, W. H., & Riefer, D. M. (1986). The statistical analysis of a model for storage and retrieval processes in human memory. *British Journal of Mathematical and Statistical Psychology, 39*, 120–149.

Batchelder, W. H., & Riefer, D. M. (1999). Theoretical and empirical review of multinomial process tree modeling. *Psychonomic Bulletin & Review, 6*, 57–86.

Chechile, R. A., & Meyer, D. L. (1976). A Bayesian procedure for separately estimating storage and retrieval components of forgetting. *Journal of Mathematical Psychology, 13*, 269–295.

Dzhafarov, E. N. (2003). Selective influence through conditional independence. *Psychometrika, 68*, 7–26.

Dzhafarov, E. N., & Kujala, J. V. (2014). On selective influences, marginal selectivity, and Bell/CHSH inequalities. *Topics in Cognitive Science, 6*, 121–128.

Dzhafarov, E. N., Schweickert, R., & Sung, K. (2004). Mental architectures with selectively influenced but stochastically interdependent components. *Journal of Mathematical Psychology, 48*, 51–64.

Erdfelder, E., Auer, T. S., Hilbig, B. E., Aßfalg, A., Moshagen, M., & Nadarevic, L. (2009). Multinomial processing tree models. *Zeitschrift für Psychologie/Journal of Psychology, 217*, 108–124.

Golumbic, M. C. (1980). *Algorithmic graph theory and perfect graphs.* New York, NY: Academic Press.

Hu, X. (2001). Extending general processing tree models to analyze reaction time experiments. *Journal of Mathematical Psychology, 45,* 603–634.

Jacoby, L. L. (1991). A process dissociation framework: Separating automatic from intentional uses of memory. *Journal of Memory and Language, 30,* 513–541.

Klauer, K. C., & Wegener, I. (1998). Unraveling social categorization in the "who said what" paradigm. *Journal of Personality and Social Psychology, 75,* 1155–1178.

Kounios, J., & Holcomb, P. (1992). Structure and process in semantic memory: Evidence from brain potentials and reaction time. *Journal of Experimental Psychology: General, 121,* 459–479.

Logan, G. D. (2002). Parallel and serial processing. In H. Pashler & J. Wixted (Eds.), *Stevens' handbook of experimental psychology: Vol. 4. Methodology in experimental psychology* (3rd edition) (pp. 271–300). New York, NY: Wiley.

Poirier, M., & Saint-Aubin, J. (1995). Memory for related and unrelated words: Further evidence on the influence of semantic factors in immediate serial recall. *Quarterly Journal of Experimental Psychology, 48A,* 384–404.

Poirier, M., Schweickert, R., & Oliver, J. (2005). Silent reading rate and memory span. *Memory, 13,* 380–387.

Roberts, F. S. (1976). *Discrete mathematical models: With applications to social, biological and environmental problems.* Englewood Cliffs, NJ: Prentice-Hall, Inc.

Roberts, S. (1987). Evidence for distinct serial processes in animals: The multiplicative factors method. *Animal Learning & Behavior, 15,* 135–173.

Schweickert, R. (1978). A critical path generalization of the additive factor method: Analysis of a Stroop task. *Journal of Mathematical Psychology, 18,* 105–139.

Schweickert, R. (1992). Constructing a stochastic critical path network given the slacks: Representation. *Mathematical Social Sciences, 23,* 343–366.

Schweickert, R., & Chen, S. (2008). Tree inference with factors selectively influencing processes in a processing tree. *Journal of Mathematical Psychology, 52,* 158–183.

Schweickert, R., Fisher, D. L., & Sung, K. (2012). *Discovering cognitive architecture by selectively influencing mental processes.* Singapore: World Scientific.

Schweickert, R., & Han, H. J. (2014). *Reaction time predictions for factors selectively influencing processes in processing trees.* (Manuscript in preparation)

Schweickert, R., & Townsend, J. T. (1989). A trichotomy: Interactions of factors prolonging sequential and concurrent mental processes in stochastic discrete mental (PERT) networks. *Journal of Mathematical Psychology, 33,* 328–347.

Schweickert, R., & Xi, Z. (2011). Multiplicatively interacting factors selectively influencing parameters in multiple response class processing and rate trees. *Journal of Mathematical Psychology, 55,* 348–364.

Stahl, C., & Klauer, K. C. (2007). HMMTree: A computer program for latent-class hierarchical multinomial processing tree models. *Behavior Research Methods, 39,* 257–273.

Sternberg, S. (1969). The discovery of processing stages: Extensions of Donders' method. *Acta Psychologica, 30,* 276–315.

Sternberg, S. (2001). Separate modifiability, mental modules and the use of pure and composite measures to reveal them. *Acta Psychologica, 106,* 147–246.

Townsend, J. T. (1972). Some results concerning the identifiability of parallel and serial processes. *British Journal of Mathematical and Statistical Psychology, 25,* 168–199.

Townsend, J. T. (1984). Uncovering mental processes with factorial experiments. *Journal of Mathematical Psychology, 28,* 363–400.

Townsend, J. T., & Ashby, F. G. (1983). *The Stochastic Modeling of Elementary Psychological Processes.* Cambridge, UK: Cambridge University Press.

Townsend, J. T., & Schweickert, R. (1989). Toward the trichotomy method of reaction times: Laying the foundation of stochastic mental networks. *Journal of Mathematical Psychology, 33*, 309–327.

Townsend, J. T., & Wenger, M. J. (2004). The serial-parallel dilemma: A case study in a linkage of theory and method. *Psychonomic Bulletin & Review, 11*, 391–418.

Wolk, E. S. (1962). The comparability graph of a tree. *Proceedings of the American Mathematical Society, 13*, 789–795.

Wu, H., Myung, J. I., & Batchelder, W. H. (2010). Minimum description length model selection of multinomial processing tree models. *Psychonomic Bulletin & Review, 17*, 275–286.

Yang, H., Fifić, M., & Townsend, J. T. (2014). Survivor interaction contrast wiggle predictions of parallel and serial models for an arbitrary number of processes. *Journal of Mathematical Psychology, 58*, 21–32.

6 Simple Factorial Tweezers for Detecting Delicate Serial and Parallel Processes

Mario Fifić

Over the last fifty years, work regarding the theoretical foundations governing the organization of mental processes has centered on the formal properties of various hypothesized mental networks. Such networks are defined in terms of their fundamental properties: processing order, stopping rule, and process dependency. Pivoting on the work of James Townsend and other essential contributors such as Richard Schweickert and Ehtibar Dzhafarov, these efforts resulted in the creation of the Systems Factorial Technology (SFT), a suite of methodological tools for directly investigating the fundamental properties of cognitive operations. The SFT approach rests on rigorously tested mathematical tools for discriminating between serial and parallel processing, exhaustive and self-terminating stopping rules, and stochastic independence and dependence, as well as for discerning the capacity of an investigated system, all in a non-parametric (distribution-free) manner. The present chapter is focused on further refining recent advances in the SFT methodology and on the development of new tools for use with mental networks consisting of more than two processes. The present study also seeks to integrate these advances with the factorial tools developed to explore non-homogeneous mental networks, which may consist of both serial and parallel processes (so called serial-parallel networks).

One of the essential tasks of cognitive psychology is to learn how mental processes are organized in various cognitive tasks. Over the last several decades, cognitive psychologists have been trying to validate various cognitive models by asking questions such as: What is the order of the completion of these mental processes (e.g., serial or parallel)? Can a cognitive system be terminated when only a few or all processes have been completed (e.g., self-termination and exhaustiveness)? Do processes of interest depend on each other (e.g., process interdependency)? What is a system's processing capacity (e.g., limited, unlimited, or super capacity)? These questions focus on the aspects of processing that are all referred to as the *fundamental properties* of mental processes.

There has been a constant development of methodologies to uncover the fundamental properties of mental processes. An important early contributor, Donders (1868/1969), devised a subtraction method, which measures processing time durations. In this method, two tasks are used with the only difference between the tasks being that in the second task, an additional process has been inserted. The duration of the *inserted* mental process is inferred by subtracting the times needed to complete two tasks.

With the rise of modern cognitive psychology in the 1960s, a new approach was developed; the "additive factor method" explored the fundamental properties of mental processes such as serial and parallel processing order. Unlike the subtraction method, which worked via inserting processes, the method proposed by Sternberg (1966, 1969) was based on affecting the duration of processes within an unknown mental network (with the motto "Stretching processes rather than inserting them," after Schweickert, Fisher, & Sung, 2012). Sternberg proposed that, by the virtue of selective influence, it should be possible to elongate the processing durations. The selective influence was (and is) considered as the critical conditional assumption of the methodology. This served as the experimental manipulation that would affect the duration of only one of the processes and leave the other processes in the network unaffected. In the additive factor method, a factor is defined as an experimental variable that affects the duration of a single process of interest. The advantage of the additive factors over the subtraction method is that researchers do not need to change the structure of the mental network under investigation.[1]

In practice, the additive factor method employs an analysis of variance (ANOVA) to test for an interaction between factors. Serial and parallel processing are tested simply by observing the absence or presence of the interaction between experimental factors, respectively.

In his seminal work on distinguishing between serial and parallel processing in short-term memory (STM), Sternberg (1966, 1969) proposed a combination of his additive factors and Donders's subtraction methods. Some processes were stretched (e.g., imposing a mask on a target) and some other processes were inserted (e.g., by varying the number of digits to be memorized across different conditions' also called workload). In his STM studies, Sternberg concluded a strict serial processing of memorized units based on the following findings: (a) The interaction effects of the key experimental factors were not significant, thus showing additivity. From Sternberg's point of view, the additive effects meant that the effects of either adding, subtracting, or stretching processes independently affected overall response-time in a STM task. The additivity supports the hypothesis that the selective influence held. (b) The reaction time (RT) showed the linearly increasing trend as a function of the number of memorized items (linear RT function of workload). This finding supported that the scanning time per one item was constant over the memory load and, consequently, supported the hypothesis that the memorized items were scanned in a serial fashion. Sternberg believed it would be possible to discriminate between pure serial and parallel processing by analyzing the shape of the RT-workload function: The landmark signature of the serial system should be a linearly increasing RT-workload function. That is, by adding more processes, the system should slow down at a constant rate. In contrast, the parallel system should exhibit a flat RT-workload function. By adding more processes that are analyzed in parallel, the system should not slow down processing, as all processes occur simultaneously.

6.1 The Theoretical Breakthrough

In the original Sternberg STM paradigm, one of the key experimental manipulations is the number of memorized units (workload). By manipulating workload, a researcher directly increases or decreases a size of the mental network that makes a STM store and consequently affects the number of conducted processes. For example, if a subject has to memorize four items, then the search for the target item should include $N = 4$ of target-to-item comparisons.

Essentially, the workload manipulation is based on the insertion method, which has been criticized in the post-Dondersian era as having the potential to invite confounding variables (e.g., Townsend, 1971a; Townsend & Ashby, 1983). For example, by inserting a number of memorized units, thus adding more items to be memorized, one would also be affecting the capacity of STM storage. If the system is of limited capacity, then it is to be expected that stored items should receive part of a shared amount of resources. So as workload increases, it is likely that a cognitive system with limited capacity would distribute fewer processing resources per memorized unit. One could argue that such capacity limitations would not prevent the serial processing system from exhibiting its landmark signature—the linearly increasing RT-workload function. Provided that each processing unit receives the same amount of shared limited capacity, the RT-workload function should increase linearly as more items are processed in a strictly serial fashion.

However, the parallel system under the same capacity limitation would fail to leave the classical parallel processing signatures: the flat RT-workload function. The problem is that, quite naturally, parallel models whose channels become less efficient as workload increases can make predictions identical to those of serial models—this is the well-known *model mimicking dilemma*. The groundbreaking work for solving the model mimicking was laid out by the work of James Townsend and his colleagues (e.g., Townsend, 1969, 1971b, 1972; Townsend & Ashby, 1983, Chapter 14).

80 *Mario Fifić*

6.2 Pure Stretching Method

The work that followed Sternberg's studies was focused on designing the new methodologies to explore the fundamental properties of mental processes. Built on the work of James Townsend and other essential contributors, such as Richard Schweickert and Ehtibar Dzahfarov, the efforts resulted in a creation of the Systems Factorial Technology (SFT), a suite of methodological tools aimed at discovering the fundamental properties of cognitive operations. The SFT approach rests on rigorously tested mathematical tools for discerning serial from parallel processing, exhaustive from self-terminating processing, process (in)dependence, and the capacity of the system under investigation. During the three decades following the cognitive revolution in the 1960s, James Townsend worked on refining the non-parametric mathematical methods that constitute the SFT suite of methodologies.

The breakthrough in the work of James Townsend (Townsend & Ashby, 1983; Townsend & Nozawa, 1995) was the theoretical definition and application of the so-called *pure stretching method* approach (Schweickert et al., 2012). In the pure stretching approach, no processes are inserted, and the analysis of the underlying mental network is conducted on a fixed number of processes. The pure stretching approach avoids possible confounds due to the capacity issue in exploring serial or parallel systems' properties using the insertion method. As a result, the pure stretching method improves model selection by reducing the possible mimicking between different models.

6.3 Single Factor Manipulation: Stretching One Process

To explain the effect of stretching of a certain mental process over time, I will define an internal psychological function h that affects the speed of mental process X by either slowing it down or speeding it up. I will also define a binary-valued variable $x \in \{x_{low}, x_{high}\}$ such that this set is ordered $x_{low} < x_{high}$. If x is a fixed factor, then it is operationalized as an external manipulation that exclusively affects only the process of interest X, providing the previously mentioned selective influence. The effect of the manipulation of x on the speed of a mental process t_X is determined by the $h(X;x)$. The following conditions should apply so that the stretching manipulation could be used in the SFT approach:

(a) Selective influence holds. This means that each experimental manipulation always works to affect only one process of interest (Sternberg, 1966, 1967).
(b) Stochastic order holds. The stochastic order of the effect of h on a mental process duration is preserved for different magnitudes of

external manipulation. Assume an underlying process of interest X whose duration is affected by $h(X)$. Assume that the process X is selectively influenced by binary-valued experimental factor x across different levels (low and high) then it should always hold that $E[t_X; x_{\text{low}}] \geq E[t_X; x_{\text{high}}]$. In other words, the manipulation of a factor x at a low level should always lead to an equal or a slower expected processing rate of the process X than when x was at the high level. An even stronger test for stochastic ordering (stochastic dominance) is conducted by looking at the order of corresponding survivor functions of reaction times, thus replacing the expectation times with the survivor function: $S(t_X; x_{\text{low}}) \geq S(t_X; x_{\text{high}})$.

(c) Process independence between processes holds. This means that the rate of processing of a single process (say X) does not depend on any other process in a mental network (say Y and Z).

In practice, the stretching manipulation via the function h is usually achieved either by selective visual masking (Sternberg, 1969), stimulus brightness (Townsend & Nozawa, 1995) in the cases of external visual search, or by inter-item similarity in the case of an internal memory search or categorization (Fifić, Little, & Nosofsky, 2010; Townsend & Fifić, 2004; Townsend & Nozawa, 1995).

The stretching effect of process X is presented here as a first-order difference operator Δ applied on the h function of the mental process X, for the parameter x: $\Delta h(X; x)$ (see also Townsend & Thomas, 1994). In case the function operates at the expected time value of the process X,

$$\Delta E[t_X; x] = E[t_x; x_{\text{low}}] - E[t_x; x_{\text{high}}] > 0. \tag{6.1}$$

Or at the survivor function level,

$$\Delta S(t_X; x) = S(t_x; x_{\text{low}}) - S(t_x; x_{\text{high}}) > 0 \tag{6.2}$$

for all t_X.

In practice, the first-order difference effect on mean reaction times indicates whether the mental process of interest was affected by experimental manipulation.

6.4 Double Factorial Manipulation: Stretching Two Processes

Here we consider a minimal size mental network made of two processes that allows for assessment of all fundamental properties. To assess properties of mental networks, a researcher orthogonally combines the manipulated variable levels (for more details, see Anderson & Whitcomb, 2000). In SFT, the h function that operates on two variables (t_X, t_Y)

orthogonally combines the binary values of each experimental factor (low, high). Thus the following *second-order* difference operator is defined as:

$$\begin{aligned}
\Delta^2 h(t_X, t_Y; x, y) &= \Delta(\Delta(t_X, t_Y; x_{\text{low}}, x_{\text{high}}, y_{\text{low}}, y_{\text{high}})) \\
&= \Delta(h(t_X, t_Y; x_{\text{low}}, y_{\text{low}}, y_{\text{high}}) - h(t_X, t_Y; x_{\text{high}}, y_{\text{low}}, y_{\text{high}})) \\
&= \Delta h(t_X, t_Y; x_{\text{low}}, y_{\text{low}}, y_{\text{high}}) \\
&\quad - \Delta h(t_X, t_Y; x_{\text{high}}, y_{\text{low}}, y_{\text{high}}) \\
&= h(t_X, t_Y; x_{\text{low}}, y_{\text{low}}) - h(t_X, t_Y; x_{\text{low}}, y_{\text{high}}) \\
&\quad - (h(t_X, t_Y; x_{\text{high}}, y_{\text{low}}) - h(t_X, t_Y; x_{\text{high}}, y_{\text{high}})).
\end{aligned} \qquad (6.3)$$

This second-order difference $\Delta^2 h(X,Y;x,y)$ is also known as the interaction contrast used to measure between-factor ANOVA interactions. The substantial literature is devoted to the nature of factorial tests in research (Anderson & Whitcomb, 2000; Maxwell & Delaney, 1999). The second-order difference in this form results in the four conditions corresponding to the four h functions in Equation 6.3. One can observe that the four conditions are obtained by the orthogonal combination of the levels of the manipulated values of the factors (low and high). I will abbreviate the four conditions in the following fashion: LL, LH, HL, and HH, corresponding to the last line of Equation 6.3. For example, LH means that the first manipulated stretching factor affecting the first variable t_X was at the low level = L, and the second manipulated stretching factor affecting the second variable t_Y was at the high level = H.

The second-order difference of a stretching effect provides sufficient information to explore the fundamental properties of the two mental processes. First, it includes the two first-order differences, each providing information as to whether each experimental stretching manipulation affected the process of interest. Second, the information about the type of interaction between the two factors, through the second-order difference, can be used to distinguish between the fundamental properties.

6.5 SFT Statistical Tests for Two-Process Mental Networks (N = 2): MIC and SIC

The main testing tools in the SFT approach are the two statistics applied on both expected value of response-time RT, $E[RT]$, and on corresponding time survivor functions, $S(t)$, over time t.

The second-order difference Equation 6.3 can be applied on expected response-time values, and it is known as the mean interaction contrast (MIC). The MIC statistic calculates the interaction between the factors similarly to an ANOVA (Sternberg, 1969; see also Schweickert, 1978; Schweickert & Townsend, 1989):

To calculate MIC for the two processes, the second-order difference is derived for two variables (X,Y), each belonging to a distinct process within an unknown mental network:

$$\Delta^2 E[t_X, t_Y; x, y] = E[t_X, t_Y; x_{\text{low}}, y_{\text{low}}] - E[t_X, t_Y; x_{\text{low}}, y_{\text{high}}]$$
$$- (E[t_X, t_Y; x_{\text{high}}, y_{\text{low}}] - E[t_X, t_Y; x_{\text{high}}, y_{\text{high}}]).$$

In the case of multiple processes, one has to verify whether the first-order difference of the first variable (t_X) aggregated over the levels of the other variable shows the expected mean order difference between low and high levels or not:

$$\Delta E[t_X, t_Y; x, y] = E[t_X, t_Y; x_{\text{low}}, y] - E[t_X, t_Y; x_{\text{high}}, y].$$

When stretching is in place, the expected response-time expectation is that the average response of the process X takes longer when the level of stretching manipulation was low than when the level is high, across all levels of the y process manipulations:[2]

$$E[t_X, t_Y; x_{\text{low}}, y] - E[t_X, t_Y; x_{\text{high}}, y] > 0.$$

The analogous check is done across the levels of y factor.

A strong stochastic ordering (stochastic dominance) is verified by looking at the order of corresponding survivor functions. The expectations are replaced with the survivor functions, and we check whether the difference between two marginal survivor functions satisfies the inequality for both x and y:

$$S(t_X, t_Y; x_{\text{low}}, y) - S(t_X, t_Y; x_{\text{high}}, y) > 0$$

for all t_X.

An even stronger test that the stochastic ordering is preserved is to check that the high and low effect on stretching of probability density functions cross exactly once (or an odd number of times (Schweickert et al., 2012; Schweickert, Giorgini, & Dzhafarov, 2000; Townsend & Nozawa, 1995; H. Yang, Fifić, & Townsend, 2014).

The aforementioned second-order difference (Equation 6.3) on mean RTs can be written in the more popular form as the so-called double-factorial test in SFT:

$$\begin{aligned} \text{MIC} &= (RT_{LL} - RT_{LH}) - (RT_{HL} - RT_{HH}) \\ &= RT_{LL} - RT_{LH} - RT_{HL} + RT_{HH}. \end{aligned} \quad (6.4)$$

RT stands for mean reaction time, and the left and right subscripts refer to the stretching levels of the first and the second mental process of interest, correspondingly. For example, HL indicates a condition where the first factor (processing the first item) is at the high level and the second factor (processing of the second item) is at the low level. The resulting design could be referred to as a 2 × 2 factorial design (as employed in ANOVA).

Completely analogously to deriving the mean interaction contrast, Equation 6.4, one can compute the survivor interaction contrast (SIC). By replacing the mean RTs for each condition by the survivor functions, at each value of t, one computes:

$$\begin{aligned} \text{SIC}(t) &= (S_{LL}(t) - S_{LH}(t)) - (S_{HL}(t) - S_{HH}(t)) \\ &= S_{LL}(t) - S_{LH}(t) - S_{HL}(t) + S_{HH}(t). \end{aligned} \quad (6.5)$$

In practice, when the double-factorial SFT test is used, it is necessary to check whether the four factorial conditions satisfy the following order at the mean reaction times:

$$M(RT_{LL}) \geq \{M(RT_{LH}), M(RT_{HL})\} \geq M(RT_{HH}).$$

And a stronger test can be done by inspecting the order of the survivor functions. It is important to keep in mind that, in order to apply SFT, the ordered survivor functions should not intersect when plotted (for statistical tests, see Houpt, Blaha, McIntire, Havig, & Townsend, 2014; Houpt & Townsend, 2010; H. Yang et al., 2014):

$$S_{LL}(t) \geq \{S_{LH}(t), S_{HL}(t)\} \geq S_{HH}(t)$$

for all t.

The SIC has a close relationship with the results from the MIC because the value of the MIC is simply the integral of the SIC over all values of t. This follows from the fact that the integral of the survivor function for a random variable yields the mean of that random variable. Because the survivor interaction contrast is simply a linear contrast of individual survivor functions, the integral of the SIC is a linear contrast of the means of the corresponding random variables (i.e., the MIC).

The showcase of the distinct diagnostic predictions of MIC and SIC patterns for several types of mental networks made of two processes ($N = 2$) are displayed in the first column of Figure 6.1A. The depicted mental networks could be characterized as canonical networks, as they possess only one processing order and one stopping rule. The MIC value is presented in each signature's upper-right corner.

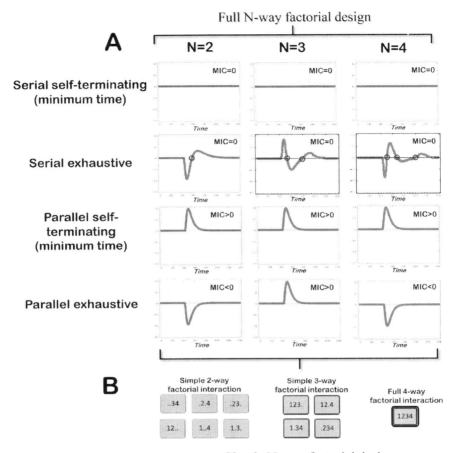

Figure 6.1 (A) The showcase of the distinct diagnostic predictions of MIC and SIC patterns for each mental network (rows) of a size up to four processes (columns) for full-factorial research designs (top row). For the serial-exhaustive mental network, the circles emphasize the intersection points of the SIC function and x-axis. (B) The bottom row indicates the type of simple interaction factorial test, derived from the 4-way full-factorial design. Each column indicates 2-way simple, 3-way simple, and 4-way full-factorial designs, and corresponding diagnostic predictions of MIC and SIC patterns. Note that all six 2-way simple interaction designs predict equivalent SICs and MICs for different mental networks. The same holds for the four 3-way simple interaction designs. Both (A) and (B) predicted MIC and SIC results are only relevant for the homogeneous mental networks (see the text for more details).

It is important to note that the SIC provides more diagnostic power than MIC, as the SIC is a function of time, while MIC is the integrated value of that function over time. For example, certain classes of models cannot be distinguished using the MIC, but can be successfully distinguished using the SIC.[3]

Although the MIC test has less diagnostic power, MICs are more practical to use than SICs, because one requires fewer trials to achieve stable estimates of the mean RT statistics than to get good estimates of the corresponding RT-survivor functions. So there is a trade-off between practical applicability and statistical power when using MIC and SIC.

From Equations 6.4 and 6.5, it is immediately clear that the SFT method, based on the pure stretching method, bypasses the confounding concerns that challenged the application of Sternberg's insertion procedure in a STM search task. By using SFT, there is no need to insert processes to learn whether processing is serial or parallel. Instead, an experimental situation with a fixed number of processes ($N = 2$ in Figure 6.1A) is sufficient. This way, the SFT approach addresses the serial/parallel mimicking problem (mentioned earlier) that arises from the confounding of the workload manipulation and the network's capacity.

The SFT tools are primarily considered as being meta-theoretical tools (or a meta-theory). The SFT does not formally represent any specific model of cognitive operations. Instead SFT tools are primarily used for the operations of validation and/or falsification of cognitive models and also as exploratory tools to learn about new, underlying cognitive operations.

The SFT models' validation/falsification power has been successfully utilized across different fields of cognitive psychology. The results challenged the standard expectations of some models to predict outcome of cognitive operations. For that purpose, SFT has been used in the context of various cognitive tasks and domains: perceptual processes (e.g., Eidels, Townsend, & Pomerantz, 2008; Fifić, Nosofsky & Townsend, 2008; Johnson, Blaha, Houpt, & Townsend, 2010; Townsend & Nozawa, 1995; C.-T. Yang, 2011; C.-T. Yang, Chang, & Wu, 2013), visual and memory search tasks (e.g., Egeth & Dagenbach, 1991; Fifić, Townsend, & Eidels, 2008; Sung, 2008; Townsend & Fifić, 2004; Wenger & Townsend, 2001, 2006), face perception tasks (Fifić & Townsend, 2010; Ingvalson & Wenger, 2005), and classification and categorization (e.g., Fifić et al., 2010; Little, Nosofsky, & Denton, 2011; Little, Noskfsky, Donkin, & Denton, 2013). The SFT tools were recognized as potentially the most important and promising methodology in understanding cognitive processes (Greenwald, 2012).

Another use of the SFT tools is to define minimal research design complexity criteria that are necessary to learn about cognitive operations of interest (Fifić, 2014). In other words, the SFT can define the benchmark for the size of the research design that must be used to correctly recognize the network underlying cognitive operations. The question posed here is: How complex should a research design be in order to make valid inferences from the study about the fundamental mental properties (see Fifić, 2014, for more details)? The answer to that question depends on the number of mental processes under investigation. So to learn about a mental network of two processes ($N = 2$), the SIC/MIC tests require at least two manipulated variables that are cross-combined at the two process-stretching levels (high and low). Then the number of experimental conditions is $2^2 = 4$. To learn about the larger mental networks made of $N = 3$ processes, the number of experimental conditions should be $2^3 = 8$. In general, to test more complex mental networks made of the N process, one has to employ at least 2^N experimental conditions.

6.6 SFT Statistical Tests for Two-Process Mental Networks ($N = 2$): The Principle Limitations

The development of the SFT tests for assaying networks of only two processes has helped in the validation of various cognitive models. However, the confinement of the SFT approaches to only $N = 2$ two processes has limited the applicability of the SFT tools. Many cognitive tasks were originally designed to explore mental networks of larger sizes. For example, a STM task usually involves modeling a search for up to six stored memorized units; thus the proposed number of processes is $N = 6$. Similar designs involving more than two processes ($N > 2$) under investigation are typical in visual search and some decision-making studies.

The main motivation behind extending the SFT approach to testing mental networks of larger sizes was to expand the application in different domains of cognitive tasks. The general extension of the SFT to an arbitrary number of mental processes has been published and detailed in recent work (H. Yang et al., 2014).

6.7 N-Factorial SIC for Homogeneous Systems: Advances to Higher Factorials

The present section summarizes the extension of the SFT method to larger size networks ($N > 2$) that are considered to be the homogeneous systems of mental networks. Homogeneous mental networks are here defined as a set of processes that are organized under a single processing order (serial or parallel) and under a single stopping rule (self-terminating or exhaustive). For example, Sternberg's serial STM processing model (Ratcliff, 1978; Sternberg, 1967) is a homogeneous mental network employing only one type of processing order and one stopping rule for all elements. Ratcliff's

88 *Mario Fifić*

(1978) parallel model of memory retrieval is a homogeneous mental network as well.[4]

By definition, any mental network made of two processes (N = 2) is a homogeneous network as long as there is only one processing order and one stopping rule that could be used. Adding at least one more process to an N = 2 network could lead to multiple processing orders and stopping rules.

6.8 Statistical Tests, the SIC General Form

In both MIC and SIC statistics, the N-order difference function over the set of variables of interest is denoted as Δ^n.

The N-order factor difference at the level of survivor functions is defined as:

$$\Delta S^N\left(t_{X_1\cdots N}; x_{1\cdots N}\right),$$

where $t_{X_1\cdots N}$ represents a set of response-time variables for processes from 1 to N.

This N-order difference function is also denoted as $SIC^N(t) = \Delta S^N(t_{X_1\cdots N}; x_{1\cdots N})$, as the SIC function can be generalized to the case for arbitrary N processes. The SIC functions for N = 2, 3, and 4 processes are derived next.

Second-order difference:

$$SIC^2(t) = \Delta^2 S(t_X, t_Y; x, y) = [S_{LL}(t) - S_{LH}(t)] - [S_{HL}(t) - S_{HH}(t)]$$

Third-order difference:

$$\begin{aligned} SIC^3(t) &= SIC^2(t; \{L, H\}) = SIC^2(t; L) - SIC^2(t; H) \\ &= \{[S_{LLL}(t) - S_{LLH}(t)] - [S_{LHL}(t) - S_{LHH}(t)]\} \\ &\quad -\{[S_{HLL}(t) - S_{HLH}(t)] - [S_{HHL}(t) - S_{HHH}(t)]\} \end{aligned}$$

Fourth-order difference:

$$\begin{aligned} SIC^4(t) &= SIC^3(t; \{L, H\}) = SIC^3(t; L) - SIC^3(t; H) \\ &= \{[S_{LLLL}(t) - S_{LLLH}(t)] - [S_{LLHL}(t) - S_{LLHH}(t)]\} \\ &\quad -\{[S_{LHLL}(t) - S_{LHLH}(t)] - [S_{LHHL}(t) - S_{LHHH}(t)]\} \\ &\quad -\{[S_{HLLL}(t) - S_{HLLH}(t)] - [S_{HLHL}(t) - S_{HLHH}(t)]\} \\ &\quad -\{[S_{HHLL}(t) - S_{HHLH}(t)] - [S_{HHHL}(t) - S_{HHHH}(t)]\} \end{aligned}$$

Figure 6.1A shows the SIC functions for different mental networks up to the size of four processes (N = 4). The SIC shapes for the higher-order mental networks that are larger than four processes can be derived by induction from the related theorems (H. Yang et al., 2014). As it can be seen from Figure 6.1A, the SIC signatures show a remarkable regularity in changing their shapes as the number of processes under investigation increases. The serial minimum-time and the parallel self-terminating processing networks both show self-repeating patterns as a function of the size of a mental network (N). The serial minimum-time SIC signature remains a flat function, while the parallel self-terminating SIC signature remains a positive unimodal function. These two SIC signatures could be characterized almost as having fractal properties, as the output of these functions would recurrently generate the same SIC patterns regardless of the size of the network. To some extent, the self-repeating patterns are also evident in the case of parallel exhaustive systems: The SIC function predicts the same shape, albeit the function flips around the x-axis as with each new process (N). Thus the SIC is strictly negative for an even number of processes and is strictly positive for an odd number of processes under investigation.

The serial exhaustive network shows the distinct coiling behavior around the principle x-axis: For the simplest serial network of two processes, the SIC function is first negative then positive under the condition that the two areas are equal. The serial exhaustive processing for $N = 2$ intersects the x-axis only once, thus introducing diagnostic property of $N - 1$ zero-crossings. By adding more processes, the SIC function flips around the x-axis and coils once more around the x-axis, thus exhibiting another regular shape change, "flips and coil," while the total sum of positive and negative areas is always zero.

The results of the recent extension of SFT to multiple processes (H. Yang et al., 2014) provide new opportunities for extended exploration of fundamental properties of larger mental networks, and they provide means for validation/falsification operations in various cognitive tasks.

6.9 Limitations

The diagnostic SIC signatures derived for homogeneous mental networks (H. Yang et al., 2014) are subject to two general limitations that can lead to diminishing the SFT diagnostic power:

(1) Non-unique SIC patterns: Upon visual inspection of Figure 6.1A, it could be observed that there are some cases of different mental architectures predicting the same shape of the SIC function. Some mental networks are made of different fundamental mental properties that have an identical SIC signature for the same N. For example, Figure 6.1A shows that both the parallel minimum-time and the parallel exhaustive network make the same SIC signature prediction when the number of processes is odd ($N = 3, 5, 7, \ldots$)[5].

90 *Mario Fifić*

(2) The diagnostic SIC signatures derived for homogeneous mental networks cannot be generalized to all types of mental networks. One such case is the class of non-homogeneous networks of larger sizes ($N > 2$), which combines different processing properties within one mental network. For example, a case of a non-homogeneous network has some mental operations conducted in serial and some conducted in parallel.[6]

In the current chapter, I provide new evidence and insights that could be used to address the concerns raised by the apparent limitations of the current SFT methods on the exploration of homogeneous systems consisting of more than two processes ($N > 2$). These efforts could be seen as another extension of the SFT methods and as a suggestion about the new approaches that test even more complex mental networks. In order to unlock potentially more powerful diagnostic features of the SFT approach, I will integrate some previous approaches with the novel ideas. The ideas will be reported in the form of proposals and their proofs in the following section. Within some of the proposals, I will provide the analysis of illustrative cases.

6.10 Simple Factorial SIC Functions for Homogeneous Systems

The existence of non-unique SIC signatures reduces the diagnostic power of SFT of homogeneous systems, which are made of an arbitrary number of processes ($N > 2$). Note that each SIC function in Figure 6.1A is obtained by the analysis of the full-factorial SFT design. That is, if the number of processes analyzed in the underlying mental network was N, then N variables were engaged in the full-factorial SFT design. I argue here that the application of the lower-level interaction tests unlocks the additional diagnostic power of SFT tools. The argument is based on the finding that the simple interaction tests would provide more evidence for distinguishing between different types of mental networks.

Claim: Applying a simple interaction factorial analysis on a full-factorial data set improves the diagnosticity of the SFT when applied on homogeneous mental networks of sizes larger than two under the conditions specified.

Evidence: One can derive the new sets of SIC signatures for the lower-level factorial designs within a full-factorial design. This is achieved by marginalization of the effects of some factors in a full-factorial design and by inspection of the SIC signatures obtained. For example, a four-process network, which is investigated by the four factors, full-factorial design, can also be investigated by the four three-way factorial designs and six two-way factorial designs by means of marginalization of single factors.

The procedure for deriving low-level interactions is equal to the one conducted in factorial ANOVA. Marginalization is equal to averaging out the effect of unwanted factors.[7] Given that a factor in an SFT design represents a single process of interest, it could be in either a low or high state (selectively influenced by the experimental manipulation). Its marginalization would lead to excluding this factor from the design by averaging its effect across other factors.

In practice, marginalization of the factors leads to having to combine the results from conditions of the high and low stretching into a single condition. Assume a network is made of three processes (X, Y, and Z); then the third-order difference function is shown in a simpler form:

$$SIC^3(t) = \{[S_{LLL}(t) - S_{LLH}(t)] - [S_{LHL}(t) - S_{LHH}(t)]\} - \{[S_{HLL}(t) - S_{HLH}(t)] - [S_{HHL}(t) - S_{HHH}(t)]\}.$$

Each of the three subscript letters represent a different variable (X, Y, Z). Each variable represents a single process that could be in either a low (L) or high (H) state based on a stretching manipulation. In the experimental study, each term represents an empirical survivor function of one experimental condition consisting of a sample of repeated RT trials.

To derive the low-level interaction contrast functions of the second-order differences, one has to marginalize the effect of one variable in the equation. To find the second-order difference of the SIC function of the two processes between Y and Z, one has to marginalize the effect of X. To marginalize the variable X, which is the first variable in the subscript, one has to aggregate the low and high conditions for the first variable, which leads to the following second-order difference between the two variables, Y and Z:

$$\begin{aligned} SIC^{2(.,Y,Z)}(t) &= [S_{LLL+HLL}(t) - S_{LLH+HLH}(t)] \\ &\quad - [S_{LHL+HHL}(t) - S_{LHH+HHH}(t)] \\ &= [S_{.LL}(t) - S_{.LH}(t)] - [S_{.HL}(t) - S_{.HH}(t)] \end{aligned} \quad (6.6)$$

The dot indicates a marginalized factor. The plus sign represents the operation of uniting the data sets from the two different conditions (for example, .LL=LLL + HLL). A similar procedure is used to find the other two second-order difference SIC functions ($SIC^{2(X,.,Z)}(t)$ and ($SIC^{2(X,Y,.)}(t)$). We will refer to these as the *simple interaction SIC tests*.

This form (Equation 6.6) of the simple interaction SIC test is equivalent to the form of the full-factorial interaction test. The second row in Equation 6.6 is the result of the first variable marginalization. This outcome is equivalent to the second-order difference

$$SIC^2 = [S_{LL}(t) - S_{LH}(t)] - [S_{HL}(t) - S_{HH}(t)].$$

One can show that derivation of the simple interaction SIC test of any factorial design will lead to the equation forms that are equivalent to the full-factorial SIC forms lessened by the number of marginalized factors.

92 Mario Fifić

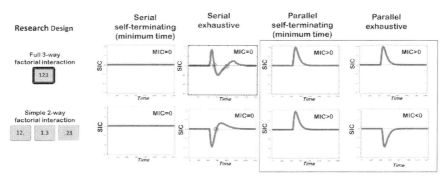

Figure 6.2 The simple interaction SIC test for the three-factorial research design. The research design, starting with the full-factorial design, is displayed in the first column, crossed with the different types of mental networks. Although the full-factorial SIC cannot distinguish between parallel minimum-time and parallel exhaustive models (the first row, SICs of the models are in a box), the simple 2-way factorial SIC (the second row, boxed) can distinguish between the two.

By using simple interaction SIC tests and marginalization of variables, it is possible to derive all possible lower-order differences for any full-factorial design. The relevant SIC predictions for each distinct mental network, of a size up to four processes, are presented in Figure 6.1B.

The analysis of simple interactions shown in Figure 6.1B directly addresses the issue raised by the non-unique SIC pattern limitation when the SFT full-factorial designs were used. For example, in the case of the shared SIC signature between the minimum-time parallel model and the parallel exhaustive model for the odd number of processes under an investigation, the simple interaction factorial analysis now provides the set of simple SIC interaction contrast functions for each full-factorial design (Figure 6.1B). For example, take the case of $N = 3$ SIC signatures, presented in Figure 6.2. Although the third-order difference SIC functions are shared (thus non-unique) between parallel minimum-time and parallel exhaustive models, the derived simple interactions (two-way) show distinct SIC patterns. In the case of the parallel minimum-time model, the two-way simple SICs are all positive, whereas for the exhaustive parallel model of the corresponding two-way simple SICs are all negative.

6.11 Limitations

The SFT methodologies described so far are confined to the exploration of homogeneous mental networks. The examples of homogeneous networks are pure serial or pure parallel processing systems in which one stopping rule (either OR or AND) is applied on all network processes. Unfortunately, the SFT signature predictions would no longer hold valid if a

Simple Factorial Tweezers for Detecting Delicate Serial 93

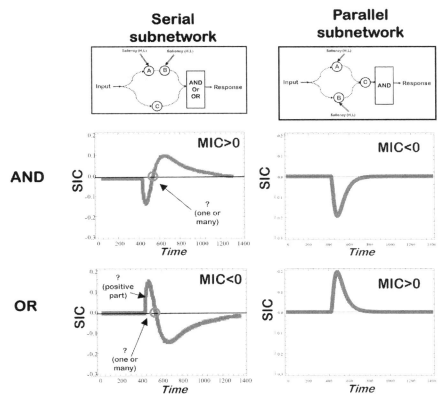

Figure 6.3 SIC function predictions for the serial and parallel subnetworks, crossed with the minimum-time stopping rule (OR) and exhaustive stopping rule (AND). The factorially manipulated processes (indicated by the arrows in the first row), are embedded in the serial-parallel network. The SIC shape expectations are not exact because they are the result of not-so-strict inequalities (Dzhafarov, Schweickert, & Sung, 2004; Schweickert et al., 2000). The unknown properties are indicated by the question signs.

non-homogenous mental network (such as a serial-parallel network) is analyzed.

Although the research literature proposes many homogenous mental networks (e.g., Ratcliff, 1978; Sternberg, 1967), many researchers have provided evidence that shows that it is not realistic to assume that the fundamental processing properties are always homogeneously distributed across larger mental networks. In fact, it is plausible to assume that larger mental networks could combine several fundamental properties within a single mental network.

94 Mario Fifić

6.12 N-Factorial SIC for Non-Homogeneous Networks

One formal way to describe a cognitive system that can combine different fundamental properties is a directed acyclic network (Townsend & Schweickert, 1985; Schweickert et al., 2000). For example, the networks depicted in the first row of Figure 6.4 combine both serial and parallel processing. These mental networks utilize either an OR or an AND stopping rule. This means that the network will wait for the completion of both items before proceeding to the next stage (AND = exhaustive processing), or it will terminate on completion of a single process (OR = processing termination is possible).

Take, for example, a model of STM. The original Sternberg model was later challenged by the results that showed a strong serial position recency effect in memory scanning. That is, recently stored items were analyzed faster than the older items in the set. The recency effect suggested that recent items may be stored in a different way than the older items. To account for the recency effect, several alternative models were published that proposed the idea that STM processing consists of two subnetworks, serial and parallel. It was proposed that STM consists of two distinct temporal stores, so the items stored can have different accessibility rates (Burrows & Okada, 1971; Clifton & Birenbaum, 1970; Forrin & Cunningham, 1973; Posner & Taylor, 1969; Waugh & Norman, 1965; see also, Oberauer, 2002; Oberauer & Bialkova, 2009).

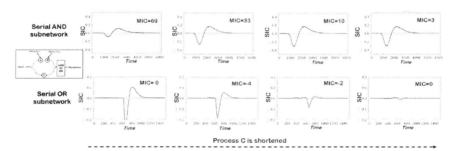

Figure 6.4   The simulation results of the serial-parallel network depicted in the first column for two different stopping rules (AND and OR). The subnetwork of interest is made of two serial processes and one in parallel with the first two. Across columns, the duration of the third parallel process is manipulated, such that the process is shortened, whereas the two processes in serial are of fixed parameter value time duration. In the simulation model, each processing time completion was determined by a simple random walk process with two bounds and probability *p* stepping to one of the bounds. Ten thousand trials were conducted per factorial condition.

Simple Factorial Tweezers for Detecting Delicate Serial 95

Work on the identification of acyclic serial-parallel networks has been conducted by Richard Schweickert, Ehtibar Dzhafarov, and a group of collaborators (Dzhafarov et al., 2004; Schweickert, Fisher, & Goldstein, 2010; Schweickert et al., 2000; for an overview, see Schweickert et al., 2012). The initial idea sprung from the seminal work of James Townsend and Richard Schweickert on identifiability of the serial-parallel networks (Townsend, & Schweickert, 1985). I will summarize the main findings of the SIC predictions in regard to the serial-parallel networks.

6.13 Statistical Tests and Subnetwork Decomposability

When an underlying processing system is non-homogeneous, one can expect that the N-factorial SIC test will become less diagnostic with the increasing number of processes and level of heterogeneity. For example, imagine a large-size network of up to four processes in which some of them form serial and some form parallel subnetworks, each of which could utilize different stopping rules. Let us assume that the described three-process network is a directed acyclic network not known to researchers. The researcher's task is to reveal the network in terms of the fundamental mental properties (processing order, stopping rule, dependency).

Theoretically, the three-process network, which could be either serial or parallel, can be organized in many ways. If the mental network is homogeneous, then there is only a single solution about how to organize them: by using one processing order with one stopping rule. If the three-process mental network is non-homogeneous, then that number could be rather high: the number of different ways to organize them is close to one hundred combinations.[8]

Although the SFT analysis could be employed at the full-factorial level, it is immediately striking that such a high number of possible mental network organizations would generate too many three-factorial SIC predictions. In the best case, some of these three-process combinations would generate unique SIC patterns that could be used to clearly distinguish them from other possible combinations. However, it is more likely that many such combinations would produce identical SIC shape predictions, thus with the potential to diminish applicability in differentiating subnetworks.

In the earlier section on the sample interactive factorial tests, we learned that more diagnostic power is achieved by analysis of the lower-level factorial interactions. The SFT analysis of the non-homogeneous system should proceed from the full-factorial to a simple-factorial analysis. In fact, the strategy of factoring out some processes from the full-factorial design proves to be effective when applied in SFT factorial analysis. As in the aforementioned homogeneous network analysis case (Figure 6.2), the marginalization of the effects of some processes allows us to reach the simplest subnetworks, consisting of only two processes ($N = 2$), which are the homogeneous networks by definition. The converging idea here is that a simple-factorial analysis should improve diagnosis of possible different subnetworks within a more complex non-homogeneous one, thus helping to improve the diagnostic power of the SFT analysis.

An immediate concern here is that even though we can isolate and analyze small-size subnetworks within a more complex one, what SIC predictions should we expect to see? For example, a two-process serial subnetwork may be embedded within a system of parallel processes inside the entire network. The question here is whether the identification of such a small serial subnetwork would be affected because of the connecion to other heterogeneous parts of the network. This concern is reasonable, because the observed data about the small-size network is based on the response of the entire mental network.

A large body of such a work has already been conducted (Dzhafarov et al., 2004; Schweickert et al., 2000), and it is possible to summarize. The work is limited to the so-called serial parallel-networks in which a single dominant stopping rule is used, but the processes can be organized in either serial, parallel, or combined subnetworks (e.g., Schweickert et al., 2000). The general theorems apply to many cases in a distribution-free manner.

6.14 Findings

Under the same conditions specified earlier, the summary of the SIC function expectations is presented in this section and in Figure 6.3. In the case of detection of a parallel subnetwork ($N = 2$) connected to a serial process(es) within a larger network, with either AND or OR gates, the SIC function predictions are identical to those of an isolated parallel two-process network (Theorem 4, case 1, from Schweickert et al., 2000). That is, the diagnostic SIC shape of the parallel subnetwork does not change its shape with the presence of another serial process within the same network (in Figure 6.3). Thus in the case of the parallel AND-gate, the SIC function is negative for all times. In the case of the parallel OR gate, the SIC function is positive for all times.

In contrast, predictions for the serial subnetworks are less specific than those for the parallel subnetworks. In the case of the serial subnetwork ($N = 2$) connected to a parallel process(es) within a larger network, the SIC functions are not identical to those of isolated two-process serial networks. In the AND serial subnetwork ($N = 2$), the area under the SIC function is negative for a short period of time (Theorem 5, Schweickert et al., 2000; Theorem 6.2, Dzhafarov et al., 2004) and then changes its sign at least once. Overall, the area under the SIC curve is equal to or greater than zero (Theorem 6.1 from Dzhafarov et al., 2004; Figure 6.3). In the serial-OR subnetwork ($N = 2$), the area under the SIC curve is equal to or lesser than zero (Theorem 5, Schweickert et al., 2000; Theorem 6.1, Dzhafarov et al., 2004; Figure 6.3)

6.15 Limitations

The theorems and proofs (Dzhafarov et al., 2004; Schweickert et al., 2000) provide the general diagnostic shapes of SIC functions for small-size ($N = 2$) mental networks embedded in a larger serial-parallel network. The prediction results are of limited diagnostic power for detecting unknown subnetworks. The reason is that in some cases, different types of subnetworks would predict the same SIC under the general specifications and the listed conditions. The formal proofs operate at the level of non-strict inequalities. For example, such approaches cannot be used to distinguish between the serial-AND subnetwork and the parallel-OR subnetwork or between the serial-OR subnetwork and the parallel-AND subnetwork. These two pairs cannot be disentangled given the SIC results in an unknown underlying mental network.

6.16 Putting It All Together: Homogeneous and Non-Homogeneous Subnetworks $N = 2$

It is still possible to recuperate more of the diagnostic power (Theorem 5, Dzhafarov et al., 2004; Schweickert et al., 2000) from an SFT analysis. The SFT signatures are shared between different serial and parallel subnetworks that utilize different stopping rules (AND and OR). In many cases in research studies, it is possible to fix the stopping rule methodologically. Such examples are target-present or target-absent responses, which are designed by a researcher. Provided high accuracy in subjects' responses, a researcher is able to analyze target-present responses as likely candidates of using the OR rule and target-absent response as using the AND rule. In other words, a researcher can separate experimental conditions in which the AND rule or OR rule are used. If the stopping rules are fixed by the researcher and analyzed separately in target-present and target-absent conditions, then the SIC signatures can be used to distinguish between the serial and parallel processing subnetworks, as depicted in Figure 6.3.

The question is: Why do parallel subnetworks ($N = 2$) embedded in a serial network predict the same SIC results as a homogeneous parallel network of the same size ($N = 2$) while, at the same time, the serial system subnetwork ($N = 2$) embedded in a parallel processing network doesn't predict the same SIC results as a homogeneous serial network of the same size?

Consider the case depicted in Figure 6.3, left column, which shows that the two serial processes, *A* and *B*, are combined in parallel with the third process *C*. If *A* and *B* are selectively influenced by the corresponding factorial stretching manipulations (to produce HH, HL, LH, and LL), then what should be the predicted SIC function for the two serial processes?

The proof (Dzhafarov et al., 2004; Schweickert et al., 2000) shows that, depending on the stopping rule, the SIC function for the two serial processes ($t_A + t_B$) should be zero or largely positive if the AND gate is used as the stopping rule; that is, the system waits for the slower of the two components, max($t_A + t_B$, t_C). The SIC function should span the areas below and above the x-axis that are either zero or negative (they can have positive values too, but the total sum of the spanned areas is negative). If the OR gate is used, that is, the system stops on the first completed component, max($t_A + t_B$, t_C), the approximate SIC shape is not really known; the number of x-axis crossings of the SIC function is not known. What is known is that the total area spanned by the SIC is either positive (AND) or negative (OR). In other words, the corresponding MIC values should be positive (AND) or negative (OR).

An alternative perspective into the result of the SIC function can be used by analyzing the MIC values of the double factorial difference on the situation depicted in Figure 6.3, the first subnetwork (AND) on the left.

For example, for the subnetwork max($t_A + t_B$, t_C), it is possible to state the following:

$$\mathrm{E}[\max(t_A + t_B, t_C); a, b, c] = p\mathrm{E}[t_A + t_B; a, b] + (1 - p)\mathrm{E}[t_C; c].$$

That is, the total time to complete processing in the serial-parallel network depicted in Figure 6.3, left panel, is equal to the probability mixture of the two events: one, when the slowest component is with probability p, and two, from the slowest component coming from the parallel process with probability $(1 - p)$.

Another observation is that the random variable in the underlying process C has a fixed rate (not stretched), while the rates for $A + B$ depend on the factorial stretching effects imposed on processes A and B ($a, b \in$ {low and high}).

In the parallel system, probability p is defined as the probability that process $A + B$ has completed before the second parallel process C. Here it is shown as the integral over the completion density function of the $t_A + t_B$ (that is, $t_A + t_B$ completed first, thus the subscript 1) and the survivor function specifying that the process C has not been completed yet (has not completed first, thus the subscript 1).

$$p\langle AB, C \rangle = \int_0^\infty f_{AB_1}(t) S_{C_1}(t) dt.$$

Because we are focused on the sign of the MIC value (that reveals the area under the SIC function) of the two serial processes A and B,

$$\Delta^2 \mathrm{E}[t = \max(t_A + t_B, t_C); a, b, c]$$
$$= \Delta^2 \{p\mathrm{E}[t_A + t_B; a \in \{\text{low, high}\}, b \in \{\text{low, high}\}] + (1 - p)\mathrm{E}[t_C; c]\},$$

which implies

$$\text{MIC}(t = \max(t_A + t_B, t_C)) =$$
$$p_{LL}\text{E}[t_A + t_B; LL] + (1 - p_{LL})\text{E}[t_C; c] -$$
$$p_{LH}\text{E}[t_A + t_B; LH] + (1 - p_{LH})\text{E}[t_C; c] -$$
$$p_{HL}\text{E}[t_A + t_B; HL] + (1 - p_{HL})\text{E}[t_C; c] +$$
$$p_{HH}\text{E}[t_A + t_B; HH] + (1 - p_{HH})\text{E}[t_C; c].$$

One can immediately infer that the rate of process C would directly affect the MIC sign through the value of the parameter p. One can expect that the probability of the processing order p will change depending on the relative speeds of the parallel processes $A + B$ and C. For example, in the AND system, if the process C is very fast (p is approaching 1), then the system will stop more frequently on the serial $A + B$ completion times; if the process C is very slow (p is approaching 0) then the system is more likely to stop on completion time of the process C. It is an interesting observation that, in this case, the MIC value is a probability mixture of different factorial conditions (HH, HL, LH, and LL) that are unequally weighted with the probability p. That is, the value of p is different for each factorial condition ($p_{LL}, p_{LH}, p_{HL}, p_{HH}$) depending on the relative rate of completion of both the $A + B$ and C components. We know from the proof of Schweickert et al. (2000) that the SIC function for such a mental network is mainly a positive function, thus the MIC > 0.

In order to observe the shape of the SIC function of such a mental network, I provided the converging evidence by simulation. The results are based on the extensive simulations of a random walk process with absorbing boundaries, which are used to characterize the completion rate of each process in the subnetwork. The simulations were conducted across different values of parameters. Here the converging result is that, in the serial-AND subnetwork, the SIC is an S-shaped function that has only one x-axis crossing with a larger positive area than negative area (MIC > 0; see Figure 6.4, first row). The simulation results add to the converging evidence from the simulation using the class of exponential distributions (Dzhafarov et al., 2004; Schweickert et al., 2000). The simulation results in Figure 6.4 show that depending on the relative speed of the parallel processes, the SIC shapes undergo the expected transformation: As the process C becomes faster, the revealed SIC and MIC shapes indicate a pure serial N = 2 mental network. This is because as C becomes very fast, the network finishes mostly on the completion of the serial processes $A + B$.

The simulation results for serial-OR subnetworks (Figure 6.3, left panel the second row) showed one crossing S-shaped SIC function, similar to those of the serial-AND subnetwork. As shown in a series of simulations based on the duration of the parallel process, the faster it becomes, the more likely it is that the subnetwork will finish on a parallel process first and will not wait for the completion of the two serial processes. The result is that the SIC shape becomes more squished, showing some small negative MICs, until it completely dissolves into a straight line.

In contrast, the serial-parallel AND network depicted in Figure 6.3 (second column) shows the parallel subsystem embedded in the serial network. The predicted MIC value and SIC function are equivalent to the pure (homogeneous) parallel-AND model for the $N = 2$ number of processes. (The proofs are straightforward and are presented in Schweickert et al., 2000, p. 502, Case 2; and also in Fifić, 2006, Appendix). Also, when the OR gate is used in the same network, both the MIC and SIC make the same predictions as the pure (homogeneous) parallel-OR model for the $N = 2$ number of processes.

6.17 Discussion

There has been a great deal of progress over the last fifty years in both the theoretical development of various cognitive models and in developing methods of validation of such models. The building blocks of cognitive models are defined as the fundamental properties of mental processes. These are processing order, stopping rule, process dependency, and processing capacity.

The current dominant approaches to exploring underlying cognitive models rely mostly on formal parametric descriptions of the cognitive models. So the cognitive models are seen as a family of a finite number of distributions that are described by a set of parameters. Consequently, cognitive models have been tested by examining the parameter values, observing the parameter values that are the most likely to generate data (least-square and maximum likelihood estimations), by applying the model selection procedures (AIC, BIC) or by using more advanced techniques to account for prior parameter values, such as in the Bayesian model analysis (for a short review, see Liu & Smith, 2009).

Such approaches provide an invaluable set of tools for model exploration. However, these approaches depend on the parametric assumptions of the models. In many cases, the model exploration is carried out by very time-consuming and computer-intensive methods. In order to find the best fitting model's parameters, one has to employ optimization searches for parameters, which are, even nowadays, limited by computational power. Even the most advance methods, such as Bayesian inference and model selection (Lee & Wagenmakers, 2013; Raftery, Gelman, Rubin, & Hauser, 1995) require a simulation method known as Markov Chain Monte Carlo (MCMC), which is not immune from days of sampling simulated data from the unknown parameter values.

The groundbreaking work of James Townsend and other essential contributors led to the creation of the Systems Factorial Technology (SFT)—a suite of methodological tools for directly investigating the fundamental properties of cognitive operations. The SFT approach, created by James Townsend, rests on rigorously tested mathematical tools for discriminating between serial and parallel processing, exhaustive and self-terminating stopping rules, and stochastic independence and dependence, as well as for discerning the capacity of an investigated system, all in a parameter-free manner.

SFT is an alternative to exploring a parameter space for the process of interest. The SFT requires factorial research designs of N-number of binary-valued factors that selectively stretch the processes of interest and requires the response-time measure. The response-time results are either aggregated (mean) or used to estimate the survivor functions across the respective factorial conditions. The N-order difference function is applied on the results and two statistics are obtained, MIC and SIC. The MIC and SIC are examined to make inferences about the fundamental properties of processes. The stronger statistic here—the SIC function—reveals different signatures for different fundamental properties.

The present study is focused on further refining recent advances in SFT methodology (H. Yang et al., 2014) and on the development of new tools for use with larger mental networks. The motivation for this chapter was to address and remove the two limitations of the current SFT methods when applied on larger mental networks. The first concern was revealed when SFT was applied on the increasing number of processes under investigation (H. Yang et al., 2014): The predicted SIC signatures were shared between different cognitive models. This concern was addressed by inclusion of simple interaction SIC tests conducted on $N = 2$ subnetworks. The simple-interaction SIC tests were carried over by ignoring some variables in a higher-order factorial design ($N > 2$) and dropping them from the factorial design. The second concern was that the main results so far have been confined to the class of the homogeneous mental networks and neglect the possibility that underlying mental networks are non-homogeneous (such as serial-parallel networks).

To address this concern, the present study integrated the results of the simple interaction SIC analysis for the higher-order factorial design ($N > 2$) with the factorial tools developed to explore non-homogeneous mental networks, which may consist of both serial and parallel processes (so-called serial-parallel networks; Dzhafarov et al., 2004; Schweickert et al., 2000). The results of the integration are summarized so that the SIC signature expectations for various $N = 2$ subnetworks were generated. The current chapter also provided converging evidence from simulations regarding the detailed SIC expectations.

As a strong alternative to parameter-dependent, model-testing approaches, the SFT is a powerful tool to analyze processes underlying any cognitive activities. This study calls for further exploration of more complicated serial-parallel mental networks and further studies that should extend to the current ongoing revolution in the analysis of neural networks (e.g.,

Agliari et al., 2015; Lewis-Peacock, Drysdale, Oberauer, & Postle, 2012; Lisman & Idiart, 1995; Pooresmaeili, Bach, & Dolan, 2014; Raghavachari et al., 2001; Rushworth, Kolling, Sallet, & Mars, 2012; Verwey, Shea, & Wright, 2015; Ward, 2003; Woodman & Luck, 2003; for a review of the current cognitive methods borrowed by the neural approaches, see Caplan, 2009). Future studies on how to use SFT could provide an important window in the organization of mental process and model validation procedures, which would not be easily paralleled by the other approaches.

Notes

1. Insertion of a process could presumably force subjects to change their ways of doing the task by employing different strategies across comparable conditions.
2. In the language of ANOVA, this would correspond to the finding of the main effect of the first variable (e.g., Maxwell & Delaney, 1999).
3. Such a case would be the distinction between the parallel minimum-time model and the coactive model or its close cousin the parallel interactive model. The MIC predicts positive values for all three model classes, but the SIC functions would differ. The SIC predicts small negative function values for early times for only the coactive and parallel interactive models. Consideration of such cases is out of the scope of the current paper, and more information is provided in other publications (Townsend & Nozawa, 1995).
4. In a typical standard STM task (Ratcliff, 1978; Sternberg, 1969), the trials are divided so that there is a total of half target-present and half target-absent trials. The target-present condition could employ a self-terminating search rule. That is, a subject would stop searching for the target as soon as it was found. In the target-absent condition, all trials must be searched, employing the exhaustive stopping rule to make the correct rejection. Both proposed models of STM search (Ratcliff, 1978; Sternberg, 1969) assumed that a single stopping rule is used in either of the conditions (target-present of target-absent) and that the single processing order was employed. Thus the proposed models are the variants of the class of homogeneous mental networks.
5. Self-repeating SIC patterns across different sizes N: For some mental networks, the SIC signatures appears of identical shape across different mental network sizes. For example, the unimodal positive SIC function, which is used to indicate the presence of the parallel minimum-time processing network, could not be used to differentiate whether the system used 2, 3, 4, or N number of processes. The self-repeating patterns could be characteristic of this function of having fractal properties. The solution for the self-repeating SIC patterns is provided by the experimental method. The size of the network is manipulated by an experimenter and is specified in the experimental method.
6. Another example would be the case of probability mixtures of homogeneous mental networks such that a subject would switch from one type of homogeneous mental network to another type on each new trial. For example, switching from pure serial to pure parallel in repeated experimental trials. Although the class of probability mixtures of the homogeneous mental network is an important case, it will not be covered in the current chapter.
7. Another approach would be to condition rather than to marginalize, but it is not addressed in this work.
8. To get the correct number of possible combinations of organization of three processes, one has to take into account that each process can be either serial

or parallel (eight combinations for three processes) and that each process could be assigned either the OR or AND stopping rule (another eight combinations), thus making a total of 8 × 8 = 64 combinations.

References

Agliari, E., Barra, A., Galluzzi, A., Guerra, F., Tantari, D., & Tavani, F. (2015). Hierarchical neural networks perform both serial and parallel processing. *Neural Networks, 66*, 22–35.

Anderson, M. J., & Whitcomb, P. J. (2000). *DOE simplified: Practical tools for effective experimentation*. Portland, OR: Productivity.

Burrows, D., & Okada, R. (1971). Serial position effects in high-speed memory search. *Perception & Psychophysics, 10*, 305–308.

Caplan, D. (2009). Experimental design and interpretation of functional neuroimaging studies of cognitive processes. *Human Brain Mapping, 30*(1), 59–77.

Clifton, C., & Birenbaum, S. (1970). Effect of serial position and delay of probe in a memory scan task. *Journal of Experimental Psychology, 86*(1), 69–76.

Donders, F. C. (1868/1969). Over die snelheid van psychische processen (trans. W. G. Koster). *Acta Psychologica, 30*, 412–431.

Dzhafarov, E. N., Schweickert, R., & Sung, K. (2004). Mental architectures with selectively influenced but stochastically interdependent components. *Journal of Mathematical Psychology, 48*, 51–64.

Egeth, H., & Dagenbach, D. (1991). Parallel versus serial processing in visual search: Further evidence from subadditive effects of visual quality. *Journal of Experimental Psychology: Human Perception and Performance, 17*, 551–560.

Eidels, A., Townsend, J. T., & Pomerantz, J. R. (2008). Where similarity beats redundancy: The importance of context, higher order similarity, and response assignment. *Journal of Experimental Psychology: Human Perception and Performance, 34*(6), 1441–1463.

Fifić, M. (2006). *Emerging holistic properties at face value: Assessing characteristics of face perception* (Unpublished doctoral dissertation). Indiana University, Bloomington.

Fifić, M. (2014). Double jeopardy in inferring cognitive processes. *Frontiers in Psychology, 5*(1130).

Fifić, M., Little, D. R., & Nosofsky, R. M. (2010). Logical-rule models of classification response times: A synthesis of mental-architecture, random-walk, and decision-bound approaches. *Psychological Review, 117*, 309–348.

Fifić, M., Nosofsky, R. M., & Townsend, J. T. (2008). Information-processing architectures in multidimensional classification: A validation test of the Systems Factorial Technology. *Journal of Experimental Psychology. Human Perception and Performance, 34*, 356–375.

Fifić, M., & Townsend, J. T. (2010). Information-processing alternatives to holistic perception: Identifying the mechanisms of secondary-level holism within a categorization paradigm. *Journal of Experimental Psychology: Learning, Memory, and Cognition, 36*, 1290–1313.

Fifić, M., Townsend, J. T., & Eidels, A. (2008). Studying visual search using systems factorial methodology with target-distractor similarity as the factor. *Perception & Psychophysics, 70*, 583–603.

Forrin, B., & Cunningham, K. (1973). Recognition time and serial position of probed item in short-term memory. *Journal of Experimental Psychology, 99*(2), 272–279.

Greenwald, A. G. (2012). There is nothing so theoretical as a good method. *Perspectives on Psychological Science, 7*, 99–108.

Houpt, J. W., Blaha, L. M., McIntire, J. P., Havig, P. R., & Townsend, J. T. (2014). Systems Factorial Technology with R. *Behavior Research Methods, 46*, 307–330.

Houpt, J. W., & Townsend, J. T. (2010). The statistical properties of the survivor interaction contrast. *Journal of Mathematical Psychology, 54*, 446–453.

Ingvalson, E. M., & Wenger, M. J. (2005). A strong test of the dual-mode hypothesis. *Perception & Psychophysics, 67*, 14–35.

Johnson, S. A., Blaha, L. M., Houpt, J. W., & Townsend, J. T. (2010). Systems Factorial Technology provides new insights on global-local information processing in autism spectrum disorders. *Journal of Mathematical Psychology, 54*, 53–72.

Lee, M. D., & Wagenmakers, E.-J. (2013). *Bayesian cognitive modeling: A practical course*. New York: Cambridge University Press.

Lewis-Peacock, J., Drysdale, A. T., Oberauer, K., & Postle, B. R. (2012). Neural evidence for a distinction between short-term memory and the focus of attention. *Journal of Cognitive Neuroscience, 24*(1), 61–79.

Lisman, J. E., & Idiart, M. A. (1995). Storage of 7 ± 2 short-term memories in oscillatory subcycles. *Science, 267*(5203), 1512-1515.

Little, D. R., Nosofsky, R. M., & Denton, S. E. (2011). Response-time tests of logical-rule models of categorization. *Journal of Experimental Psychology: Learning, Memory, and Cognition, 37*, 1–27.

Little, D. R., Nosofsky, R. M., Donkin, C., & Denton, S. E. (2013). Logical rules and the classification of integral-dimension stimuli. *Journal of Experimental Psychology: Learning, Memory, and Cognition, 39*, 801–820.

Liu, C. C., & Smith, P. L. (2009). Comparing time-accuracy curves: Beyond goodness-of-fit measures. *Psychonomic Bulletin & Review, 16*(1), 190–203.

Maxwell, S. E., & Delaney, H. D. (1999). *Designing experiments and analyzing data: A model comparison perspective*. Mahwah, NJ: Lawrence Erlbaum Associates.

Oberauer, K. (2002). Access to information in working memory: Exploring the focus of attention. *Journal of Experimental Psychology: Learning, Memory, and Cognition, 28*(3), 411–421.

Oberauer, K., & Bialkova, S. (2009). Accessing information in working memory: Can the focus of attention grasp two elements at the same time? *Journal of Experimental Psychology: General, 138*(1), 64–87.

Pooresmaeili, A., Bach, D. R., & Dolan, R. J. (2014). The effect of visual salience on memory-based choices. *Journal of Neurophysiology, 111*(3), 481–487.

Posner, M. I., & Taylor, R. L. (1969). Subtractive method applied to separation of visual and name components of multiletter arrays. *Acta Psychologica, 30*, 104–114.

Raftery, A. E., Gelman, A., Rubin, D. B., & Hauser, R. M. (1995). Bayesian model selection in social research. *Sociological Methodology, 25*, 111–184.

Raghavachari, S., Kahana, M. J., Rizzuto, D. S., Caplan, J. B., Kirschen, M. P., Bourgeois, B., . . . Lisman, J. E. (2001). Gating of human theta oscillations by a working memory task. *The Journal of Neuroscience, 21*(9), 3175–3183.

Ratcliff, R. (1978). A theory of memory retrieval. *Psychological Review, 85*, 59–108.

Rushworth, M. F. S., Kolling, N., Sallet, J., & Mars, R. B. (2012). Valuation and decision-making in frontal cortex: One or many serial or parallel systems? *Current Opinion in Neurobiology, 22*, 946–955.

Schweickert, R. (1978). A critical path generalization of the additive factor method: Analysis of a Stroop task. *Journal of Mathematical Psychology, 18*, 105–139.

Schweickert, R., Fisher, D. L., & Goldstein, W. M. (2010). Additive factors and stages of mental processes in task networks. *Journal of Mathematical Psychology*, 54(5), 405–414.

Schweickert, R., Fisher, D. L., & Sung, K. (2012). *Discovering cognitive architecture by selectively influencing mental processes*. Singapore: World Scientific.

Schweickert, R., Giorgini, M., & Dzhafarov, E. (2000). Selective influence and response-time cumulative distribution functions in serial-parallel task networks. *Journal of Mathematical Psychology*, 44, 504–535.

Schweickert, R., & Townsend, J. T. (1989). A trichotomy: Interactions of factors prolonging sequential and concurrent mental processes in stochastic discrete mental (PERT) networks. *Journal of Mathematical Psychology*, 33, 328–347.

Sternberg, S. (1966). High-speed scanning in human memory. *Science*, 153, 652–654.

Sternberg, S. (1967). Retrieval of contextual information from memory. *Psychonomic Science*, 8(2), 55–56.

Sternberg, S. (1969). Memory scanning: Mental processes revealed by reaction time experiments. *American Scientist*, 4, 421–457.

Sung, K. (2008). Serial and parallel attentive visual searches: Evidence from cumulative distribution functions of response times. *Journal of Experimental Psychology: Human Perception and Performance*, 34(6), 1372–1388.

Townsend, J. T. (1969, April). *Mock parallel and serial models and experimental detection of these*. (Paper presented at the Purdue Centennial Symposium on Information Processing, West Lafayette, Indiana, Purdue University).

Townsend, J. T. (1971a). A note on the identifiability of parallel and serial processes. *Perception & Psychophysics*, 10, 161–163.

Townsend, J. T. (1971b). Theoretical analysis of an alphabetic confusion matrix. *Perception & Psychophysics*, 9, 40–50.

Townsend, J. T. (1972). Some results concerning the identifiability of parallel and serial processes. *British Journal of Mathematical and Statistical Psychology*, 25, 168–199.

Townsend, J. T., & Ashby, F. G. (1983). *The Stochastic Modeling of Elementary Psychological Processes*. Cambridge, UK: Cambridge University Press.

Townsend, J. T., & Fifić, M. (2004). Parallel versus serial processing and individual differences in high-speed search in human memory. *Perception & Psychophysics*, 66, 953–962.

Townsend, J. T., & Nozawa, G. (1995). Spatio-temporal properties of elementary perception: An investigation of parallel, serial, and coactive theories. *Journal of Mathematical Psychology*, 39, 321–359.

Townsend, J. T., & Schweickert, R. (1985). Interactive effects of factors prolonging processes in latent mental networks. In G. d'Ydewalle (Ed.), *Cognition, Information Processing, and Motivation*, Vol. 3 (pp. 255–276). XXIII International Congress of Psychology. Amsterdam: North Holland.

Townsend, J. T., & Thomas, R. D. (1994). Stochastic dependencies in parallel and serial models: Effects on systems factorial interactions. *Journal of Mathematical Psychology*, 38, 1–34.

Verwey, W. B., Shea, C. H., & Wright, D. L. (2015). A cognitive framework for explaining serial processing and sequence execution strategies. *Psychonomic Bulletin & Review*, 22(1), 54–77.

Ward, L. M. (2003). Synchronous neural oscillations and cognitive processes. *Trends in Cognitive Science*, 7(12), 553–559.

Waugh, N. C., & Norman, D. A. (1965). Primary memory. *Psychological Review*, 72, 89–104.

Wenger, M. J., & Townsend, J. T. (2001). Faces as gestalt stimuli: Process characteristics. In M. J. Wenger & J. T. Townsend (Eds.), *Computational, geometric, and process perspectives on facial cognition: Contexts and challenges* (pp. 229–284). Mahwah, NJ: Lawrence Erlbaum Associates.

Wenger, M. J., & Townsend, J. T. (2006). On the costs and benefits of faces and words: Process characteristics of feature search in highly meaningful stimuli. *Journal of Experimental Psychology: Human Perception and Performance, 32*, 755–779.

Woodman, G. F., & Luck, S. J. (2003). Serial deployment of attention during visual search. *Journal of Experimental Psychology: Human Perception and Performance, 29*(1), 121–138.

Yang, C.-T. (2011). Relative saliency in change signals affects perceptual comparison and decision processes in change detection. *Journal of Experimental Psychology: Human Perception and Performance, 37*, 1708–1728.

Yang, C.-T., Chang, T.-Y., & Wu, C.-J. (2013). Relative change probability affects the decision process of detecting multiple feature changes. *Journal of Experimental Psychology: Human Perception and Performance, 39*, 1365–1385.

Yang, H., Fifić, M., & Townsend, J. T. (2014). Survivor interaction contrast wiggle predictions of parallel and serial models for an arbitrary number of processes. *Journal of Mathematical Psychology, 58*, 21–32.

7 Identifying Spatiotemporal Information

Joseph S. Lappin

This chapter develops the following ideas about information for sensory, perceptual, and cognitive processes:

1. The existence and transmission of information require corresponding relational structures in separate systems. The problem of identifying information is identifying the relational structures that satisfy the required correspondence. The generic problem of representing variations in one system by those in another occurs in many areas of science and technology—e.g., measurement theory, perception, cognition, robotics, and neurophysiology. Indeed, this is a generic problem of knowledge.
2. Information is not an objective "thing." Its transmission involves a relationship between sender and receiver, a coordination of observer and observed. Perception involves an observer's active and selective organization of information.
3. Relational structures of continuous spatiotemporal patterns are qualitatively different from those involving sets of discrete elements, such as symbols, objects, etc. A theory of optical information about local surface shape is now available. Optical information about spatial relations between separate surfaces is not yet well understood, however.
4. The effectiveness of a representation can be evaluated by empirical criteria: (a) resolution (precision of correspondence), (b) invariance under observational transformations, and (c) context invariance. Specific examples illustrate the nature and power of these empirical tests.
5. Context invariance entails both experimental and theoretical challenges. Much of the research by Jim Townsend and colleagues concerns models and methods for evaluating context interactions and context invariance. Further development of these methods is needed to reveal (a) the structure of information in spatiotemporal patterns and (b) the shaping of information by context.

7.1 Introduction: From Stimulation to Information

S. S. Stevens (1951) pointed out that the key scientific problem in psychology is to define the stimulus: "In a sense there is only one problem of psychophysics, namely, the definition of the stimulus. In this same sense there is only one problem in all of psychology — and it is the same problem" (Stevens, 1951, p. 31).

When Stevens developed that idea in his chapter on "Mathematics, Measurement, and Psychophysics" for the *Handbook of Experimental Psychology*, psychology was commonly considered the scientific study of "responses" to "stimuli." A stimulus was the cause, and a response was the effect.

Now, however, cause-effect relations are understood differently in psychology and other areas of science and engineering. Sensory input is often called "information" rather than stimulation; and the resulting processes are also described in terms of operations on this information. Nevertheless, despite profound changes in the concepts, methods, and theories of psychological science, Stevens's cogent statement about the decisive role of the sensory information remains relevant and insightful.

If we substitute "information" for "stimulus" in Stevens's statement, then his claim about the necessity for defining the sensory input expresses a central theme of the present chapter. Two ideas implicit in his statement are that (a) defining the stimulus is critical for understanding the psychological processes that lead to observable behavior and (b) that definition of the stimulus is not self-evident, that it requires investigation. Similar ideas hold for the critical importance of identifying information in studies of perception, cognition, decision-making, and action.

When Stevens was writing about the rationale and methods of psychophysics, profound changes in the conception of causal relations were underway in psychology and in many areas of science and engineering. Shannon's (1948) "mathematical theory of communication" (often called "information theory") was one of the landmarks in this intellectual transformation. Related developments at about the same time included Wiener's (1961) treatise on *Cybernetics, Or Control and Communication in the Animal and the Machine*, development of the transistor (by physicists and engineers at Bell Labs, where Shannon worked), and the first general-purpose electronic computer in 1946 (Electronic Numerical Integrator And Computer, ENIAC, by the Army Ballistic Research Lab and University of Pennsylvania). (Gleich (2011) and Wiener (1954) provide stimulating nontechnical accounts of this intellectual history.) Increasing evidence of the insufficiency of scientific behaviorism and stimulus-response concepts made psychology receptive to the new ideas about information and information processing.

7.1.1 Information Involves Organization

As suggested by the word itself, information is "in the formation"—in a physical organization rather than physical energy or matter as such. Information is transmitted by corresponding structures of variation in physically separate systems. Information-carrying variations occur in many different physical formats, spatial and temporal as well as symbolic.

Information is sometimes misunderstood as a property based exclusively on symbolic representation. By definition, the physical forms of symbols are unrelated to what they represent. In optics, vision, acoustics, and hearing, however, information is often intimately associated with the organization of patterns in spacetime. The spatial patterns of optical images and the spatiotemporal organization of acoustic patterns are essential carriers of environmental information for humans and other animals. Wiener (1954) pointed out that scientific concepts of information and communication emerged in the 17th century physics of Fermat, Huygens, and Leibniz, concerned with optical images. In sensory, neural, perceptual, and motor systems, information involves primarily spatiotemporal patterns rather than symbols.

Actually, the information acquired by sensory and neural systems is often unspecified. Questions about whether this information is symbolic or spatiotemporal are seldom directly addressed. The elementary forms and variations that carry information are seldom identified.

Intuitions about the nature of information are often implicitly symbolic. Symbolic and spatiotemporal representations, however, entail different mechanisms for acquiring and using information. Symbolic information is associated with logical operations and rules of inference—the validity of which is independent of spatial or temporal parameters and independent of natural laws governing motion, mass, or energy. In contrast, spatiotemporal information involves energy distributed over time and space.

Symbolic and spatiotemporal representations of information are associated with different conceptual frameworks and different research strategies. Examples of both approaches are found throughout science and engineering. In research on perception, intellectual tensions between ecological and inferential approaches derive partly from differing assumptions about symbolic and spatiotemporal structures of information (Lappin, 2013). Similar tensions appear in other sciences of information processing, from robotics to neuroscience.

Context has a very different influence on information embodied in symbols versus spatiotemporal patterns. The definition of a local symbol is generally independent of its context, even when its meaning within a message is context dependent. Visual symbols—letters, words, etc.—usually have discrete spatial positions that may be specified independently of their context. Such context invariance is appealing for representing complex patterns as sets of distinctive features. Pattern recognition is easier when input information can be represented by sets of symbols.

Context effects impose more difficult computational problems, however, when information is embodied in spatiotemporal patterns. The challenge of such problems is exemplified by the persisting difficulties of computer vision and robotics in solving problems of sensory perception in natural environments—problems that appear to be easily and reliably solved by virtually all active animals. Brooks (e.g., 1990, 1991) argues that basic computational difficulties arise from representing information as sets of symbols and from computations using symbol manipulation.

The present chapter aims to develop a theory of information in spatiotemporal structure. This is certainly not the first such effort. Many of the present ideas about spatiotemporal information and about the senses as perceptual systems are related to James Gibson's approach (e.g., Gibson, 1950, 1966, 1979).

The present extension focuses on a representational theory of spatiotemporal information. A central concern is the empirical criteria for evaluating and comparing possible representations.

7.1.2 Information Structured by Surfaces

As an illustrative example, *surface structure* is an important class of spatiotemporal information. Surfaces are especially important in optics and visual perception.

Surfaces of 3-D objects are 2-D manifolds. They can be described by spatial derivatives. The same is true for images of surfaces in eyes, photographs, paintings, and other media. Images of surfaces are also surfaces, and their differential geometries are related to one another—indeed, linearly related! Such geometrical correspondences between objects and images do not hold for many other spatial elements and relations, such as coordinate positions, relative lengths, and angles. Images of surfaces, therefore, are visually important information about the structure of the 3-D world.

Psychophysical research supporting this idea has focused mainly on the precision and robustness of visually perceived local surface shape (Section 7.2.3). Surfaces and their images also carry visual information about additional aspects of environmental structure.

First, surfaces are 2-D boundaries between regions of 3-D space occupied by different material substances—air, water, rock, wood, skin, fur, metals, glass, fabrics, vegetation, etc. Spatial variations in the color spectrum of light reflected, scattered, absorbed, and transmitted by surfaces carry optical information about these materials. Images of surfaces provide optical information about both the materials and shapes of environmental objects.

Second, surfaces also generate a topology of the visual world by segregating, arranging, and nesting volumes of space. By structuring the spatial layout of the environment, surfaces are critical for guiding navigation and action. The locations, directions, and smoothness of runways, paths, stairs, walls, doorways, furniture, trees, traffic, and so forth are informative about environmental constraints and opportunities for active observers. Designing surfaces and spaces to support and facilitate human activities is the central aim of architecture.

Third, surfaces are also critical in transmitting information—by converting energy and information from one medium to another. The human senses and brain depend on such energy transduction at surfaces arrayed with sensory receptors (in eye, ear, skin, etc.) that interface the nervous system to the outside world at membranes separating individual cells from their electrical and chemical surroundings, at synapses between nerve cells, and at muscle fibers that convert electro-chemical events into mechanical action. In short, the structure and dynamics of surfaces shape the structure and dynamics of information in senses, brains, and muscles.

7.1.3 Information and Uncertainty

A counterintuitive but fundamental contribution of Shannon's (1948; Shannon & Weaver, 1949 *Mathematical Theory of Communication* and Wiener's (1961)) *Cybernetics* involves the explicit role of probability in defining information. As Garner (1974) expressed it, "Information theory has provided psychology with the basic concept of information itself, and it has clarified that information is a function not of what the stimulus is, but rather of what it might have been, of its alternatives" (Garner, 1974, p. 194).

This conception of sensory information clashes with the intuitive primacy of stimuli in causal sequences of physical, chemical, and physiological processes in the senses and brain: (1) Sensory information defined by possible rather than actual events differs from classical physics of mass and energy. (2) Defining information by an observer's uncertainty about what might happen is implicitly subjective rather than objective. (3) How can probabilities have a causal role in the biophysics of the senses and brain? Not surprisingly, intuitions about the causal primacy of the stimulus have persisting influence.

Nevertheless, contemporary psychology also offers widespread support for a concept of information that departs from classical concepts of physics and psychology. Signal detection theory (SDT) is a well-established example of the power of statistical descriptions of sensory information and processes. SDT represents both physical and physiological sensory events as random variables described by probability distributions. According to SDT, sensory detection results from statistical evidence favoring one alternative relative to another—in contrast to the notion of a threshold response to a given physical stimulus.

Further, observed behavioral effects of such sensory processes are represented as *choices* among alternatives. Indeed, the whole array of physiological, perceptual, and decision processes that transform sensory input into behavioral output involves variability and relations among alternatives. Contemporary psychology is inconceivable without such relativistic concepts.

Stochastic process models developed by Townsend and colleagues are a notable application of probabilistic conceptions of perceptual processes (e.g., Eidels, Townsend, Hughes, & Perry, 2015; Houpt & Townsend, 2012a; Townsend, 1972, 1976, 1990a, 1990b; Townsend & Ashby, 1983; Townsend & Eidels, 2011; Townsend & Nozawa, 1995; Townsend, Solomon, & Spencer-Smith, 2001; Townsend & Wenger, 2004a, 2004b). The continuing promise of this framework is documented by the present collection of recent research.

7.1.4 Information Requires Correlation

Another counterintuitive but basic aspect of information involves the conjoint relation between source and destination of transmitted information between an observer and the objects of observation. Transmission of information requires a correlation between structures of variation in physically separate systems. In other words, information is not a "thing," but a structural correlation. Information entails a relationship between separate systems.

Defining information as a relationship rather than an objective structure or variation may seem conceptually awkward. Does information exist independently of its transmission? Efforts to define information independently of a correspondence between input and output involve inevitable ambiguities. For systems designed by nature and evolution rather than by human engineers, the specific structural variations that convey information are often uncertain or unknown. Correlated variations are necessary for identifying and defining information.

Perception and action in natural environments often involve behavioral performance that exceeds current understanding of sensory information and sensory mechanisms. So-called means-end analysis (Simon, 1996) is an effective research strategy in many such cases: One begins with the observed performance and then deduces the information that could guide that performance. This research strategy is also exemplified by James Gibson's approach (e.g., Gibson, 1966).

The correlational nature of information was implicit in Shannon's (1948) model of communication. "The fundamental problem of communication is that of reproducing at one point either exactly or approximately a message selected at another point" (Shannon, 1948, p. 379).

Communication obviously involves a correlation between the source and destination, but what about "information?" As Shannon pointed out, the content and meaning of a message are irrelevant to the engineering problem defined by his communication theory. "The significant aspect is that the actual message is one selected from *a set* of possible messages" (Shannon 1948, p. 379).

Identifying information was not a problem in Shannon's communication systems. His communication systems were designed by human engineers rather than by nature and evolution. Sets of possible messages and signals were known to both source and destination before transmitting any information. The receiver was uncertain beforehand about which particular signals would be transmitted, but was not uncertain about the set of alternative signals.

In natural environments, however, identifying information is a critical problem. What constitutes information is often unknown to a scientist, engineer, or observer outside the system.

In studying natural systems relevant to biology, perception, and cognition, one finds everyday performance that is difficult to explain. Attempted explanations sometimes invoke sensory processes with a magical quality, guidance by evolution, unspecified intelligence and prior learning, or Bayesian inference supplemented by hypothesized knowledge of prior odds. Often, no process is specified for transforming sensory measures into observed performance.

Engineering designs of robotic systems are often confronted with similar problems in specifying how physical signals can be transformed into desired performance. The history of unanticipated challenges in computer vision and robotics demonstrates the counterintuitive difficulty of this problem.

Computational problems in perceiving environmental objects, spaces, and events may be regarded as problems of identifying information. Information-carrying signals are not "given"; they must be discovered.

Structural correspondence of input and output is a criterion for identifying and defining information. The research strategy using this approach is discussed in Sections 7.2 and 7.3.

The present approach exemplifies a strategy common in engineering, known as "means-end" analysis (Simon, 1996). Specifically, desired output performance can be used as a basis for identifying information that can enable this performance. The present approach might also be recognized as phenomenological—using perception to infer the information and processes that provide this perception. This means-end strategy differs from the method of classical psychology that begins with a physical "stimulus" as an objective start of a causal sequence.

7.1.5 *Information, Capacity, and Selective Attention*

Information acquired through sensory, perceptual, and cognitive processes depends on attention. Two widely accepted ideas about attention are that (a) capacities of human observation are limited and much less than the total information available in a given task environment and (b) active observers select information. The concepts of *information, attention*, and *capacity* are interlinked. Each concept involves the others.

Thus acquired information is shaped by attention. Information entering the senses, awareness, comprehension, and memory depends on the observer's prior knowledge, interests, and performance goals, as well as on the context of information about surrounding objects and events, risks, and opportunities. The observer's influence is especially important in acquiring information from natural environments, but is also critical in controlled experiments. Speed and accuracy of performance depend on the observer's cooperative attention to tasks set by the experimenter. Many experiments indicate that perception requires attention (e.g., Mack & Rock, 1998; Simons & Chabris, 1999).

The concept of selective attention, however, raises questions about what exactly is "selected." One aim of attention research has been to identify the sensory elements selected by attentional processes—e.g., stimuli, features, objects, or spatial positions. Research on visual search has often suggested that attention selects and integrates elementary features revealed by "pre-attentive" vision (e.g., Treisman & Gelade, 1980; Wolfe, Cave, & Franzel, 1989; Wolfe & Horowitz, 2004). This conception of visual attention is not well supported (see Lappin, Morse, & Seiffert, submitted for publication). Nevertheless, representing visual information as an array of elements is conceptually and methodologically convenient, so the idea persists.

Alternatively, visual information and attention may involve geometric organizations of spatial and temporal relationships rather than sets of discrete elements. Problems of information identification include (a) perception of 3-D space in natural scenes, (b) perception of motion and moving structures, (c) perception of solid shapes and surfaces, and (d) recognition of configurations such as faces. Townsend and colleagues have sought to identify computational processes for recognizing geometric structures in patterns such as faces (e.g., Ashby & Townsend, 1986; Kadlec & Townsend, 1992; Thomas, 1995; Wenger & Townsend, 2001).

The concept of attentional capacity requires identification of the structure and quantity of sensory information. Efforts to define perceptual capacities were made in the 1950s and 1960s by applying Shannon's measure of transmitted information to quantify a perceptual "channel capacity" (e.g., Eriksen & Hake, 1955a, 1955b; Garner, 1962; Hyman, 1953; Miller, 1956). The early promise of this method faded, however, due to its limited applicability to geometric structures of spatiotemporal patterns (Section 7.2).

Research on visual working memory points to capacity limits defined mainly by a number of independent spatial forms (e.g., Alvarez & Franconeri, 2007; Averbach & Coriell, 1961; Eriksen & Lappin, 1967; Lappin, 1967; Luck & Vogel, 1997; Sperling, 1960; Woodman & Vogel, 2008). Capacity limits of visual attention are not restricted to tasks involving working memory, however (Lappin et al., submitted for publication).

Generalized methods for quantifying the complexity of spatiotemporal patterns are not yet available. And without methods for quantifying input information, the concept of an attentional capacity is theoretically vague.

7.1.6 Quantifying Information

At the center of Shannon's theory of communication were his elegant formulas for quantifying the complexity of a set of signals and rate of information transmission. For the case of discrete signals, the average information, $H(X)$, associated with selections of signals x_i from a set of categories, X, is given by his familiar formula

$$H(X) = -\sum_i p(x_i)\log_2 p(x_i), \tag{7.1}$$

where $\Sigma_i p(x_i) = 1.0$. The units of $H(X)$ are *bits*—corresponding to the average number of binary discriminations required to uniquely identify individual signals.

The population of possible signals, X, is a set of mutually exclusive subsets, A_i, such that $\Sigma_i p(A_i) = 1.0$. Importantly, the relational structure of these subsets involves merely *nominal* categories. The relation between any pair of signals, x_i and $x_j \in X$, is merely *same* or *different*, depending on whether these signals are members of the same or different subsets. The categories may be subdivided into smaller, hierarchically nested, and potentially overlapping subsets, at varied scales of resolution. At any scale of resolution, the total probability for all signals is unity, $\Sigma_i p(x_i) = 1.0$.

In Shannon's theory, relations among signals such as adjacency, connectedness, order, or proximity are irrelevant for quantifying information. The theory can apply to any variations, discrete or continuous, symbolic or geometrical, involving any type of physical or mathematical relationship, but it does not describe such relational structures.

Shannon's *fundamental theorem* established the existence of a fixed limiting *channel capacity*, C, on the rate (*bits/s*) at which any given communication channel can transmit information. (Different rates for different channels.) This important theorem is valid regardless of the topological structure of relations among alternative signals. (Conditional probabilities of one signal given the occurrence of others are directly relevant, however.) The generality of this quantification is a significant and widely applied strength.

The same generality, however, limits its usefulness for describing information in natural systems. Information in nature often involves the structure of images and other patterns with order, connectedness, proximity, continuity, and other topological relations in space, time, energy, or other dimensions. Unlike the engineered systems in Shannon's communication theory, the relational structure of information in natural systems is often unknown. As Stevens (1951) suggested, a principal scientific problem is to identify that information.

Identifying the sensory information for everyday capabilities of active animals in natural scenarios is scientifically challenging. Achievements in coordinating perception and action with changing environmental conditions demonstrate that sufficient sensory information exists to enable this performance. In contrast, the limited capabilities of current robots illustrate the challenges in identifying this sensory information.

Shannon's theory does not address these problems. The theory does not describe or quantify spatiotemporal structure.

7.1.7 Meaning

As Shannon (1948) made clear, the content and meaning of a message are irrelevant to the engineering problem defined by his theory of communication:

> Frequently, the messages have *meaning*; that is they refer to or are correlated according to some system with certain physical or conceptual entities. These semantic aspects are irrelevant to the engineering problem. The significant aspect is that the actual message is one *selected from a set* of possible messages.
>
> (p. 379)

Informal usage of the term "information," in science as well as everyday language, often involves notions of content, meaning, and functional significance for both animal and human receivers. Shannon regarded "information theory" as a misleading label for his theory of communication.

Meaning is inherent and inextricable from information acquired by natural systems. In the general case, the set of possible signals has not been specified beforehand. In general, information associated with a specific physical event involves relationships with potential alternatives that might have occurred. The structure of possibilities is given by the observer's prior knowledge, beliefs, and perceptions of context—past, present, and future, here and now and then and there. Knowledge facilitates the perception of patterns and enhances the information offered by pieces of patterns.

Information conveyed by music, visual arts, language, and images necessarily entails observers' knowledge. Information and meaning derive from fields of relations surrounding specific events. The same is true for both natural and artificial systems.

7.2 Visual Representations of Spatiotemporal Variation

Two themes of the preceding discussion of information are: (1) Information is based on corresponding relational structures in physically separate systems. By virtue of such structural correspondence, variations in one system are an image of those in another. And (2), identifying information is central to the investigation of sensory, perceptual, cognitive, decision, and action processes. Representing the information for a system constitutes a hypothesis about its effective input and output. Such hypotheses must be tested in relation to alternatives.

The effectiveness of a representation can be evaluated empirically. Evaluation is based on the correspondence of variations in two domains involving the amount of information transmitted from input to output.

Two classes of empirical criteria for evaluating correspondence of two structures of variation are *resolution* and *invariance*. Lappin, Norman, and Phillips (2011) used these criteria to identify information for perceiving solid shape; and Lappin (2014) used them to identify the structure of binocular disparity as input to stereopsis. Similar ideas apply to a wide range of problems involving representation of a relational structure in one system by that in another.

The present concepts of "resolution" and "invariance" are related to the *representation* and *uniqueness theorems* used in theories of measurement (Krantz, Luce, Suppes, & Tversky, 1971; Scott & Suppes, 1958; Suppes & Zinnes, 1963). The logic of representing qualitative empirical relations by numerical relations guided the present approach.

The problem of identifying corresponding variations in two physical systems is less well defined than the problem of numerical representation. Measurement problems arise within a broader context of research, however, with questions about which objects and variables to observe, about methods of observation, and so forth. Numerical representation is an aspect of larger theories of representation involving identification of the elementary objects and relations of observed nature.

The primary present concern is the structure of information in spatiotemporal optical patterns—where the relational structures often are not obvious. The present approach is based on corresponding relational structures.

Optical images of environmental objects and spaces offer relevant examples. Spatial relations in the environment are obviously represented in the images, but equally obvious are fundamental discrepancies between 3-D environmental structures and 2-D image structures. Many spatial relations in the environment—e.g., distances, angles, and slants—are not represented in the images. The effectiveness of vision, photography, and painting in guiding perception demonstrates that important spatial information is preserved in optical images, however.

If two structures of variation are *isomorphic*, then a certain structure of relations is the same in both systems. If two relational structures are isomorphic, then variations in one system constitute information about variations

118 Joseph S. Lappin

in the other. How, then, can one decide whether two structures of variation are isomorphic?

7.2.1 Numerical Representation

The representational theory of measurement (Krantz et al., 1971; Scott & Suppes, 1958; Suppes & Zinnes, 1963) exemplifies the general problem of representation. In measurement theory, a *relational structure* is a set of *elements*, a set of *relations* among those elements, and, often, *operations* that combine or transform elements to others in the set.

Consider the use of a balance beam to evaluate the relative masses of objects placed at the two ends of the beam. Let A be the collection of objects to be compared, with $a, b, c \in A$. The balance beam provides two empirical binary relations—*equality*, $a \approx b$, and *order*, $a < b$—plus a *concatenation* operation, $\oplus$, that combines two or more objects in the same balance pan, where $a \oplus b \approx c$ or $a \oplus b > c$ or $c > a \oplus b$ (ternary relations). Empirical equality, $\approx$, is commutative and transitive; order $>$ is transitive; and concatenation $\oplus$ is commutative and associative.

To prove a *representation theorem*, one shows that a specific numerical relational structure is isomorphic with a particular (qualitative) empirical structure. The isomorphism requires axioms that define the elements and relations and specify assumptions about their properties. If $\langle A, R_i, \oplus \rangle$ is an empirical relational structure, and if $\phi \langle A, R_i, \oplus \rangle \rightarrow \langle \mathscr{R}, S_i, + \rangle$ is a representation in the real numbers, $\mathscr{R}$, then the representation theorem establishes an isomorphism such that for all $a, b \in A$, and all $\phi(R_i) \rightarrow S_i$, then $a\, R_i\, b$ iff $\phi(a)\, S_i\, \phi(b)$. Note that the isomorphism applies to the relations, not to the objects and numbers. Multiple objects may be assigned the same number, as in the weighing example earlier, which includes relations of equality. The isomorphism does not include many other irrelevant properties and relations, such as the sizes, shapes, and materials of objects to be weighed.

Measurement also involves a *uniqueness theorem* that identifies permissible transformations of the numerical assignments. For the preceding example of measuring relative mass, when the set of objects is sufficiently large and dense, the numerical assignments can provide a *ratio scale*—where the numerical assignments are unique up to multiplication by a scalar.

To interpret this scale as a measure of *mass* requires additional evidence involving invariance of the empirical relations under transformations of (a) physical context and properties such as object volume and shape and (b) observational conditions such as the velocity and acceleration of the balance beam and objects. The concept of "mass" is part of a larger physical theory.

7.2.2 Structures in Spatiotemporal Continua

The relational structure of continuous spatiotemporal patterns is less obvious than that of a set of discrete objects. Indeed, a long-standing problem in phenomenological philosophy is to identify component elements in spatiotemporal continua (see Albertazzi, 2002). Related issues are found in physics and psychophysics involving distinctions between local elements, objects, and energy on one hand versus field theories on the other.

Such issues motivated research on visual motion perception. Is optical motion (a relationship in spacetime) a fundamental visual attribute, or is it derived from the spatial and temporal positions of distinct objects? Converging experimental evidence shows that motion is visually fundamental, not derived (e.g., Johansson, 1973; Lappin, Bell, Harm, & Kottas, 1975; Lappin & van de Grind, 2002). Experiments with motion patterns composed of many texture elements also demonstrate that vision is sensitive to the statistical coherence of a global motion field rather than individual element motions (Bell & Lappin, 1973; Lappin & Bell, 1976; van de Grind, van Doorn, & Koenderink, 1983).

How, then, should we represent the visually relevant relational structure of optical images of natural scenes projected on the eyes of moving animals or robots? Optical information for vision involves corresponding relational structures in at least two other distinctly different physical systems. First, the images constitute information about the observer's environment. Second, the image information must also be accessible to the visual system. Thus spatiotemporal image information involves corresponding relational structures of images, environment, and visual system.[1]

Isomorphism is transitive. Thus isomorphisms of spatiotemporal variations in the environment and optical images and between the images and visual system also imply isomorphism between the visual system and environment.

The idea that visual information involves corresponding structures of variation in environments, images, neurophysiology, and perception is contrary to the conception of visual and cognitive processes as causal sequences that begin with a physical stimulus. Nevertheless, the present argument is that such corresponding variations are necessary, both mathematically and physically, for transmitting information among these different physical domains. This theoretical argument is also supported by experimental evidence reported by Lappin and Craft (2000) and Lappin, et al. (2011), and briefly described in the following section.

Alternative hypotheses have proposed that (a) optical image information is insufficient to specify the perceived environment, and (b) visual discriminations of environmental structures are more reliable than the correlations between images and environments. These ideas violate both physical and computational principles concerning reductions of entropy in closed systems.

Image information involves spatiotemporal variations *within* images and *between* different images of different environmental objects, motions, and scenes. Representing the spatiotemporal structure of information within images is the more challenging problem and is a necessary prerequisite for representing relations between images. The present focus is on the

120 *Joseph S. Lappin*

structure of image information about (a) the spatial structure of surfaces and (b) spatial relations between separate surfaces. As indicated in Section 7.1.2, surface structure is especially important for visual perception.

7.2.3 Surface Structure and Image Structure

A principal insight about optical image structure is that optical images are images of surfaces. James Gibson (1950, 1966) emphasized the importance of surface structure for visual perception in contrast to conventional understanding that perceived surfaces are inferred from more fundamental properties of visual stimuli. Koenderink & van Doorn (e.g., 1976a, 1976b, 1976c, 1980, 1992a, 1992b, 1992c, 1997; Koenderink, 1990) clarified the fact that differential structures of surfaces and their images are approximately isomorphic.[2]

The present discussion of the differential geometry of surfaces and images is necessarily just a brief overview. In addition to the seminal articles by Koenderink & van Doorn, Koenderink's book on *Solid Shape* (1990) gives a thorough description of the differential geometry of surface shape. Lappin and Craft (2000), Lappin et al. (2011), Lappin (2014), Phillips and Todd (1996), and Todd (2004) also review theoretical ideas and supporting psychophysical evidence that human vision is directly sensitive to surface structure.

Theoretical ideas about the differential structure of surfaces and their images include:

1. Environmental surfaces and their optical images are both *2-D manifolds*, described at any point by spatial derivatives in two principal orthogonal directions.
2. Differential structures of environmental surfaces are approximately isomorphic ("*diffeomorphic*") with the differential structures of spatiotemporal images formed by rotating the surface in depth and/or by binocular disparity. The inter-image disparities between two or more images of surfaces viewed from neighboring vantage points constitute a vector field with a differential structure that is isomorphic with that of an environmental surface.[3]
3. The structures of the surface and its image are related by a *local linear coordinate transformation*. Let $\mathbf{dS} = (ds_1, ds_2)$ be a column vector representing a small spatial displacement on the surface, where ds_1 and ds_2 are the differentials in two surface coordinates. And let the corresponding retinal image of this vector be $\mathbf{dR} = (dr_1, dr_2)$. Then the linear transformation from the environmental surface to the retinal image is given by

    $$\mathbf{dR} = \mathbf{V}\mathbf{dS}, \qquad (7.2)$$

where the coordinate transformation, **V**, is a 2×2 matrix with entries $\partial r_i / \partial s_j$ $i, j = \{1,2\}$. The inverse transformation from image to surface is written in the same way: $d\mathbf{S} = \mathbf{V}^{-1} d\mathbf{R}$, where the entries of $\mathbf{V}^{-1}$ are the differentials $\partial s_i / \partial r_j$.

These coordinate transformations are local; their definition and computational estimation do not depend on the global shape. Nevertheless, surface structures in neighboring image areas are not independent. The coordinate transformations vary smoothly over both the surface and its image.

4. *Information about local surface shape* is given by the 2-D second-order differential structure of surfaces and their images. This local structure involves the relative value of the maximum and minimum curvatures in orthogonal directions. Curvature in a particular direction is given by a second order spatial derivative associated with the rate of change in the direction of the surface normal (though surface normals are not used in the image computations).

   The relational structure of this local shape operator is fourth order—involving spatial relations among five neighboring regions. (A first-order spatial derivative involves a binary relation between two neighboring points; a second-order derivative involves a relation among three points—a difference of differences—in either 1-D or 2-D. In the literature, the image structure associated with local surface shape is often referred to as "second order," though it involves relative values of two second-order derivatives.) Image measures in at least three directions are necessary, however, because the principal curvature directions are not generally known beforehand.

   Figure 7.1 gives a schematic illustration of the local linear image structure associated with local surface shape. For simplicity, one of the principal directions is aligned with the vertical axis of rotation, but such alignment is not general. As may be seen, rotation in depth yields image information about local shape by image deformations in two dimensions—changing (a) relative alignments parallel with the rotation axis and (b) bilateral symmetries in the direction of rotation. This image information involves 2-D symmetries of the optical field around each point on a smooth surface.

5. Local shape is *intrinsic* to the surface—independent of a 3-D reference frame with coordinates in depth. Local shape involves *relative* curvatures in two principal directions. Measures of curvature or depth are not required to measure shape.

6. Koenderink (1990) and Koenderink and van Doorn (1992c) proposed a specific *shape index* as a convenient one-dimensional measurement scale for local shape. This scale has useful properties and has been used effectively in psychophysical studies (Perotti, Todd, Lappin, & Phillips, 1998; van Damme & van de Grind, 1993). The shape index,

Figure 7.1 Schematic illustrations of deformations of 2-D second-order image structure produced by rotation of a surface around a central vertical axis. Before the rotation, each of these image patches was circular. The central point in each diagram is a central reference point that does not move. The deformation involves relative horizontal displacements of the surrounding image points. As may be seen, the five surface shapes, from left to right, are a plane, horizontal cylinder, vertical cylinder, ellipsoid, and saddle. The shapes are defined by the relative surface curvatures in the two principal coordinate directions, direction of minimum and maximum curvature, which are horizontal and vertical in this illustration for purposes of simplicity. Thus planes have zero curvature in both directions, cylinders (parabolic patches) have zero curvature in one axis, ellipsoids (elliptic patches) have the same sign of curvature in both axes, and saddle shapes (hyperbolic patches) have opposite signs of curvature in the principal directions. These second-order deformations are invariant under transformations of lower-order structure, such as image translations, 2-D rotation, dilation, and shear (produced by surface slant). (Copyright ©2000 by the American Psychological Association. Reproduced with permission.) The official citation that should be used in referencing this material is Lappin and Craft (2000, Fig. 3, p. 14). The use of APA information does not imply endorsement by APA.)

S, is defined as

$$S = \frac{-2}{\pi} \arctan \left[\frac{\kappa_{max} + \kappa_{min}}{\kappa_{max} - \kappa_{min}} \right], \tag{7.3}$$

where curvature in a given direction is measured as the reciprocal of the radius of curvature, $\kappa = 1/r$, and κ_{max} and κ_{min} are the two principal curvatures—positive or negative depending on whether the curvature is convex or concave. This shape index is an interval scale in the range $(-1, +1)$. Scale values in the range $(0.5, +1)$ represent convex "hills"; values in the range $(-1, -0.5)$ are concave "valleys"; and values in the range $(-0.5, +0.5)$ have both concave and convex curvatures, saddle-shaped. Values of S with opposite signs of curvature are effectively "negatives" of each other. As $\kappa_{max} - \kappa_{min} \to 0$, then $S \to \pm 1$, where curvature is equal in all directions (spherical), is convex at $S = +1$ and concave at $S = -1$.

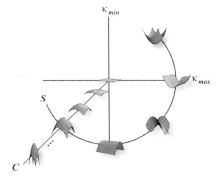

Figure 7.2 Koenderink & van Doorn's shape index, S, and curvedness index, C, describe a two-dimensional space. The angular measure represents shape, and the radius represents curvedness. (Copyright ©1996 by the American Psychological Association. Reproduced with permission.) The official citation that should be used in referencing this material is Phillips and Todd (1996, Fig. 5, p. 933). (The use of APA information does not imply endorsement by APA.)

The shape index can be illustrated in polar coordinates as an angular direction in a Cartesian (κ_{max}, κ_{min}) plane, as in Figure 7.2.

Radial distance from the origin of this space, at $\kappa_{max} = \kappa_{min} = 0$ (a planar patch with no curvature and, effectively, no shape), measures the total "curvedness." C. Koenderink's (1990) curvedness measure is given by

$$C = \left[\frac{\kappa_{max}^2 + \kappa_{min}^2}{2}\right]^{1/2}. \tag{7.4}$$

This curvedness scale measures the depth variation at a given surface location. Importantly, these measures of shape and curvedness are independent of one another. Curvedness entails an embedding in 3-D coordinates, but shape does not require 3-D depth.

7. *Boundary contours in images* are especially informative about intrinsic local surface shape. These 2-D image contours appear at surface points where the viewing direction (the ray between the eye's focal point and the surface boundary) is tangent or nearly tangent to the surface, thereby determining the surface orientation at that point. As a result, curvature of the 2-D image contour and the 3-D surface curvature are closely related (Koenderink, 1984a; Koenderink, 1990, p. 431–437).

Specifically, let κ_r be the radial curvature of the surface in the visual direction, and let κ_t be the transverse surface curvature perpendicular to the plane of the radial curvature. When the viewing direction is

124 *Joseph S. Lappin*

sufficiently distant that the visual ray is tangent to the surface, the surface normal is at the intersection of the κ_r and κ_t planes, and the κ_t curvature is the visible curvature of the image contour. In this case,

$$K = \kappa_r \kappa_t, \text{ and } \kappa_t = K/\kappa_r, \tag{7.5}$$

where $K = \kappa_{max}\kappa_{min}$ is the Gaussian curvature (Koenderink, 1984a). (Gaussian curvature is a basic characteristic in differential geometry, a numerical representation of local surface shape.) Thus the sign of the curvature of the image contour equals the sign of the Gaussian curvature! Thus if $\kappa_t 0$, then $K > 0$ corresponding to an elliptic (ovoid) surface shape (convex, because surface concavities cannot yield boundary contours); if $\kappa_t < 0$, then $K < 0$, then the shape is hyperbolic (saddle-shaped), and if $\kappa_t = 0$, then $K = 0$, and the local shape is parabolic, an inflection between elliptic and hyperbolic regions. If viewing distance is sufficiently small so that visual directions are not quite tangent to the surface, then a slight adjustment of Equations 7.5 accounts for the effect of the viewing distance (Koenderink, 1984a, 1990).

A famous drawing by Picasso (*Fragment de corps de femme*) in Figure 7.3 illustrates this image information about surface shape. The drawing illustrates three qualitatively different surface shapes—

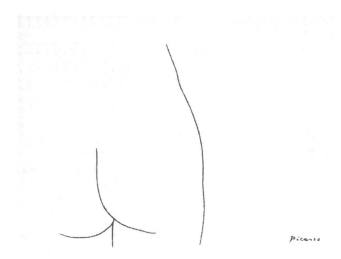

Figure 7.3 A famous drawing by Pablo Picasso, *Fragment de corps de femme*, elegantly illustrates correspondence between the curvature of 2-D boundary contours and 3-D surface shape.

ovoids ($K > 0$), saddle ($K < 0$), and curvature inflections ($K = 0$). Contour inflections are suggested at two points along the mostly convex contour at the right boundary, and these inflections also occur at the ends of the boundary, of the right buttock.

8. *Resolution-invariant image estimates of surface structure*: In practice, images have limited resolution, influenced by viewing distance, illumination, field of view, refractive focus, photoreceptor density, stereopsis, motion blur, visual attention, etc. Image information about environmental spatial structures is necessarily limited by image resolution. Is information about surface shape independent of image resolution?

   Koenderink (1984b; 1990, p. 496-508) and Koenderink and van Doorn (1992a) show that the answer is yes: Image resolution can be represented by a single parameter, independent of image variations due to shape. Moreover, there is only one way to do this. Specifically, image resolution should be represented by 2-D Gaussian blur, with resolution specified by a standard deviation, σ. Image estimators for differential surface structure can then be formed from spatial derivatives of Gaussians (Koenderink & van Doorn, 1992a). These local image measures satisfy the requirement that decreasing image resolution never yields increased structural complexity—i.e., no spatial aliasing or moiré artifacts. The Gaussian blur operators are the unique solution to this requirement.

9. *Direct measures of higher-order differential structure*: Intuitively, higher-order spatial derivatives might seem to derive from more basic measures of lower-order relations. Because the variance of a difference between two independent variables is the sum of their variances, higher-order differential structure might seem too unreliable to be practical. This intuition is mistaken. Estimators for higher-order image structure can be formed from derivatives of Gaussians, yielding subregions with opposite signed weights. Thus spatial variations can be estimated by integration rather than differentiation (see Koenderink, 1990, p. 37-40; Koenderink & van Doorn, 1992a).

   - *General comments:* Geometric relations between surfaces and their images are simpler and more informative than traditionally assumed. Image information about local surface shape is directly provided by the radial symmetry of spatial organization around any given point. Psychophysical experiments (Lappin & Craft, 2000) find that vision obtains more precise information about this property than about seemingly simpler, lower-order structures, such as retinal position, depth, spatial frequency, or surface slant. Lower-order properties are less informative, because they vary with the observer's vantage point relative to the surface.

7.2.4 Spatial Relations Between Objects

Surface shapes involve spatial variations in depth, but those variations do not derive from measures of depth. Surfaces serve to segment spaces, but otherwise impose few restrictions on spatial relations between surfaces. What is the image information about spatial relations between separate objects? The answer is not yet clear; many issues are unresolved.

Two-dimensional images in eyes, photographs, and paintings obviously provide valuable information about 3-D scenes, but they cannot give a reliable representation of 3-D spatial relations among separate objects. Neither the optical information nor the ambiguities of the projective maps between image space and environmental space are adequately understood.

The study of space perception extends well beyond psychology and beyond the scope of the present chapter. Many reviews are available, however, including Baird (1970), Cutting and Vishton (1995), Foley (1978), Gibson (1950), Gillam (1995), Howard (2002), Howard and Rogers (2002), Indow (1991), Sedgwick (1986), Suppes (1995), and Suppes, Krantz, Luce, and Tversky (1989, Chs. 12, 13). A striking characteristic of this literature is its inconsistency—experimentally and theoretically. Selected aspects include the following:

1. *Space as an abstract extrinsic framework*: Intuitively, space often seems an abstract framework independent of its contents. Both Newtonian physics and classical vision research conceived of space as an a priori framework that defines positions, motions, and spatial relations. This conception applied to spatial structures in the environment, image, and perception.

   The spatial structure of retinal images is often assumed to be a scalar field with coordinate positions supplied by anatomy, independent of image content. Marr (1982), among others, regarded this representation as obvious. But it is a hypothesis—with basic consequences for spatial vision.

   Binocular disparity, for example, is often defined as a difference between the two monocular retinal positions of a given image feature. Experiments show that this representation is not valid, however. Stereoscopic "hyperacuity" for very small relative differences between the two monocular images remains invariant under noisy image transformations that disrupt binocular correspondence of retinal positions (see Lappin & Craft, 1997, 2000, and other references therein). Similar comments apply to image motion. Spatial positions in the images, therefore, are defined by intrinsic image topology, not extrinsic retinal coordinates.

   Much of the literature on visual space perception has concerned *depth* perception, involving egocentric distances and relative depth differences between objects. Visual space is often conceived as an abstract framework with three orthogonal axes—two in the azimuth and elevation of visual direction and a third for radial distance in depth. Spatial relations in the retinal image are often treated as if in a Euclidean metric plane, where lengths and angles are invariant under translations and rotations. In fact, the visual field is not a plane. The spherical surface of the retina specifies a conic bundle of visual directions. A planar approximation is often adequate in a restricted central area about the size of a standard computer monitor. As peripheral eccentricity increases, however, environmental distances and directions are increasingly distorted in the planar approximation.[4]

Distances in depth are sometimes regarded as inferred from a collection of "cues." This paradigm for depth perception defines spatial relations by a reference frame in which the depth scale is inferred, not perceived directly.

This spatial reference frame varies with the vantage point, however. Regardless of our intuitions about an objective constancy of physical space in which we operate, visual space varies with our vantage point. A common (but not universal) experimental result is that judged lengths in depth are substantially reduced relative to the frontal plane (e.g., Todd, Oomes, Koenderink, & Kappers, 2001; Todd, Tittle, & Norman, 1995; Wagner, 1985).

Several lines of research support the hypothesis that visual space is *affine* (e.g., Todd et al., 2001, 1995; Wagner, 1985). Like Euclidean space, affine spaces are also metric, but allow different scales for different axes. Affine models of visual space perception permit a reduced scale factor for the depth axis relative to those for the retinal image. Todd et al. (2001) found support for an affine model in the internal consistency of observer's bisections of apparent distances between pairs of marked locations in different directions. The adjusted points need not be physically collinear or bisections to satisfy internal affine consistency, and indeed they were not.

Wagner (1985), Gibson (1950), and others concluded that perceived space in fully illuminated natural scenes with ample depth cues approximates a Euclidean structure—where relative lengths and angles are invariant with the observer's vantage point. This idea agrees with our intuitions of a space that remains constant independent of our movements.

Athletic coordination of perception and action in ball-playing sports reinforces the same intuition. Indeed, a computational account of such phenomena seems daunting without that idea. Nevertheless, coordinating visual perception and action in ball-playing sports is a simpler problem than it first appears. The computational problem is greatly simplified by representing spatial information relative to the vantage point of the moving athlete. Visual images of the ball then provide simple reliable information for anticipating intersection of the ball and athlete (Lappin, 2013).

2. *Alternatives to the intuitive model of exocentric space:* Egocentric directions and distances are not the only possible representation of perceived space. Alternative relational structures include (a) intrinsic local topology, (b) congruence under motion, and (c) incidence of perceived lines and points.

The intrinsic topological structure of retinal images offers many qualitative relations that are local, non-metric, and often independent of the observer's vantage point. Binary relations of connectedness and of ordered relative positions as well as ternary relations of betweenness and collinearity are examples of potentially informative visual structures. Such simple topological properties may suffice to support reliable perception and action for many cases.

Riemannian geometry is based on local relations. Integration of the local relations generates metric structures. This Riemannian approach contrasts with the globally consistent *homogeneous* geometries of Euclidean, spherical, and hyperbolic space, which have dominated theories of visual space. The Riemannian approach to perceived spatial relations warrants further study.

Congruence under motion induces a homogeneous space. Thus perceived congruence of a moving form can be used to design and generate 3-D spaces in local regions of 2-D images (Lappin & Wason, 1993). The art of M. C. Escher offers many compelling graphic illustrations of the effectiveness of congruent shapes for perceiving metric structures in 3-D. The power of congruence as spatial information is also indicated by the perceived rigidity of moving 3-D structures in movie and TV screens, despite large perspective distortions that vary with the viewer's location (Cutting, 1987).

In certain conditions, e.g., when a planar shape rotates on a slanted plane, congruence under motion can serve as a visual basis for perceiving metric relations among spatial arrays of objects or points (Lappin & Ahlström, 1994; Lappin & Fuqua, 1983; Lappin & Love, 1992; Lappin & Wason, 1993). Mathematically, however, congruence under motion does not generally induce rigid 3-D structure from motions of solid shapes. Accordingly, Norman and Todd (1993) demonstrated that human observers could not perceive violations of rigid structure of a solid shape rotating in depth.

Incidence relations between lines and points, e.g., two points define a unique line and the incidence of two lines define a unique point, are among the simplest spatial relations. These incidence relations plus collinearity are preserved under projective transformations from one plane onto another. Koenderink, van Doorn, Kappers, and Todd (2002) tested a higher-order consistency property, known as the Pappus condition, that holds for a configuration of three collinear sets of three points. If the Pappus condition is added (as an axiom) to the basic incidence relations among points and lines, then it induces projective geometry and guarantees congruence under motion. Koenderink et al. found that the Pappus condition held for visually judged collinearities of objects in the horizontal plane of a natural scene in "full-cue" conditions with a wide field of view, although judged collinearities clearly deviated from physical collinearity. This result suggests a potential geometric foundation for the visual representation of spatial relations among objects.

3. *Context effects:* A general finding of the extensive literature on visual space is that judged spatial relations vary with the context of the observational setting. In the classical literature, context effects were typically viewed as artifacts that interfered with judgments of the hypothetically pure visual framework. Blank (1953) emphasized that constrained observational conditions—e.g., "tiny points in the dark, fixed head,"—were required for estimating the underlying space (which he believed to be hyperbolic, as theorized by Luneburg, 1947). For the past 25 years or so, however, research has studied normally viewed natural settings. Context effects remain largely unexplained but important characteristics of visual space perception (Lappin, Shelton, & Rieser, 2006).

Context dependence generally contradicts the concept of visual space as an abstract framework for the spatial structure of visual information. Perceived relations vary with what the setting affords. The classic moon illusion is an illustration: A full moon appears strikingly larger when near the horizon than when overhead, even though the retinal images are the same size. Paradoxically, the horizon moon also seems closer than the moon overhead.

The conclusions of three experts summarize the general situation: Gibson (1950): "*visual* space, unlike abstract geometrical space, is perceived only by virtue of what fills it" (p. 5). Indow (1991): Visual space "is dynamic, not a solid empty container into which various percepts are put without affecting its contours and intrinsic structure" (p. 450). Suppes (1995): "the most important general feature of visual space is that it is context dependent, a characteristic of physical systems rather than classical geometrical ones. ". . . no reasonably simple set of axioms . . . can be given for the structure of visual space" (p. 37).

4. *Dependence on task and attention:* Perceived spatial relations also vary with demands of the task environment and the observer's attention. Indeed, perceived spatial relations are often inconsistent among different vantage points and even inconsistent among different spatial

characteristics of the same objects. Visual awareness is ordinarily quite tolerant of such inconsistencies, but they may be easily seen if one attends to them.

Inconsistencies may be seen, for example, in apparently "foreshortened" relative depths and lengths among far objects as compared to near objects. For example, when driving on an interstate highway, one can notice that the lines between lanes appear to be much shorter in the distance—perhaps only 20% of the length of lines near the car. But ordinarily one does not notice this inconsistency.

One can notice countless examples of such visual flexibility and tolerance involving not only spatial vision but also nearly all other aspects of perception. Koenderink (2001) refers to such phenomena as evidence for a "multiple-visual-worlds hypothesis" and argues that theses phenomena are commonplace.

Visual attention may be regarded as an organizing process for recognizing coherent structures of variation. The same object may be represented within multiple potential spatial structures. Different contexts, different observers, and different tasks all afford different possible spatial structures. The problem of identifying optical information is a problem in representing optical relations that correlate with those of visually guided discriminations and actions.

7.3 Empirical Criteria: Resolution and Invariance

Two central ideas in this chapter are that (a) information is defined by corresponding structures of variation, not by the physical characteristics of individual events and objects, and (b) representations of information constitute hypotheses about the specific variations that satisfy a map from input and output. Thus identifying information requires comparative evaluation of multiple alternative hypotheses of alternative representations of input and output.

The analysis of perception, cognition, decision making, action, and other computational processes rests on identifying the information that coordinates input and output. Representations vary in their effectiveness in revealing transformations from input to output. Accordingly, criteria for evaluating and comparing alternative representations of visual information concern (a) the precision and speed with which the input and output information can be coordinated, and (b) the generality of this coordination.

These two classes of criteria are here termed *resolution* and *invariance*. Both criteria are empirically testable; both can guide experiments and observational methods. These criteria seldom receive explicit attention in psychological literature on research methods, although versions have been used previously. The discussion that follows aims to show why these two criteria for perception and performance are essential for identifying and evaluating acquired information. The present chapter expands ideas developed by Lappin and Craft (2000) and Lappin et al. (2011) for testing hypotheses about the optical information for perceiving surface shape.

7.3.1 Resolution, Precision, and Variability

Experiments on perception, psychophysics, and performance typically do not focus on the variability of multiple responses by the same observer to the same stimulus in the same conditions. The ANOVA model of experimental design is a guide for standard practice. Investigations usually focus on differences between experimental conditions, with performance in a particular condition estimated by averaging over individual observers and trials.

Nevertheless, response variability—of independent responses to the same stimulus[5] by the same observer in the same condition—is a basic and theoretically important index of acquired information. The precision of an observer's resolution of input variations is limited by the variability of responses to any given input. The amount of difference needed to discriminate between stimuli can be estimated from the variability of responses to a given stimulus.

The precision and accuracy of responses are different and independent measures of performance. Accuracy involves comparisons of average responses in a given condition with a physically defined reference standard. Variability of responses to the same input, on the other hand, involves resolution of variations in input. The quality and quantity of information transmitted from input to output depends on this resolution.

Resolution is limited by both external and internal random noise. Manipulating external variability offers a method for evaluating the relative influence of internal and external variability. Three examples of this method are (a) the classic experiments of Hecht, Shlaer, and Pirenne (1942) on the role of photonic variability in visual detection thresholds, (b) Green's (1964) study of judgmental consistency in auditory detection experiments, and (c) Lu & Dosher's (1998) studies of the role of attention in modulating internal noise.

Variations of stimulus parameters may or may not produce response variations depending on whether these parameters are part of the relevant information for a given task. Thus one can identify the controlling information by testing whether discriminations of that information remain invariant with random variations in ostensibly irrelevant parameters. Illustrative applications of this research method are in studies by Perotti et al. (1998) and Lappin and Craft (1997, 2000), and they are discussed in Section 7.3.2.

7.3.1.1 What Do Humans See Best?

Empirical methods for identifying information involve comparative evaluations of performance in multiple tasks that depend on different forms of information. A basic empirical question is "What do humans see best?"

Two basic facts about human performance: (a) we can do many different things; and (b) we can do some things better than others.

A) We can voluntarily attend to and coordinate actions in many ways with many different patterns of information. Within any given task environment, observing, thinking, and acting can be guided by many forms of information. Our wide-ranging flexibility in acquiring and using information is fundamental for psychological science and for the arts and sciences more generally.

B) We are more sensitive to some environmental and sensory patterns than others and are more efficient at some cognitive and behavioral tasks than others. Our sensory, cognitive, and motor skills enable and limit our coordination of perception and action.

What, exactly, do humans see best? For a given set of alternative actions, what form of input information optimizes performance? In Shannon's communication theory, the information transmitted from input to output, $T(X:Y)$, can be quantified by the formula

$$T(X:Y) = H(X) - H(X \mid Y), \tag{7.6}$$

where X represents a set of alternative input signals, Y is a set of alternative output responses, $H(X)$ is the input uncertainty defined by Equation 7.1, and $H(X|Y)$ is the contingent uncertainty of the input when the output is known. The research question, "what do observers see best?" is an optimization problem about what relational structure of inputs, X, maximizes information transfer, $T(X:Y)$, where the output responses, Y, are fixed. The optimization criterion is the measure $T(X:Y)$, in units of *bits*, or $T(X:Y)/s$ in *bits/s*.

7.3.1.2 Quantifying Resolution of Ratio-Scaled Variables

Performance measures other than Shannon's information transmission are preferable for many specific applications. For positive ratio-scaled variables, such as spatial lengths, a frequently useful measure is the *coefficient of variation*, $S(y)/M(y)$, where $S(y)$ and $M(y)$ are the standard deviation and mean of a random variable, $y \in Y$.

Suppose that variable y refers to the set of estimated length bisections given by an observer in response to an individual stimulus length $x \in X$ selected by an experimenter. The values of y, $M(y)$, and $S(y)$ might be obtained from an observer's active adjustments, or $M(y)$ and $S(y)$ might be approximated from the psychometric function of a series of binary judgments (e.g., "greater than" or "less than") in a discrimination experiment.

In psychophysics, the coefficient of variation is a *Weber fraction*, W = $\Delta(x)/x = S(x)/M(x)$, where $\Delta(x) = S(x)$ is a just-discriminable difference in a physical variable such as spatial length.[6] This measure is a dimensionless ratio applicable to any positive ratio-scaled stimulus or response variable. Because of its generality, the Weber fraction is valuable for quantifying and comparing resolution for a wide variety of stimulus variables and experimental conditions. Lappin et al. (2011) used Weber fractions to compare visual resolutions of various forms of information evaluated by different experimenters with different methods in different conditions.

Related and comparable measures of resolution are also used in signal detection theory. The widely used measure of discrimination accuracy is

$$d' = \frac{[\mu_1(y) - \mu_2(y)]}{\sigma(y)}, \qquad (7.7)$$

where $\mu_1(y) - \mu_2(y)$ is a theoretically inferred difference in the means of two values of a hypothetical sensory variable, y, and $\sigma(y)$ is the inferred standard deviation of the sensory variable y. The experimenter usually does not directly observe the quantities $\mu_1(y)$, $\mu_2(y)$, or $\sigma(y)$, but the ratio d' defined by Equation 7.7 may be reliably estimated from observed discrimination performance. Like the Weber fraction, the discrimination measure d' is also a dimensionless ratio scaled in units of standard deviation.

Note that the Weber fraction may be estimated from d' for discriminations between two physical stimulus variables x_1 and x_2. In this case, we can express d' as a ratio of observed values of physical variables, x_1, x_2:

$$d' = \frac{M(x_2) - M(x_1)}{S(x)},$$

where $M(x_2)$, $M(x_1)$, and $S(x)$ are the empirically estimated means and standard deviation of x. Let the expected value of the difference in the observed sample means equal the difference in the physical values

$$E[M(x_2) - M(x_1)] = x_2 - x_1. \qquad (7.8)$$

Then

$$d'(x_1, x_2) = \frac{x_2 - x_1}{S(x)}.$$

If the empirical estimate of discrimination is $d' > 0$, then

$$S(x) = \frac{x_2 - x_1}{d'}.$$

134 Joseph S. Lappin

Let the average of the two physical values be $m(x) = (x_1+x_2)/2$. Then we can write the Weber fraction, W, as

$$W = \frac{S(x)}{m(x)} = \frac{x_2 - x_1}{d' \cdot m(x)}$$
$$= \left[\frac{x_2 - x_1}{x_1 + x_2}\right] \cdot \frac{2}{d'}. \tag{7.9}$$

The quantity $C = (x_2-x_1)/(x_1+x_2)$ is the familiar *contrast ratio* or *Michelson contrast*, which is widely used in optics and visual psychophysics. If the contrast ratio C is used to quantify a just detectable difference in intensities of two stimuli—e.g., the smallest detectable difference between the minimum and maximum intensities of a cosine grating—then the value of the contrast ratio is half that of the Weber fraction, $W = 2C$.

In other words, there are close family relations between the coefficient of variation and three psychophysical measures, the Weber fraction (W), contrast ratio (C), and signal detection (d'). All are dimensionless ratios, applicable to a wide range of physical variables and psychophysical methods. Like the coefficient of variation, W and d' are scaled by standard deviations, and the same discrimination scale is also applicable to contrast thresholds, C. All four measures involve binary relations invariant under scalar transformations of the physical stimulus variable. All four are valuable for comparing resolution of different variables in different conditions.

7.3.1.3 Quantifying Resolution by Response Speed

Response speeds for discriminating or classifying stimuli offers another useful measure of resolution. Response times (RTs) are quite variable but also quite sensitive to input information and to task demands. Three sets of factors influence response times: (a) resolution of the input variations, (b) attentional workload, and (c) compatibility of relational structures of stimulus input and response output.

Analyses of RTs typically focus on differences in means to evaluate effects of stimulus and task conditions. In the frameworks of both ANOVA and the "additive factor method" (Sternberg, 1969), the relational structure of RTs is usually represented by differences in mean RTs for varied task conditions. RT variances are sometimes regarded as measurement error—often correlated with the means and not directly relevant.

For example, RTs are often used to study visual search for a target in a display with distractors. An analogous paradigm is a memory search task, where the search set is displayed before the target and not simultaneously visible with the target. In both paradigms, mean RT usually increases linearly with the size of the search set. The slope of the linear-function-relating mean RT and set size (ms/item) is commonly regarded as a measure of the rate of visual or cognitive scanning (e.g., Schneider & Shiffrin, 1977;

Sternberg, 1966, 1969; Treisman & Gelade, 1980; see reviews by Logan, 2004, Wolfe & Horowitz, 2004, and Eckstein, 2011).

The linear relation between RT and set size is often interpreted as an effect of serial processing. The serial-process interpretation entails representations of the relational structures of stimulus input as a set of discrete elements and response output as differences in mean RT. Both representations are questionable. The same result is also consistent with a limited-capacity parallel process (Townsend, 1971, 1972, 2001).

The temporal structure of response times can be represented more effectively, however, by hazard rates than by RT means and variances (see Chechile, 2003; Houpt & Townsend, 2012b; Lappin et al., under review; Luce, 1986; Townsend, 1990b; Townsend & Ashby, 1983; Townsend & Eidels, 2011; Townsend & Wenger, 2004a; Wenger & Gibson, 2004).

The hazard rate evaluates the rate of change in the temporal probability distribution of an event, such as a detection response. Let $S(t) = 1 - F(t)$ be the survival function, the probability that a given event (e.g., target detection) has not yet occurred at time t. If $f(t)$ is the probability density of the event, then the hazard rate, $h(t)$, is $h(t) = f(t)/S(t)$.[7]

The hazard function at a given time is conveniently estimated by the slope of the integrated hazard function, $H(t)$. Thus

$$H(t) = \int_0^t h(t')dt' = -\log_2 S(t). \tag{7.10}$$

The integrated function, $H(t)$, is simply a logarithmic transformation of the cumulative distribution function, F(t), preserving the ordinal structure of the RTs. Whereas $F(t)$ is generally S-shaped, $H(t)$ is more linear, with smaller changes in slope. The units of $H(t)$ are bits, which increase monotonically with RT.[8] Accordingly, the derivative of $H(t)$, the hazard rate $H(t)$, is in bits/s. Thus $H(t)$ estimates the detection rate at a given point in time. Lappin et al. (submitted for publication) recently found that stable estimates of hazard functions were obtained from difference ratios $\Delta H(t)/\Delta t$ at four successive quintiles of $F(t)$: 10–30%, 30–50%, 50–70%, and 70–90%.

The temporal shape of the hazard function describes the temporal structure of information processing. It reflects both the processing architecture and the structure and dynamics of input information. For example, serial search among equally discernible independent items will produce monotonically increasing hazard rates, increasing as the unsearched items decrease. In a task resembling visual search, we recently found that the hazard functions demonstrated parallel processes—despite a linear relation between set size and mean RT (Lappin et al., submitted for publication).

Hazard functions offer significant advantages for describing the temporal structure of acquired information (see Chechile, 2003; Godwin, Walenchok, Houpt, Hout, & Goldinger, 2015; Lappin et al., submitted for publication; Luce, 1986; Townsend, 1990c; Townsend & Ashby, 1983; Townsend & Eidels, 2011; Townsend & Nozawa, 1995; Townsend & Wenger, 2004a; Wenger & Gibson, 2004), including the following:

1. Estimates of hazard rates and relative hazard rates are nonparametric—involving no assumptions about RT distribution parameters or underlying stochastic process.
2. Inferences about effects of task conditions on process speeds are stronger when based on hazard functions than on distribution parameters, such as mean RTs: If $H_a(t) > H_b(t)$ for all t, then $\text{Mean}_a(t) < \text{Mean}_b(t)$, but the converse is not true (Townsend, 1990c).
3. The hazard rate, $h(t)$, is a ratio scale of process rate. Ratios of hazard rates at two times or in two conditions, say $h(t_1)/h(t_2)$ or $h_a(t)/h_b(t)$, are dimensionless, scale-invariant. Thus relational structures of hazard functions can describe multiplicative and divisive relations among conditions—an expansion of the additive factor method. Similarly, ratio-scaled relations among hazard functions permit estimates of processing capacity.

In short, the temporal structure of hazard rates is an effective representation of temporal processes for acquiring and resolving information. Experimental research using hazard functions is still limited, but the developing results demonstrate that this method is significantly more powerful than analyses of mean RTs, revealing more details of the temporal process than seen with mean RTs.

7.3.2 Invariance as a Criterion for Defining Structure and Information

Invariance is basic in the definition of information. To identify the specific variables that carry information, one must know how these variables can be transformed without changing the correspondence between input and output.

This approach is not common in psychological science, but it is often regarded as fundamental in theoretical physics and in pure and applied mathematics (e.g., Stewart, 2007). As Lederman and Hill (2004, p. 98) put it, "the laws of physics are essentially *defined by symmetry principles!*" Conservation of energy, for example, is equivalent to invariance of physical interactions under translations in the time at which they are observed. And Einstein's theory of special relativity is equivalent to invariance of the speed of light under relative motions of the observer. Stewart (2007) provides a related historical account of how the invention of a method for describing symmetry of mathematical equations led to theories of symmetry used throughout pure and applied mathematics. In general, patterns of the natural world are described by their symmetries, by invariance under transformations.

After stating that the central problem of psychology is to define the stimulus, Stevens (1951, p. 32) also pointed out that the definition required identification of invariants:

> The complete definition of the stimulus to a given response involves the specification of all the transformations of the environment... that leave the response invariant.... It is easy enough, of course, to decide upon arbitrary definitions of "stimulus objects" (e.g., a given pattern of lines, a quantity of luminous flux, an acoustic waveform, etc.), but the question is: what properties of these objects do the stimulating?

Thus the "stimulus"' is a *category*—a set of objects and events that can occur at different times and places, in different environmental contexts, and are observable by different observers from different vantage points, with the same functionally effective structure that distinguishes one stimulus from another. "Information" seems a better term than "stimulus," but the definitions of both rest implicitly on invariance. Similar comments apply to the term "response."

Investigations of invariance are not common in psychology, but notable examples include Gibson's (1950) study of *The Perception of the Visual World* converging operations to distinguish perceptual from response factors (Garner, Hake, & Eriksen, 1956), ROC curves in signal detection theory (Green & Swets, 1966), and the uniqueness theorem in measurement theory (Krantz et al., 1971). Invariance is inextricably linked to the concept of information and, therefore, also to concepts of perception, cognition, and action.

Here we consider two types of invariance involved in information—invariance under observational transformations and context invariance. These two aspects of invariance are important, but do not exhaust the topic. Sensory information about different environmental properties involves different groups of transformations. The present focus is on information about spatial structure. Specifically, what spatial relations remain invariant with observational transformations of viewing position and motion and with contextual changes in surrounding objects and motions?

7.3.3 Invariance Under Observational Transformations

If an optical pattern on the eyes constitutes information about the spatial structure of an object, event, or scene, then that pattern must be independent of at least some variations in who observes it and when, where, and how it is observed. The optical images of environmental objects in observers' eyes change dramatically with the observer's vantage point and motion. Sizes, shapes, relative positions, and motions of objects are very different in 3-D environmental space and in 2-D optical image space. Nevertheless, if the spatiotemporal structure of retinal images provides information about

138   *Joseph S. Lappin*

environmental structures, locations, and motions, then some correspondence between spatial relations in environments and images must be invariant with the group of 3-D motions of the observer's viewing position relative to the object. This observational invariance is empirically testable.

Such an invariant correspondence between objects and images, however, does not preclude basic spatial ambiguities. For example, second-order local image structure corresponds to local surface shapes of environmental objects, but image cues about relative depths, lengths of contours, and lines, angles, and surface slants of environmental objects are ambiguous, and they vary with the observer's vantage point. Such spatial properties do not necessarily *appear* ambiguous, but experiments find that judgments of these properties are quite unreliable (see Lappin et al., 2011).

Image information requires structural correspondences between environmental objects and their retinal images. For the case of environmental surfaces and their images, this correspondence has been identified (Section 7.2.3). This correspondence was identified by use of the observational invariance criterion, involving invariance under transformations of viewing position.

7.3.3.1 *Invariance of Shape Perception*

The experimental problem involves (a) evaluating human resolution of the hypothesized image information and (b) demonstrating that resolution is invariant under the image transformations associated with 3-D motions of viewing position. Lappin and Craft (1997, 2000) and Perotti et al. (1998) provided such psychophysical tests. Their experiments demonstrated precise discriminations of the 2-D second-order structure of stereoscopic and moving images corresponding to local surface shape. Importantly, these discriminations were invariant with image transformations produced by 3-D motions of viewing position.

Lappin and Craft (1997, 2000) independently perturbed the two monocular images of stereoscopic patterns with rapid random image transformations (10/s) that disrupted specific structural correspondences between the two images. Random uncorrelated horizontal and vertical translations of the two monocular images, for example, disrupted correspondence between the two monocular retinal image positions of individual points, but did not alter stereoacuity for very small binocular disparities in the relative positions of multiple points. Stereoacuities for detecting differences in relative depth were approximately 10 *arcsec*, despite random image perturbations more than an order of magnitude larger. This result contradicts the representation of binocular disparity as a difference between the monocular retinal positions of a given image feature. Instead, binocular positions and disparities are topological, defined by relations among neighboring points.

Experimental tests of stereoscopic acuities for binocular disparities of higher-order structure involving pairs, triples, and five-tuples of points were also tested by other image transformations. Random dilations and

2-D rotations of the two monocular images perturbed binocular correspondences between pairs of points in each image. Precise stereoacuity was maintained under both of these image perturbations. Thus binocular disparity of image structure is not based on binary relations—e.g., autocorrelation spectrum or Fourier power spectrum.

Dichoptic image transformations involving "pure shear" are associated with surface slant and deform triangular surface patches. These image perturbations as well had only small effects on stereoacuity. And this result contradicts representations of binocular disparity based on triangular configurations (first-order relations in 2-D).

Image transformations that preserve 2-D second-order relations (Figures 7.2 and 7.3) maintain stereoacuity for detecting a depth displacement of a point from a smooth surface. Perturbations of that structure, however, destroy the precision of stereoacuity (Lappin & Craft, 1997). Lappin and Craft (2000) found essentially the same hyperacuities for both motion parallax and stereoscopic patterns and the same invariance under image transformations produced by observer motions in 3-D space.

Observers in a study by Perotti et al. (1998) adjusted the two principal curvatures of stereoscopic patterns so as to match a randomly generated shape specified by rigid rotation in depth. This method tested invariance of perceived shapes from motion parallax and from stereopsis. Invariance tests involved comparing shape adjustments for motion patterns with added image motions due to rotation, expansion, or pure shear (slant), keeping the total motion energy constant across conditions. Shape discriminations based on the ratio of principal curvatures were nearly perfect in all conditions. Correlations between simulated and adjusted shapes were $R^2 = 0.995$ with no added image perturbations, and $R^2 = 0.997, 0.998$, and 0.993 with added rotation, expansion, and shear, respectively. Judgments of curvedness in depth were imprecise in all conditions: $R^2 = 0.550$ with no added image transformations, and $R^2 = 0.604, 0.564$, and 0.470 with added rotation, expansion, and shear, respectively.

Results of these and other studies demonstrate that precise shape discriminations are preserved under image transformations produced by changes in viewing position. Judgments of relative depth, surface slant, and curvedness, however, are consistently unreliable. Lappin and Craft (2000), Lappin, et al. (2011), Lappin (2014), and Todd (2004) review the accumulating literature on the perception of surface shape from spatiotemporal patterns.

7.3.3.2 Invariance of Perceived Spatial Relations Among Separate Objects

The study of visual space has many unsolved problems. We do not yet know what perceived spatial relations remain invariant under arbitrary observer motions.

Research on visual space perception has usually investigated metric relations, such as egocentric and relative distances, perpendicularity, parallelism, and congruence. Spaces in which metric relations are congruent under motion are *homogeneous* spaces (with constant curvature)—Euclidean, elliptic, or hyperbolic. Luneburg's theory of hyperbolic visual space (1947; Blank, 1953) illustrates the mathematical appeal of such observationally invariant structure, but reviews by Indow (1991, 1997), Suppes (1995), Suppes et al. (1989), and others find that visual space does not have invariant metric structure.

Research on visual space is now often conducted in "full-cue" natural environments with a fully visible ground surface, objects, and spatial layout. This contemporary approach contrasts with classical research in "reduced-cue" settings with disconnected points of light in the dark. Issues that motivate contemporary research include (a) how actions in space—walking, reaching, ball-playing, etc.—are guided by visual information, and (b) perceived spatial relations among visible objects in natural scenes. Observational invariance is a fundamental issue in both issues.

Loomis, DaSilva, Philbeck, and Fukusima (1996) proposed that a basic spatial invariant is perceived *location*—as jointly specified by egocentric directions and distances. Presumably, egocentric directions in full-cue environments are visually primitive information from which other spatial characteristics may be derived. Judgments of both egocentric and exocentric distances at a given viewing position, however, are known to be inaccurate, imprecise, and vary with viewing position and environmental context. Loomis et al. have evaluated the accuracy of pointing to perceived locations of objects before and after walking blindfolded in a different direction from the initial egocentric target direction. Because changes in egocentric target directions depend on egocentric distances as well as the distance and direction of the blindfolded locomotion, information about the perceived egocentric distances may be inferred by triangulating the pointing directions before and after locomotion. In full-cue settings, the pointing directions are found to be generally accurate and without systematic error. Loomis and colleagues concluded that perceived spatial locations are dissociated from perceived exocentric distances. This is an important result. Further study with such methods is needed, of course.

In contrast to the preponderance of research on metric relations, Koenderink et al. (2002) have studied the feasibility for a simpler, non-metric geometry for visual space based only on perceived collinearities and incidence of lines and points. Koenderink and colleagues tested whether visual space satisfied an internal consistency requirement known as the Pappus condition, which is an axiomatic requirement for projective space. The Pappus configuration involves three sets of three collinear points in a 2-D space of constant curvature. The psychophysical tests involved observers' adjustments of object locations to be (a) collinear with a given pair of widely separated objects and (b), in separate tests, to coincide with the intersection of lines between two given pairs of points. The Pappus condition was empirically verified, despite clear departures from physical collinearity that varied with viewing distance and observers.

This important result warrants further investigation. Koenderink et al. found that perceived collinearities probably are not invariant with the vantage point. Nevertheless, the internal consistency of the projective space at any given vantage point might be maintained across changes in vantage point. Evidence is needed. More evidence is also needed about the precision with which observers can detect violations of the Pappus condition. An important hypothesis is that the structure of visual space is based on the projective invariance of points, lines, and their incidences. This hypothesis demands tests.

7.3.4 Context Invariance

Context invariance is another functional criterion associated with the concept of information. This criterion applies especially to the representation of information as a set of elementary symbols, stimuli, features, or dimensions. If a particular stimulus is a causal element in the input information to perception, then, intuitively, its causal influence should be separable and independent of variations in its context.

Thus distinctions between information and context are involved in problems such as quantifying the informational complexity of stimulus patterns, quantifying rates and capacities of information processing, characterizing selective attention, and distinguishing serial and parallel processing. For these and other reasons, context invariance is a basic concern in research on most aspects of human information processing. The present focus is the use of context effects as empirical criteria for identifying information.

If sensory information is represented as a multidimensional structure of discrete stimulus elements, then one can test whether the probability distribution of responses to variations in one dimension depends on either the values of other dimensions or on the observer's responses to these values. Mathematical models and experimental tests based on this approach are found throughout Townsend's research. Good examples include Ashby and Townsend (1986), Kadlec and Townsend (1992), Thomas (1995), Townsend (1981), Townsend and Ashby (1983), and Townsend, Hu, and Ashby (1980); Townsend, Hu, and Evans (1984). As demonstrated in these papers, perceptual independence can be defined and tested in various ways, involving both response probabilities and response times.

How does the concept of information developed in Sections 7.1 and 7.2 affect concepts of information, context, and context invariance? Three ideas are relevant:

1. *Relativity of information and choice:* (a) perceptual information is based on the relational structure of a set of alternative events, and

142   *Joseph S. Lappin*

(b) responses are choices among a set of alternatives. That is, the information associated with particular stimulus and response events depends entirely on the context of their alternatives. This broad principle is uncontroversial, widely accepted in contemporary psychology, and implicit in all the models and methods developed by Townsend and colleagues to evaluate perceptual independence. Nevertheless, this broad principle contradicts the intuitive idea of causal relations between individual stimuli and responses independently of the alternatives that did not occur.

2. *Sensory information is often nonsymbolic, often carried by continuous spatiotemporal variations*: Analyses of perceptual independence often involve representations of sensory information based on relations among discrete elements and variables such as features, dimensions, and other objects that can be represented symbolically. Context, contextual interactions, and perceptual independence are more easily modeled when the elements of information can be symbolically represented than when information is embodied in the structure of variations continuous in spacetime. Important classes of such spatiotemporal information include optical information about (a) the spatial structure of surfaces and (b) spatial relations between separate surfaces.

   As discussed in Section 7.2.3, optical and visual information about the shapes of environmental surfaces can now be identified. The relational structure of this information involves deformations of higher-order spatial relations among a five-tuple of neighboring spatial regions. This informational structure satisfies a type of context-invariance criterion, insofar as information about local surface shape is defined *locally*, without reference to a global shape or cues. At the same time, however, the local surface shape varies smoothly over the surface. Perceived local structure is, therefore, constrained by the smoothly varying structure of the surrounding spatial neighborhood. Neighboring spatial regions are certainly not perceptually independent. Boundary contours in the image of a surface are especially important and influential.

   Perceptual information about spatial relations between separate objects, however, is poorly understood, as discussed in Sections 7.2.4 and 7.3.3. *Perceived spatial relations between separate objects are context dependent*. Indeed, variables that describe global context cannot now be distinguished from those associated with local spatial relations. Current models of perceptual independence do not apply to context effects in visual space perception.

3. *Information involves corresponding relational structures in separate systems. The observer plays an active role in selecting and organizing information about the task environment*: The interdependence of the observer and the observed has a profound influence on the nature of acquired information and context. The observer's *prior knowledge* and

selective attention both influence what is information and what is context.

7.3.4.1 Selective Attention

Selective attention is a principal influence on acquired information. Attention is a decisive influence because (a) observers have limited capacities of attention, perception, and cognition, and (b) natural task environments generally provide sources and forms of information that exceed observers' acquisition rates. If information were an objective structure or quantity independent of the observer, then attention could be modeled as a filter that admits some items and rejects others, and information could be distinguished from its context. Such a conception is implicit in much of the research on human attention. But information is not objective; it depends on what is available and needed in the task environment.

A study conducted some years ago (Lappin, 1967) illustrates this influence. The purpose was to determine how attention to one particular object or feature influenced the perception of others. (At the time, little evidence about such issues was available. Since then, Townsend and colleagues have systematically investigated this basic aspect of visual information.)

Individual "*objects*" were circles with three independent dimensions: *size* (small, medium, large), *color* (red, purple, blue), and *angle* of a line through the circle (down, middle, up—20°, 45°, 70° from horizontal). Each display contained nine such objects around a central fixation point. Observers identified three items on each trial designated by easily visible pointers. On each trial, an array of randomly varied objects appeared simultaneously with the pointers for about 50 ms, with display time adjusted for each of four observers to produce about 75% correct identifications for a single dimension of a single object. Identification accuracy was evaluated in five main conditions: *single object* (requiring identifications of the three dimensions of one object), *multiple objects and dimensions* (size of one, color of the second, angle of the third), and three conditions involving a *single dimension* (three sizes, three colors, or three angles of three different objects).

The serial order of the three identified features was always clockwise and always size, color, and angle. The five main conditions were each tested in separate blocks of trials, so the four well-practiced observers always knew what the task required in a given block of trials.

For present purposes, the relevant striking finding was that (for all four individual observers) within all five conditions, *accuracies of the three identified features are always mutually independent*, despite very large and clear differences in performance across conditions. Performance was substantially better in the *single-object* condition than any of the *multiple-objects* conditions and was better in all the *same-dimension* conditions than in the condition with *multiple objects and dimensions*.

Thus comparing across task conditions, multiple objects and dimensions were perceptually highly interdependent. Within a given task, however, the three objects and features were always perceptually independent components of the acquired information.[9] Evidently, acquired information was structured to fit the needs of the task.

7.3.4.2 Prior Knowledge

An explicit and fundamental aspect of Shannon's famous mathematical theory of communication is that information is defined by a probability distribution over a set of alternatives. The information associated with any given stimulus event is associated with the observer's uncertainty about what *might have happened*. The observer's prior knowledge about the context of a given stimulus event is a basic factor in the quantity of information in that context.

This principle is sufficient to account for many of the well-established findings that both speed and accuracy of detection decrease as the number of alternative signals increases. Such effects can occur in both forced-choice and yes/no signal detection experiments, as well as in both visual search and memory search experiments. Such effects of stimulus uncertainty can be explained equally well by serial and parallel processes, as Townsend and colleagues have shown, but many of the results can also be explained by normative statistical models with no limitations at all on the observer's processing capacity. Signal detection theory (e.g., Green & Swets, 1966; Tanner Jr., 1956) and Luce's Choice Theory (e.g., Lappin & Uttal, 1976; Luce, 1963) provide similar explanations based on the statistical context of a given stimulus event.

Scientific understanding of human information processing requires a representation of the information for processing. The information associated with any given "stimulus" involves a structure of relationships with alternatives, and that structure depends on the observer's knowledge about the context in which a given stimulus event occurs.

7.4 Conclusion

As Stevens (1951) might have said: *In a sense there is only one problem of psychophysics, namely, the identification of information. In this same sense there is only one problem in all of psychology—and it is the same problem.*

Acknowledgments

Preparation of this manuscript has significantly benefited from editorial comments and suggestions by an anonymous reviewer, Joe Houpt, and Gordon Logan. Development of these ideas has also been influenced by discussions with Jim Townsend, Charles Eriksen, Jan Koenderink, Jim Todd, Farley Norman, Flip Phillips, Bill Warren, Ehtibar Dzhafarov, Liliana Albertazzi, and Gordon Logan.

Notes

1. The term "visual system" is used here as shorthand for multiple structures of neural variations as well as various cognitive and perceptual representations. All these representations are here conceived as corresponding structures of spatiotemporal variations. Presumably, none of these representations is symbolic.
2. The isomorphism is "approximate" due to noisy perturbations in the imaging system. Present use of "isomorphism" should be understood as an implicit approximation affected by physical noise. The isomorphism applies to a restricted set of spatial relations, not to physical objects or geometric properties in general.
3. These inter-image disparities are defined on intrinsic image structure, not retinal coordinates.
4. Rogers and Naumenko (2015) provide a powerful illustration of the counter-intuitive spherical image of a physically straight line in 3-D Euclidean space—between the sun and the moon. The projection of this straight line is a great circle on the sphere of visual directions, but this curvilinearity appears paradoxical and in conflict with the horizon, which is also a great circle, but projects as a straight line at eye height.
5. Physical stimulation is never really the *same* across separate presentations of a given stimulus event by an experimenter or environmental source. The context varies. And both external environment and internal processes add random physical "noise." Percepts and responses are also not generally independent, due to learning, for example.
6. The numerator of the Weber fraction is often based on a 75% correct "threshold" for binary responses in a discrimination task. The standard deviation is a more general measure that is also related to d'.
7. The base of the logarithm is arbitrary, affecting only the numerical scale: $\log_2(x) = In(x)/In(2)$. The natural log, $ln(x)$, is conventional in the literature, but scaling $h(t)$ in bits/s is heuristically useful. Note that the reciprocal, $1/h(t)$, in s/bit, is the detection half-life at time t.
8. $H(t)$ and $h(t)$ both measure distributions of RTs, not stimuli. One bit corresponds to a 50% reduction of the undetected targets, $S(t)$. Larger values of $h(t)$ describe RT distributions with less variability.
9. The probability that any pair or all three of the responses would be correct was always close to the product of the marginal hit rates for each response.

References

Albertazzi, L. (2002). *Unfolding perceptual continua*. Philadelphia: John Benjamins.
Alvarez, G. A., & Franconeri, S. L. (2007). How many objects can you track? Evidence for a resource limited attentive tracking mechanism. *Journal of Vision, 7*, 1–10.
Ashby, F. G., & Townsend, J. T. (1986). Varieties of perceptual independence. *Psychological Review, 93*, 154–179.
Averbach, E., & Coriell, A. S. (1961). Short-term memory in vision. *Bell System Technical Journal, 40*, 309–328.

Baird, J. C. (1970). *Psychophysical analysis of visual space*. Oxford: Pergamon.

Bell, H. H., & Lappin, J. S. (1973). Sufficient conditions for the discrimination of motion. *Perception & Psychophysics, 14*, 45–50.

Blank, A. A. (1953). The Luneburg theory of binocular space perception. *Journal of the Optical Society of America, 43*, 717–727.

Brooks, R. (1990). Elephants don't play chess. *Robotics and autonomous systems, 6*, 3–15.

Brooks, R. (1991). New approaches to robotics. *Science, 253* (5025), 1227–1232.

Chechile, R. A. (2003). Mathematical tools for hazard function analysis. *Journal of Mathematical Psychology, 47*, 478–494.

Cutting, J. E. (1987). Rigidity in cinema seen from front row, side isle. *Journal of Experimental Psychology: Human Perception and Performance, 13*, 323–334.

Cutting, J. E., & Vishton, P. M. (1995). Perceiving layout and knowing spaces: The integration, relative potency, and contextual use of different information about depth. In W. Epstein & S. Rogers (Eds.), *Perception of space and motion* (pp. 69–117). San Diego: Academic Press.

Eckstein, M. P. (2011). Visual search: A retrospective. *Journal of Vision, 11*, 1–36.

Eidels, A., Townsend, J. T., Hughes, H. C., & Perry, L. A. (2015). Evaluating perceptual integration: uniting response-time- and accuracy-based methodologies. *Attention, Perception, & Psychophysics, 77*(2), 659–680.

Eriksen, C. W., & Hake, H. W. (1955a). Absolute judgments as a function of stimulus range and number of stimulus and response categories. *Journal of Experimental Psychology, 49*, 323–332.

Eriksen, C. W., & Hake, H. W. (1955b). Multidimensional stimulus differences and accuracy of discrimination. *Journal of Experimental Psychology, 50*, 153–160.

Eriksen, C. W., & Lappin, J. S. (1967). Selective attention and very short-term recognition memory for nonsense forms. *Journal of Experimental Psychology, 73* (3), 358–364.

Foley, J. M. (1978). Primary distance perception. In R. Held, H. S. Leibowitz, & H.-L. Teuber (Eds.), *Handbook of sensory physiology: VIII. Perception* (pp. 181–213). New York: Springer.

Garner, W. R. (1962). *Uncertainty and structure as psychological concepts*. New York: Wiley & Sons.

Garner, W. R. (1974). *The processing of information and structure*. Potomac, MD: Lawrence Erlbaum Associates.

Garner, W. R., Hake, H. W., & Eriksen, C. W. (1956). Operationism and the concept of perception. *Psychological Review, 63*, 149–159.

Gibson, J. J. (1950). *The perception of the visual world*. Boston: Houghton Mifflin.

Gibson, J. J. (1966). *The senses considered as perceptual systems*. Boston: Houghton Mifflin.

Gibson, J. J. (1979). *The ecological approach to visual cognition*. Boston: Houghton Mifflin.

Gillam, B. (1995). The perception of spatial layout from static optical information. In W. Epstein & S. Rogers (Eds.), *Perception of space and motion* (pp. 23–67). San Diego: Academic Press.

Gleich, J. (2011). *The information*. New York: Vintage Books.

Godwin, H. J., Walenchok, S. C., Houpt, J. W., Hout, M. C., & Goldinger, S. D. (2015). Faster than the speed of rejection: Object identification processes during visual search for multiple targets. *Journal of Experimental Psychology: Human Perception and Performance, 41*, 1007–1020.

Green, D. M. (1964). Consistency of auditory detection judgments. *Psychological Review, 71*(5), 392–407.

Green, D. M., & Swets, J. A. (1966). *Signal detection theory and psychophysics.* Oxford, England: John Wiley.
Hecht, S., Shlaer, S., & Pirenne, M. H. (1942). Energy, quanta, and vision. *Journal of General Physiology, 25,* 819–840.
Houpt, J. W., & Townsend, J. T. (2012a). Statistical measures for workload capacity analysis. *Journal of Mathematical Psychology, 56*(5), 341–355.
Houpt, J. W., & Townsend, J. T. (2012b). Statistical measures for workload capacity analysis. *Journal of Mathematical Psychology, 56,* 341–355.
Howard, I. P. (2002). *Seeing in depth: Vol. 1. basic mechanisms.* Toronto: I. Porteous.
Howard, I. P., & Rogers, B. J. (2002). *Seeing in depth: Vol. 2. depth perception.* Toronto: I. Porteous.
Hyman, R. (1953). Stimulus information as a determinant of reaction time. *Journal of Experimental Psychology, 45,* 188–196.
Indow, T. (1991). A critical review of Luneburg's model with regard to global structure of visual space. *Psychological Review, 98,* 430–453.
Indow, T. (1997). Hyperbolic representation of global structure of visual space. *Journal of Mathematical Psychology, 41*(1), 89–98.
Johansson, G. (1973). Visual perception of biological motion and a model for its analysis. *Perception & Psychophysics, 14*(2), 201–211.
Kadlec, H., & Townsend, J. T. (1992). Implications of marginal and conditional detection parameters for the separabilities and independence of perceptual dimensions. *Journal of Mathematical Psychology, 36,* 325–374.
Koenderink, J. J. (1984a). What does the occluding contour tell us about solid shape? *Perception, 13,* 321–330.
Koenderink, J. J. (1984b). The structure of images. *Biological Cybernetics, 50,* 363–370.
Koenderink, J. J. (1990). *Solid shape.* Cambridge, MA: MIT Press.
Koenderink, J. J. (2001). Multiple visual worlds (guest editorial). *Perception, 30,* 1–7.
Koenderink, J. J., & van Doorn, A. J. (1976a). Geometry of binocular vision and a model for stereopsis. *Biological Cybernetics, 21,* 29–35.
Koenderink, J. J., & van Doorn, A. J. (1976b). Local structure of movement parallax of the plane. *Journal of the Optical Society of America, 66,* 717–723.
Koenderink, J. J., & van Doorn, A. J. (1976c). The singularities of the visual mapping. *Biological Cybernetics, 24,* 51–59.
Koenderink, J. J., & van Doorn, A. J. (1980). Photometric invariants related to solid shape. *Optica Acta, 27,* 981–986.
Koenderink, J. J., & van Doorn, A. J. (1992a). Generic neighborhood operators. *IEEE Transactions on Pattern Analysis and Machine Intelligence, 14,* 597–605.
Koenderink, J. J., & van Doorn, A. J. (1992b). Second-order optic flow. *Journal of the Optical Society of America. A, 9,* 530–538.
Koenderink, J. J., & van Doorn, A. J. (1992c). Surface shape and curvature scales. *Image and Vision Computing, 10,* 557–564.
Koenderink, J. J., & van Doorn, A. J. (1997). The generic bilinear calibration-estimation problem. *International Journal of Computer Vision, 23,* 217–234.
Koenderink, J. J., van Doorn, A. J., Kappers, A. M., & Todd, J. T. (2002). Pappus in optical space. *Perception & Psychophysics, 64*(3), 380–391.
Krantz, D. H., Luce, R. D., Suppes, P., & Tversky, A. (1971). *Foundations of measurement, volume I.* New York: Academic Press.
Lappin, J. S. (1967). Attention in the identification of stimuli in complex visual displays. *Journal of Experimental Psychology, 75*(3), 321–328.

Lappin, J. S. (2013). *Inferential and ecological theories of visual perception.* In L. Albertazzi (Ed.) *Handbook of experimental phenomenology: Visual perception of shape, space and visual perception* (pp. 39–69). Oxford, UK: John Wiley & Sons.

Lappin, J. S. (2014). What is binocular disparity? *Frontiers in Psychology, Perception Science.* http://journal.frontiersin.org/Journal/10.3389/fpsyg.2014.00870/full

Lappin, J. S., & Ahlström, U. B. (1994). On the scaling of visual space from motion —in response to Pizlo and Salach-Golyska. *Perception & Psychophysics, 55*(2), 235–242.

Lappin, J. S., & Bell, H. H. (1976). The detection of coherence in moving random-dot patterns. *Vision Research, 16,* 161–168.

Lappin, J. S., Bell, H. H., Harm, O. J., & Kottas, B. (1975). On the relation between time and space in the visual discrimination of velocity. *Journal of Experimental Psychology: Human Perception and Performance, 1*(4), 383–394.

Lappin, J. S., & Craft, W. D. (1997). Definition and detection of binocular disparity. *Vision Research, 37,* 2953–2974.

Lappin, J. S., & Craft, W. D. (2000). Foundations of spatial vision: From retinal images to perceived shapes. *Psychological Review, 107*(1), 6–38.

Lappin, J. S., & Fuqua, M. F. (1983). Accurate visual measurement of three-dimensional moving patterns. *Science, 221,* 480–482.

Lappin, J. S., & Love, S. R. (1992). Planar motion permits perception of metric structure in stereopsis. *Perception & Psychophysics, 51*(1), 86–102.

Lappin, J. S., Morse, D. L., & Seiffert, A. E. ((under review) for publication). *Evenly divided visual awareness of multiple moving objects.*

Lappin, J. S., Norman, J. F., & Phillips, F. (2011). Fechner, information, and shape perception. *Attention, Perception, & Psychophysics, 73*(8), 2353–2378.

Lappin, J. S., Shelton, A. L., & Rieser, J. J. (2006). Environmental context influences visually perceived distance. *Perception & Psychophysics, 68*(4), 571–581.

Lappin, J. S., & Uttal, W. R. (1976). Does prior knowledge facilitate the detection of visual targets in noise? *Perception & Psychophysics, 20,* 367–374.

Lappin, J. S., & van de Grind, W. A. (2002). Visual forms in space-time. In L. Albertazzi (Ed.), *Unfolding perceptual continua* (pp. 119–146). Philadelphia: John Benjamins Publishing.

Lappin, J. S., & Wason, T. D. (1993). The perception of geometrical structure from congruence. In S. R. Ellis (Ed.), *Pictorial communication in virtual and real environments* (2nd ed., pp. 425–448). Washington, D. C.: Taylor & Francis.

Lederman, L. T., & Hill, C. T. (2004). *Symmetry and the beautiful universe.* Amherst, NY: Prometheus Books.

Logan, G. D. (2004). Cumulative progress in formal theories of visual attention. *Annual Reviews of Psychology, 55,* 207–234.

Loomis, J. M., DaSilva, J. A., Philbeck, J. W., & Fukusima, S. S. (1996). Visual perception of location and distance. *Current Directions in Psychological Science, 5*(3), 72–78.

Lu, Z.-L., & Dosher, B. A. (1998). External noise distinguishes attention mechanisms. *Vision Research, 38,* 1183–1198.

Luce, R. D. (1963). Detection and recognition. In R. D. Luce, R. R. Bush, & E. Galanter (Eds.), *Handbook of mathematical psychology* (Vol. 1, pp. 103–189). New York: Wiley.

Luce, R. D. (1986). *Response times.* New York: Oxford University Press.

Luck, S. J., & Vogel, E. K. (1997). The capacity of visual working memory for features and conjunctions. *Nature, 390*(6657), 279–281.

Luneburg, R. K. (1947). *Mathematical analysis of binocular vision*. Princeton, NJ: Princeton U. Press.
Mack, A., & Rock, I. (1998). *Inattentional blindness*. Cambridge, MA: MIT Press.
Marr, D. (1982). *Vision*. New York: W. H. Freeman.
Miller, G. A. (1956). The magical number seven, plus or minus two: Some limits on our capacity for processing information. *Psychological Review, 63*(2), 81–97.
Norman, J. F., & Todd, J. T. (1993). The perceptual analysis of structure from motion for rotating objects undergoing affine stretching transformations. *Perception & Psychophysics, 53*, 279–291.
Perotti, V. J., Todd, J. T., Lappin, J. S., & Phillips, F. (1998). The perception of surface curvature from optical motion. *Perception & Psychophysics, 60*(3), 377–388.
Phillips, F., & Todd, J. T. (1996). Perception of local three-dimensional shape. *Journal of Experimental Psychology: Human Perception and Performance, 22*(4), 930–944.
Rogers, B., & Naumenko, O. (2015). The new moon illusion and the role of perspective in the perception of straight and parallel lines. *Attention, Perception, & Psychophysics, 77*(1), 249–257.
Schneider, W., & Shiffrin, R. M. (1977). Controlled and automatic human information processing: I. Detection, search, and attention. *Psychological Review, 84*(1), 1–66.
Scott, D., & Suppes, P. (1958). Foundational aspects of theories of measurement. *Journal of Symbolic Logic, 23*, 113–128.
Sedgwick, H. A. (1986). Space perception. In K. R. Boff, L. Kaufan, & J. P. Thomas (Eds.), *Handbook of perception and human performance* (Vol. 1, pp. 21.1–21.57). New York: Wiley.
Shannon, C. E. (1948). A mathematical theory of communication. *The Bell System Technical Journal, 27*, 623-656, 379–423.
Shannon, C. E., & Weaver, W. (1949). *The mathematical theory of communication*. Urbana: University of Illinois Press.
Simon, H. A. (1996). *The sciences of the artificial, 3rd edition*. Cambridge, MA: MIT Press.
Simons, D. J., & Chabris, C. F. (1999). Gorillas in our midst: Sustained inattentional blindness for dynamic events. *Perception, 28*, 1059–1074.
Sperling, G. (1960). The information available in brief visual presentations. *Psychological Monographs: General and Applied, 74*(11), 1–29.
Sternberg, S. (1966). High-speed scanning in human memory. *Science, 153*, 652–654.
Sternberg, S. (1969). The discovery of processing stages: Extensions of Donders' method. *Acta Psychologica, 30*, 276–315.
Stevens, S. S. (1951). Mathematics, measurement, and psychophysics. In S. S. Stevens (Ed.), *Handbook of experimental psychology* (ch. 1, pp. 1–49). New York: John Wiley.
Stewart, I. (2007). *Why beauty is truth, a history of symmetry*. New York: Basic Books.
Suppes, P. (1995). Some foundational problems in the theory of visual space. In R. D. Luce, M. D. D'Zmura, D. D. Hoffman, G. J. Iverson, & A. K. Romney (Eds.), *Geometric representations of perceptual phenomena: Papers in honor of Tarow Indow on his 70th birthday* (pp. 37–45). Hillsdale, N. J.: Lawrence Erlbaum Associates.
Suppes, P., Krantz, D., Luce, D., & Tversky, A. (Eds.). (1989). *Foundations of measurement, vol. II: Geometrical, threshold, and probabilistic representations*. New York: Academic Press.

Suppes, P., & Zinnes, J. L. (1963). Basic measurement theory. In R. D. Luce, R. R. Bush, & E. Galanter (Eds.), *Handbook of mathematical psychology* (Vol. 1, pp. 1–76). New York: John Wiley & Sons.

Tanner Jr., P., W. (1956). Theory of recognition. *Journal of the Acoustical Society of America, 28*, 882–888.

Thomas, R. D. (1995). Gaussian general recognition theory and perceptual independence. *Psychological Review, 102*, 192–200.

Todd, J. T. (2004). The visual perception of 3d shape. *Trends in Cognitive Science, 8*, 115–121.

Todd, J. T., Oomes, A. H., Koenderink, J. J., & Kappers, A. M. (2001). The affine structure of perceptual space. *Psychological Science, 12*, 191–196.

Todd, J. T., Tittle, J. S., & Norman, J. F. (1995). Distortions of three-dimensional space in the perceptual analysis of motion and stereo. *Perception, 24*, 75–86.

Townsend, J. T. (1971). A note on the identifiability of parallel and serial processes. *Perception & Psychophysics, 10*, 161–163.

Townsend, J. T. (1972). Some results concerning the identifiability of parallel and serial processes. *British Journal of Mathematical and Statistical Psychology, 25*, 168–199.

Townsend, J. T. (1976). Serial and within-stage independent parallel model equivalence on the minimum completion time. *Journal of Mathematical Psychology, 14*, 219–238.

Townsend, J. T. (1981). Some characteristics of visual whole report behavior. *Acta Psychologica, 47*, 149–173.

Townsend, J. T. (1990a). Serial vs. parallel processing: Sometimes they look like Tweedledum and Tweedledee but they can (and should be) distinguished. *Psychological Sciences, 1*, 46–54.

Townsend, J. T. (1990b). Truth and consequences of ordinal differences in statistical distributions: Toward a theory of hierarchical inference. *Psychological Bulletin, 108*, 551–567.

Townsend, J. T. (2001). A clarification of self-terminating versus exhaustive variances in serial and parallel models. *Perception & Psychophysics, 63*(6), 1101–1106.

Townsend, J. T., & Ashby, F. G. (1983). *The Stochastic Modeling of Elementary Psychological Processes*. Cambridge, UK: Cambridge University Press.

Townsend, J. T., & Eidels, A. (2011). Workload capacity spaces: A unified methodology for response-time measures of efficiency as workload is varied. *Psychonomic Bulletin & Review, 18*, 659–681.

Townsend, J. T., Hu, G. G., & Ashby, F. G. (1980). A test of visual feature sampling independence with orthogonal straight lines. *Bulletin of the Psychonomic Society, 15*(3), 163–166.

Townsend, J. T., Hu, G. G., & Evans, R. (1984). Modeling feature perception in brief displays with evidence for positive interdependencies. *Perception & Psychophysics, 36*, 35–49.

Townsend, J. T., & Nozawa, G. (1995). Spatio-temporal properties of elementary perception: An investigation of parallel, serial, and coactive theories. *Journal of Mathematical Psychology, 39*, 321–359.

Townsend, J. T., Solomon, B., & Spencer-Smith, J. (2001). The perfect Gestalt: Infinite dimensional Riemannian face spaces and other aspects of face perception. In M. J. Wenger & J. T. Townsend (Eds.) *Computational, geometric, and process perspectives of facial cognition: Contexts and challenges* (pp. 39–82). Mahwah, NJ: Lawrence Erlbaum Associates.

Townsend, J. T., & Wenger, M. J. (2004a). The serial-parallel dilemma: A case study in a linkage of theory and method. *Psychonomic Bulletin & Review, 11*, 391–418.

Townsend, J. T., & Wenger, M. J. (2004b). A theory of interactive parallel processing: New capacity measures and predictions for a response-time inequality series. *Psychological Review, 111,* 1003–1035.

Treisman, A. M., & Gelade, G. (1980). A feature-integration theory of attention. *Cognitive Psychology, 12,* 97–136.

van Damme, W. J., & van de Grind, W. A. (1993). Active vision and the identification of three-dimensional shape. *Vision Research, 33*(11), 1581–1587.

van de Grind, W. A., van Doorn, A. J., & Koenderink, J. J. (1983). Detection of coherent movement in peripherally viewed random dot patterns. *Journal of the Optical Society of America, 73,* 1674–1683.

Wagner, M. (1985). The metric of visual space. *Perception & Psychophysics, 38*(6), 483–495.

Wenger, M. J., & Gibson, B. S. (2004). Using hazard functions to assess changes in processing capacity in an attentional cuing paradigm. *Journal of Experimental Psychology: Human Perception and Performance, 30,* 708–719.

Wenger, M. J., & Townsend, J. T. (2001). Faces as gestalt stimuli: Process characteristics. In M. J. Wenger & J. T. Townsend (Eds.), *Computational, geometric, and process perspectives on facial cognition: Contexts and challenges* (pp. 229–284). Mahwah, NJ: Lawrence Erlbaum Associates.

Wiener, N. (1954). *The human use of human beings.* Boston: Houghton Mifflin.

Wiener, N. (1961). *Cybernetics, or control and communication in the animal and the machine* (2nd ed.). Cambridge, MA: MIT Press.

Wolfe, J. M., Cave, K. R., & Franzel, S. L. (1989). Guided search: An alternative to the feature integration model for visual search. *Journal of Experimental Psychology: Human Perception and Performance, 15,* 419–433.

Wolfe, J. M., & Horowitz, T. S. (2004). What attributes guide the deployment of visual attention and how do they do it? *Nature Reviews, Neuroscience, 5,* 1–7.

Woodman, G. F., & Vogel, E. K. (2008). Selective storage and maintenance of an object's features in visual working memory. *Psychonomic Bulletin & Review, 15,* 223–229.

8 Models of Intertemporal Choice

Junyi Dai and Jerome R. Busemeyer

This chapter surveys a variety of formal models of intertemporal choice, with emphasis on probabilistic and dynamic models. Intertemporal choices are decisions involving trade-offs among costs and benefits occurring at different times (Frederick, Loewenstein, & O'Donoghue, 2002). For example, one may need to decide whether to spend a certain amount of money immediately or save it for future expenditure. Such decisions are ubiquitous in economic and everyday activities because almost every decision has nontrivial future consequences. As a result, both economists and psychologists have invested much effort to develop and test various models of intertemporal choice in an attempt to provide an accurate description of how people make such decisions. Currently, the most popular theory of intertemporal choice among economists is Samuelson's (1937) discounted utility (DU) model, and the counterpart among psychologists is the hyperbolic discounting model proposed by Mazur (1987). The former was built upon axiomatic analysis, whereas the latter was developed to better fit behavioral data. The axiomatic analysis requires that people's preference between two options occurring at different times should not change when time passes. As a natural consequence of different analysis frameworks, the critical difference between the DU model and the hyperbolic discounting model lies in their predictions on time consistency. Specifically, the DU model entails time-consistent preferences between payoffs at different times as time elapses. To the contrary, the hyperbolic discounting model may predict a preference reversal under the same condition, a result frequently found in empirical studies. Stated otherwise, the hyperbolic discounting model can accommodate the finding that people prefer the later option when two options are in the far future, but prefer the sooner option when the passage of time brings both options closer together.

According to the DU model, the utility of a delayed payoff is discounted relative to its instantaneous utility and, the degree of discounting is governed by the following exponential discount function,

$$D(t) = exp(-kt), \tag{8.1}$$

where t represents the delay duration of the payoff and k is a discount rate parameter. Similarly, the hyperbolic discounting model uses the following hyperbolic discount function to specify the degree of delay discounting:

$$D(t) = \frac{1}{1+kt}, \qquad (8.2)$$

where t and k have the same meaning as in the DU model. Both models suggest that the discounted utility of a delayed payoff with monetary amount v and delay duration t equals

$$DU(v, t) = u(v)D(t), \qquad (8.3)$$

where $u(v)$ represents the instantaneous utility of the payoff if it occurred immediately and $D(t)$ denotes the discount function in either model. Furthermore, both models prescribe that, among a set of immediate or delayed payoffs, the payoff with the highest discounted utility should be preferred.

Despite the popularity of the DU model and hyperbolic discounting model, they are inadequate to capture the full range of observed patterns in behavioral studies on intertemporal choice. For example, it is well known that the DU model cannot accommodate the empirical finding of preference reversal in intertemporal choice, at least in its original form. To make the DU model capable of capturing the preference reversal, it has to be further assumed that larger payoffs suffer less from delay discounting than smaller payoffs, contradicting the DU model's assumption of unitary time preference. Similarly, recent work by Luhmann (2013) suggested that the discounting of delayed rewards does not follow the hyperbolic form specified by Equation 8.2. Specifically, the result of Luhmann's study showed that participants did become more patient when the front-end delay was increased, but not as patient as the hyperbolic discount function would suggest.

What is more important is that both the DU and hyperbolic discounting models assume a delay discounting perspective on intertemporal choice, which involves three implicit but questionable views on the topic, that is, the deterministic, static, and alternative-wise views. First of all, the deterministic view implies that each payoff has a fixed discounted utility across trials. Consequently, when the same set of payoffs are presented multiple times, a person should always prefer and choose the same payoff. However, as a form of preferential choice, intertemporal choice is very likely to be probabilistic as is risky choice (Rieskamp, 2008). Therefore, an appropriate model of intertemporal choice should be capable of making probabilistic rather than only deterministic predictions on choice responses. Second, the static view of the delay discounting perspective makes the DU and hyperbolic discounting models silent on the deliberation time underlying explicit intertemporal choice and thus is unable to explain response-time data. Consequently, dynamic intertemporal choice models, which provide an account for both choice and response-time data, are needed to improve our understanding of this important topic. Finally, the alternative-wise view of the delay discounting perspective suggests that each payoff is independently evaluated before a final choice is made. A number of studies by Read and colleagues (e.g., Roelofsma & Read, 2000; Scholten & Read, 2010; Scholten, Read, & Sanborn, 2014), however, showed that the empirical data actually favored an attribute-wise approach to intertemporal choice. As a result, we need distinct models that assume an attribute-wise instead of an alternative-wise view on the topic. In summary, the traditional delay discounting perspective is insufficient to provide appropriate explanations for various empirical findings on intertemporal choice, and thus new approaches should be explored to gain more insights into the topic.

8.1 Probabilistic Models of Intertemporal Choice

To examine whether intertemporal choice is actually probabilistic, dynamic, and attribute-wise, Dai and Busemeyer (2014) conducted three experiments and compared the fitting performance of various models with regard to the observed data. Participants in the experiments were required to choose between pairs of intertemporal options, where each choice pair was presented multiple times to detect choice variability. It turned out that all the participants switched their choice between one or more choice pairs when they were presented repeatedly, strongly supporting a probabilistic perspective on intertemporal choice. Subsequently, Dai and Busemeyer developed and compared a total of 57 probabilistic models of intertemporal choice in an attempt to find a single best model in terms of model fitting. All of the models could be categorized in terms of how they transformed objective value and time into subjective ones, their core theories, and their stochastic specifications. In what follows, we will describe each component in detail to show how different probabilistic models of intertemporal choice can be generated.

8.1.1 Transformations of Objective Value and Time

It has long been recognized that the subjective value or utility of a monetary payoff is neither identical nor even a linear function of its objective amount. Consequently, many choice models involve a utility function that transforms the objective amount of a payoff into its subjective value. The most popular form of transformation in this respect appears to be the power transformation involved in prospect theory (Kahneman & Tversky, 1979). This kind of transformation in general prescribes a nonlinear relationship between objective and subjective values. Similarly, the role of time perception in intertemporal choice has recently been increasingly emphasized in the literature (e.g., Takahashi, Oono, & Radford, 2008; Zauberman, Kyu Kim, Malkoc, & Bettman, 2009). For example, Zauberman et al. found that people's subjective perceptions of prospective duration are nonlinear and concave in objective time, and this disparity between objective and subjective times provides an alternative explanation for hyperbolic discounting. This suggests that an appropriate model of intertemporal choice should also assume a certain form of nonlinear transformation on objective time. As a result, Dai and Busemeyer (2014) explored models with either identity or power transformations of both objective value and time. In this way, the resultant set of competing models would include both previously popular models, such as the original DU and hyperbolic discounting models with identity time transformation, and recent models that also consider the impact of time perception.

8.1.2 Core Theories

The deterministic special case of a probabilistic model is called its core theory (Loomes & Sugden, 1995). Dai and Busemeyer (2014) examined probabilistic models of intertemporal choice built upon four types of core theories. Two of these were alternative-wise models derived from the exponential and hyperbolic discount functions (i.e., Equations 8.1 and 8.2), and the others were attribute-wise models assuming an attention-switch mechanism. By introducing a time transformation function into the exponential and hyperbolic discounting functions, respectively, the authors first generalized the DU model and hyperbolic discounting model to create two alternative-wise core theories. Specifically, according to the generalized DU model, a decision maker should prefer a smaller-but-sooner (SS) option, denoted as (v_s, t_s), against a larger-but-later (LL) option, denoted as (v_l, t_l), if and only if

$$d = DU_{LL} - DU_{SS} = u(v_l)exp(-kp(t_l)) - u(v_s)exp(-kp(t_s)) \quad (8.4)$$

is negative and prefer the LL option when d is positive. The function $p(t)$ in Equation 8.4 is the aforementioned time transformation function that transforms objective time duration, t, into its subjective perception, $p(t)$. Similarly, the generalized hyperbolic discounting model suggests that people should prefer the SS option when

$$d = DU_{LL} - DU_{SS} = \frac{v_l}{(1 + kp(t_l))} - \frac{u(v_s)}{(1 + kp(t_s))} \quad (8.5)$$

is negative and prefer the LL option when d is positive. Note that the generalized models are still deterministic and thus can serve as core theories of probabilistic intertemporal choice models. Note also that a couple of more complex hyperbolic discounting models, such as Rachlin's (2006) two-parameter hyperbola model and Myerson and Green's (1995) two-parameter hyperboloid model, are actually special cases of the generalized hyperbolic discounting model (i.e., Equation 8.5).

On the other hand, Dai and Busemeyer (2014) presented two attribute-wise deterministic models of intertemporal choice by exploiting an attention-switch mechanism borrowed from Decision Field Theory (DFT; Busemeyer & Townsend, 1993). Specifically, it was assumed that, when facing a choice between two intertemporal options, people would first make intra-attribute comparisons and then combine the results to make a decision. In addition, their attention was assumed to switch between the two attributes, that is, money and time, during the deliberation process. When people paid attention to the money attribute, the preference level for the LL option increased because it provided a higher amount of reward and thus was an advantageous option. By contrast, when the time or delay attribute was attended, preference shifted toward the SS option. The final decision was determined by the average of the two preferences weighted by the amounts of attention allocated to the relevant attributes. In summary, the alternative-wise models assume that people process intertemporal choice by evaluating each option independently and then comparing the independent evaluations to make a decision. To the contrary, the attribute-wise models suggest that each option is evaluated relative to the other option at an attribute level, and the attribute-wise comparisons are then combined for a final decision.

One natural issue arising from the attribute-wise approach to intertemporal choice is how the intra-attribute comparison is performed. Dai and Busemeyer (2014) examined two primary modes of comparison, that is, a direct comparison and a relative comparison. A direct comparison entails that the advantage/disadvantage of an option on a given attribute is evaluated in terms of the simple difference between the two attribute values. For example, when the identity utility function is used, the advantage on the money attribute for a payoff of twenty dollars in ten days over a payoff of ten dollars in five days is 20 − 10 = 10 units. By contrast, a relative comparison involves a proportional evaluation of the advantage/disadvantage. For the same pair of options mentioned earlier, the advantage of the LL option on the money attribute equals $\frac{20-10}{10} = 100\%$. Note that the local minimum on the money attribute is used as the normalizer when transforming direct advantage/disadvantages into relative ones. The same also holds for the time attribute. The rationale for this setting comes from previous research (Weber et al., 2007) showing that people tend to use the SS option as a reference point in intertemporal choice. In summary, according to the attribute-wise core theory with direct comparisons, a decision maker should prefer the LL option when

$$d = w(u(v_l) - u(v_s)) - (1-w)(p(t_l) - p(t_s)) \tag{8.6}$$

is positive and prefer the SS option when d is negative. The w parameter in Equation 8.6 represents the relative amount of attention to the money attribute and $(1-w)$ is the relative amount of attention to the delay attribute. It is worth noting that, according to this core theory, the direct differences are drawn after objective value and time are transformed into subjective ones. Similarly, the attribute-wise core theory with relative comparisons entails a preference for the LL option when

$$d = w(u(v_l) - u(v_s))/u(v_s) - (1-w)(p(t_l) - p(t_s))/p(t_s) \quad (8.7)$$

is positive and a preference for the SS option when d is negative.

8.1.3 Stochastic Specifications

To accommodate choice variability in empirical data, deterministic choice models should be extended so that they are capable of predicting moderate choice probabilities. A variety of stochastic specifications have been applied to deterministic risky choice models, such as the Cumulative Prospect Theory (Tversky & Kahneman, 1992), to generate probabilistic extensions (e.g., Stott, 2006). Similarly, Dai and Busemeyer (2014) extended their core theories by equipping them with different stochastic specifications so that they can be fit to the probabilistic intertemporal choice data and compared against each other with regard to their fitting performance. The following is a list of probabilistic models of intertemporal choice with different stochastic specifications explored by Dai and Busemeyer.

8.1.3.1 Constant Error Model

The constant error model (Harless & Camerer, 1994), which assumes a "trembling hand" mechanism for the choice variability in observed data, is the simplest possible probabilistic choice model. According to this model, people have a true preference between options, but there is a fixed probability that they choose the undesirable option from time to time. Let ε be the probability of "trembling hand" on each trial, then the choice probability of the truly preferred option is $1-\varepsilon$, and the choice probability of the other option is just ε. One distinct feature of such a model is that it predicts an abrupt change in choice probability around crossing points just like a deterministic choice model. Also, this type of model only allows for two fixed choice probabilities across choice pairs, that is, ε and $1-\varepsilon$ (and 0.5 if indifference between options is allowed).

8.1.3.2 Fechner Model

Like constant error models, Fechner models (Becker, DeGroot, & Marschak, 1963) also assume that people have true preferences among options. However, the latter attributes choice variability in observed data to random processing errors and thus predicts varying choice probabilities among different choice pairs (Loomes & Sugden, 1995). According to the original conceptualization of Fechner models, the choice probability of option A from a pair of options {A, B} is

$$Pr(A|\{A,B\}) = Pr(u_A - u_B + \varepsilon > 0) \tag{8.8}$$

in which u_A and u_B represent the true utilities of the two options, respectively, and ε denotes the random amount of processing error. The specific types of Fechner models examined by Dai and Busemeyer (2014) were logistic models that assumed a logistic distribution on processing error; in this case,

$$Pr(A|\{A,B\}) = 1/(1 + exp(-gd)), \tag{8.9}$$

where d represents the difference in true utility for alternative-wise models (i.e., Equations 8.4 and 8.5) or the weighted average of intra-attribute differences for attribute-wise models (i.e., Equations 8.6 and 8.7), and g is a free parameter reflecting the degree of choice variability. Note that the attribute-wise logistic models are a generalization of the original logistic models built upon the concept of utility.

8.1.3.3 Random Utility Model

Random utility models are another class of probabilistic choice models that accommodate choice variability by introducing random components into relevant deterministic utility models (e.g., Becker et al., 1963). The main difference between deterministic and random utility models lies in the way of assigning utility to each option. The former class assumes fixed utility for each option across repeated trials, whereas the latter class allows for different utilities from trial to trial. As a result, the former always predicts the same preference and choice across trials, but the latter is compatible with probabilistic choice patterns. According to a random utility model, the probability of choosing option A from a pair of options {A, B} is

$$Pr(A|\{A,B\}) = Pr(U_A - U_B > 0) \tag{8.10}$$

in which U_A and U_B are the random utilities of the two options, respectively.[1] One common practice in developing random utility models is to specify a reasonable joint distribution of the random utilities so that the exact probability of choosing each option can be derived from Equation 8.10. For example, we may assume that the utilities of two intertemporal options follow a bivariate normal distribution with independent components and same variances. This will lead to a widely adopted random utility model, that is, Thurstone's Case V model (Thurstone, 1927). Specifically, Thurstone's Case V model assumes that $U_{LL} - U_{SS} \sim N(d, \sigma^2)$, where d represents the mean difference in random utility between the two options and σ is a measure of variability in utility difference. With this joint distribution of random utilities, we have

$$Pr(LL|\{SS, LL\}) = \Phi(d/\sigma), \tag{8.11}$$

where Φ represents the standard normal cumulative distribution function. In general, a probabilistic model with a stochastic specification represented by Equation 8.11 is called a Probit model. Note again that when Equation 8.11 is used to generate attribute-wise probabilistic models (i.e., substituting the d parameter in Equation 8.11 with the right side of Equation 8.6 or 8.7), the resultant models are actually a generalization of the original random utility models.

In more complicated cases, different options may have different utility variances. Consequently, the parameter σ in Equation 8.11 may depend on attribute values of the options and other aspects of the model of concern. For example, Dai and Busemeyer (2014) tried a model that assumed that the longer an option is delayed, the more uncertain its random utility will be. Consequently, for alternative-wise models derived from Equations 8.4 and 8.5, the authors set

$$\sigma = \sqrt{c(p(t_s) + p(t_l))} \tag{8.12}$$

to formulate this assumption in which c is a free-scaling parameter to be estimated. For attribute-wise models based on Equations 8.6 and 8.7, the concept of utility (and thus utility variance) was no longer valid, but it was not difficult to derive a measure of σ from the attention-switch mechanism to generalize Equation 8.11. Specifically, it was assumed that the probability of sampling from a certain attribute at any time equals its relative attention weight, and this sampling process produces variability in instantaneous evaluation with a standard deviation equal to

$$\sigma = w(1-w)\sqrt{u(v_l) - u(v_s) + p(t_l) - p(t_s)} \tag{8.13}$$

for attribute-wise models with direct differences and

$$\sigma = w(1-w)\sqrt{\frac{u(v_l) - u(v_s)}{u(v_s)} + \frac{p(t_l) - p(t_s)}{p(t_s)}} \tag{8.14}$$

for attribute-wise models with relative differences. By replacing parameters d and σ in Equation 8.11 with Equations 8.4–8.7 and Equations 8.12–8.14, respectively, one could generate four more classes of probabilistic intertemporal choice models.

Yet another way to develop random utility models from deterministic core theories is to introduce variability into the principal parameter of the core theories. The resultant models are usually referred to as random preference models because each random realization of the principal parameter leads to a random preference relation among the options (Loomes & Sugden, 1995). To develop random preference models from the four core theories, Dai and Busemeyer (2014) assumed that the k parameter in Equations 8.4 and 8.5 and the w parameter in Equations 8.6 and 8.7 can vary from trial to trial. In other words, discount rates (for alternative-wise models) and attention weights (for attribute-wise models) were allowed to change across trials to accommodate choice variability in empirical data. Specifically, Dai and Busemeyer assumed that $exp(-k)$ in the generalized DU model follows a normal distribution truncated between zero and one, the k parameter in the generalized hyperbolic discounting model follows a log-normal distribution, and the attention weight parameter, that is, w, in the attribute-wise models follows a normal distribution truncated between zero and one. With these settings, various random preference models were generated and fit to the observed data.

8.1.3.4 Diffusion Model

The last class of probabilistic models examined by Dai and Busemeyer (2014) were diffusion models that differed fundamentally from the others. As a special case of sequential sampling models, diffusion models assume an evidence or preference accumulation process that eventually leads to the explicit choice. Consequently, they are capable of predicting both choice probability and distribution of decision times, whereas the other models examined by Dai and Busemeyer are all static and thus silent on the issue of decision time.

Diffusion models suggest that, at each time point, evidence for or against each option is sampled and accumulated until the preference strength for one option reaches a threshold first. This very option is then chosen and the decision time, together with the time for nondecisional components, determines the total response time. A diffusion model of binary choice usually involves five parameters. The first is the parameter of mean drift rate, d, which denotes the average rate of preference accumulation. The second parameter is the diffusion parameter, σ, which represents the standard deviation in the instantaneous preference accumulation rate. The third parameter, θ, represents the threshold on preference strength. The higher it is, the more time it requires to make a decision. The fourth parameter, z, reflects the initial preference level before the accumulation process starts. It provides a measure of bias toward a specific option. The final parameter, T_{er}, denotes the amount of nondecisional time that is required for predicting response-time distribution. The following formula specifies the choice probability of an option in a binary choice task given its parameter values:

$$Pr(d, \sigma, \theta, z) = \frac{1 - exp(-2d(\theta + z)/\sigma^2)}{1 - exp(-4d\theta/\sigma^2)}. \tag{8.15}$$

See Ratcliff (1978) and Busemeyer and Diederich (2009) for the formula of the probability distribution of the predicted distribution of decision times given the parameter values.

As for other stochastic specifications mentioned earlier, Dai and Busemeyer (2014) applied the stochastic specification of diffusion models to the four core theories to generate corresponding probabilistic intertemporal choice models. Specifically, Equations 8.4–8.7 were used to determine the value of parameter d in Equation 8.15, and σ was either treated as a free parameter or determined by Equations 8.12–8.14. The z parameter was fixed at zero to generate simplified unbiased models, and θ was set as proportional to σ. The latter setting is common practice when applying DFT to choice tasks. The rationale is that, when the instantaneous accumulation rate varies considerably across times (i.e., for a larger σ), a higher preference threshold is necessary to guarantee a relatively high choice probability for the option favored by the core theory (i.e., the option with a positive d). As a result, the actual free parameter to estimate was $\theta^* = \theta/\sigma$ instead of θ per se. According to the attribute-wise diffusion models, when facing a binary intertemporal choice, a decision maker samples as evidence the difference in either money or delay attribute one at a time and switches his or her attention between the two attributes during the preference accumulation process until the preference level of one option reaches a threshold first, thus triggering an explicit choice. A similar interpretation can be applied to the alternative-wise diffusion models, in which case a decision maker switches his or her attention between the two options with equal weights.

8.1.4 Other Probabilistic Intertemporal Choice Models

With the two sets of value and time transformation functions, four core theories, and seven stochastic specifications, Dai and Busemeyer (2014) generated 56 probabilistic models of intertemporal choice by factorially combining the three components. As mentioned earlier, the resultant set of models covers a wide range of existing ones as well as new models incorporating recent insights into intertemporal choice. However, this model set is by no means exhaustive. There are also alternative approaches to generating probabilistic intertemporal choice models. For example, the proportional difference (PD) model (González-Vallejo, 2002) can be conveniently applied to intertemporal choice to create probabilistic models thereof. According to the PD model, when choosing between two options with multiple attributes, people would process the intra-attribute differences in a proportional way and sum up the proportional differences to make an overall evaluation. For the pair of SS and LL options mentioned earlier, this means that

$$d = \frac{v_l - v_s}{v_l} - \frac{t_l - t_s}{t_l} \tag{8.16}$$

plays a critical role in determining the general tendency of choosing the LL option against the SS option. The quantity d in the equation can be interpreted as the amount of proportional advantage of the LL option over the SS option. The PD model further assumes that (1) the proportional advantage of an option is susceptible to a normally distributed error term with a mean of zero and a standard deviation of σ, and (2) each decision maker has a personal decision threshold δ that determines the amount of proportional advantage required for an option to be chosen more frequently. As a result, the choice probability of the LL option equals

$$Pr(LL|\{SS, LL\}) = \Phi\left(\frac{d-\delta}{\sigma}\right). \tag{8.17}$$

Furthermore, the choice probability of the SS option is just one minus that of the LL option.

Yet another promising model of intertemporal choice is the tradeoff model (Scholten & Read, 2010; Scholten et al., 2014). This model also assumes an attribute-wise approach to intertemporal choice, although the intra-attribute differences are supposed to be evaluated in a direct rather than proportional way. According to the tradeoff model, the outcome advantage of one option (e.g., that of an LL option for two delayed rewards) is weighted against the time advantage of the other option (e.g., that of an SS option for two delayed rewards), and the option with the greatest advantage should be chosen. For two delayed rewards, the outcome advantage of the LL option is referred to as the effective compensation and measured as $u(v_l) - u(v_s)$,[2] and the time advantage of the SS option is called the effective interval and measured as $w(t_l) - w(t_s)$. The intra-attribute weighing functions $u(v)$ and $w(t)$ in the tradeoff model play similar roles as the value and time transformation functions in the probabilistic models examined by Dai and Busemeyer (2014). On the other hand, $u(v)$ and $w(t)$ in the tradeoff model assume different functional forms than the value and time transformation functions by Dai and Busemeyer. Specifically, in the tradeoff model,

$$u(v) = \frac{1}{\gamma} \log(1 + \gamma v), \tag{8.18}$$

$$w(t) = \frac{1}{\tau} \log(1 + \tau t). \tag{8.19}$$

Furthermore, the tradeoff model suggests that the effective compensation is weighted against the effective interval using a tradeoff function, Q, and a decision maker will be indifferent between the SS and LL options if

$$Q(w(t_l) - w(t_s)) = u(v_l) - u(v_s). \tag{8.20}$$

Although presented initially as a deterministic model of intertemporal choice, the tradeoff model was later equipped with the following stochastic specification to make it probabilistic:

$$Pr(LL|\{SS, LL\}) = \frac{(u(v_l) - u(v_s))^{1/\varepsilon}}{(Q(w(t_l) - w(t_s)))^{1/\varepsilon} + (u(v_l) - u(v_s))^{1/\varepsilon}}. \quad (8.21)$$

The parameter ε in Equation 8.21 is a noise parameter; the larger it is, the more random the choice will be. Because the tradeoff model says nothing about the underlying processes leading to the explicit intertemporal choice, it is also static and thus can be applied only to the choice data.

8.1.5 Summary of Probabilistic Intertemporal Choice Models

In total, Dai and Busemeyer (2014) examined 57 probabilistic models of intertemporal choice, including 56 models generated by factorially combining the three components as well as the PD model for intertemporal choice. The tradeoff model was not investigated by Dai and Busemeyer, but was examined to the same degree in a couple of follow-up studies. Most of these models are static except for the various diffusion models, especially those derived from DFT assuming mechanisms of attention shift and sequential evidence accumulation. The static models were fit only to choice data because they provided no account for decision time, whereas the dynamic models were fit to both choice responses and response times to exploit more information from the observed data.

8.2 Results of Model Fitting and Comparisons

The various probabilistic models of intertemporal choice mentioned earlier were fit to empirical data from a number of experiments using maximum-likelihood estimation, and their performances were compared with one another (Dai, 2014; Dai & Busemeyer, 2014). These experiments were designed to examine a variety of phenomena in intertemporal choice, such as the common difference effect, the magnitude effect, and the nonadditivity in delay discounting. Choice pairs for investigating different phenomena usually had distinct structures. For example, choice pairs for examining the common difference effect had the same direct differences, but varying relative differences in delay duration. In contrast, choice pairs for the magnitude effect had the same relative differences, but varying direct differences in reward amount. Furthermore, in some studies, the SS options were always delayed whereas, in others they might be either immediate or delayed.

To partly address the issue of model complexity in selecting among competing models, Akaike Information Criterion (AIC) and Bayesian Information Criterion (BIC) indices were used as major measures of relative performance of the models. In general, attribute-wise models built upon the attention-shift mechanism (i.e., Equations 8.6 and 8.7) performed better than alternative-wise models generalized from the traditional DU and hyperbolic discounting models. Among attribute-wise models, those considering direct differences usually outperformed the corresponding models involving relative differences. Furthermore, dynamic models, that is, diffusion models assuming an evidence accumulation process, generally performed better than static models, such as Probit models, even when only choice data were fit. Results from follow-up studies (Dai, 2014) involving the tradeoff model also suggested that several diffusion models outperformed the tradeoff model. When both choice and response-time data were considered, the single best model appeared to be the attribute-wise diffusion model with direct differences, power transformations of objective value and time, and a varied σ contingent on attribute values of each choice pair and the attention weight parameter (i.e., Equation 8.13). Finally, constant error models that attribute choice variability to a "trembling hand" always performed poorly, if not the worst, in fitting the observed data.

The results of model fitting and comparisons listed earlier have a number of implications for understanding intertemporal choice. First, although the DU model has long been the standard model of intertemporal choice for economists and many psychologists adopt the hyperbolic discounting model in empirical studies, their implicit alternative-wise approach to intertemporal choice might be unrealistic, at least for choices between two single-dated outcomes. Instead, it seems that people tend to first compare the options within each attribute and then combine the results to make a decision. In other words, there is no "discounted utility" associated with each delayed payoff based on which an intertemporal choice is made. Second, when comparing options within an attribute, most people evaluate each option's advantage or disadvantage by simply taking the direct difference between the subjective values or times. The impact of relative differences seems to be negligible compared with that of direct differences. Third, DFT provides a solid foundation for developing dynamic and attribute-wise probabilistic models of intertemporal choice. Such models can predict not only choice probability of each option but also the related distribution of response times, with the winning model serving as an excellent example of this model class. The winning model can account for a number of empirical effects in intertemporal choice, such as the magnitude effect and common difference effect, as well as the observed relationship between choice proportions and response times, that is, choice pairs with moderate choice probabilities tending to require more response times than those with extreme choice probabilities. These capabilities give the winning model a remarkable advantage over traditional deterministic, alternative-wise, and static models of intertemporal choice, including the popular DU model and hyperbolic discounting model. Last, but not least, the "trembling hand" mechanism assumed by constant error models does not provide a good explanation for the probabilistic nature of intertemporal choice. When attribute values were manipulated to reveal various intertemporal choice effects, the change in choice probability was more systematic than what was expected from constant error models. Instead, the pattern of change was also highly contingent on the varying attribute values and the underlying processes.

8.3 Mental Architectures and Stopping Rules of Intertemporal Choice

The various probabilistic models of intertemporal choice described earlier also imply different mental architectures and stopping rules (Townsend & Ashby, 1983; Townsend, Yang, & Burns, 2011; Townsend, Yang, & Van Zandt, 2012). For example, the winning DFT model in Dai and Busemeyer (2014) assumes a coactive mental architecture by which difference in subjective value or time is sampled one at a time and sequentially accumulated into a single channel until the evidence level in that channel reaches a threshold. The order of sampling is essentially random, and the relative frequency of sampling either difference is determined by the corresponding attention weight. For intra-attribute comparisons, the winning model does not specify a particular processing type; either serial or parallel sampling of attribute values and related subjective perceptions across options is possible, followed by the operation of subtracting one from the other. The concept of stopping rule does not apply to the winning DFT model due to its coactive processing (Townsend & Nozawa, 1995). The same is true for all the other attribute-wise and alternative-wise diffusion models examined by Dai and Busemeyer.

For the static models, such as logistic models and the tradeoff model, the underlying mental architecture is not well defined since they are not intended to be process models of intertemporal choice. On the other hand, they do imply an exhaustive stopping rule, because these models stipulate that discounted utilities of both options or differences within both attributes are considered before a decision is made. The order of processing discounted utilities or intra-attribute differences is trivial in these models. In summary, all the aforementioned models assume virtually a random order of processing; the diffusion models suggest a coactive mental architecture, whereas the static models are mute on this issue. For those models with a clear specification of mental architecture and stopping rules, it is possible to empirically test the relevant assumptions.

Given that all the models presented so far adopt either an exhaustive stopping rule or a coactive mental architecture, it is natural to ask whether intertemporal choice can instead be processed in a self-terminating way. To answer this question, let us first look at how risky choice can be modeled using a self-terminating stopping rule. One such attempt is the priority heuristic (Brandstätter, Gigerenzer, & Hertwig, 2006), which was later generalized to create the probabilistic priority model (Rieskamp, 2008). According to the priority heuristic, when facing a choice between gambles, people will first consider the difference in minimum outcome between the gambles. If the difference is larger than one-tenth of the maximum outcome across the gambles, a decision is made to choose the gamble with a higher minimum outcome. Otherwise, people will proceed to process the difference in the probability of obtaining the minimum outcome. If the difference is larger than one-tenth, then people will choose the gamble with a lower probability of obtaining the minimum outcome. Finally, if neither of the previous two considerations leads to a decision, people will always choose the gamble with the highest maximum outcome. The same concept can be easily applied to intertemporal choice to make self-terminating models. Furthermore, the stochastic specification of the priority model can also be used to generate probabilistic models of intertemporal choice. Whether such models can achieve the same level of fitting performance as the previous winning model remains to be examined. It is worth noting that the priority model of risky choice turned out to perform worse in fitting empirical data than the corresponding model built upon DFT. Also, future theoretical and empirical research is necessary to develop a reasonable account of response-time for a priority model of intertemporal choice so that more information from empirical data can be utilized to distinguish between exhaustive and self-terminating intertemporal choice models.

8.4 Equivalence Between Intertemporal Choice Models

Yet another significant issue in developing intertemporal choice models is the potential equivalence between models presumably generated with distinct assumptions (see van der Maas, Molenaar, Maris, Kievit, & Borsboom, 2011, for examples related to item response theory). General equivalence of parallel and serial models has been intensively investigated by Townsend and colleagues (e.g., Anderson, 1976; Townsend, 1976; Townsend & Wenger, 2004). This might also occur with intertemporal choice models assuming different mental architectures and stopping rules. With regard to the model comparison by Dai and Busemeyer (2014), a more prominent possibility is the equivalence between probabilistic models with the same core theories, but different stochastic specifications. For example, Equation 8.15 specifies the choice probability of an option based on the assumption of diffusion processes. If we further assume that $z = 0$ (i.e., there is no initial bias toward choosing either option) and σ is fixed across trials, Equation 8.15 reduces to the following:

$$Pr(d, \sigma, \theta, z) = \frac{1}{1 + exp(-2d\theta/\sigma^2)}, \quad (8.22)$$

which is equivalent to the logistic function (i.e., Equation 8.9) given that $g = 2\theta/\sigma^2$. In other words, the diffusion model assuming no initial bias and fixed σ leads to the same prediction on choice probabilities as the logistic model that does not have a dynamic structure. If data exists only on choice responses, then these two models are indistinguishable. Fortunately, we can always set these two models apart by collecting response-time data as well. With data on both choices and response times, the logistic model can be discarded as an inadequate model or modified to develop prediction on response-time distribution so that these two models can be compared with regard to more information from the observed data.

When two models assume different core theories, but the same stochastic specification, it is possible that they make the same predictions on both choice probabilities and response-time distribution. In this case, collecting response-time data will no longer be sufficient to distinguish between the models. For example, the attribute-wise core theory with direct differences (i.e., Equation 8.6) might be re-expressed as

$$\begin{aligned} d &= w(u(v_l) - u(v_s)) - (1 - w)(p(t_l) - p(t_s)) \\ &= [wu(v_l) - (1 - w)p(t_l)] - [wu(v_s) - (1 - w)p(t_s)]. \end{aligned} \quad (8.23)$$

The right-hand side of Equation 8.23 suggests an alternative-wise core theory with the discounted utility of an option equal to

$$DU(v, t) = wu(v) - (1 - w)p(t). \quad (8.24)$$

If we further assume the stochastic specification of a diffusion model with fixed σ across trials, the resultant alternative-wise and attribute-wise models are not distinguishable, even if we have both choice and response-time data. It could always be argued that Equation 8.24 does not appear to be a reasonable formulation of discounted utility, but this is a different issue. The good news is that the winning model from Dai and Busemeyer (2014) assumes varied σ across trials. In this case, σ is dependent on attribute values and an attention weight parameter as specified by Equation 8.13. By contrast, the equation for the corresponding alternative-wise diffusion model with regard to the σ parameter is

$$\sigma = \{[wu(v_l) - (1 - w)p(t_l)] - [wu(v_s) - (1 - w)p(t_s)]\}/2. \quad (8.25)$$

Clearly Equation 8.13 differs from Equation 8.25 and, thus, the two related models in general make distinct predictions on both choice and response time. However, the issue of model equivalence may loom larger if future endeavors in developing intertemporal choice models suggest a different type of model that is susceptible to this issue.

8.5 Concluding Comments

Intertemporal choice has long been investigated from a deterministic, static, and alternative-wise perspective, leading to the widely adopted DU model and hyperbolic discounting model. Recent theoretical and empirical work (e.g., Dai & Busemeyer, 2014; Scholten & Read, 2010; Scholte et al., 2014), however, suggests a paradigmatic shift toward a probabilistic, dynamic, and attribute-wise approach to the topic. In this chapter, we review a large number of deterministic and probabilistic models of intertemporal choice and present the results of fitting the probabilistic models to empirical data. Both the empirical data and results of model comparisons suggest that intertemporal choice is essentially probabilistic just like risky choice, and it should be understood through a dynamic lens. Consequently, future research should focus on process models of intertemporal choice that provide an account for both choice probability and response-time distribution. In this way, we can understand intertemporal choice more deeply, and different models can be distinguished with more information from empirical data.

Notes

1. Equation 8.10 is built upon the assumptions of a two-alternative, forced-choice paradigm and zero probability of having no preference between the two options. See Regenwetter and Davis-Stober (2012) for a more general form of random utility models.
2. Note that here we use $u(v)$ instead of $v(x)$ as in the original formulation to make consistent notations in this chapter.

References

Anderson, J. R. (1976). *Language, memory, and thought*. Hillsdale, NJ: Lawrence Erlbaum Associates.

Becker, G. M., DeGroot, M. H., & Marschak, J. (1963). Stochastic models of choice behavior. *Behavioral Science, 8*, 41–55.

Brandstätter, E., Gigerenzer, G., & Hertwig, R. (2006). The priority heuristic: Making choices without tradeoffs. *Psychological Review, 113*, 409–432.

Busemeyer, J. R., & Diederich, A. (2009). *Cognitive modeling*. Thousand Oaks, CA: Sage Publications.

Busemeyer, J. R., & Townsend, J. T. (1993). Decision field theory: A dynamic-cognitive approach to decision making in an uncertain environment. *Psychological Review, 100*, 432–459.

Dai, J. (2014). *Using test of intransitivity to compare competing static and dynamic models of intertemporal choice* (Unpublished doctoral dissertation). Indiana University, Bloomington.

Dai, J., & Busemeyer, J. R. (2014). A probabilistic, dynamic, and attribute-wise model of intertemporal choice. *Journal of Experimental Psychology: General, 143*, 1489–1514.

Frederick, S., Loewenstein, G., & O'Donoghue, T. (2002). Time discounting and time preference: A critical review. *Journal of Economic Literature, 40*(2), 351–401.

González-Vallejo, C. (2002). Making trade-offs: A probabilistic and context-sensitive model of choice behavior. *Psychological Review, 109*, 137–155.

Harless, D., & Camerer, C. F. (1994). The predictive utility of generalized expected utility theories. *Econometrica, 62*, 1251–1289.

Kahneman, D., & Tversky, A. (1979). Prospect theory: An analysis of decision under risk. *Econometrica, 47*, 263–291.

Loomes, G., & Sugden, R. (1995). Incorporating a stochastic element into decision theories. *European Economic Review, 39*, 641–648.

Luhmann, C. C. (2013). Discounting of delayed rewards is not hyperbolic. *Journal of Experimental Psychology: Learning Memory and Cognition, 39*(4), 1274–1279.

Mazur. (1987). An adjusting procedure for studying delayed reinforcement. In M. J. Commons, J. E. Mazur, J. A. Nevin, & H. Rachlin (Eds.), *Quantitative analysis of behavior: Vol 5. the effect of delay and intervening events on reinforcement value* (pp. 55–73). Mahwah, NJ: Lawrence Erlbaum Associates.

Myerson, J., & Green, L. (1995). Discounting of delayed rewards: Models of individual choice. *Journal of Experimental Analysis of Behavior, 64*, 263–276.

Rachlin, H. (2006). Notes on discounting. *Journal of Experimental Analysis of Behavior, 85*, 425–435.

Ratcliff, R. (1978). A theory of memory retrieval. *Psychological Review, 85*, 59–108.

Regenwetter, M., & Davis-Stober, C. P. (2012). Behavioral variability of choice versus structural inconsistency of preferences. *Psychological Review, 119*, 408–416.

Rieskamp, J. (2008). The probabilistic nature of preferential choice. *Journal of Experimental Psychology: Learning Memory and Cognition, 34*, 1446–1465.

Roelofsma, P. H. M. P., & Read, D. (2000). Intransitive intertemporal choice. *Journal of Behavioral Decision Making, 13*, 161–177.

Samuelson, P. (1937). A note on measurement of utility. *The Review of Economic Studies, 4*, 155–161.

Scholten, M., & Read, D. (2010). The psychology of intertemporal tradeoffs. *Psychological Review, 117*, 925–944.

Scholten, M., Read, D., & Sanborn, A. (2014). Weighing outcomes by time or against time? Evaluation rules in intertemporal choice. *Cognitive Science, 38*, 399–438.

Stott, H. P. (2006). Cumulative prospect theory's functional menagerie. *Journal of Risk and Uncertainty, 32*, 101–130.

Takahashi, T., Oono, H., & Radford, M. H. B. (2008). Psychophysics of time perception and intertemporal choice models. *Physica A, 387*, 2066–2074.

Thurstone, L. L. (1927). The law of comparative judgment. *Psychological Review, 34*, 273–286.

Townsend, J. T. (1976). Serial and within-stage independent parallel model equivalence on the minimum completion time. *Journal of Mathematical Psychology, 14*, 219–238.

Townsend, J. T., & Ashby, F. G. (1983). *Stochastic modeling of elementary psychological processes*. Cambridge, UK: Cambridge University Press.

Townsend, J. T., & Nozawa, G. (1995). Spatio-temporal properties of elementary perception: An investigation of parallel, serial, and coactive theories. *Journal of Mathematical Psychology, 39*, 321–359.

Townsend, J. T., & Wenger, M. J. (2004). The serial-parallel dilemma: A case study in a linkage of theory and method. *Psychonomic Bulletin & Review, 11*, 391–418.

Townsend, J. T., Yang, H., & Burns, D. M. (2011). Experimental discrimination of the world's simplest and most antipodal models: The parallel-serial issue. In H. Colonius & E. Dzhafarov (Eds.), *Descriptive and normative approaches to human behavior in the advanced series on mathematical psychology* (pp. 271–302). Singapore: World Scientific.

Townsend, J. T., Yang, H., & Van Zandt, T. (2012). Information processing architectures: Fundamental issues. In J. D. Wright (Ed.), *Encyclopedia of social and behavioral sciences* (pp. 7460–7464). Oxford: Pergamon.

Tversky, A., & Kahneman, D. (1992). Advances in prospect theory: Cumulative representation of uncertainty. *Journal of Risk and Uncertainty, 5*, 297–323.

van der Maas, H. L. J., Molenaar, D., Maris, G., Kievit, R. A., & Borsboom, D. (2011). Cognitive psychology meets psychometric theory: On the relation between process models for decision making and latent variable models for individual differences. *Psychological Review, 118*, 339–356.

Weber, E. U., Johnson, E. J., Milch, K. F., Chang, H., Brodscholl, J. C., & Goldstein, D. G. (2007). Asymmetric discounting in intertemporal choice: A query-theory account. *Psychological Science, 18*, 516–523.

Zauberman, G., Kyu Kim, B., Malkoc, S. A., & Bettman, J. R. (2009). Discounting time and time discounting: Subjective time perception and intertemporal preferences. *Journal of Marketing Research, 46*, 543–556.

9 Variations on the Theme of Independence
Tasks and Effects of Stroop, Garner, and Townsend

Daniel Algom

The objects that inhabit people's perceptual world are many dimensional. The books on your shelf come in certain colors, sizes, and weights; the cars on our roads vary in color, shape, size, and speed. Two fundamentally important problems ensue. The first concerns selective attention to an individual attribute of the perceived object. Although the objects are multidimensional, in everyday life, people typically attend to a single dimension that is relevant to the task at hand. When crossing the road, people must attend to the speed of the approaching car, ignoring momentarily attributes such as the car's color or make. When buying a car, by contrast, the relevant attribute may well be the car's color. One should realize that a modicum of ability to attend selectively is essential for performing the simplest of tasks. In the absence of selectivity, one cannot concentrate on reading the newspaper in the cafeteria, comprehend a presentation in class, or conduct a conversation with a friend. Facility at isolating the target attribute is indispensable for adaptation and survival. The question of consequence is this: Can one focus on the target information, excluding distractions from other, task-irrelevant pieces of information? If one cannot, how do failures of target selection arise? And, once they do, how does one measure the degree of the failure to attend selectively?

The second fundamental problem ensuing from the fact that the objects in the field of view are many dimensional is determining how the various dimensions combine in perceptual processing. How is your perception of the car's speed affected by your perception of its size? Is your perception of the book's height contingent on your perception of its width? In general, how do the constituent dimensions combine to produce your perception of the object called book? These questions converge on the notion of perceptual independence. At an informal level, the notion of independence in perception is easily stated. The components Height and Width of the book are perceived independently if the perception of one attribute does not depend on the perception of the other attribute, and hence they do not interact in perceptual processing of the book. A more formal definition can be based on the multiplication rule of probability: Height and Width are independent in perception if and only if the joint probability of perceiving them equals the product of the probabilities of perceiving each component separately. This rule already provides a way for assessing the presence of perceptual independence, although many others are possible.

It is worth pausing to reexamine the questions posed with respect to selective attention and then with respect to perceptual independence. A remarkable feature is their close affinity, tractable to the following logical contingency. Selective attention to an individual attribute of the object is possible only if perceptual independence is present across the various attributes of the object. Or, in the absence of perceptual independence, selective attention to any one attribute is impossible. Perceptual independence is a necessary attendant condition for the possibility of selective attention.

Given the kinship, it may come as a surprise that the two concepts have heretofore led separate lives. For the sake of proper disclosure, I borrowed the set of questions with respect to selective attention from the article by Melara and Algom (2003), introducing the Tectonic Theory of Stroop effects. I borrowed the second set of questions from the article by Ashby and Townsend (1986), inaugurating the General Recognition Theory of perceptual independence. The term perceptual independence is missing from the Melara and Algom article, and the term selective attention is missing from the Ashby and Townsend article. It is noticeable in this respect that Ashby and Townsend do not mention the Stroop effect, psychology's oldest and best known measure of selectivity (commendably, they do discuss several Garner effects). My goal in this chapter is to rectify this situation. In particular, my goal is first to make explicit the argument that perceptual independence is necessary for selective attention and, then, to explicate the implications of this contingency for measurement. Consequently, I explore the overlapping nature of the operationalization of the pertinent concepts in the domains of selective attention and perceptual independence.

A note of caution seems warranted at this point. The close association between selective attention and perceptual independence pertains to the pertinent theoretical constructs. The association granted, the practical experimental approaches and statistics developed to measure the respective constructs differ as a matter of course. I highlight these differences, but they should not obscure the relationships that exist at the conceptual level.

9.1 Selective Attention and Perceptual Independence: A Bit of History

Taking a long view of the history of psychology, both selective attention and perceptual independence are newcomers into the discipline of cognition, although the former is older than the latter. Selective attention features prominently in William James's celebrated chapter on attention (James, 1890). Consider the opening sentences of the chapter: "Strange to say, so patent a fact as . . . selective attention has received hardly any notice from psychologists of the English empiricist school ... in the pages of such writers as Locke, Hume, Hartley, the Mills, and Spencer the word hardly occurs" (James 1890, p. 265). It is the stated goal of James to rectify the situation and to introduce the concept into the science of psychology. He did so with characteristic persuasiveness and great success. Of more significance, James's famous definition of attention is that of selective attention. Thus, "Focalization [is] its essence. It implies withdrawal from some things in order to deal effectively with others" (James 1890, p. 266). Successful selection means avoiding "distraction" (James's term!). James's definition of selective attention is essentially governing its measurement today: the ability to focus on the task-relevant attribute while ignoring distraction from task-irrelevant information. The Stroop (1935) and the Garner (1974) measures of selectivity are direct offsprings of James's view.

Perceptual independence is a younger concept. I was not able to find the term or the concept in James's *Principles of Psychology* (James, 1890). I note though that the term "independence" appears in David Hume's "Treatise" (Hume 1739/1962), scrutinized extensively by philosophers. However, Hume uses the term to stress the (relative) freedom of perception from mere sensory datum or early sense impression. Hume also employs the adjective "separable" (e.g., Hume 1739/1962 p. 69), which can be construed, with excusable exaggeration, as a precursor of Garnerian separability.

Early discussions of independence within psychology date back to the 1960s and are closely associated with an unresolved issue (at the time) in information theory (Attneave, 1959; Garner, 1962, 1974). When does the addition of a dimension to a given set of stimuli improve their identification, or, in the language of information theory, increase total transmitted information? For example, people can accurately identify 6 lines that vary in length, but they can identify close to 14 such lines once we paint each in a different color. However, in other cases, adding a dimension does not improve identification. For example, adding a different dose of a new chemical to each of a given set of chemicals may not affect identification (the taste thus created may well act as a single new perceptual dimension). It was at this juncture that the notion of perceptual independence emerged as a diagnostic tool for deciding when an added dimension does or does not improve performance. Garner was among the first students of information theory to notice the critical role of independence: Only "if any two communication acts provide completely independent information, then the total information provided is simply the sum of the two separate amounts of information" (Garner 1962, p. 85). And again, "as long as the dimensions are perceptually independent, then addition of new dimensions will increase total discrimination and information transmission" (Garner 1962, p. 127). Garner's book also marks the first appearance of the notion of perceptual independence in a major contribution (but see Eriksen & Hake, 1955; Tanner Jr., 1956). The term appears as a subtitle in a couple of chapters and is discussed substantively in yet other chapters.

Of most significance, the concept is not studied as an isolated (if interesting) phenomenon, but rather it is incorporated into a larger theoretical framework.

Having identified a function of perceptual independence, Garner was increasingly drawn to exploring the concept of independence in ever-greater depth. In a significant (and grossly underreported) effort, Garner and Lee (1962) interrogated several possible models of perceptual independence. Eventually, Garner's continual interest led to the seminal Garner and Morton (1969) paper, concluding that perceptual independence is not a unitary concept and hence that it cannot be assessed by any one measurement procedure. Subsequently, Townsend has taken Garner's lead, uncovering, stratum by stratum, the multiple sources of perceptual independence. In their formative study, Ashby and Townsend (1986) reached the same conclusion as did Garner: Perceptual independence is not a unitary concept; indeed, it is not even an empirically observable concept. At best, it can be supported, to various degrees, by empirical measures. A major contribution of Ashby and Townsend's General Recognition Theory (GRT) has been the integration of these various measures into a tight network.

A less salutary side effect of these explorations has been to render the relationship between selective attention and perceptual independence fuzzy, if not altogether opaque. If perceptual independence is multifaceted and can be assessed in a variety of ways, and if selectivity, too, can be measured by alternative means, it is not clear just how a particular pair of measures carries the connection. Nevertheless, the network of measures notwithstanding, the logical relationship between the selectivity of attention and perceptual independence is inescapable. In this instance, too, Garner was the first theorist to notice the relationship. For one illustration, Garner pondered the property of a set of stimuli "that allows the subject to attend selectively in such a way that he obtains independent information" (Garner 1962, p. 87). In the Garner and Morton (1969) paper, too, there is a (brief) reference to Broadbent (1958) filter processes in the context of models of perceptual independence. These inchoate ideas have motivated the growing acknowledgment of the association. The title of the relevant chapter in the Macmillan and Creelman (2005) book on detection theory includes the twin terms, "attention and [perceptual] interaction" (p. 187). The authors then proceed to note that "classification designs are extensively used to study two important topics: (a) independence versus interaction between . . . aspects of a stimulus, and (b) [selective] attention" (p. 187). Notably, in the end of the chapter, the authors concluded that "loss due to attention depends on whether the dimensions on which the stimuli vary are independent or interacting" (Macmillan & Creelman 2005, p. 209). With this much granted, the association is yet to be worked out in sufficient detail. This chapter is a step in that direction.

The selection-independence yoke, I maintain, is a key datum of human information processing because it bridges theorems, measures, and observations from two traditions. The logical implications, I repeat, are compelling: Selective attention is possible only in the presence of perceptual independence in some sense of the term. In this chapter, I address this "some sense" or meaning with respect to three widely employed measures of selectivity and independence: the Stroop effect, Garner interference, and perceptual separability. The first two have been conceived within the tradition of selective attention, whereas the third comes from the tradition of independence discussed within the structure of the GRT (cf. Ashby & Townsend, 1986; Kadlec & Townsend, 1992a, 1992b).

Concerning the three measures, one should note the following corollary: Given the linkage of selectivity and independence, measures of selective attention simultaneously bear on the presence of perceptual independence. For example, the absence of Stroop or Garner effects (i.e., good selectivity of attention) implies the presence of perceptual independence in (at least) one of its empirical incarnations. Of course, this statement is contingent on the presence of decisional separability, a condition assumed to hold under many a standard testing.

9.2 General Recognition Theory and the Selectivity of Attention

I assume some familiarity with the theory in the current discussion, especially as acquaintance with the GRT now extends beyond the close-knit community of mathematical psychologists. The current synopsis is meant to restate the basic assumptions, focusing on the definition of several key GRT notions. I consider then the relationship between GRT and (measures of) selective attention.

Following signal detection theory (SDT; Graham, Kramer, & Yager, 1987; Green & Swets, 1966; Macmillan & Creelman, 2005; Swets, Tanner Jr., & Birdsall, 1961; Tanner Jr., 1956), the perceptual effect produced by a given stimulus does not remain constant over its repeated presentations. If the stimulus is composed of two dimensions, the trial-to-trial variation can be captured by a bivariate probability distribution of the percepts. Suppose that four stimuli are created by the factorial combination of the binary levels of two dimensions. The perceptual features (the means and variances on each dimension, as well as their covariance or correlation) determine then the (relative) placement of each distribution in the pertinent perceptual space. A convenient representation is created by slicing the distributions at a fixed value of probability, thereby creating equal likelihood contours for each. With bivariate normal distributions, these equal density contours are always circles or ellipses with their major and minor axes aligned with the coordinate axes. If (a) the covariance term is zero and (b) the variances are equal, the contours are circles, otherwise they are ellipses. For the latter, when the variances are unequal, the contours are wider in the direction of one of the coordinate axes. With a nonzero covariance, the degree of correlation determines the slope of the major axis.

Following SDT further, the percept produced by a given stimulus on a given presentation passes through a decision process that determines the response. This process is captured within GRT by a perceptual space that is parsed via decision bounds into regions associated each with a different response. These decision bounds, like the response criteria in ordinary one-dimensional SDT, are lines or curves that separate one response region from another. On a trial, the response to the stimulus depends on the region that the pertinent percept happens to fall.

The central assertion of GRT is that the generic concept of perceptual independence is neither unitary nor observable. Three theoretical notions of independence are identified: perceptual independence (in a definite sense), perceptual separability, and decisional separability. These notions, too, are unobservable, but they can often be evaluated by features in the data. These data typically issue from an identification experiment entailing the factorial combination of the binary values of a pair of dimensions (resulting in four two-dimensional stimuli).

Perceptual independence holds for a pair of components in a stimulus if and only if the respective perceptual effects are statistically independent. When the probability distribution is bivariate normal, this definition means that the covariance parameter is zero. Consequently, the contour of equal likelihood for this stimulus is a circle or an ellipse in which the major and minor axes are parallel to the coordinate axes. Note that perceptual independence is a property of a single stimulus (i.e., it can hold for one stimulus in the matrix but not for another). *Measurement*: The empirical property most closely associated with perceptual independence, sampling independence, derives from the multiplication rule of probability. Sampling independence in a two-dimensional stimulus holds if and only if the probability of reporting both dimensional features is equal to the probability of reporting one feature (across all levels of the other dimension) times the probability of reporting the other feature (across all levels of the first dimension). In other words, the joint probability of two perceptual events equals the product of the marginal probabilities of each event—if the events are independent. I note in passing that a case has been made recently for replacing "sampling independence" by "report independence" to highlight that it is a measure based on what the observer reports and not directly on perceptual processes. Finally, perceptual independence comprises a symmetric relationship, applying equally to both dimensions. The other two theoretical concepts can be asymmetric with respect to the constituent dimensions.

Perceptual separability holds if the perceptual effects of a given level of one dimension do not depend on the level of the other dimension.

Consequently, perceptual separability is a property of the entire set of stimuli. This relation need not be symmetric: One dimension can be perceptually separable from another dimension, but the reverse may not hold. *Measurement*: The empirical procedure most closely associated with perceptual separability is an SDT sensitivity analysis performed with respect to the marginal distributions. In particular, if one dimension is perceptually separable from the other dimension, then the marginal d's for this dimension will be equal across levels of the other dimension (see Theorem 8.4, Kadlec & Townsend, 1992b). Another test with an intuitive association with perceptual separability is marginal response invariance. Marginal response invariance does not employ SDT analysis, but rather refers directly to the data. Marginal response invariance for one dimension holds across the levels of the other dimension if and only if the probability of recognizing the first dimension does not depend on the level of the second dimension. When two dimensions are perceptually separable from one another, a rectangular configuration of the means (or the contours around the means) of the four stimuli results. In general, perceptual separability is what determines the position of the stimuli in the perceptual space.

Finally, *decisional separability* holds if and only if the decision about the level of one dimension does not depend on the perceptual effects associated with levels of the other dimension. Decisional separability, too, can be symmetric or asymmetric. *Measurement*: The empirical procedure most closely associated with decisional separability is an SDT response-bias analysis performed with respect to the marginal distributions. For example, if decisional separability holds for both dimensions and perceptual separability holds for one of the dimensions, then the marginal βs for that dimension will be equal across levels of the other dimension (see Theorem 8.5, Kadlec & Townsend, 1992b).

The network of GRT theorems (Ashby & Townsend, 1986; Kadlec & Townsend, 1992a, 1992b) relate the three theoretical aspects of independence to the various empirical properties observed in the data. Typically, the presence of a theoretical feature is a sufficient condition for observing a given empirical property, but the presence of the same feature does not comprise a necessary condition for that empirical observation. In general, the logical implications go from the unobservable theoretical aspects to the observable measures. Nevertheless, positive observation of a given empirical property provides weak support for the presence of the relevant theoretical feature in the sense that the data do not falsify it (when they could have falsified it). In this sense, if sampling independence holds, support for perceptual independence is indicated. Similarly, equal marginal d's for a dimension across levels of a second dimension provides support for perceptual separability (for the first dimension). By contrast, the data can logically imply the failure of a theoretical feature. Thus unequal d's in the previous example do imply the failure of perceptual separability.

9.2.1 GRT as an Enabler of Selective Attention

GRT is seldom presented in the context of selective attention (but see Ashby & Townsend, 1986, pp. 163–166). However, I will show that it plays a pivotal role in that context.

First, consider the typical experimental task used in GRT studies. It is identification, entailing full report of the momentary values of both dimensions. If the tested dimensions are color and shape, the participant reports on each trial the specific color and the specific shape of the presented stimulus. Clearly, this task is that of divided attention, not of selective attention. It already defeats the possibility of selective attention to any one dimension in the GRT experiment. Selective attention, one recalls, refers to exclusive focusing on a single, task-relevant dimension, while ignoring the task-irrelevant dimension. In the GRT task, there are no relevant and irrelevant dimensions—both dimensions are relevant and must be attended in order to perform in the experiment. This feature of the GRT task has been largely overlooked or downplayed in most presentations.

This brief scrutiny makes it clear that the GRT experiment itself cannot be used to test selectivity. However, the GRT results play a role in assessing the possibility of selective attention in other contexts. Suppose that the dimensions of color word and ink color are subjected to full identification within the framework of a GRT experiment (cf. Kadouri-Labin, 2007). Suppose further that perceptual independence is supported by the data such that sampling independence is found for all of the color-word combinations with decisional separability in force. Given the strong support for perceptual independence, exclusive focus on any one of the constituent dimensions is possible (although it is not strictly mandated by the sheer presence of perceptual independence). In other words, it is possible that the participant will be able to name ink colors without suffering intrusions from the task-irrelevant words. Given the GRT results, one can expect (but one is not compelled by logic to expect) the absence of a Stroop effect (to be defined) for these color-word stimuli (cf. Algom, Dekel, & Pansky, 1996; Eidels, Townsend, & Algom, 2010; Melara, & Algom, 2003; Pansky & Algom, 1999, 2002; Sabri, Melara, & Algom, 2002). Note that I ignore for the moment the difference between non-speeded GRT responses and speeded Stroop responses. For another example, suppose that perceptual separability for color is supported within the GRT with respect to shape (such that the marginal d' for color remains invariant across shapes and that some other conditions hold). Given this GRT result, the absence of Garner interference (to be defined) and presence of Garnerian separability for color with respect to shape are likely (although not strictly mandated by the GRT results) when the same stimuli are exposed for this test of selective attention.

At this point, let me restate the logical relationship asserted at the outset: The presence of good selective attention implies the presence of perceptual independence. Note that I do not argue the converse—namely, that the presence of perceptual independence implies the presence of good selective attention. This explains my guarded comments with respect to the pertinent conclusions in the previous examples. Because perceptual independence is logically prior to selective attention, the inferences are unreservedly valid when they proceed in the other direction. Nevertheless, there is weak support for the predictions as they are stated in the sense that they are not falsified (when they could have been falsified by violation of perceptual independence/separability).

The GRT data form then a powerful basis for enabling (or disabling) selective attention. Recall, too, that perceptual independence and/or perceptual separability (when they hold) are attained under quite inauspicious circumstances. These markers tap autonomous performance (per dimension) in the face of trial-to-trial variation in both dimensions. The difficulty is compounded by the request to respond to both dimensional values. Perceptual independence/separability obtained in this situation is all the more impressive. It documents considerable analytic capacity on the part of the observer that can be expressed, in turn, as good selectivity (in other tests).

This selection-independence picture is complicated by the fact that all species of independence are not tapped by the GRT. A hallmark of the GRT experiment is random trial-to-trial variation in both dimensional values. The rich network of GRT notions, measures, and theorems are derived under this regime of incessant variation. However, a trivial source for the breakdown of perceptual separability can be this variation itself. This source, one notes, cannot be tested within the GRT framework simply because variation is always present. Suppose that color (red, green) and shape (circle, triangle) are the dimensions tested in a GRT identification experiment and that interest is focused on perceptual separability for color. Now perceptual separability for color may fail for no other reason than the random variation in shape that the observer was unable to ignore or filter out. This source can be tapped by considering a pair of control conditions in which shape is held constant (at circle or at triangle) throughout the experimental trials (responding to shape is gratuitous in these "shape constant" conditions, of course). Note that the pair of "shape constant" conditions still permit the calculation of marginal d's for color (between red and green once with circle and once with triangle as the constant irrelevant stimulus) as well as the calculation of marginal response invariance (again, for each color across the two shapes). Therefore, perceptual separability can be assessed in the control conditions (given that decisional separability holds). If perceptual separability is supported in the control conditions but fails in the GRT experiment, then irrelevant variation is implicated for its failure in the GRT experiment (cf. Algom & Edelstein, 1998).

The last point is notable. The breakdown of separability by irrelevant variation is not tested within the GRT structure, but irrelevant variation forms a major tool for assaying selectivity, the Garner paradigm. An immediate corollary is that GRT separability and Garnerian separability are not fully comparable measures of independence or separability in perception.

Throughout this discussion, I referred to the critical role of decisional separability. The conclusions with respect to the selectivity-independence association are contingent on the presence of decisional separability. Recently however, Silbert and Thomas (2013) identified serious problems of indeterminacy with respect to decisional separability. The authors showed that when linear bounds do not satisfy decisional separability within the framework of a given model, there always exists an alternative model that does. Because the two models make the same predictions (relying on the same data), decisional separability is not testable within the standard GRT identification experiment. I cannot expand on Silbert and Thomas's challenge within the confines of this chapter (mean-shift integrality, rotation, and affine- and shear-transformation are key concepts in their development); it is clear though that their conclusions pose a threat to the validity of GRT. The current argument is also affected: If one cannot identify with certainty decisional separability, then perceptual separability and independence are also suspect.

A few specific results in Silbert and Thomas's development should nonetheless give one pause. Although inferences based on marginal SDT analysis (comparisons of d's and of βs or cs, measures of sensitivity and response bias, respectively) are suspect on grounds of uniqueness, those based on marginal response invariance are informative and valuable. Moreover, Silbert and Thomas (2013) identified a hitherto unnoticed relationship between marginal response invariance and the parameters of marginal SDT analysis: If the former holds, the latter are equal. A final important result for the current interest concerns perceptual separability. Although the presence of perceptual separability in the initial model is not unique (a transformation imposing decisional separability no longer entails perceptual separability), its absence practically is. One cannot transform (linearly) the data so that the resulting model entails separability or independence when those were absent initially.

What are the implications of the Silbert and Thomas (2013) development for the current argument connecting selective attention to GRT separability and independence? Clearly, one must be very circumspect when basing inferences on marginal SDT results. A straightforward solution of sorts (and one recommended by Silbert and Thomas) is to assume decisional separability, given that this assumption is "practically useful and less presumptive than assumptions of perceptual separability and independence" (Silbert & Thomas, 2013, p. 15). In this case, of course, all GRT theorems and the current argument stand unchanged. Another consequence is the augmented role of marginal response invariance: If it holds, then marginal values of d' and c are (should be) equal so that perceptual separability is (weakly) supported. Finally, violation of perceptual separability is (practically) unique, so that this result also facilitates analysis (e.g., one expects appreciable effects of Garner and Stroop).

For a final take on this issue, I note that a recent review of GRT asserts that the Silbert and Thomas challenge actually is "not catastrophic" (Ashby & Soto, 2015, p. 18). Ashby and Soto offer several insights and remedies, one of which is augmenting GRT by additional experimental manipulations that ameliorate the difficulty of decidability. It is fair to note though that Silbert and Thomas themselves suggest using experiments outside the GRT protocol to enable "explicit modeling of possible failures of decisional separability" (Silbert & Thomas, 2013, p. 15). This solution opens up a surprising role for the Stroop and Garner effects discussed in this assay. Among their other functions, Stroop and Garner studies can serve as part of the extra-GRT arsenal of experiments, helping to specify decisional separability in a unique fashion.

Finally, I alluded to the difference in response mode that complicates the selection-independence complementarity. The response measure is accuracy in GRT but it is reaction time (RT) in the great bulk of selectivity paradigms. Harnessing RT as a response measure within the GRT framework has been attempted by Ashby and Maddox (1994), Maddox and Ashby (1996), and more recently by Townsend, Houpt, and Silbert (2012), but neither avenue fully alleviates problems of comparison. Using accuracy as the response measure means that the stimuli are imperfectly discriminable in any GRT study. This also means that, in most applications, stimuli do not appear as they do in natural extra-experimental settings, but rather are degraded by various means (e.g., short exposure, visual noise, inconspicuous contours, increased similarity). These manipulations introduce a certain atmosphere of artificiality into the experiment that can pose a threat to ecological validity. Imperfect discriminability likely is a legacy from the early research by Tanner Jr. (1956). However, the purview of perceptual independence theory includes perfectly discriminable stimuli that people deal with in the vast majority of cases.

The upshot is, the independence-selectivity bond is compelling, but specific instantiations should be approached with caution, recognizing the stipulations that apply. I now turn attention to selective attention, examining the notorious Stroop effect.

9.3 The Stroop Effect and Perceptual Separability

The Stroop effect (SE) is a prime example of the human failure to attend selectively to a single attribute of the stimulus (for reviews, see MacLeod, 1991; Melara & Algom, 2003). When naming the ink color in which color words are printed, people are unable to overcome their tendency to read the carrier words even when engaging the words can hurt color performance. Inevitably, exclusive focusing on the ink color is compromised. The

Stroop effect gauges the degree of this failure to attend fully selectively to the target dimension. It is defined as the difference (RT, error) in naming the color of congruent (e.g., the word RED printed in red color) and incongruent (GREEN in red) stimuli. Formally,

$$SE = MRT(incongruent) - MRT(congruent), \qquad (9.1a)$$

where MRT is the mean reaction time to name the ink color. An analogous formula exists for error. In terms of response probability, P, the effect can be written as,

$$SE(t) = P(RT \leq t \mid congruent) - P(RT \leq t \mid incongruent). \qquad (9.1b)$$

Concerning Equation 9.1, had people attended exclusively to the target color, there would not have been a content-dependent difference in performance (i.e., the Stroop effect). The presence of the effect betrays the engagement of the task-irrelevant dimension of word, thereby compromising fully selective attention to color. By contrast, a zero Stroop effect documents absolutely undivided attention to color.

At its root, the Stroop effect is an item-specific phenomenon (cf. Jacoby, Lindsay, & Hessels, 2003). It exists and is calculable for each single word and color included in the stimulus ensemble. Take the color word RED for an example. The item-specific Stroop effect for this word is given by the RT difference in color responses between trials in which the word appeared printed in red (congruent combination) and trials in which it appeared printed in green (incongruent combination). The published Stroop effects are actually the average of all the item-specific effects lurking in the stimulus matrix. This feature underscores the strong experimental design sustaining the Stroop effect. Because the same word appears printed in the various colors, all lexical and other extraneous variables are radically controlled (cf. Algom, Zakay, Monar, & Chajut, 2009). The effect, when it exists, is solely attributable to the failure of full selective attention to color.

Simultaneously, I maintain, the same task and effect comprise a measure of perceptual separability. Here is why. The Stroop effect is measured in a single block of trials where the participant names, while timed, the ink color in which each word appears. The task itself is an austere psychophysical task of sensory identification (of color) that does not engage semantic- or high-level processing. Given the single-block testing and the undemanding task, it is eminently plausible that decisional separability holds (i.e., it does not change across the experimental trials and the ink colors). Consequently, a zero Stroop effect for error (Equation 9.1a) and, in particular, a zero effect for the individual colors, indicates that marginal response invariance holds. In a matrix entailing all four combinations of two color words (RED, GREEN) and the corresponding ink colors (red, green), the parity means that the d's for discriminating red from green remain invariant across RED and GREEN. Collectively, a zero Stroop effect is consistent with perceptual separability of the ink color with respect to the word.

The intuition gained from the preceding analysis is that positive values of the Stroop effect signal the breakdown of selective attention to the relevant attribute and, simultaneously, the failure of perceptual separability across attributes. In other words, the Stroop effect is incompatible with perceptual separability. What causes the disruption of selectivity? A cursory survey of the vast Stroop literature implicates semantic clash or agreement between the attributes as the root cause of the effect. Stroop interference (or facilitation) derives from a single source—semantic processing of the tested dimensions. For a trivial example, the Stroop effect does not exist in a situation in which the color-word stimuli come in a language unfamiliar with the participant. For another demonstration, the closer the association of non-color words with the domain of color, the longer it takes to name their color (e.g., it takes longer to name the incongruent ink color of SKY or of GRASS than that of TABLE or BOTTLE; Klein, 1964). The Stroop effect is a thoroughly semantic phenomenon.

The last point is important when assessing the potential use of the Stroop effect as a universal yardstick for assaying selectivity (or separability). A glimpse at Equation 9.1 makes it clear that the Stroop effect can only be calculated for stimuli that can be characterized as congruent or incongruent. The defining feature of this class of stimuli is the presence of a logical relationship, compatibility or incompatibility, between the stimulus attributes. To enable the logical relationship, one of the constituent dimensions (at least) must be semantic (i.e., possess meaning via association to referent non-presented properties). Therefore, every Stroop stimulus falls into the one of the mutually exclusive and exhaustive subsets of congruent or incongruent combinations. Take the original dimensions of ink color and color word for an example. All conceivable combinations of a color word and an ink color must result in either a congruent (the word naming its color) or an incongruent (word and color mismatch) stimulus. Precluded is any other type of combination. The same partition applies to all members of the large class of Stroop-like stimuli from combinations of a picture and a word to those of direction and location of an arrow to the words MALE and FEMALE spoken by a male or a female speaker. Formally, any two dimensions whose values combine to produce stimuli characterized as either congruent or incongruent are Stroop-generating dimensions and the stimuli are Stroop stimuli (see Algom, Chajut, & Lev, 2004, for details).

Given the logical structure of the Stroop stimulus, it follows that congruent and incongruent stimuli exist pre-experimentally, independent of the observer's performance. The person may or may not exhibit the Stroop effect, but the particular empirical results do not alter the a priori classes of congruent and incongruent combinations. Acknowledgment of this point supports the well-known Garnerian dictum that everything, including the Stroop conflict, resides in the stimulus (Garner, 1974; see also Eidels, 2012; Eidels et al., 2010).

The unique structure of Stroop objects might explain the immense popularity of the Stroop effect. These objects stand at the intersection of two separate branches of philosophy, perception and logic. On the one hand, the Stroop object is a perceptual stimulus that impinges on the sensory surface like any other physical stimulus. On the other hand, the Stroop object carries a logical relationship between its constituent dimensions. The apparent oxymoron—logico-perceptual object—characterizes all Stroop stimuli. I believe that this property (unrecognized by most students of the Stroop effect) is at the root of the continuous fascination with the phenomenon.

It is immediately apparent that all multidimensional stimuli are not also Stroop stimuli. A red triangle is not a Stroop stimulus. It is neither more nor less congruent or incongruent than a blue circle. Because the quality of congruity does not apply to non-Stroop stimuli, the Stroop effect is not defined or computable for such stimuli. However, the key issue of selective attention and perceptual separability applies with equal force to Stroop and non-Stroop stimuli alike. Can people attend selectively to color while ignoring shape? Does perceptual separability hold for vertical elevation of a stimulus with respect to its horizontal position? Another measure is needed to gauge selectivity and separability with such stimuli. This measure is Garner interference and Garnerian separability. It is of virtually unlimited generality, applying to Stroop and non-Stroop stimuli alike.

To recap, the Stroop effect is psychology's oldest and still best-known measure of selective attention. Given its role in understanding central aspects of human attention and automatic action, the effect has evolved into the single most popular phenomenon in current cognitive science (cf. Eidels et al., 2010). The enormous amount of research dedicated to all aspects of the Stroop effect (almost a century after its conception!) justifies its title as "the gold standard" of all attention measures (MacLeod 1992, p. 12). This much granted, Equation 9.1 shows that the effect is of limited applicability. It is with this liability in mind that I now turn to examine the Garner measures of attention and separability.

9.3.1 Garnerian Separability and GRT Separability

The task for the observer is the same in Stroop and Garner settings: to respond as quickly and accurately as possible to a single task-relevant dimension of the stimulus. Beyond the shared task of selective attention, however, the two paradigms diverge in structure and analysis. For one, the Garner paradigm includes several blocks of trials, whereas the Stroop effect is typically measured within a single block of trials. Therefore, the Stroop effect is a within-block result (with few exceptions), whereas the Garner effect is a between-block result. Given the task of selective attention in the Garner paradigm, the same task-relevant dimension varies in a random fashion in all of the blocks. The observer's task also remains the same: to respond to the momentary value of this target dimension. Consequently, the various blocks differ by what happens to the task-irrelevant dimension, the dimension which the observer is instructed to ignore (explicitly or implicitly). In the Baseline block, the irrelevant dimension is held at a constant value throughout all trials. In the Filtering block, the irrelevant dimension varies from trial-to-trial in an orthogonal fashion. Now if performance is worse in Filtering than at Baseline, fully selective attention to the target dimension has failed. The decrement shows that irrelevant variation took a toll on selective performance. In contrast, comparable performance in Filtering and Baseline indicates perfect selective attention to the target dimension. The parity shows that the observer classified values along the target dimension as fast and as accurately with the irrelevant dimensions varying in a random fashion, as when the irrelevant dimension was held constant. The difference in performance between Filtering and Baseline taps the extent of (the failure of) selective attention to the task-relevant dimension. This difference is known as Garner interference (GI; Pomerantz, 1983):

$$GI = MRT(Filtering) - MRT(Baseline), \qquad (9.2a)$$

where MRT is the mean reaction time to classify the value of the relevant dimension. Another formula exists for error. In terms of response probability, P, the effect can be written as,

$$GI(t) = P(RT \leq t \mid Baseline) - P(RT \leq t \mid Filtering). \qquad (9.2b)$$

Concerning Equation 9.2 (see Equation 2, Ashby & Maddox 1994, for an analogous formula), the baseline measure can be based on one Baseline block or represent the average of the two Baseline blocks (with the irrelevant dimension held constant at a different value in each). A positive value in Equation 9.2 indicates the failure of selective attention. Moreover, the greater this value, the greater the breakdown of selectivity.

For the sake of a complete account, Garner's Speeded Classification Paradigm includes additional conditions. An important one is the Correlation or Redundancy condition. In that block, like in the Filtering block, the irrelevant dimension also varies from trial-to-trial, but now in a corresponding manner with the target dimension. The Correlation condition is fraught with problems of indeterminacy (it is not clear which dimension actually sustains the observer's responses; cf., Ashby & Maddox, 1994) and with a changing decision strategy (Maddox, 1992; Maddox & Ashby, 1996). Because this condition is not critical for the current argument, I do not discuss it further in this chapter.

The difference depicted in Equation 9.2 forms a singularly successful tool for measuring the failure of selective attention for a large variety of dimensions. Moreover, the results are consistent: When a given pair of dimensions exhibited an appreciable amount of Garner interference (note that the interference need not be symmetric), it did so repeatedly under fairly variable dimensional values. Conversely, the absence of Garner interference for other dimensions proved similarly resilient in the face of variability in testing and stimulus specification. The outcome—presence or absence of Garner interference—seems a fixed property of the stimulus dimension. These conclusions are bolstered by converging evidence (Garner, Hake, & Eriksen, 1956) from other methods of measurement. For a given set of dimensions, the absence of Garner interference in speeded classification occurs in tandem with a city-block metric in similarity scaling and with an additive outcome in information transmission. For other dimensions, a positive Garner interference is associated with a Euclidian metric in the similarity space and with less-than-fully additive information transmission. The upshot is, Garner interference is a *theoretical* result, not merely a particular experimental result.

Garner (1970; 1974, 1976; Garner & Felfoldy, 1970) elected to couch these results in terms of a partition between separable and integral dimensions (see also Shepard, 1964; Torgerson, 1958). The absence of Garner interference (along with other measures) indicates the separability of the dimensions, whereas the presence of Garner interference taps integral dimensions. Selective attention is perfect with separable dimensions; the observer is able to dissect mentally the stimulus onto its constituent dimensions. Selective attention fails for integral dimensions; the observer is unable to respond to one attribute without noticing simultaneously the other attribute. The separability-integrality partition forms a pillar of modern cognitive science (see Figure 9.1).

9.4 Garnerian Separable Dimensions and GRT Perceptual Separability

Two points that should be obvious are the difference in task and in response mode. For the former, the Garner task, like the Stroop task, is that of selective attention in which the observer's partial report is confined to the task-relevant dimension. The GRT task, by contrast, is one of divided attention in which the observer provides full report on both dimensions of the stimulus. For the other difference, Garner's is a speeded task, whereas no time limit is imposed on the observer in the GRT task. The difficulties, though, are not insurmountable.

The first thing to note is that a fair number of GRT analyses can be performed on data collected within the Garner paradigm (mainly with accuracy as the variable of interest). The reason is that Garnerian filtering and GRT identification entail exactly the same design. Both comprise the factorial combination of the binary values of two stimulus dimensions (known also as the

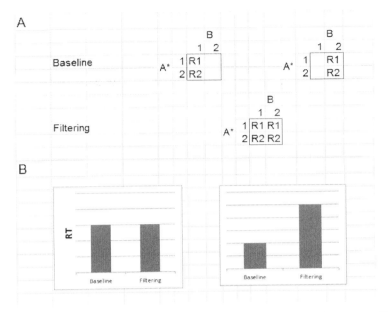

Figure 9.1 Panel A: The Baseline (two blocks of trials) and the Filtering conditions of the Garner paradigm. The asterisk indicates that dimension A is the relevant dimension for responding. Panel B: Two general patterns of results. Performance in Baseline and Filtering is comparable in the left-hand graph, indicating separable dimensions. Performance is worse in Filtering than at Baseline in the right-hand graph, the difference—Garner interference—indicating integral dimensions.

feature complete design). In both designs, there is random, independent variation from trial-to-trial of both dimensional values. Now, the partial reporting in the Garner task already suffices to derive the marginal d's and marginal response invariance for the relevant dimension. Furthermore, the experimenter can subsequently swap the roles of the dimensions and define the previously irrelevant dimension as the relevant one in that part of the experiment. The same GRT measures can then be derived for the second dimension. The outcome is amenable to standard GRT interpretation.

This tactic was used in a study on pain by Algom and Edelstein (1998). The authors concluded that electric pain and auditory pain are not perceptually separable, regardless of whether shock or (loud) tone was the attended attribute of the shock-tone compounds (delivered, respectively, to the wrist and the ears at the same time). This conclusion was reinforced by Garner and Stroop effects calculated with respect to the same stimuli. These results on the perception of multicomponent pain are interesting given that the same pains were found to combine in an additive manner in studies employing Anderson's (1981) method of Functional Measurement (e.g., Algom, 1992; Algom, Raphaeli, & Cohen-Raz, 1986, 1987). The relationship between Functional Measurement and GRT is complex and has not been fully worked out (but see Algom, 2007). The issues with respect to pain itself are fascinating, but their explication unfortunately falls outside the confines of this chapter (see Algom, 2004, for review and discussion).

GRT analyses of Garner data are not confined to Filtering (a replica of the GRT experiment). Their application to Baseline turns out to be most revealing. Suppose that color is the relevant dimension with respect to shape. Then one merely contrasts performance across the two Baseline blocks to derive a pair of d's for color, one from the block in which shape was *held constant* as triangle and another from the block in which shape was *held constant* as circle. Marginal response invariance can also be tested across the two Baseline blocks. At this point, a comparison is invited between the indices at Baseline and the same indices in GRT. The implications of this comparison are profound.

In GRT, the marginal d's are derived *ex post facto*, so to speak: The experimenter selects subsets of the results (e.g., all the trials in which the triangle was presented) for analysis following data collection. In the experiment itself, one recalls, color and shape vary unpredictably from trial-to-trial, and the d's actually come from this situation facing the observer. In contrast, the d's derived from the Garnerian Baseline blocks are planned a priori. These d's are derived in an experimental situation in which the observer does not face irrelevant variation. Suppose that the marginal d's are equal at Baseline and that marginal response invariance holds, but that neither is the case in GRT. These results implicate variability of the opponent variable as the root cause of the breakdown of perceptual separability in the GRT experiment. One must be circumspect, though, because variability may carry less force with the non-speeded responses in GRT; also, in the Garner experiment, errors are usually very few. More research on this topic is needed, but variability may well prove an important source of the failure of perceptual separability within GRT.

The Garner paradigm suffers from a known liability: It lacks a decision component. Consequently, the previous conclusions are valid only if decisional separability holds. The assay of Garner interference itself is valid only if decisional separability holds. Fortunately, the problem is less severe in practice than in theory. Maddox (1992) adduced arguments to the effect that decisional separability holds in Filtering and, hence, that Garner interference is a good test of perceptual separability (see also Ashby & Maddox, 1994). Subsequently, Maddox and Ashby (1996) produced empirical evidence in support of this conclusion. Ashby and his colleagues (Ashby & Gott, 1988; Ashby & Maddox, 1990) have similarly concluded that perceptual separability is a property of a stimulus dimension (but that decisional separability is under the observer's discretion).

The argument of the preceding paragraphs has been conclusive: GRT analyses can be performed on data collected within the Garner paradigm.

However, the truly decisive question concerns the relationship between Garner interference and perceptual separability. Are Garnerian separability and GRT perceptual separability comparable? Despite the common nomenclature, close scrutiny shows that they are not. Although both measures tap the ability of an observer to exempt target performance from influence by a second dimension, they do so by different means. The Garner measure, one recalls, derives from comparing target performance across different blocks of trials. In the Baseline block, the entire world comes to a halt apart from the to-be-responded dimension. In Filtering, there exists task-irrelevant variation while the observer responds to the same target dimension. Garner interference thus registers the fact that the task-irrelevant variation was noticed and took a toll on target performance. Now irrelevant variation is always noticed in the GRT given that the observer reports all dimensional values on each trial. Clearly, the source and operational definition of the failure of separability expressed by Garner interference differ from that underlying the failure of perceptual separability in GRT. What then causes the failure of perceptual separability in GRT? One possibility, I alluded, is sheer variation of the opponent dimension, a source that cannot be tested within the current form of the GRT task. A widely held view implicates the integrality of the dimensions. The difficulty with this interpretation is that integral dimensions are originally defined within the Garner paradigm. The problem surfaces in an acute form when the results for the same pair of dimensions differ in the GRT and Garner tests. Suppose that perceptual separability holds in the GRT test but not in the Garner test. Are the dimensions separable or integral? The few empirical studies that derived both Garner and GRT measures (Algom & Edelstein, 1998; Fitousi, 2013, 2014; Fitousi & Wenger, 2013; Kadouri-Labin, 2007) yielded inconclusive results: Garner interference and failure of perceptual separability tended to occur in tandem, but individual variability was large. Comparing the sources of Stroop and Garner effects sheds light on the issue.

The nub of the Stroop-Garner relationship is the occurrence (or lack thereof) of semantic analysis. The Garner measure does not rely on semantic processing of the stimuli; it merely registers the presence of task-irrelevant variation. The Stroop effect, by contrast, is a quintessentially semantic phenomenon; it registers the kind of task-irrelevant variation on a trial-to-trial basis (otherwise congruent and incongruent cases lose psychological reality). Because one cannot attend to kinds of variation without noticing variation, the Stroop effect implies Garner interference, although the reverse is not true (Algom et al., 1996; Melara & Mounts, 1993). This brings us back to ponder the nature of the failure of perceptual separability in GRT. Like the Garner paradigm, GRT does not rely on semantic analysis (virtually all stimuli tested in studies of GRT entailed simple physical features that did not possess meaning). On the other hand, the GRT task, like the Stroop task, entails the momentary identification of both dimensional values (in the Stroop task the identification of the irrelevant dimension is implicit, revealed by the Stroop effect). In GRT, identification occurs with non-Stroop stimuli. Let us then take stock of the three species of interference. Stroop interference (or facilitation) is semantic. Garner interference is not semantic. What kind of interference is failure of perceptual separability? At first glimpse, it is not semantic, yet the requirement to identify the exact momentary value of the opponent dimension may mandate (a modicum of) semantic processing. If so, the failure of perceptual separability taps a unique case: semantic interference that is not Stroop. The shared and distinct features of the three tests of selectivity or separability are summarized in Table 9.1.

Table 9.1 Summary of Shared and Different Features of STROOP, GARNER, and TOWNSEND (GRT) Measures

Feature	STROOP	GARNER	TOWNSEND
Experimental Task	Selective Attention	Selective Attention	Divided Attention
Attended Dimension	Single, Relevant	Single, Relevant	Both
Participant's Report	Partial	Partial	Full
Major Measure of Performance	RT	RT	Accuracy
Design and Context	A single block of trials with random variation	Multiple blocks of trials with the irrelevant dimension either constant or varying	A single block of trials with random variation
Major Comparison	Across subsets of the stimuli defined by corresponding and conflicting values	Constant versus varying presentation of the irrelevant dimension	Across subsets of the stimuli defined by values of the opponent variable
Calculating Dimensional Separability	Contrasting subsets of congruent and incongruent stimuli	Contrasting blocks with the irrelevant dimension held constant or varying	Contrasting subsets at different levels of the opponent dimension
Decision Mechanism	Absent	Absent	Present
Pre-Experimental Relationship Between the Tested Dimensions	Logical	Immaterial	Immaterial

9.5 Conclusion

In this remaining section, I wish to highlight the meaning and some logical relations connecting the three methods. The GRT notion of perceptual independence and the associated measure of sampling independence are direct applications of the mathematical definition of independence of two variables, X and Y, as follows:

$$P(X) = P(X|Y). \tag{9.3a}$$

The multiplication rule at the root of perceptual independence is merely another form of Equation 9.3a. The GRT notion of perceptual separability also comes close to the mathematical definition of independence as stated in Equation 9.3a, which for the special case of Y having just two possible values can be stated as,

$$P(X|Y_1) = P(X|Y_2), \tag{9.3b}$$

showing the invariance of X for various levels of Y.

If instead of the probability of reporting or of detection, P, one considers $D(X)$, the ability to discriminate between two values of X, then a closely associated equality should be satisfied if X and Y are independent.

$$D(X_i|Y_1) = D(X_i|Y_2) \tag{9.4a}$$

or, using the discrimination measure from SDT,

$$d'(X_i|Y_1) = d'(X_i|Y_2). \tag{9.4b}$$

It may come as a surprise that the Stroop measure is also subserved by Equation 9.3b with one notable caveat: X and Y carry meaning such that they are either congruent or incongruent. In particular, one examines if the following equation is satisfied:

$$P(X_1|Y_1) = P(X_1|Y_2), \tag{9.5}$$

where the same subscripts in X and Y indicate congruent combinations and different subscripts incongruent ones. Therefore, the Stroop test of separability is the same as that of GRT's, subject to the proviso that X and Y are bonded by a preexisting logical relationship of conflict or correspondence.

The Garner measure introduces a concept foreign to both GRT and Stroop: variation, in particular irrelevant variation. It tests the equality

$$P(X|Y \text{ constant at } j) = P(X|Y \text{ varies across values of } j) \tag{9.6}$$
$$j = 1, 2.$$

The right-hand term of Equation 9.6 depicts the standard condition tested in Stroop and GRT studies; indeed it is the only condition tested. The left-hand term depicts a condition tested only in the Garner paradigm. It provides the yardstick against which one can assess the effect of variation itself. Both dimensional values are presented on every trial of the Garner paradigm, too. However, the task-irrelevant values are held at a constant level in a pair of blocks, but vary in a random fashion in another block. Therefore, Garnerian separability, defined by satisfying Equation 9.6, differs appreciably from perceptual separability, defined by satisfying Equation 9.4b (with other stipulations respected).

The notion of separability is a fundamental organizing principle of human attention to multidimensional stimuli. However, critical analysis shows that separability (indeed, its failure) can derive from distinct sources. It remains to be seen if the GRT and Garner tests exhaust all sources of interference, especially in light of the semantic analyses tapped by the Stroop test.

9.6 Epilogue: The Marriage of Selectivity and Independence Gets Personal

Scientific issues have faces. For me, they are those of Wendell Garner and Jim Townsend. The merger of selectivity and independence vetted in this chapter is, on a personal level, a merger of ideas by these scientific role models. I had been under the influence of Garner's ideas on selectivity and separability when I came across Ashby and Townsend's seminal paper on "Varieties of Perceptual Independence." I immediately recognized, intuitively at first, the close relationship between the pertinent issues. So I ventured a tentative foray into this treacherous territory by examining pain (experimentally delivered pain that is—I was still a psychophysicist) and deriving GRT, Stroop, and Garner effects. When preparing the results for a conference talk, I was apprehensive since my audience was composed of psychophysicists (this endangered species is still alive; it certainly was at that time).The audience knew of the Garner of psychoacoustics (I cited the Garner and Miller paper from 1947 in my own dissertation on temporal integration in hearing). They were aware of the Garner of information theory, but had heard next to nothing of the latter-day Garner of attention and structure. Needless to add, virtually none had an idea of the GRT. With this in mind, I prepared a listener-friendly presentation. This proved a prudent gamble—well almost. Scientific encounters often come cloaked in improbable disguises. As it happened, I was heckled in the talk by this gentleman asking all sorts of uncomfortable questions. I was dismissive at first, thinking of the best way to get free of this gadfly. But the comments continued, and, of more concern, they were thoughtful if not directly intimidating. Well, you guessed it, the heckler was Jim Townsend. As they say, the rest is history. However, the marriage of selectivity and independence, like all marriages, proved fraught with all sorts of difficulties. We were walking the streets of Tel-Aviv when I first sounded the idea to Jim. I was dismayed by his unenthusiastic response. He was speaking the foreign language (apart from his English, that is) of channels, stochastic versus other forms of independence, and things of that kind. He was correct, of course. Because perceptual independence is such a multilayered concept, one must be very careful when examining each individual case of contingency.

Let me conclude by noting that the influence of these role models reached beyond the issues discussed in this chapter. During my last meeting with Garner (a couple years before his death), I noted (tongue in cheek) that there are actually three Garners, meaning his contributions to psychophysics, information theory, and attention. He retorted, "You're wrong Danny, there are five Garners." As usual, he was correct; I left out (at the least) the Garner of figural goodness and art and the Garner of baseball (his best-selling book from 1951 with a second edition in 1966). I don't know if there are five Townsends, but there are certainly multiple Townsends. Apart from his immense contributions to the mathematical specification of human information processing, there is the Townsend of chaos theory, the Townsend of methodology and statistics, and the Townsend of face perception. And I did not mention the Townsend of yachts and sailings, the ever risk-seeking adventurer.

Hopefully, it is not taken as a breach of modesty when I mention the company of these men. It has been a pleasure to enjoy it, and I will be ever grateful for their friendship and inspiration.

Acknowledgments

I thank Ami Eidels and Danny Fitousi for helpful comments on earlier drafts of this chapter. Further special thanks go to Danny Fitousi for alerting me to some relevant passages in the writings of David Hume. Thanks are also due to an anonymous reviewer for pinpointing an error in the logic of the argument in several places and to Joe Houpt for many insightful comments on various portions of the text and the development. Preparation of this chapter was supported by Israel Science Foundation grant, ISF-646-12.

References

Algom, D. (1992). Psychophysical analysis of pain: A functional perspective. In H.-G. Geissler, S. W. Link, & J. T. Townsend (Eds.), *Cognition, information processing, and psychophysics* (pp. 267–292). Hillsdale, NJ: Lawrence Erlbaum Associates.

Algom, D. (2004). Pain psychophysics: Its role in measuring, validating, and understanding pain. *Psychologica, 37*, 15–34.

Algom, D. (2007). Functional measurement and perceptual independence. *Teorie & Modelli, 1–2,* 77–86.

Algom, D., Chajut, E., & Lev, S. (2004). A rational look at the emotional Stroop phenomenon: A generic slowdown, not a Stroop effect. *Journal of Experimental Psychology: General, 133,* 323–338.

Algom, D., Dekel, A., & Pansky, A. (1996). The perception of number from the separability of the stimulus: The Stroop effect revisited. *Memory & Cognition, 24,* 557–572.

Algom, D., & Edelstein, A. (1998). Selective attention to pain stimuli. In S. Grondin & Y. Lacouture (Eds.), *Fechner day 98.* Quebec, Canada: International Society for Psychophysics.

Algom, D., Raphaeli, N., & Cohen-Raz, L. (1986). Integration of noxious stimulation across separate somatosensory communication systems: A functional theory of pain. *Journal of Experimental Psychology: Human Perception and Performance, 12,* 92–102.

Algom, D., Raphaeli, N., & Cohen-Raz, L. (1987). Pain combines additively across different sensory systems: A further support for the functional theory of pain. *Perceptual and Motor Skills, 65*(2), 619–625.

Algom, D., Zakay, D., Monar, O., & Chajut, E. (2009). Wheel chairs and arm chairs: A novel experimental design for the emotional Stroop effect. *Cognition & Emotion, 23,* 1552–1564.

Anderson, N. H. (1981). *Foundations of information integration theory.* New York: Academic Press.

Ashby, F. G., & Gott, R. E. (1988). Decision rules in the perception and categorization of multidimensional stimuli. *Journal of Experimental Psychology: Learning, Memory, and Cognition, 14,* 33–53.

Ashby, F. G., & Maddox, W. T. (1990). Integrating information from separable psychological dimensions. *Journal of Experimental Psychology: Human Perception and Performance, 16,* 598–612.

Ashby, F. G., & Maddox, W. T. (1994). A response-time theory of separability and integrality in speeded classification. *Journal of Mathematical Psychology, 38,* 423–466.

Ashby, F. G., & Soto, F. A. (2015). Multidimensional signal detection theory. In J. R. Busemeyer, Z. Wang, J. T. Townsend, & A. Eidels (Eds.), *The Oxford handbook of computational and mathematical psychology.* Oxford: Oxford University Press.

Ashby, F. G., & Townsend, J. T. (1986). Varieties of perceptual independence. *Psychological Review, 93,* 154–179.

Attneave, F. (1959). *Applications of information theory to psychology.* New York: Holt, Reinhart, & Winston.

Broadbent, D. E. (1958). *Perception and communication.* New York: Pergamon.

Eidels, A. (2012). Independent race of colour and word can predict the Stroop effect. *Australian Journal of Psychology, 64,* 189–198.

Eidels, A., Townsend, J. T., & Algom, D. (2010). Comparing perception of Stroop stimuli in focused versus divided attention paradigms: Evidence for dramatic processing differences. *Cognition, 114,* 129–150.

Eriksen, C. W., & Hake, H. W. (1955). Absolute judgments as a function of the stimulus range and number of stimulus and response categories. *Journal of Experimental Psychology, 49,* 323–332.

Fitousi, D. (2013). Mutual information, perceptual independence, and holistic face. *Attention, Perception & Psychophysics, 75,* 983–1000.

Fitousi, D. (2014). On the internal representation of numerical magnitude and physical size. *Experimental Psychology, 61,* 149–163.

Fitousi, D., & Wenger, M. J. (2013). Variants of independence in the perception of facial identity and expression. *Journal of Experimental Psychology: Human Perception and Performance, 39*, 133–155.

Garner, W. R. (1962). *Uncertainty and structure as psychological concepts.* New York: Wiley & Sons.

Garner, W. R. (1970). The stimulus in information processing. *American Psychologist, 25*, 350–358.

Garner, W. R. (1974). *The processing of information and structure.* Potomac, MD: Lawrence Erlbaum Associates.

Garner, W. R. (1976). Interaction of stimulus dimensions in concept and choice processes. *Cognitive Psychology, 8*, 98–123.

Garner, W. R., & Felfoldy, G. L. (1970). Integrality of stimulus dimensions in various types of information processing. *Cognitive Psychology, 1*, 225–241.

Garner, W. R., Hake, H. W., & Eriksen, C. W. (1956). Operationism and the concept of perception. *Psychological Review, 63*, 149–159.

Garner, W. R., & Lee, W. (1962). An analysis of redundancy in perceptual discrimination. *Psychological and Motor Skills, 15*, 367–388.

Garner, W. R., & Morton, J. (1969). Perceptual independence: Definitions, models, and experimental paradigms. *Psychological Bulletin, 72*, 233–259.

Graham, N., Kramer, P., & Yager, D. (1987). Signal detection models for multidimensional stimuli: Probability distributions and combinations rules. *Journal of Mathematical Psychology, 31*, 192–206.

Green, D. M., & Swets, J. A. (1966). *Signal detection theory and psychophysics.* Oxford, England: John Wiley.

Hume, D. (1739/1962). *A treatise of human nature. Book 1: Of the understanding.* New York: The World Publishing Company.

Jacoby, L. L., Lindsay, D. S., & Hessels, S. (2003). Item-specific control of automatic processes: Stroop process dissociations. *Psychonomic Bulletin & Review, 10*(3), 638–644.

James, W. A. (1890). *The principles of psychology.* New York: Holt.

Kadlec, H., & Townsend, J. T. (1992a). Implications of marginal and conditional detection parameters for the separabilities and independence of perceptual dimensions. *Journal of Mathematical Psychology, 36*, 325–374.

Kadlec, H., & Townsend, J. T. (1992b). Signal detection analyses of dimensional interactions. In F. G. Ashby (Ed.), *Multidimensional models of perception and cognition* (pp. 181–227). Hillsdale, NJ: Lawrence Erlbaum Associates.

Kadouri-Labin, S. (2007). *Is perceptual separability separable?* (Unpublished doctoral dissertation). Tel-Aviv University.

Klein, G. S. (1964). Semantic power measured through the interference of worlds with color naming. *American Journal of Psychology, 77*, 576–588.

MacLeod, C. M. (1991). Half of a century research on the Stroop effect: An integrative review. *Psychological Bulletin, 109*, 163–203.

MacLeod, C. M. (1992). The Stroop task: The gold standard of attentional measures. *Journal of Experimental Psychology: General, 121*, 12–14.

Macmillan, N. A., & Creelman, C. D. (2005). *Detection theory.* Mahwah, NJ: Lawrence Erlbaum Associates.

Maddox, W. T. (1992). Perceptual and decisional separability. In F. G. Ashby (Ed.), *Multidimensional models of perception and cognition* (pp. 147–180). Hillsdale, NJ: Lawrence Erlbaum Associates.

Maddox, W. T., & Ashby, F. G. (1996). Perceptual separability, decisional separability, and the identification–speeded classification relationship. *Journal of Experimental Psychology: Human Perception and Performance, 22*(4), 795–817.

Melara, R. D., & Algom, D. (2003). A tectonic theory of Stroop effects. *Psychological Review*, *110*, 422–471.

Melara, R. D., & Mounts, J. R. (1993). Selective attention to Stroop dimensions: Effects of baseline discriminability, response mode, and practice. *Memory & Cognition*, *21*, 627–645.

Pansky, A., & Algom, D. (1999). Stroop and Garner effects in comparative judgment of numerals: The role of attention. *Journal of Experimental Psychology: Human Perception and Performance*, *25*, 39–59.

Pansky, A., & Algom, D. (2002). Comparative judgment of numerosity and numerical magnitude: Attention preempts automaticity. *Journal of Experimental Psychology: Learning, Memory, and Cognition*, *28*, 259–274.

Pomerantz, J. R. (1983). Global and local precedence: Selective attention in form and motion perception. *Journal of Experimental Psychology: General*, *112*(4), 516–540.

Sabri, M., Melara, R. D., & Algom, D. (2002). A confluence of contexts: Asymmetric versus global failure of selective attention to Stroop dimensions. *Journal of Experimental Psychology: Human Perception and Performance*, *27*, 515–537.

Shepard, R. N. (1964). Attention and the metric structure of the stimulus space. *Journal of Mathematical Psychology*, *1*(1), 54–87.

Silbert, N. H., & Thomas, R. D. (2013). Decisional separability, model identification, and statistical inference in the general recognition theory framework. *Psychonomic Bulletin & Review*, *20*, 1–20.

Stroop, J. R. (1935). Studies of interference in serial verbal reactions. *Journal of Experimental Psychology*, *18*(6), 643–662.

Swets, J. A., Tanner Jr., W. P., & Birdsall, T. G. (1961). Decision processes in perception. *Psychological Review*, *68*, 301–340.

Tanner Jr., P., W. (1956). Theory of recognition. *Journal of the Acoustical Society of America*, *28*, 882–888.

Torgerson, W. S. (1958). *Theory and methods of scaling*. New York: Wiley.

Townsend, J. T., Houpt, J. W., & Silbert, N. H. (2012). General recognition theory extended to include response times: Predictions for a class of parallel systems. *Journal of Mathematical Psychology*, *56*, 476–494.

10 Modeling Interactive Dimensions in a Component Comparison Task Using General Recognition Theory

Robin D. Thomas, Noah H. Silbert, Emily Grossman, and Shawn Ell

10.1 Introduction

Long is the list of seminal contributions to our understanding of perception and cognition that has been made by Jim Townsend, our friend and mentor, as this volume attests. Perhaps two of the most important lines of work on this list include the development and extension of statistical decision theory to multiple stimulus dimensions (Ashby & Townsend, 1986; Kadlec & Townsend, 1992a, 1992b; Townsend, 1984; Townsend & Landon, 1982) and the mathematical and statistical analysis of the structure of mental architectures (selected works include Johnson, Blaha, Houpt, & Townsend, 2010; Schweickert & Townsend, 1989; Townsend, 1972, 1984, 1990; Townsend & Nozawa, 1995; Townsend & Schweickert, 1989; Townsend & Thomas, 1994), with recent efforts to integrate these perspectives (e.g., Eidels, Townsend, Hughes, & Perry, 2015; Townsend, Houpt, & Silbert, 2012). Core characteristics of all of this work are the careful attention to logical distinctions among key concepts and the mathematical rigor of the analysis (especially Ashby & Townsend, 1986; Townsend, 1984).

We report research in this chapter that draws elements from both of these sides of Jim's research "personality." We describe the application of General Recognition Theory (GRT; also described as multidimensional signal detection theory) with aspects of mental architecture (e.g., serial versus parallel processing systems) to a selective-attention version of the classic same-different judgment task, which we call component same-different. This extends the work of Thomas (1996), who examined predictions of accuracy and response-time distributions in this task, assuming separability and independence for two specific types of decision processes. In the current chapter, we explore the case of perceptual integrality and add optimal responding to the slate of decision processes applied to component same-different judgments.

In the sections that follow, we review the basics of the GRT and the constructs of interaction defined within it. Following this, we present the extension to the same-different judgment task initially described in Thomas (1996; see also MacMillan & Creelman (1991, for similar ideas in the unidimensional case), focusing specifically on a selective attention version that is useful for identifying interactions among stimulus attributes. The important theoretical extension to interactive attributes follows in the form of simulation work in which different decision models of the task produce responses and response times.

10.2 GRT and the Same-Different Task

10.2.1 Basic Concepts of the GRT

We briefly review the basic structure of the GRT as detailed presentations can be found in numerous places (Ashby & Townsend, 1986; Kadlec & Townsend, 1992a; 1992b; Thomas, 1995; and Chapters 6, 7, 8, and 16 of Ashby, 1992). Assume the stimulus is composed of two components, A and B, each taking on a finite number of levels. Denote the stimulus by A_iB_j, where the subscripts refer to the physical level of the corresponding component. For example, if A denotes form (1 = circle, 2 = square) and B denotes color (1 = red, 2 = green), the stimulus A_1B_2 would be a green circle. As it was originally developed for perceptual identification, the GRT assumes that on any given trial, the presentation of a stimulus leads to a perceptual effect representable as a point in multidimensional space where the dimensions in this psychological space correspond to the physical components of the stimulus (e.g., pitch corresponds to frequency). The observer divides this space into mutually exclusive and exhaustive regions, demarcated by decision bounds, which are associated with different responses required by the task. If a percept falls in a particular region, the observer deterministically emits the associated response. Over trials, due to inherent noise in the perceptual stimulus, there is variability in the percept so that the stimulus, say A_iB_j, over the course of the experiment can be represented as a probability density function of perceptual effects, $f_{A_iB_j}(x,y)$ over two perceptual dimensions X and Y. Response probabilities are computed as the integrals of these densities over the regions associated with the responses. Marginal densities for a given stimulus associated with each one of the components are found by ignoring effects of the other (integrating over the other perceptual component). For instance, $g_{A_iB_j}(x)$ denotes the marginal density for effects of component A, and $h_{A_iB_j}(y)$ denotes those of B. Figure 10.1 diagrams the basic GRT representation for a two-component, two-levels-each factorial identification design.

A key value of the GRT concerns its utility in allowing precise definitions of how stimulus dimensions may interact during processing. For example, component A is *perceptually separable* from B if and only if $g_{A_iB_1}(x) = g_{A_iB_2}(x)$ for all x and $i = 1, 2$. That is, physical variation of component B does not change the perceptual representation of component A. A similar definition for B separable from A can be offered. *Perceptual independence* of dimensions within a stimulus requires $f_{A_iB_j}(x,y) = g_{A_iB_j}(x)h_{A_iB_j}(y)$. As in

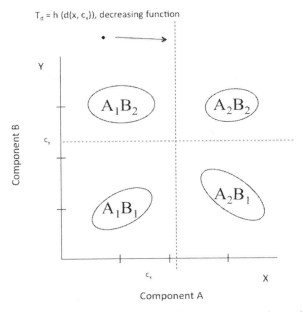

Figure 10.1 Basic GRT configuration with RT-distance hypothesis illustrated.

unidimensional signal detection theory (SDT; Green & Swets, 1966), decision is logically distinct from perception, so separability can be defined for decision as well. In the identification task, decisional separability holds if and only if the decision regarding the identity of one component does not depend on the perceptual effect of, nor the decision regarding, the other. In the canonical task, this renders decision bounds parallel to the perceptual axes. When the GRT is extended to tasks other than identification, different decision models need to be articulated, and analogous concepts derived with respect to these new models should embody decisional separability.

When response times (RTs) are the measures to be collected, one type of auxiliary assumption has been made to accommodate this dependent variable: the *RT-distance hypothesis* (Ashby & Maddox, 1991; 1994; Maddox & Ashby, 1996; Murdock, 1985). Simply stated, identification time on a given trial is inversely related (decreases monotonically) to the (Euclidean) distance from the percept to the decision bound. Overall RT for the trial is assumed to be the sum of the identification time and some independent base time, T_b. A common function that is used to model decision time and that embodies this assumption is the exponential $T_d = \alpha \exp[-\beta \, \text{dist}(x, c_x)]$, where dist() is the distance from the percept, x, and the decision criterion, c_x. All other terms are parameters to be adjusted. Justification for the empirical validity of this hypothesis, much of which comes from unidimensional signal detection theory, is given in Ashby and Maddox (1991, 1994) and, for multidimensional stimuli, in Ashby, Boynton, and Lee (1994).

As an example of experimental tasks that have been commonly used to define separability-employing response times, consider the speeded classification tasks of Garner (Garner, 1974; Garner & Felfoldy, 1970; Posner, 1964). One type of speeded classification task is the *filtering test* in which observers classify values along one dimension (the *relevant* dimension). In the control condition for this test, the irrelevant dimension is held constant, whereas in the experimental or orthogonal condition, it is varied in an orthogonal manner to the relevant dimension. The logic is that pairs of interacting dimensions (i.e., integral) should lead to interference (in terms of speed and accuracy) in the orthogonal condition when compared to control. It is believed that observers cannot or will not selectively attend to the relevant dimension, or filter out irrelevant information, thus experiencing "Garner interference." On the other hand, if observers are able to ignore variations in the irrelevant dimension, then the dimensions are deemed separable. The other speeded classification task, the *redundancy test*, is used to provide converging evidence of integrality. In this task, the observer, again, classifies on the basis of only one dimension, but the stimulus dimension values are correlated across stimuli in the experimental condition, thus providing redundant information. If performance improves in the correlated or redundant condition relative to a control, (i.e., there is a redundancy gain), then the dimensions are said to be integral.

Ashby and Maddox (1994) provide a precise description of the structure of the speeded classification tests, the mathematical foundation for their use within the GRT framework, and the often unstated assumptions that underlie them. In addition to comparing filtering performance in the orthogonal condition to the control condition, one can compare the classification performance across specific pairs of stimuli to assess separability in finer detail. Recall that if perceptual separability holds, then the representation of a stimulus along a given dimension is invariant across levels of the opposing dimension (i.e., the marginal perceptual distributions are equal). Ashby and Maddox showed that, together with the assumption of decisional separability and the RT-distance hypothesis, perceptual separability of stimulus components would imply that the entire response-time distribution for classifying a stimulus according to the value of a relevant dimension would be invariant across physical levels of the irrelevant component. Support for separability can be found in two ways. First, one can confirm invariance in the response-time distributions in the orthogonal condition when observers are asked to selectively attend to a focal attribute. Second, a more extensive evaluation could be made using the speeded classification task and several control conditions. For details, see Ashby and Maddox (1994).

The role of decisional separability in the redundancy conditions was a focal concern of Ashby and Maddox. For example, if we suppose that the observer is responding optimally in the positive redundancy condition (that is, when the physical dimensional values are positively correlated), then decisional separability would generally not be satisfied. For example, if the perceptual distributions are extremely simple (e.g., Gaussian with covariance matrix equal to the identity), then the optimal decision bound would tilt toward the left resulting in an RT redundancy gain (see Theorem 6 and Figure 5 of Ashby & Maddox, 1994). Thus a conclusion of integrality with respect to the perceptual aspects of the stimulus may be unwarranted if a redundancy gain is observed. Decisional integrality such as this is a common finding among experienced observers in both psychophysical and categorization tasks (Ashby & Gott, 1988; Ashby & Lee, 1991; Ashby & Maddox, 1990; Ashby & Maddox, 1992; Mckinley & Nosofsky, 1995; Thomas, 1998). Maddox and Ashby (1996) conducted experiments employing the various filtering and redundancy conditions using traditionally separable dimensions (form and color). They were able to establish separability in the filtering conditions, but their observers, with practice, did show significant redundancy gains in the correlated dimensions condition as would be expected with optimal responding.

10.2.2 Same-Different Comparison

An earlier extension of the GRT to the same-different comparison task included two types of decision processes: subclassification and distance-based (Thomas, 1996; again see MacMillan & Creelman 1991, for these constructs in unidimensional SDT). We add optimal responding in this work following the discussion of these two. Decision processes differ in their assumptions concerning how the observer compares the perceptual representations of the pair of stimuli presented. The *subclassification* model assumes that the observer classifies/identifies each presented stimulus separately and responds the "same" if those classification labels are the same; otherwise, he or she responds "different." Because the subclassification model contains two mini-identification processes, the previously defined concepts of decisional separability and the RT-distance hypothesis of Ashby & Maddox (as pertains to the individual identifications) carry over. However, we need additional consideration of processing architecture when the overall response-time predictions are to be made. When faced with a pair of stimuli on a trial, the observer could first classify (i.e., locate the perceptual effect in the space) one stimulus and then classify the other in series (*serial classification*). Alternatively, he or she might concurrently identify each stimulus (*parallel classification*). Finally, in the case of sequential presentations where RT is measured upon presentation of the second stimulus, the observer may have already classified the first stimulus so that measured RT is determined only by one classification time (*one classification*). In this case, the response-time results of Ashby and Maddox (1991, 1994) apply. Figure 10.2A outlines the basics of the subclassification same-different

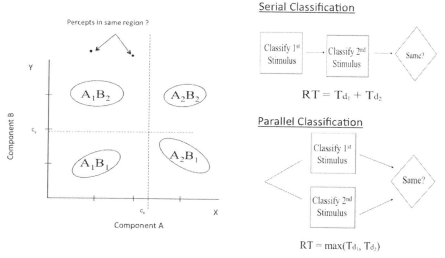

Figure 10.2 Subclassification GRT model of same-different judgments. When applied to the selective-attention component task, only one of the decision criteria is relevant.

model and Figure 10.2B its architectural options for response-time predictions.

Alternatively, if the observer assesses a difference between the percepts generated and responds "same" if that difference is less than some threshold and otherwise responds "different" if the difference is greater, then we say they are using a *distance-based* decision process (e.g., Ennis & Ashby, 1993; Takane & Sergent, 1983). Decision times can be derived by examining how far from the threshold the distance between the stimulus percepts is. For example, we could let $d = \text{dist}(S_i, S_j)$ denote the distance between the percepts generated by S_i and S_j and let τ denote the criterion against which this distance is evaluated to determine sameness or difference, $T_d = h(|d-\tau|)$, with h monotonic decreasing. For example, $\alpha \exp[-\beta|d-\tau|]$ would be a reasonable response-time model.

If the decision strategy is distance-based (as depicted in Figure 10.3), then no decision bounds are referenced in the perceptual space, so new concepts of decisional separability need to be introduced. Thomas (1996) argued that a good definition of decisional separability for any model ought to entail that separate decisions are made with respect to the individual components. Thus, for the distance-based models, decisional separability holds if and only if there are separate decisions to respond "same" or "different" on each component and those individual decisions do not depend on each other. Thus if both components are relevant (as in standard

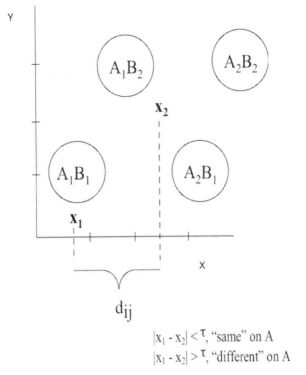

Figure 10.3 Component same-different judgment on *A* according to distance-based DS.

applications of the same-different task) and decisional separability holds, a decision to respond "same" for a given pair of stimuli would result from an internal decision to respond "same" on component *A* and "same" on component *B*. Also, the criterion for each component decision cannot be a function of the perceived level, decision, or identity of the other component. The processing time required for each decision process is assumed to be a monotonic decreasing function of the difference between the two perceptual effects on the given dimension from the decision criterion for that component. Thus for "different" trials, observation pairs whose distances in perceptual space are great (and greater than the criterion) are responded to quickly. In contrast, those observation pairs whose distance between their percepts is around the decision criterion are responded to the slowest.

In general, when decisional separability is not assumed (e.g., a Euclidean metric is used to assess difference between stimuli as in, e.g., Ennis & Ashby, 1993) and then RT is assumed to be a monotonic decreasing function of the difference between the distance and the criteria used for same-different evaluations (for similar modeling of RT in the same-different task, see Takane & Sergent, 1983 and Podgorny & Garner, 1979). Here, again, processing architecture comes into play when decisional separability for this model is assumed. First, each dimension could be classified as "same" or "different" in series (*serial decision*) or in parallel (*parallel decision*). If we are concerned only with the special case of same-different judgments for one dimension—a selective-attention version of the comparison task (see next section), we do not need to explore possible stopping rules for this distance-based decision strategy such as self-terminating or exhaustive here. The reason is, if decisional separability is assumed and one is performing a selective attention (component) same-different task, distances are taken with respect to only the relevant dimension.

To outline an *optimal decision* strategy, we note that the structure of the same-different task can be described as an example of the general pattern classification problem (e.g., Dai, Versfeld, & Green, 1996; Fukunaga, 1990; Pao, 1989;). For n-dimensional stimuli, on a given trial, the pattern to be classified is a $2n$-dimensional vector $\mathbf{w} = (u_1, u_2, \ldots, u_n, v_1, v_2, \ldots, v_n)$ where $\mathbf{u} = (u_1, u_2, \ldots, u_n)$ is the percept for the first stimulus, S_i (either spatially or sequentially) and $\mathbf{v} = (v_1, v_2, \ldots, v_n)$ is the percept for the second, S_j. The task maps $\mathbf{w}$ into the binary response set {Same, Different}. Because there is variability in the percepts across trials, let $\mathbf{W}$ represent the random observation vector. Let $f(\mathbf{W} \mid S_i \cap S_j)$ denote the density of the observation vector when stimuli S_i and S_j are presented. For a given observation, $\mathbf{W} = w$, if the payoff matrix is symmetric, or if one is simply attempting to maximize accuracy, then the optimal response rule is to classify w as Same whenever

$$\Pr(\text{Same} \mid \mathbf{W} = w) > \Pr(\text{Different} \mid \mathbf{W} = w)$$

or, equivalently, taking prior probabilities into account and using Bayes's rule

$$\frac{\Pr(\mathbf{W} = w \mid \text{Same})\Pr(\text{Same})}{\Pr(\mathbf{W} = w \mid \text{Different})\Pr(\text{Different})} > 1.$$

Let π equal the prior probability of a Same trial. Suppose there are k stimuli in the stimulus set. Let B_i be the (conditional) prior probability that the stimulus pair S_i and S_i are presented given a Same trial with ($\Sigma_{i=1}^{k} B_i = 1$). Let γ_{ij} = (conditional) prior probability of the stimulus pair S_i and S_j (with $j \neq i$) given a Different trial, $\left(\sum_{j \neq i}^{k} \sum_{i=1}^{k} \gamma_{ij} = 1\right)$. If the observations from each stimulus in the pair are independent, then the optimal rule is to respond "Same" whenever

$$\frac{\sum_{i=1}^{k} B_i f(u_1, u_2, \cdots, u_n \mid S_i) f(v_1, v_2, \cdots, v_n \mid S_i)}{\sum_{j \neq i}^{k} \sum_{i=1}^{k} \gamma_{ij} f(u_1, u_2, \cdots, u_n \mid S_i) f(v_1, v_2, \cdots, v_n \mid S_j)} > \frac{1 - \pi}{\pi}$$

or otherwise respond "Different." In the usual, but special case, $B_i = 1/k$, $\gamma_{ij} = 1/k(k-1)a$, this becomes

$$\frac{(k-1)\sum_{i=1}^{k} f(u_1, u_2, \cdots, u_n \mid S_i) f(v_1, v_2, \cdots, v_n \mid S_i)}{\sum_{j \neq i}^{k} \sum_{i=1}^{k} f(u_1, u_2, \cdots, u_n \mid S_i) f(v_1, v_2, \cdots, v_n \mid S_j)} > \frac{1-\pi}{\pi}.$$

When incorporating response times into these models, we incorporate a distance-like device, assuming that the farther away from the comparison criterion the log-likelihood ratio of the perceptual effect is, the faster the decision time. For example, let L represent the left-hand side of the aforementioned decision rule for the optimal model, and let $c = \ln 1-\pi/\pi$. A good model for decision time could be $T_d = \alpha \exp(-\beta |\ln L - c|)$. In the case of equally likely trial types ($\pi = .5$), this becomes $T_d = \alpha \exp(-\beta |\ln L|)$.

10.2.3 Adaptation to Selective Attention (Component) Comparison Task

The same-different decision models described earlier can be tailored to a selective-attention version of the comparison task. In this task, the observer is asked to make comparison judgments along only one relevant dimension and to ignore variation on any other stimulus attribute. This is a same-different analogue of the Garner speeded classification task. Using comparisons rather than classification labels for response alternatives may be useful to avoid any linguistic effects such labels could introduce (see, e.g., Townsend, Hu, & Kadlec, 1988).

For the subclassification model, a component judgment would require classifications along the relevant attribute. The response region would then be divided only into regions associated with levels of the relevant component (in Figure 10.2, only c_x would be used if the observer were attending to component A; see also Ashby & Maddox, 1994). All other assumptions carry forward in the logical manner. For the distance-based decision model, assuming a decisionally separable process (see the aforementioned), distances would be taken along the relevant dimension. Assumptions relating distance to decision time are as described earlier. Figure 10.3 clarifies how the distance-based model can be adapted to the component same-difference task assuming decisional separability.

Within this framework, Thomas (1996) established the following results for accuracy and response times with respect to separability. Consider a stimulus set constructed from the factorial combination of two components taken at two levels each: A_1B_1, A_1B_2, A_2B_1, and A_2B_2. In the component same-different task, on each trial, a pair of stimuli is selected randomly (with replacement) from the set and presented. Thus there are sixteen possible stimulus pairings (not collapsing across order). The following two conditions are run:

(i) Same-different filtering A (SDA). The observer's task is to indicate whether the stimulus pair matches on component A.
(ii) Same-different filtering B (SDB). The observer's task is to indicate whether the stimulus pair matches on component B.

Let $A_iB_j \cap A_kB_m$ indicate that A_iB_j and A_kB_m were presented on a trial. Under the joint hypotheses of perceptual and decisional separability for component A, for both subclassification and distance-based strategies, for $i,k = 1,2$,

$$P_{SDA}(\text{Same} \leq t \mid A_iB_1 \cap A_kB_1) = P_{SDA}(\text{Same} \mid A_iB_2 \cap A_kB_2)$$
$$= P_{SDA}(\text{Same} \mid A_iB_1 \cap A_kB_2)$$
$$= P_{SDA}(\text{Same} \mid A_iB_2 \cap A_kB_1)$$

and

$$P_{SDA}(RT_{\text{Same}} \leq t \mid A_iB_1 \cap A_kB_1) = P_{SDA}(RT_{\text{Same}} \leq t \mid A_iB_2 \cap A_kB_2)$$
$$= P_{SDA}(RT_{\text{Same}} \leq t \mid A_iB_1 \cap A_kB_2)$$
$$= P_{SDA}(RT_{\text{Same}} \leq t \mid A_iB_2 \cap A_kB_1).$$

Similar invariances hold in the case of separability for component B. We suspect that in the case of optimal responding, if the additional assumption of perceptual independence is made, these equalities hold as well. Later in the chapter, when independence does not hold but perceptual separability does, optimal responding in the component same-different task predicts response-time distributions that are very nearly indistinguishable from these that assume separability.

10.3 Perceptual Interactions and Component Comparisons

In Sections 10.2.2 and 10.2.3, we described model structures within the GRT framework that could be used to understand the same-different judgment task, particularly applied to component (selective-attention) comparisons. In this section, we investigate the theoretical consequences of perceptual interactions on response-time distributions assuming the GRT model architectures for the component same-different task described earlier. We limit our investigation to one type of integrality—the mean-shift integrality (e.g., Ashby & Maddox, 1994; Macmillan & Ornstein, 1998)—and separability with a within-stimulus correlation. For the latter, only the optimal response strategy is investigated, as the

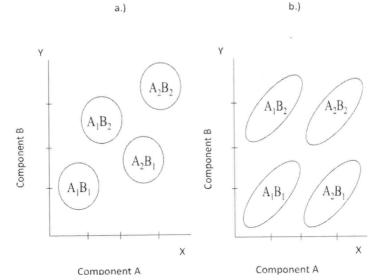

Figure 10.4 a) Mean-shift integrality on both dimensions. b) Separability with positive perceptual correlation.

other two decision models (subclassification and distance-based) with decisional separability will not detect correlations; the theorems of Thomas (1996) hold. To relax the assumption of decisional separability in these models does not provide guidance on what the strategy might be if not decisional separability—an infinite number of options arise. We chose the most sensible alternative to DS—the optimal response strategy. Our plan is to derive RT distributions for component same-different judgments assuming the presence of integrality or perceptual correlation. We describe the assumed stimulus configurations and results of our simulations next.

10.3.1 Mean-Shift Integrality and Perceptual Correlation

When attributes interact in the perception of a stimulus, many possibilities exist for how this comes to be. One type of perceptual interaction that has been investigated is a *mean-shift integrality*, in which the stimulus means no longer form a rectangle (as in PS configurations) but shift to a parallelogram type arrangement (Macmillan & Ornstein, 1998; Maddox, 1992; Silbert & Thomas, 2013; Thomas & Silbert, 2014). Figure 10.4 illustrates such a mean-shift integrality on the X dimension only. As the physical component B increases from level 1 to 2, the mean for the perceptual effect of A (on the X dimension) shifts to the right, even though component A has not changed. Figure 10.4(a) diagrams a possible mean-shift integrality on both dimensions.

Another possible type of perceptual interaction is non-independence of dimensions within a stimulus. Within the GRT framework, perceptual independence holds if and only if the joint density of perceptual effects for a given stimulus is equal to the product of the corresponding marginal densities (see "Introduction"). Contours of equal likelihood for such a case will either be circular (if both variances are equal) or elliptical with major and minor axes aligned with the perceptual axes. When dependence exists, these contours will exhibit tilt away from the axes. Figure 10.4(b) illustrates a case in which all stimulus distributions exhibit positive correlation between the components within stimuli, but are perceptually separable across stimuli. In earlier work, Thomas (2001; Thomas, Altieri, Silbert, Wenger, & Wessels, 2015) found perceptual correlations among features of faces that also exhibited separability in classification, identification, and uncertainty judgments. Hence these two types of perceptual interaction can be distinguished both theoretically and empirically.

10.3.2 Simulating Mean-Shift Integrality and Perceptual Correlation

In this section, we simulate performance in the component same-different task, assuming bivariate normal perceptual distributions, for the mean-shift integrality and perceptual correlation cases illustrated in Figure 10.4. These simulations allow us to derive response-time distribution predictions for three types of decision models: subclassification, distance-based, and optimal. All three decision processes are applied to the mean-shift integral scenario of which there are two subcases: mean shift on dimension X only, and mean shift on both. Only the optimal response strategy is applied to perceptually correlated attributes. This is because, in the absence of integrality, the theorems of Thomas (1996) presented in Section 10.2.3 earlier indicate that subclassification and distance-based processing with decisional separability will not detect correlations. The task to be modeled is same-different judgments on component A.

We assume a two-component, two-levels-each stimulus set yielding four possible stimuli. There are 16 possible pairs of stimuli that can be sampled with equal probability. Half of these pairs will yield a "same-on-component-A" designation. Once a pair of stimuli out of the 16 possible pairs is selected, bivariate percepts are generated according to the stimulus distribution parameters for that configuration. Table 1 houses the parameter values used in the different simulation cases. The percept values are then interrogated by the appropriate decision process to determine if a "same-on-component-A" response is warranted. Response time is computed according to the assumptions for that process as described in Sections 10.2.2 and 10.2.3. For each configuration examined, 900 simulated trials

Table 10.1 Configuration Parameters for RT Simulations

Subclassification (T : α = 1, β = 0.5)

	Type A			**Type B**		
	Shift 1 (seed = 5)			Shift 1 (seed = 4)		
Stimulus #	μ_x μ_y σ_x σ_y	Decision Criteria	Stimulus #	μ_x μ_y σ_x σ_y	Decision Criteria
1	0 0 1 1	1	1	0 0 1 1	1
2	0.3 2 1 1	1	2	1 1.73 1 1	1
3	2 0 1 1	1	3	1.73 1 1 1	1
4	2.3 2 1 1	1	4	2.73 2.73 1 1	1
	Shift 2 (seed = 6)			Shift 2 (seed = 5)		
Stimulus #	μ_x μ_y σ_x σ_y	Decision Criteria	Stimulus #	μ_x μ_y σ_x σ_y	Decision Criteria
1	0 0 1 1	1	1	0 0 1 1	1
2	0.6 2 1 1	1	2	0.75 1.85 1 1	1
3	2 0 1 1	1	3	1.85 0.77 1 1	1
4	2.6 2 1 1	1	4	2.62 2.62 1 1	1
	Shift 3 (seed = 7)			Shift 3 (seed = 5)		
Stimulus #	μ_x μ_y σ_x σ_y	Decision Criteria	Stimulus #	μ_x μ_y σ_x σ_y	Decision Criteria
1	0 0 1 1	1	1	0 0 1 1	1
2	0.9 2 1 1	1	2	0.52 1.93 1 1	1
3	2 0 1 1	1	3	1.93 0.52 1 1	1
4	2.9 2 1 1	1	4	2.45 2.45 1 1	1
	Shift 4 (seed = 8)					
Stimulus #	μ_x μ_y σ_x σ_y	Decision Criteria			
1	0 0 1 1	1			
2	1.2 2 1 1	1			
3	2 0 1 1	1			
4	3.2 2 1 1	1			

(*Continued*)

Table 10.1 (Continued)

Subclassification (T : α = 1, β = 0.5)									
Type A					**Type B**				
Distance Based, (T : α = 1)					Optimal Responding (T : α = 1, β = 0.5)				
Base Configuration, β = 0.5					PS, p = 0.7				
Stimulus #	μ_x μ_y σ_x σ_y			Decision Criteria	Stimulus #	μ_x μ_y σ_x σ_y			Decision Criteria
1	0 0 1 1			1	1	0 0 1 1			0.7
2	1.2 2 1 1			1	2	0 2 1 1			0.7
3	2 0 1 1			1	3	2 0 1 1			0.7
4	3.2 2 1 1			1	4	2 2 1 1			0.7
Extended Configuration, β = 0.5					PS, p = 0.7				
Stimulus #	μ_x μ_y σ_x σ_y			Decision Criteria	Stimulus #	μ_x μ_y σ_x σ_y			Decision Criteria
1	0 0 1 1			3	1	0 0 1 1			0.9
2	2 2 1 1			3	2	0 2 1 1			0.9
3	4 0 1 1			3	3	2 0 1 1			0.9
4	6 2 1 1			3	4	2 2 1 1			0.9
Extended Configuration, β = 0.8					Mean-Shift Integrality (type B, shift 3)				
Stimulus #	μ_x μ_y σ_x σ_y			Decision Criteria	Stimulus #	μ_x μ_y σ_x σ_y			Decision Criteria
1	0 0 1 1			3	1	0 0 1 1			0
2	2 2 1 1			3	2	0.52 1.93 1 1			0
3	4 0 1 1			3	3	1.93 0.52 1 1			0
4	6 2 1 1			3	4	2.45 2.45 1 1			0

per each of the 16 possible pairs occurred, yielding a total of 14,400 trials per simulation case. Selected simulation results are presented as decision-time distributions in Figures 10.5–10.12, as these are representative of the qualitative patterns. The legends use the numbers 1 – 4 for stimulus labels due to formatting difficulties the use of subscripts can create. These map onto the set $A_1B_1, A_1B_2, A_2B_1, A_2B_2$, respectively.

(*Subclassification*). Figures 10.5 and 10.6 collect the predicted correct decision distributions for "same on component A" when component A is at level 1 for the subclassification model with decisional separability. Due to the symmetry of the mean-shift integrality probed by these simulations,

Modeling Interactive Dimensions 211

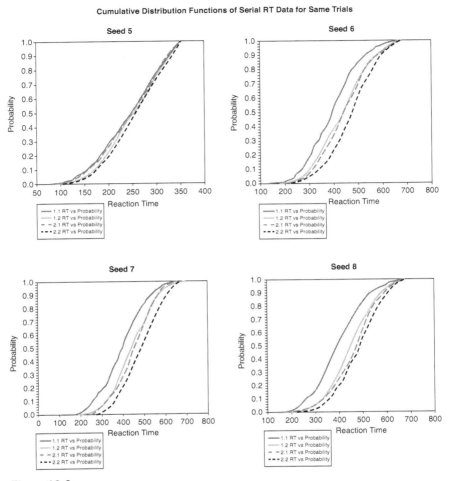

Figure 10.5

these plots are sufficient for all same-on-A pairs (e.g., stimulus pairs 4,4; 4,3; 3,4; 3,3 would directly correspond to 1,1; 1,2; 2,1; and 2,2, respectively). Recall that this model assumes that observers separately classify each stimulus and then determine if their labels are identical. The RT-distance hypothesis governs the decision-time predictions of the individual classifications. Not surprisingly, then, when both of the stimuli are far from their bound, same classification is fastest (1,1 and the unplotted but equivalent 4,4 cases). Slowest are the trials in which both stimuli are close to the decision bound. Architecture did not impact the order of the

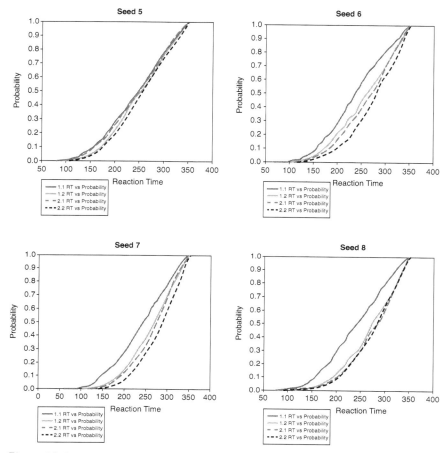

Figure 10.6

distributions, although there appears to be subtle shape differences that are unlikely to be detected in empirical data. In addition, other processes besides decision contribute to an overall response time, such as response selection and execution. These would be convolved with decision time, which would alter the shape of the cumulative function. Figures 10.7 and 10.8 illustrate the predicted distributions for correct "different-on-A" trials. Again, when stimuli are far from the decision bound, classification is fast, and it is slowest when both are near the bound (as in stimulus pair 2,3).

(*Distance-based*). Figures 10.9 and 10.10 show the predicted distributions from the distance-based model for the component-A judgments with

Modeling Interactive Dimensions 213

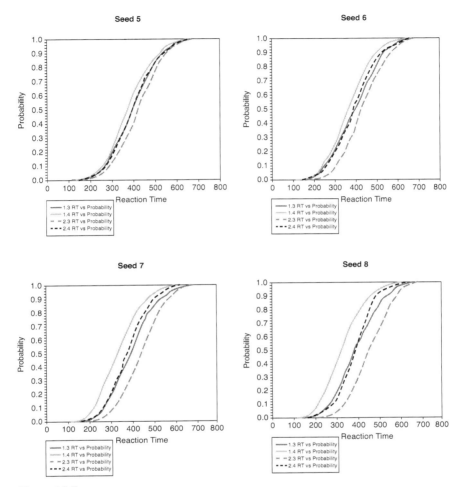

Figure 10.7

same trials in Figure 10.9 and different trials in Figure 10.10. Recall that this model suggests, when decisional separability is assumed, that percepts on dimension X generated from their respective stimuli are differenced and compared to a threshold. As can be seen in the figures, perceptual integrality influences decision time for pairs that differ on the irrelevant component because when the irrelevant component changes level, the marginal distribution for the relevant component shifts. For this model, on component-same trials, whenever the pair consists of identical stimuli, decision time

214   Robin D. Thomas et al.

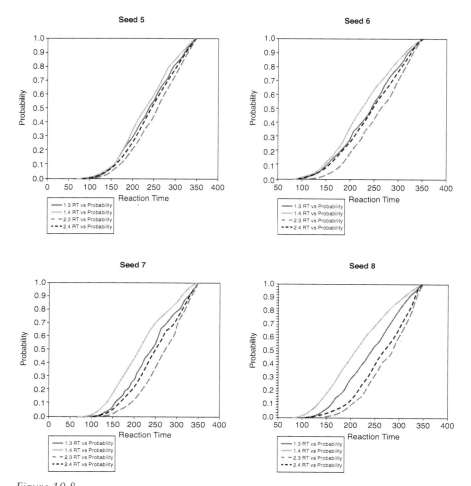

Figure 10.8

is fastest regardless of which identical pair is presented. This contrasts with predictions from the subclassification model in which the fastest identical pairs are those farther from the boundary. On different trials, distributions from the two decision models are ordered similarly and in an intuitive way. The mean-shift integrality renders stimuli 1 and 4 (A_1B_1 and A_2B_2) farthest apart on the X dimension and stimuli 2 and 3 (A_1B_2 and A_2B_1) closest together.

Modeling Interactive Dimensions 215

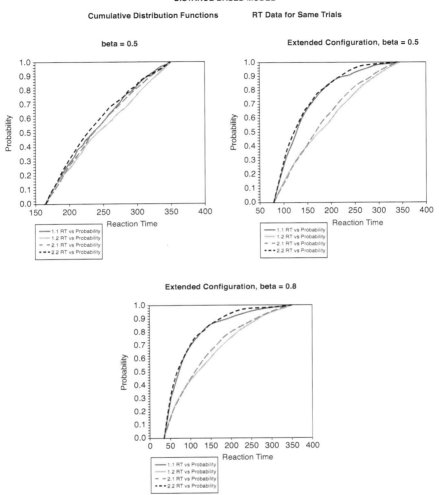

Figure 10.9

(*Optimal–Mean-Shift Integrality*). Figure 10.11 diagrams representative distributions for component-same and component-different correct trials assuming optimal response. Intriguingly, the component-same decision-time distribution predictions mimic those of the subclassification model. Why this is would require deeper analysis. Shapes of the distribution appear more similar to the parallel architecture than the serial architecture, though again, this subtle feature would be difficult to confirm empirically. Component-different trials resemble those of the other decision models.

DISTANCE BASED MODEL

Cumulative Distribution Functions   RT Data for Different Trials

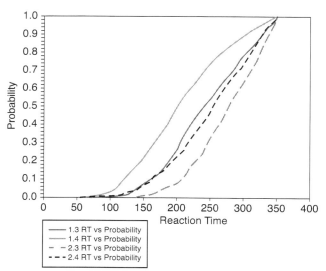

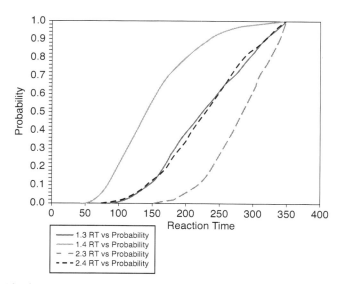

Figure 10.10

OPTIMAL MODEL

Mean-Shift Integrality

Same Trials

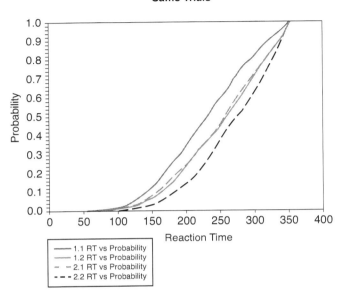

Different Trials

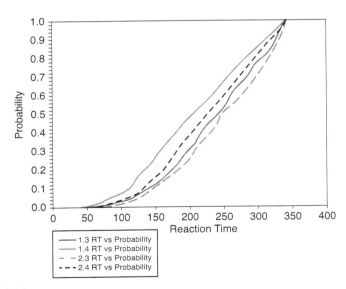

Figure 10.11

Optimal Model

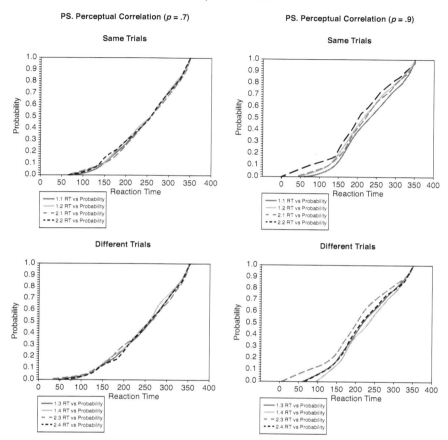

Figure 10.12

(*Optimal – Perceptual Correlation with Separability*). A priori, we did not know if a perceptual correlation would influence component comparison judgment in optimal responding given that this strategy exploits all useful features of the probability distributions. Figure 10.12 indicates, however, that when the task is to focus on component A for the comparisons, the decision-time distributions generated by the optimal process are virtually the same as would be expected given perceptual separability even with a moderately large correlation of 0.7. In the right of Figure 10.12, with an extreme perceptual correlation of 0.9, we begin to see some separation of the distributions. Figure 10.13 schematizes what an optimal partition of the stimulus space might look like for a component "same-on-A" task. This partition occurs at the intersection of the mixed density function representing stimuli with the same level of component A.

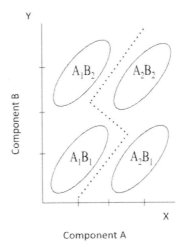

Figure 10.13 PS with positive correlation and partition induced by optimal responding in a "same-on-A" judgment task.

If the distributions plotted are to be believed, on "same-on-A" trials, stimulus pair 1,1 (A_1B_1 and A_1B_1) appear to be the slowest with stimulus pair 2,2 (A_1B_2 and A_1B_2) the quickest. Perhaps more of the distribution for the former is closer to the "boundary" than that of the latter. When the pair is 2 and 3 (A_1B_2 and A_2B_1), component-different judgments are fast, whereas when stimulus pair 1,4 (A_1B_1 and A_2B_2) occur, judgments are slowest. Evidently, the positive correlation increases the statistical distance between the former (see, e.g., Thomas, 1999) and shrinks it in the latter case. Given the assumption that decision time is a monotonic function of the strength of evidence manifest in the likelihood ratio, these orderings are understandable. However, in reality, the differences between these simulated distributions are very slight and emerged only in the case of a very high correlation between perceptual dimensions.

10.4 Conclusions

In this chapter, we have presented a theoretical integration of two of the core areas in which Jim Townsend has focused his research over many years. Specifically, we have presented an analysis of speeded classification and same-different tasks in which participants must selectively attend to single stimulus attributes. Our analysis incorporated notions and definitions of perceptual interactions from Jim and colleague's work on the GRT, as well as notions and definitions of mental architecture and stopping rules from Jim and colleague's work on response-time modeling. By rigorously analyzing the ways in which stimulus attributes may interact perceptually and, simultaneously, how observers may make decisions and select responses, we have described theoretically how the nature of perceptual representations, decision rules, and mental architectures combine to produce unique patterns of response accuracies and response-time distributions in speeded classification and component (selective attention) same-different tasks.

References

Ashby, F. G. (1992). *Multidimensional models of perception and cognition.* Hillsdale, NJ: Lawrence Erlbaum Associates.
Ashby, F. G., Boynton, G., & Lee, W. W. (1994). Categorization response-time with multidimensional stimuli. *Perception & Psychophysics, 55,* 11–27.
Ashby, F. G., & Gott, R. E. (1988). Decision rules in the perception and categorization of multidimensional stimuli. *Journal of Experimental Psychology: Learning, Memory, and Cognition, 14,* 33–53.
Ashby, F. G., & Lee, W. W. (1991). Predicting similarity and categorization from identification. *Journal of Experimental Psychology: General, 120,* 150–172.
Ashby, F. G., & Maddox, W. T. (1990). Integrating information from separable psychological dimensions. *Journal of Experimental Psychology: Human Perception and Performance, 16,* 598–612.
Ashby, F. G., & Maddox, W. T. (1991). A response-time theory of perceptual independence. In J. Doigon P. & J. Falmagne C. (Eds.), *Mathematical psychology: current developments.* New York: Springer-Verlag.
Ashby, F. G., & Maddox, W. T. (1992). Complex decision rules in categorization: contrasting novice and experienced performance. *Journal of Experimental Psychology: Human Perception and Performance, 18*(1), 50–71.
Ashby, F. G., & Maddox, W. T. (1994). A response-time theory of separability and integrality in speeded classification. *Journal of Mathematical Psychology, 38,* 423–466.
Ashby, F. G., & Townsend, J. T. (1986). Varieties of perceptual independence. *Psychological Review, 93,* 154–179.
Dai, H., Versfeld, N. J., & Green, D. M. (1996). The optimum decision rules in the same-different paradigm. *Perception & Psychophysics, 58,* 1–9.
Eidels, A., Townsend, J. T., Hughes, H. C., & Perry, L. A. (2015). Evaluating perceptual integration: Uniting response-time and accuracy-based methodologies. *Attention, Perception, & Psychophysics, 77*(2), 659–680.
Ennis, D. M., & Ashby, F. G. (1993). The relative sensitivities of same-different and identification judgment models to perceptual dependence. *Psychometrika, 58,* 257–279.
Fukunaga, K. (1990). *Introduction to statistical pattern recognition.* New York: Academic press.
Garner, W. R. (1974). *The processing of information and structure.* Potomac, MD: Lawrence Erlbaum Associates.
Garner, W. R., & Felfoldy, G. L. (1970). Integrality of stimulus dimensions in various types of information processing. *Cognitive Psychology, 1,* 225–241.
Green, D. M., & Swets, J. A. (1966). *Signal detection theory and psychophysics.* Oxford, England: John Wiley.
Johnson, S. A., Blaha, L. M., Houpt, J. W., & Townsend, J. T. (2010). Systems Factorial Technology provides new insights on global-local information

processing in autism spectrum disorders. *Journal of Mathematical Psychology, 54,* 53–72.

Kadlec, H., & Townsend, J. T. (1992a). Implications of marginal and conditional detection parameters for the separabilities and independence of perceptual dimensions. *Journal of Mathematical Psychology, 36,* 325–374.

Kadlec, H., & Townsend, J. T. (1992b). Signal detection analyses of dimensional interactions. In F. G. Ashby (Ed.), *Multidimensional models of perception and cognition* (pp. 181–227). Hillsdale, NJ: Lawrence Erlbaum Associates.

MacMillan, N. A., & Creelman, C. D. (1991). *Detection theory: A user's guide.* New York: Cambridge University Press.

Macmillan, N. A., & Ornstein, A. S. (1998). The mean-integral representation of rectangles. *Perception & Psychophysics, 60,* 250–262.

Maddox, W. T. (1992). Perceptual and decisional separability. In F. G. Ashby (Ed.), *Multidimensional models of perception and cognition* (pp. 147–180). Hillsdale, NJ: Lawrence Erlbaum Associates.

Maddox, W. T., & Ashby, F. G. (1996). Perceptual separability, decisional separability, and the identification–speeded classification relationship. *Journal of Experimental Psychology: Human Perception and Performance, 22*(4), 795–817.

Mckinley, S., & Nosofsky, R. M. (1995). Investigations of exemplar and decision bound models in large, ill-defined category structures. *Journal of Experimental Psychology: Human Perception and Performance, 21,* 128–148.

Murdock, B. (1985). An analysis of the strength-latency relationship. *Memory & Cognition, 13,* 511-521.

Pao, Y. (1989). *Adaptive pattern recognition and neural networks.* Reading, MA: Addison-Wesley Publishing Co., Inc.

Podgorny, P., & Garner, W. R. (1979). Reaction time as a measure of inter- and intraobject visual similarity: Letters of the alphabet. *Perception & Psychophysics, 26,* 37–52.

Posner, M. I. (1964). Information reduction in the analysis of sequential tasks. *Psychological Review, 71,* 491–504.

Schweickert, R., & Townsend, J. T. (1989). A trichotomy: Interactions of factors prolonging sequential and concurrent mental processes in stochastic discrete mental (PERT) networks. *Journal of Mathematical Psychology, 33,* 328–347.

Silbert, N. H., & Thomas, R. D. (2013). Decisional separability, model identification, and statistical inference in the general recognition theory framework. *Psychonomic Bulletin & Review, 20,* 1–20.

Takane, Y., & Sergent, J. (1983). Multidimensional scaling models for reaction times and same-different judgments. *Psychometrika, 48,* 393–423.

Thomas, R. D. (1995). Gaussian general recognition theory and perceptual independence. *Psychological Review, 102,* 192–200.

Thomas, R. D. (1996). Separability and independence of dimensions within the same-different judgment task. *Journal of Mathematical Psychology, 40,* 318–341.

Thomas, R. D. (1998). Learning correlations in categorization tasks using large, ill-defined categories. *Journal of Experimental Psychology: Learning, Memory, and Cognition, 24,* 119–143.

Thomas, R. D. (1999). Assessing sensitivity in a multidimensional space: Some problems and a definition of a general d'. *Psychonomic Bulletin & Review, 6,* 224–238.

Thomas, R. D. (2001). Perceptual interactions of facial dimensions in speeded classification and identification. *Perception & Psychophysics, 63*(4), 625–650.

Thomas, R. D., Altieri, N. A., Silbert, N. H., Wenger, M. J., & Wessels, P. M. (2015). Multidimensional signal detection decision models of the uncertainty task: Application to face perception. *Journal of Mathematical Psychology, 66,* 16–33.

Thomas, R. D., & Silbert, N. H. (2014). Technical clarification on Silbert & Thomas (2013). *Psychonomic Bulletin & Review, 21,* 574–575.

Townsend, J. T. (1972). Some results concerning the identifiability of parallel and serial processes. *British Journal of Mathematical and Statistical Psychology, 25,* 168–199.

Townsend, J. T. (1984). Uncovering mental processes with factorial experiments. *Journal of Mathematical Psychology, 28,* 363–400.

Townsend, J. T. (1990). Truth and consequences of ordinal differences in statistical distributions: Toward a theory of hierarchical inference. *Psychological Bulletin, 108,* 551–567.

Townsend, J. T., Houpt, J. W., & Silbert, N. H. (2012). General recognition theory extended to include response times: Predictions for a class of parallel systems. *Journal of Mathematical Psychology, 56,* 476–494.

Townsend, J. T., Hu, G. G., & Kadlec, H. (1988). Feature sensitivity, bias and interdependencies as a function of intensity and payoffs. *Perception & Psychophysics, 43,* 575–591.

Townsend, J. T., & Landon, D. E. (1982). An experimental and theoretical investigation of the constant ratio rule and other models of visual letter confusion. *Journal of Mathematical Psychology, 25,* 119–162.

Townsend, J. T., & Nozawa, G. (1995). Spatio-temporal properties of elementary perception: An investigation of parallel, serial, and coactive theories. *Journal of Mathematical Psychology, 39,* 321–359.

Townsend, J. T., & Schweickert, R. (1989). Toward the trichotomy method of reaction times: Laying the foundation of stochastic mental networks. *Journal of Mathematical Psychology, 33,* 309–327.

Townsend, J. T., & Thomas, R. D. (1994). Stochastic dependencies in parallel and serial models: Effects on systems factorial interactions. *Journal of Mathematical Psychology, 38,* 1–34.

11 Symmetry Provides a Turing-Type Test for 3D Vision

Zygmunt Pizlo

11.1 Introduction

The question of whether computers and robots will ever be able to think as well as we do has occupied researchers working in artificial intelligence for more than 50 years, ever since Alan Turing (1950) proposed his behavioral test. In this test, a computer tries to imitate a human being's use of natural language in a conversation carried on via a teletype machine back in the 1950s and via e-mails today. The human participant in this exchange is required to decide whether he is conversing with another human being or with a computer, and if it is hard for the human being to tell which it is, Turing, and some others, have concluded that the computer participating in this discussion is as intelligent as we humans are. This test has been criticized on a number of counts, with the best-known criticism coming from Searle (1980). Searle's criticism is elaborated in his "Chinese room" thought experiment, which makes it clear that even if a computer passes the Turing test by manipulating words appropriately, one is not entitled to conclude that the computer understands what is being said. Searle's criticism is clearly valid, because similar behaviors, in themselves, need not imply that similar underlying mechanisms are governing these behaviors. One should note that Searle's (1980) criticism of Turing's test is not very different from Chomsky's (1959) criticism of Skinner's behavioristic theory of language. Today, virtually everyone acknowledges that Skinner was obviously wrong, and one should find it easy to appreciate that Turing was, too.

Despite this impasse, some progress has been made toward understanding the relationship between observable behavior and the unobservable mental states that underlie perception. Signal detection theory (SDT) was devised precisely to allow us to infer the observer's percept without confounding it with other, nonperceptual of his mental states, but signal detection measures do not go nearly far enough. They do not tell us how the percept is represented in the observer's mind. They only tell us what a subject can discriminate. For example, these methods only allow us to verify whether two subjects' abilities to discriminate between two wavelengths of light are the same, but they do not allow us to find out whether the subjects' subjective experiences of color, say pure green, are actually the same. If SDT cannot do this with two subjects, there is no way it will be able to allow us to compare a human subject's percepts with a computer's. So an experiment using signal detection methodology, despite its obvious advantages over "classical" psychophysical methods cannot be, and never has been, able to serve as a Turing-type test in perception.

The present chapter describes a new way of explaining percepts, a way that will actually tell us how the percept is represented in the observer's mind or in a computer model of it. This will be explained with examples taken from the perception of 3D shapes. It is unlikely that this approach can be extended to perceptual properties other than 3D shape, but understanding why it will be hard to do this may help us develop new, perhaps analogous, ways of studying problem solving, language, and thinking. The essence of my new approach to a valid Turing-type test for perception is that it must be based on fundamental principles used to explain phenomena in the "hard" natural sciences, such as physics, rather than being based on, and confined to, observable behavior, as has been done till now. What are these fundamental physical principles, and how will they be used?

11.2 How Physicists Explain Natural Phenomena

Natural phenomena in physics are said to always be invariant under some transformations. For example, when we test Newton's second law in two different places, say in two different labs in the same building, we expect to get the same results. We do, which means that Newton's laws are invariant, or symmetric, with respect to a translation in space. Similarly, the outcome of an experiment is expected to be the same when the experiment is performed at two different times in the same laboratory, say today and tomorrow. When it is the same, this means that the law of nature is also invariant, or symmetric, with respect to a translation in time. The same is true with a rotation in space. These facts can be stated succinctly; namely, *the result of a transformed experiment is the same as the transformed result of the experiment* (Rosen & Freundlich, 1978). To illustrate, take the example of a translation in time. When the outcome of an experiment that was performed for the first time today is examined tomorrow, that is, when its outcome was translated in time from today to tomorrow, the outcome will be the same as the outcome of an identical experiment performed tomorrow, that is, when the experiment was translated in time because it was performed tomorrow, not today. So for a natural law N and a transformation, or mapping M, the following equivalence takes place: $NM = MN$. Wigner

(1967) pointed out that without such invariances (symmetries) there actually would be no such thing as science. This observation is obviously not only confined to physics. It applies equally well in biology and psychology (Narens, 2002).

The symmetry of natural laws is only one of three fundamental characteristics that are used to explain phenomena in physics. The least-action principle is the second fundamental principle. This principle states that phenomena in physics can be formulated in such a way that the cause-effect relations can be shown to minimize some quantity. More generally, some quantity is stationary (the first derivative of this quantity is zero). The Greeks way back when had some intuition about this least-action principle. In modern times, it was Fermat, then Leibniz, and later Maupertuis, Euler, Lagrange, and Hamilton who provided more and more solid formulations of this principle (see Hildebrandt & Tromba, 1996, for a lucid review). Fermat's principle is one of the most commonly known. It says that the reflection and refraction of light can be explained by assuming that light "chooses" the path that minimizes the total time traveled. Another common example, often used to illustrate an application of a least-action principle, can be found in electrical circuits where Kirchhoff's laws for currents and voltages can be derived by assuming that an electrical circuit minimizes the total amount of heat generated in its resistors.

This way of thinking in physics culminated with Noether's (1918) theorems in which the conservation laws can be derived by applying the least-action principle to the symmetries (invariances) of the natural laws. The conservation laws are the third fundamental characteristic upon which our modern physics is built. For two examples, the conservation of energy results from time symmetry, and the conservation of momentum results from position symmetry. These three fundamental aspects of physics, namely symmetry, the least-action principle, and the conservation laws allow physicists to describe and explain underlying, hidden, cause-effect relations. Furthermore, they allow abstract representations of physical phenomena that are not amenable to direct observation. They provide the basis for the model of atom, the concept of black holes, and the big bang theory. This way of thinking and proceeding will be applied to the study of visual perception in this paper (for a preliminary presentation of this idea, see the "Note Added in Proofs" in Pizlo, Li, Sawada, & Steinman, 2014). Percepts will actually be easier to deal with than atoms, black holes, and big bangs because they are not extremely small, extremely far away, or in the extremely distant past. They will, however, present one special difficulty because percepts reside in the mental, not in the physical, world. A hundred years ago this was believed to be an insurmountable obstacle because mental phenomena were thought to be outside the scope of scientific study, but modern psychological and engineering communities have been willing to take mental phenomena seriously for quite a while

11.3 Importing the Least-Action Principle Into Perception

The suggestion that the least-action principle operates in perception first appeared in Mach's (1886/1959) book on perception. Mach also discussed the ability of the human visual system to detect symmetrical patterns in this book. The important role that symmetry plays in perception will be discussed in detail in the next section. Here, only the status of the least-action principle will be evaluated. Mach was actively involved in the discussion of many new trends in physics that took place at the end of the 19th century. The extent and significance of his interests can be seen in his book on mechanics published in 1883. Mach was an unusually creative and prescient thinker. He actually claimed that the scientific laws are "constructed" by the mind of the scientist, rather than "discovered," and that the role of a scientific theory is to describe experimental data economically, rather than to describe, or to explain, the laws of nature. So if one follows Mach's lead, one can claim that the least-action principle, commonly assumed to operate in the physical world, actually originates in the scientist's mind because the scientist's mind used the least-action principle to represent the data he had on hand as economically as possible. We probably will never know whether this claim is really correct, but what is important here is that Mach was the first to claim that the least-action principle operates in the human mind. He went on to support his claim by providing concrete examples taken from visual perception. He pointed out that when a straight-line segment is projected on the observer's retina, the observer perceives a straight-line segment, rather than a circle. Both a straight-line segment and a circle are possible interpretations, but the simpler straight line segment is perceived. Mach went even one step further and pointed out that the simpler interpretation is also more likely, setting the stage for the modern equivalence of the simplicity and likelihood principles (e. g., Chater, 1996; M. Li & Vitanyi, 1994).

The Gestalt psychologists took Mach's simplicity principle very seriously and made this principle the foundation of their revolution without ever citing Mach (Koffka, 1935; Wertheimer 1923/1958). Gestalt psychologists called their simplicity principle "Prägnanz," a concept very close to what Mach meant when he talked about the economy of perceptual representation. The Gestalt psychologists deserve a lot of credit for emphasizing simplicity to a much greater extent than Mach ever did. They also deserve a lot of credit for taking the next very important step, when, in 1920, they introduced the concept of isomorphism between the physiological representation of the physical stimulus in the brain and the stimulus' perceptual representation. Wolfgang Köhler, before formally joining the Gestalt movement, received his psychological training at the University of Berlin between 1907 and 1909 under the guidance of Carl Stumpf. He also received solid training in physics at the same time under the guidance of Max Planck. So he clearly had the background needed to pick up the least-action principle where Mach left it. By 1920, Mach was dead, so Köhler did not have to give Mach credit for introducing this important idea to perception. Köhler (1920/1938) claimed that the brain acts as an electrical circuit whose minimum state represents the Prägnanz of the percept. Köhler knew that the end-state of an electrical circuit always ends with the minimal amount of heat generated by its resistors. He also knew that this least-action principle allows one to derive Kirchhoff's laws described in 1845, so for Köhler the least-action principle can act on two levels: the physiological and the mental. He was, however, not in a position to make any meaningful elaborations of the neurophysiological underpinnings of the least-action principle in the brain simply because the brain was not sufficiently understood back then. He did, unfortunately, try to do this, committing himself to the idea that the brain is a "volume conductor." This idea did not have a long life, and it distracted many contemporary neuroscientists who felt that they had to test it.

Sixty-five years after Köhler published his 1920 paper, Poggio, Torre, and Koch (1985) published a plausible physiological model of an electrical circuit that might realize the least-action principle in the brain. These authors were able to elaborate Köhler's ideas considerably, because a number of new tools were available to them, including the Theory of Inverse Problems, the Regularization method, Information Theory, as well as Rissanen's (1978) elaboration of Kolmogorov complexity that did not exist in the first half of the 20th century. Furthermore, much more was known about neural circuits in the brain in 1985 than was known to Köhler in 1920. Today, all computational models of vision take the form of the least-action principle (Pizlo, 2001, 2008), but not everyone working on them today is willing to make claims about the underlying physiological mechanisms as Köhler did. Despite such widespread skittishness, it seems highly likely that some version of what Köhler (1920/1938) had in mind, and what Poggio et al. (1985) described, is actually going on when the brain produces percepts, because visual percepts are produced very quickly. This can only happen when the minimum of some cost function is found by a physiological process resembling the least-action principle known to govern all physical and chemical events. The kind of iterative processes used by computers today cannot act fast enough to pull this off. Once this is appreciated, the brain/percept isomorphism first proposed by Köhler becomes both self-evident and necessary. Other cognitive functions, such as thinking and language, may be different. They may not make use of a physiological least-action principle, because they tend to be much slower than perception.

11.4 Bringing Symmetry Into Theories of Perception

Mach (1886/1959), as pointed out earlier, was the first to discuss the role of symmetry in vision. He used 2D mirror, rotational, and translational symmetries as examples when he did this. He pointed out that mirror symmetrical configurations are the easiest to see as being self-similar when they were compared to rotational and translational symmetrical configurations. This convinced him that mirror symmetry is special for a human observer when compared to the other types of symmetry. Wertheimer (1923/1958) made the next important contribution to the role of symmetry in visual perception when he used interwoven sine- and square-waves to illustrate what he meant by "simplicity" with the grouping principle he called "good continuation." The periodically repeating patterns of the sine- and squarewaves he used made it very easy to disambiguate the x-intersections of the two waves because of the redundancy introduced by their symmetry. This was important because Wertheimer insisted that the simplicity of a curve is not caused by its geometrical simplicity; for example, a straight line is simpler than a curved line. Its simplicity was produced by something quite different. The example he chose to illustrate this difference implies that the similarity of a pattern to itself (aka symmetry) is a better way to define the simplicity of the pattern than any geometrical measure of the pattern, such as its curvature or variation of the curvature.

From this point on, symmetry was tested, on and off, by a host of students of human vision, but only as a source of redundancy that could make it easier to store and remember symmetrical patterns. This made sense in light of Shannon's (1948) Information Theory, which had been picked up by psychologists who thought that detecting and removing redundancy was the primary task confronting the visual system (see, e.g., Attneave, 1954; Barlow, 1961; Van der Helm, 2000). This focus on symmetry as redundancy encouraged, actually forced, vision scientists to use stimuli that were symmetrical when they were presented to the observer's retina. This was unfortunate, as well as unnatural, because natural symmetrical objects are 3D, not 2D, and they almost never produce 2D symmetrical retinal images. A 2D retinal image of a 3D symmetrical object is itself symmetrical, but only for a very restricted number of viewing directions. Such viewing directions, which are called "degenerate," are so unlikely to occur in our natural lives that their probability can be said to be zero.

This was the role symmetry played in visual perception until 2006, when we showed that 3D mirror symmetry is used by the human visual system to recover 3D shapes from a single 2D retinal image (Pizlo, Li, & Steinman, 2006). The retinal image of a 3D mirror-symmetrical object is always 2D and usually asymmetrical, so assuming that 3D objects are symmetrical is the only effective way for the visual system to recover the 3D shapes of the objects from 2D retinal images. Two important facts must be noted here, namely: (i) natural objects are 3D and many of them are mirror-

Symmetry Provides a Turing-type Test for 3D Vision   229

symmetrical, and (ii) we see them as 3D and mirror-symmetrical. These facts imply that a 3D mirror reflection, which defines mirror symmetry, operates as well in the physical world as it operates in the mental world. With this established, we can use the concepts and jargon borrowed from physics introduced in Section 11.3 to elaborate this story. A 3D mirror-symmetrical object does not change under reflection. This means that the object is invariant (symmetric) under 3D reflection. The same is true with the perceptual representation of a 3D mirror-symmetrical object. Specifically, we see symmetrical objects as symmetrical, which means that a mirror reflection of the perceptual representation of a 3D mirror-symmetrical object does not change this representation. Now, let M represent a 3D reflection of a physical object or of the object's perceptual representation. Let N represent a psychophysical natural law describing how the 3D physical world is transformed into its perceptual representation in the mind of the observer. What has just been said about the symmetry of objects and the symmetry of percepts can be expressed as follows: $NM = MN$, which means that the percept of a 3D reflected symmetrical object is the same as a 3D reflected percept of the original object (see Figure 11.1). This statement is intuitively obvious, but it is far from trivial. Note that this statement would not be true if we did not perceive symmetrical objects as symmetrical. This claim will be illustrated by using Marr's theory of vision, because his theory, as all prior theories of human vision, ignored symmetry completely. Assume that the percept is like Marr's 2.5D representation, namely the observer's percept represents only the visible surfaces of a 3D opaque object. So, according to Marr, when the right half of a horse's body is facing an observer, the observer can only perceive the right half of the horse's body, and after a 3D reflection of this percept, the right half becomes the left half of the horse. This would be the result after applying the transformation "MN" to the

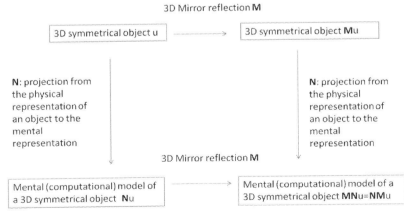

Figure 11.1 N is our natural law for mapping a 3D mirror-symmetrical object, u, to its mental representation. M is a 3D reflection.

3D horse, that is, MN(horse) = left half of the horse. Now, if we first reflect the 3D horse, we get the same horse, but the percept now, according to Marr, is the right half of the horse. This is the result of applying the transformation "NM" to the horse, that is, NM(horse) = right half of the horse. Clearly, the right half of a horse is not the same as its left half,[1] so, $NM \neq MN$ in Marr's theory. This means that Marr's theory stands no chance, whatsoever, of becoming a law of nature, so it is neither surprising nor disappointing that Marr's theory has largely been forgotten. Symmetry, simply put, cannot be ignored.

With this made clear, our discussion returns to the symmetry of objects and the symmetry of percepts. As long as we see symmetrical objects as symmetrical, the relation $MN = NM$ is satisfied for the psychophysical law describing the perception of 3D objects. This statement is very important because it is identical to the statement used in Section 11.2, where we described what it means for a law of nature to be symmetric (invariant) with respect to a transformation: "the result of a transformed experiment is the same as the transformed result of the experiment" (Figure 11.1).

To summarize, in the previous section (see Section 11.3), we established that the natural law for the perception of 3D objects is governed by the least-action principle. In this section, we established that it is characterized by invariance (symmetry) in the presence of 3D reflections. A cost function that represents the least-action principle will be described in the next section where it will be shown that when this cost function is applied to the 2D retinal image of a 3D symmetrical object, the 3D shape is "conserved." This psychophysical conservation is called "veridical" in shape perception. This way of deriving the conservation of shape through the application of a minimum principle to an object's symmetry is analogous to the manner in which Noether's theorem established a one-to-one correspondence between the symmetries of natural phenomena and the conservation laws. The fact that the 3D shape of an object remains unchanged when the 3D object undergoes a transformation between the physical world and its mental representation, provides the basis for comparing the perceptual representations of two different human observers or the perceptual representations of a robot and a human observer.

11.5 Veridicality of 3D Shape Perception Seen as a Conservation Law

Assume that we are given a 2D camera image of a set of N pairs of 3D points that form a mirror-symmetrical configuration. Call this set of 3D points a "3D object." Real objects, such as chairs, horses, and bell peppers, are not sets of points. In fact, they cannot be described adequately by points. We use points here, despite this, simply because this makes it easy to explain how our cost function leads to the veridical perception of a 3D shape. In prior work, we showed how the cost functions used could recover the shapes of a wide variety of natural objects, including birds, praying mantises, spiders, and jeeps (Pizlo et al., 2014). When we say that a set of 3D points is mirror-symmetrical, we mean that there is a plane that bisects the line segments connecting the individual symmetrical pairs of points. This plane is called the "plane of symmetry," and the lines connecting pairs of mirror-symmetrical points are called "symmetry lines." These symmetry lines are all parallel to each other, and they are orthogonal to the plane of symmetry. In the 2D camera image, the images of the symmetry lines intersect at a single point called the "vanishing point" (Sawada, Li, & Pizlo, 2015). The line connecting the center of a perspective projection of the camera with the vanishing point on the 2D camera's image is parallel to the 3D symmetry lines (Sawada, Li, & Pizlo, 2011). It follows that the position of the vanishing point in the 2D camera image uniquely determines the 3D orientation of the symmetry plane relative to the camera, but not its distance from the camera. Once we determine which pairs of points in the 2D camera image are projections of the pairs of symmetrical points in 3D, the symmetry correspondence in the image has been established (Sawada, Li, & Pizlo, 2014). Once symmetry correspondence is known, a single 2D camera image determines a unique 3D symmetrical interpretation of the 3D points up to some unknown overall size. This unknown size means that the 2D image could have been produced by a small object close to the camera, or by a large object far away. But the shape of the recovered set of 3D points is determined uniquely. By shape, here we mean the ratios of pairwise distances and the sizes of angles. According to this conventional definition, the shape of an object does not change when the object is rigidly translated, rotated, or its size is changed uniformly. Obviously, the shape of a symmetrical object will not change after a 3D reflection either. So by applying a single a priori constraint, symmetry, which only says that the 3D set of points is symmetrical, allows us to recover the 3D shape from a single 2D image. The recovered 3D shape will be veridical, which simply means that the recovered 3D shape is identical to the shape of the 3D set of points "out there." This straightforward geometrical fact is nothing short of remarkable, because it provides a solution to what has been considered for dozens, if not hundreds, of years the most difficult problem in human vision—namely, producing 3D percepts from 2D retinal images (Pizlo, 2008). We will now use this geometrical fact to explain the relation among a symmetry a priori constraint, the least-action principle, and veridical shape perception as it is used in 3D vision.[2]

Let the matrix $\mathbf{X}_{4 \times 2N}$ represent our 3D mirror-symmetrical object. The columns of $\mathbf{X}$ represent individual 3D points. We have $2N$ columns that are N pairs of symmetrical points. The first three rows of $\mathbf{X}$ represent X, Y, and Z, Euclidean coordinates of the points. The last row is a set of "ones." In this way, our matrix $\mathbf{X}$ is defined by homogeneous coordinates. Homogeneous coordinates are useful because they allow representing a perspective projection, which is a nonlinear transformation, by using matrix multiplication, which is a linear operation. Let the matrix $\mathbf{x}_{3 \times 2N}$ represent the camera image of $\mathbf{X}$. Again, we use homogeneous coordinates, so each column of $\mathbf{x}$ is a set of three numbers: $x*, y*$, and w. The usual Euclidean coordinates on the image are obtained by taking ratios: $x = x*/w, y = y*/w$. Finally, let $\mathbf{A}_{3 \times 4}$ represent a perspective projection that maps the 3D space to the 2D retinal or camera image. So the relation between the 3D object X and its camera image x is expressed as follows:

$$\mathbf{x} = \mathbf{A}\mathbf{X}. \tag{11.1}$$

If $\mathbf{A}$ were a square matrix whose inverse $\mathbf{A}^{-1}$ existed, the recovery of the 3D object $\mathbf{X}$ would have been trivial: it would have been produced by premultiplying both sides of Equation 11.1 by $\mathbf{A}^{-1}$. But in our case, the inverse $\mathbf{A}^{-1}$ does not exist, which means that without any a priori constraints, for a given camera image $\mathbf{x}$, there are infinitely many $\mathbf{X}$s that satisfy Equation 11.1. Now we define two standard terms of a cost function. The first term, E_1, evaluates how well the recovered object fits the given 2D camera (or retinal) image $\mathbf{x}$:

$$E_1 = \sum_{i=1}^{2N} \left[(\hat{x}_i - x_i)^2 + (\hat{y}_i - y_i)^2 \right], \tag{11.2}$$

where the 2D image $\hat{x}$ is produced by the recovered 3D object $\hat{X}$ using Equation 11.1.

The second term, E_2, evaluates the degree of asymmetry of the recovered object. Let $L_{2(i-1)+1}$ and L_{2i} be the distances of the corresponding 3D points of the recovered object from the symmetry plane. If the recovered 3D object is perfectly symmetrical, these two distances are equal. But remember that the family of possible 3D interpretations includes many objects that are not symmetrical, so our cost function will evaluate the asymmetry of each of them. The simplest way to evaluate asymmetry is as follows:[3]

$$E_2 = \sum_{i=1}^{N} \left(L_{2(i-1)+1} - L_{2i} \right)^2. \tag{11.3}$$

Note that if instead of discrete points we are dealing with curves, the summations in Equations 11.2 and 11.3 are substituted by integrals. The cost function E is a weighted sum of the two terms

$$E = E_1 + \lambda E_2. \tag{11.4}$$

The 3D object $\tilde{X}$ that minimizes E is the best 3D recovery. Note that the parameter λ in Equation 11.4 controls the relative importance of the symmetry a priori constraint and the 2D image. Typically, when the 2D image is unreliable, λ is set to be large. Otherwise, λ is small. Also note that if X is perfectly mirror-symmetrical, the two terms E_1 and E_2 are invariant to a 3D reflection of the object, simply because the object itself is invariant to 3D reflection. This is analogous to the properties of a Lagrangian that is used in least-action principles as employed in physics.

The cost function E closely resembles what physicists call "action," which is an integral of a Lagrangian. In this way, finding the object that minimizes E is completely analogous to how the least-action principle operates in physics. If there is no noise in the 2D image and if the 3D object X in front of the camera is perfectly symmetrical, minimizing E will produce a 3D recovery whose shape will be identical to the shape of X. This is guaranteed by the theorem described at the beginning of this section. If this recovery is done by an observer's visual system, rather than by a camera, the observer's percept of the 3D shape will be called "veridical." This is what we mean by our psychophysical shape conservation law. It is produced by applying our least-action principle to a 3D object that is mirror-symmetrical.

To summarize, when an observer looks at a 3D object, his mental representation cannot be a copy of this object simply because a mental representation does not have physical characteristics such as mass, albedo, or stiffness. But we have been able to show that the mental representation of the 3D shape of the object is a copy of the actual 3D shape of this object. Its shape did not change during the transition between the physical and the mental representations. The object's shape was conserved. It follows that the perceptual representations in the mind of two people looking at the same 3D shape will be identical. Also, if a robot is given appropriate visual equipment, namely two cameras that acquire 2D images of a 3D scene, and if the robot uses a shape recovery algorithm based on our least-action principle, the robot's perceptual representation of 3D shapes will be the same as ours.

We can conclude that the perception of shape is a law of nature in the same way that the laws of physics are laws of nature, because shape perception is governed by the same three fundamental characteristics: symmetry, a least-action principle, and conservation. This is not to say that percepts are physical phenomena. They obviously are not, but we can say that percepts have the same scientific status as the physical phenomena believed by everyone to be real. This means that there is no reason to assume any fundamental difference between the shape perception of humans and robots with visual systems designed to emulate them. Shape conservation can provide a Turing-type test for determining whether a robot can see as well as we do. The next section describes how such tests were performed with our robot, called "Čapek."

11.6 Empirical Tests Verifying That Čapek Sees as We Do

In the same year that Köhler was describing his psychophysical, least-action principle, Karel Čapek, a Czech writer, coined the term "robot" in his 1920 play "Rosumovi Univerzální Roboti," which translates into English as "Intelligent Universal Robots." We named our first robot Čapek to honor this writer. Čapek arrived in our lab in the Spring of 2010. By then we had already worked out our algorithms for the 3D recovery of shapes based on the cost function described in the previous section, so the time was right to start comparing Čapek's 3D shape perception to ours. The time had come to run our Turing-type tests. At this point, the reader will do well to look at animations illustrating several examples of these recoveries (go to http://shapebook.psych.purdue.edu/1.2/ and http://shapebook.psych.purdue.edu/2.4/demo_skeleton1.html). When you do this, you will find that the 3D shapes recovered by Čapek are identical to the shapes you see. We have published formal comparisons of Čapek's and human performance in several papers. For example, Y. Li, Sawada, Shi, Kwon, and Pizlo (2011) compared the results of four human subjects with Čapek's (our computational model) when they recovered 3D shapes from 2D images, monocularly and binocularly.

We have also compared human and our robot's performances in the recovery of 3D scenes. In these experiments, several pieces of children's furniture were placed 2–5 m away from our observers, humans and our robot. The ground truth about the positions and sizes of objects was established by using a PhaseSpace optical system with accuracy better than 2 cm, and precision 2 mm to locate the furniture within the experimental chamber. Čapek's and our human observers' recoveries of 3D scenes was compared to this ground truth, as well as to each other. Figure 11.2 is an example of one of Čapek's recoveries. The precision of Čapek's recoveries of the pairwise distances of the objects was between 7% and 10%. The average precision of each of the three human subjects, who were tested with similar scenes, was 7%, 8%, and 10%.[4] All three of the humans' results fell within Čapek's range, which is a very good fit, indeed (Kwon, Li, Sawada & Pizlo, 2015). One simply could not know whether he or she were looking at what Čapek was seeing or what one of our human subjects was seeing by looking at the data they produced.

The accuracy (absence of systematic errors) of both the human subjects and of Čapek was also tested in a task in which both were required to construct a right isosceles triangle by positioning three pieces of furniture within the chamber. Both accomplished this task with very small systematic errors. The angles of the right isosceles triangles they constructed were good

Symmetry Provides a Turing-type Test for 3D Vision 235

Figure 11.2 Top-left: A 3D indoor scene as seen from Čapek's point of view. Bottom: The top-view (floor plan) as perceived by Čapek. Black quadrilaterals show the ground truth. Grey rectangles represent Čapek's percept of individual objects. Top-right: The corresponding regions in Čapeks's 2D camera image. Individual grey polygons indicate where in the image Čapek detected objects.

enough to satisfy Euclid himself. The average right angles constructed by the three subjects were 87°, 89.8°, and 91.6°. The average right angle constructed by Čapek was 88.5°. These results show two important things. First, both the humans' and the robot's 3D shape and 3D space perception were virtually identical, and second, both the humans' and Čapek's performances were veridical. Both saw the physical world as it really is. So we have not only developed a Turing-type test of 3D vision, which clearly showed that both humans' and a machine's vision systems can see the world the same way and accurately, but we also justified the methodology underlying our success by using a formalism taken from physics. Simply put, we *explained* why our test actually worked. The extent to which this test can be generalized to other properties of visual percepts will be discussed in the concluding section. Do not expect to see very many visual applications, because the property called "shape" in visual perception is *unique* because of its complexity (Pizlo, 2008; Pizlo et al., 2014). Shape by being both complex and symmetrical is the *only* communication channel that provides us with accurate information about our external world. We, as humans, would probably not even be here as we are if shape did not permit us to see our world veridically.

11.7 Generality and Implications of Our Test

Our derivation of the veridicality of 3D shape and 3D space perception as a form of a conservation law was based on two critical facts—namely, the 3D objects are symmetrical, and the visual system recovers their shapes by applying an a priori simplicity constraint to the sensory data provided by a 2D retinal image. It follows that the approach described in this chapter (i) cannot be generalized to percepts for which symmetry cannot be defined and (ii) cannot be used if the visual system does not apply a least-action (simplicity) principle. These two criteria exclude a large fraction of possible visual percepts, perhaps all but a very few. Consider the difficulty inherent in trying to use our approach for the perception of the hues of light, say green versus blue versus red versus yellow. These perceptions (appearances) of hues rest entirely on sensory coding. There is no reason to believe that the visual system uses anything like a least-action principle to determine how a hue will be perceived. Now consider symmetry, the sine qua non, for shape. Defining the symmetry for any given physical stimulus, and the percept associated with it, requires that the stimulus and the percept are sufficiently complex. For example, it must be possible to define two halves of the percept and then verify whether they are similar. Obviously, with hues this will not work. A hue is represented by a single point on the boundary of the chromaticity diagram. There is no way to split this kind of point into two. Shape, unlike hue, has all the required properties; it is very complex both geometrically and perceptually. In the limit, one needs an infinite number of dimensions to describe the shape of an object. In the real world, it has been shown to have four hundred or more dimensions (Pizlo, 2008). This is very different from color, size, lightness, or speed. These perceptual characteristics are at most three-dimensional. So far, we have been able to extend our theory of the veridical perception of 3D shapes to the veridical perception of 3D scenes. We were able to do this because 3D shapes reside in a 3D space, and simply by assuming gravity and a common ground plane, the symmetry of 3D shape can be used to "calibrate" the Euclidean 3D space. This seems to be about as far as we can go in vision. The application of symmetry, a least-action principle and conservation may actually end right here. We know of nothing at this time outside of 3D shape and 3D space perception that can benefit from the principled approach described in this chapter, an approach that is based on how explanation is done today in the "hard sciences." Note that when we say that we cannot do more than what we have done with shape and space so far, we are actually agreeing with David Marr's definition of the goal of vision science, as stated in the introductory part of his book (Marr, 1982, p. 36). Here Marr claimed that explaining the perception of shape and space is the central task for vision science. Other visual percepts, such as color, texture, or motion are only secondary. So we agree wholeheartedly with Marr's stated goal, but we disagree completely with how he tried to achieve it (see Section 11.4).

Having reached what seemed to be an insoluble impasse in visual science, we were encouraged to ask whether there are phenomena in cognition, outside vision, that have a sufficient degree of complexity to allow symmetry to operate? There are if we accept Shepard's (1981) claim that all cognitive functions have spatial representations because they were formed, during our long evolutionary adaptation, on top of spatial representations already existing in vision. Consider three unambiguous examples. Here the Traveling Salesman Problem (TSP) stands out. This problem requires a human being to find the shortest possible tour among a number of cities. TSP is called "intractable" because finding the shortest tour often requires prohibitively long solution times. Fifteen years ago, we showed that human subjects produce near-optimal tours very quickly (Graham, Joshi, & Pizlo, 2000). We know that these solutions are so good (fast and nearly optimal) because the subjects used vision to solve the TSP. We also know that the brain uses a self-similar pyramid structure in its visual system to represent the problem on many levels of scale and resolution (Pizlo et al., 2006; Pizlo & Stefanov, 2013). One can say that the visual system can impose a self-similar structure on the problem, a structure that the problem itself did not have. Once this is done, the visual system uses self-similar (symmetrical) operations to solve the problem. Pyramids, which are hierarchical representations, are becoming widely used across many different types of problem solving, as well as in theories of human and machine learning. This is not surprising because of how important clustering, or chunking, is in cognitive operations and how common hierarchical relations are found throughout nature. Taxonomy, or biological classification, is probably the best example.

The second example that will be discussed here deals with how problems are solved in physics. Good physics students are said to be good because they solve problems well. But how they do this is not understood. Understanding a problem stated verbally and then solving it is difficult enough to have resisted, so far, many attempts to write computer algorithms that can solve these problems as well as good students do. The absence of a working theory of how to solve physics problems should not be surprising because there are no educational approaches that tell us how to teach new physics students how to solve problems. Few seem to be concerned with this educational issue, perhaps because everyone knows that solving a new problem requires

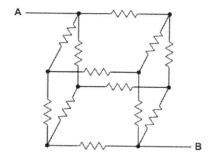

Figure 11.3 Each edge of the cube is a 1Ω resistor. Find the equivalent resistance between corners A and B.

creative thinking (aka insight), so it is expected to be very difficult, and no one is surprised when this expectation is met. But (i) once we know that physical phenomena are governed by symmetry (invariance), a least-action principle, and conservation laws and (ii) that the human mind makes use of these fundamental characteristics, it may be possible to teach students how to look for symmetries within the verbal statement of a physics problem and then infer the corresponding conservation and least-action principle. Take a simple example: "the 12 edges of the cube each contain a 1Ω resistor, and the task is to calculate what the equivalent resistance is between two opposing corners" (see Figure 11.3). This problem is not easy if one uses straight circuit analysis, but it becomes almost trivial if we recognize and make use of the symmetry of the cube's configuration. The gist of this solution is as follows: (for more details, see Rosen, 2008, pp. 114–119 or the following site: http://www.rfcafe.com/miscellany/factoids/kirts-cogitations-256.htm). The cube is rotationally symmetrical around the line connecting two opposite corners. Rotating the cube by 120° around this line maps the cube onto itself. The same is true with a rotation by 240°. This means that the current "I" entering the corner of the cube marked by A must be distributed equally between the three output branches ($I/3$ in each branch). The same must be true with the three currents flowing into corner B ($I/3$ in each branch). The remaining six branches form three pairs, each pair having input current $I/3$. Again, because of symmetry of the cube, the current in each of these six branches is half of $I/3$, which is $I/6$. Using Ohm's law, the voltage across each resistor is the resistance (here 1Ω) times the current through this resistor. Taking any of the three resistors connecting A and B gives us a total voltage of $1/3 \cdot I + 1/6 \cdot I + 1/3 \cdot I = 5/6 \cdot I$ between the corners A and B. The equivalent resistance between A and B is the total voltage (here $5/6 \cdot I$) divided by the current entering the corner marked by A (here I). So the equivalent resistance is 5/6Ω. We think that the symmetry of natural phenomena, together with the least-action principle and conservation laws, can actually provide a common denominator for solving all physics problems, including word problems. If this works out, it might even lead to the application of our approach to more general understanding of much less restricted kinds of verbal communication.

Here it must be pointed out that noticing the 3D rotational symmetry of the cube consisting of resistors (shown earlier) actually changed the representation of the problem. We started with 12 resistors, some of which are in series, whereas others are in parallel, forming six loops, with each loop sharing a resistor with another loop. After 3D symmetry was "imposed" on this set of resistors, the entire cube was split differently by using subsets of resistors that represented the rotational symmetry of the cube's configuration. This made solving the problem easy. The fact that changing the representation of a problem can make a seemingly insoluble problem easy is not news. The Gestalt psychologists (viz., Duncker & Lees, 1945; Wertheimer, 1945) made a big deal about this 70 years ago by pointing out that "Productive Thinking," which required insight, could do just this. In one of their examples, they asked the subject to construct four identical triangles, using only six wooden matches. This problem cannot be solved on a flat surface. Everyone starts by trying to do it this way and fails. The solution is actually simple once the problem is visualized in a 3D representation. Changing the representation from 2D to 3D was all that had to be done to solve what seemed, in 2D, to be an impossible problem. One might be tempted to believe that it is not a complete coincidence that the four triangles in this 3D configuration form a regular tetrahedron, one of the Platonic solids that are characterized by multiple symmetries. It is important to note that the representation of a problem can be changed when the type of symmetry already present in the problem is changed, rather than when symmetry is imposed on a problem that did not have any symmetry. The latter is the kind of problem just described earlier. We changed the type of symmetry with good effect recently when we explained how the visual system detects closed contours (Kwon, Agrawal, Li & Pizlo, 2015). The simplest closed contour is a circle, so it is not surprising that all prior approaches to the detection of closed contours started by trying to find circle-like curves on the retina. This could not work because the visual system analyzes contours in V1 in the cortex not on the retina. The retina only detects center-surround organizations. It turns out that a circle on the retina is transformed into a straight line in V1, so a rotational symmetry is transformed into translational symmetry when information is moved up in the visual system. This change of representation greatly simplifies the problem of detecting closed contours, because detecting a smooth open line in V1 can be done by finding the least-cost path. This discovery shows that the kind of symmetry used in visual processing is important when the least-action principle is applied.

The third example considers how our approach, which is based on the way phenomena are explained in the hard sciences, now including

240 *Zygmunt Pizlo*

3D vision, might be extended into less restricted forms of linguistic communication. The three texts that follow show how environments (3D scenes) were described in a hundred-year period during which the modern novel underwent a host of changes. These three authors contributed a lot to changing our novel's style, but the way they described scenes changed very little as they did this. Each text consists of 128 words. They were selected haphazardly from sections in each book with only one constraint; namely, it did not contain any dialogue.

> It was a substantial-looking farm. In the stables, over the top of the open doors, one could see great cart-horses quietly feeding from new racks. Right along the outbuildings extended a large dunghill, from which manure liquid oozed, while amidst fowls and turkeys, five or six peacocks, a luxury in Chauchois farmyards, were foraging on the top of it. The sheepfold was long, the barn high, with walls smooth as your hand. Under the cart-shed were two large carts and four ploughs, with their whips, shafts and harnesses complete, whose fleeces of blue wool were getting soiled by the fine dust that fell from the granaries. The courtyard sloped upwards, planted with trees set out symmetrically, and the chattering noise of a flock of geese was heard near the pond.
> (Flaubert, *Madame Bovary*, 1856)

> At one side of her bed stood a big yellow chest-of-drawers of lemonwood, and a table which served at once as pharmacy and as high altar, on which, beneath a statue of Our Lady and a bottle of Vichy-Célestins, might be found her service-books and her medical prescriptions, everything that she needed for the performance, in bed, of her duties to soul and body, to keep the proper times for pepsin and for vespers. On the other side her bed was bounded by the window: she had the street beneath her eyes, and would read in it from morning to night to divert the tedium of her life, like a Persian prince, the daily but immemorial chronicles of Combray, which she would discuss in detail afterwards with Françoise.
> (Proust, *Swan's Way*, 1913)

> They walked up the road together to the old man's shack and went in through its open door. The old man leaned the mast with its wrapped sail against the wall and the boy put the box and the other gear beside it. The mast was nearly as long as the one room of the shack. The shack was made of the tough bud shields of the royal palm which are called guano and in it there was a bed, a table, one chair, and a place on the dirt floor to cook with charcoal. On the brown walls of the flattened, overlapping leaves of the sturdy fibered guano there was a picture in color of the Sacred Heart of Jesus and another of the Virgin of Cobre.
> (Hemingway, *Old Man and the Sea*, 1952)

The 3D scenes described verbally in these three passages should allow all literate readers to visualize what each of the authors had in mind when these texts were written down. Why? It seems most likely that the author saw a 3D scene, rather like the one described, represented it visually in his mind, and then depicted it using words. The author chose his words to make it possible for the reader to recover the 3D scene for himself. The same could be done by an artist who produced a 2D painting, or a drawing, of a 3D scene. We all would expect that the end results would be very similar. There is a large difference in these two types of communication because the painting would be a two-dimensional image, whereas written, or spoken, sentences would have only a single dimension—each new word follows the previous one. There is another important difference. The linguistic depiction, unlike scenes represented by images, relies heavily on the reader's familiarity with the names of objects, such as "barn," "bed," "table," or "horse"; the meanings of prepositions, such as "on," "under," or "between"; and the meaning of verbs. With images, the viewer may or may not be familiar with some objects represented, but he or she would still be able to recover their 3D shapes and would also be able to recover their 3D spatial relations.

So how is familiarity exploited in linguistic communication? Familiarity with the objects and with their names conveys information to the reader about their symmetry. Note that horses, and almost all other animals, are mirror-symmetrical with the planes of symmetry almost always parallel to the direction of gravity. Beds, barns, and tables usually have rectangular bases. This means that they have at least two planes of symmetry, both vertical. Rooms are almost universally rectangular with three planes of symmetry. Walls are impenetrable, so a bed is never placed in two rooms at the same time. Objects are also impenetrable, which means that they can be next to each other, possibly touching, or on top of one another and certainly touching because of the operation of gravity. A door is almost always rectangular, and it swings around a vertical axis. The bottom of the door is usually next to the floor, while the bottom of a window is not. All objects are three-dimensional and all, except for birds and airplanes, reside on the common horizontal ground because of gravity.

Objects that are included in a linguistic description are always also included in the reader's mental representation. Not much more is included. By way of illustration, an upright piano might have been standing in the corner of the bedroom in one of the stories or just outside the barn in the other, but if the piano was not included in the linguistic description, the reader would assume that the piano was not actually in the scene described. A reader simply does not add or multiply objects or other things in his representation without a good reason. Instead, he uses a version of Occam's Razor, which will be called a simplicity principle if he happens to be a Gestalt psychologist or one of their disciples. So linguistic communication is facilitated by capitalizing on several of the natural regularities that are often prominent within our natural physical environments, namely, (i) the symmetries of familiar objects and the relationships among them, (ii) their three-dimensionality, (iii) their impenetrability, (iv) the direction of gravity, and (v) the orientation of the horizontal ground, which is usually orthogonal to the direction of gravity. These regularities are governed by an overarching simplicity principle. Noticing these regularities allows us to recover 3D scenes through a slow and often painfully conscious effort that can characterize reading or listening to linguistic descriptions. The visual system has a much easier job, and it can produce the same result by recovering 3D shapes and 3D scenes from a couple of 2D retinal images. It can do this automatically, almost instantaneously, and without any effort. This is obviously not the entire story because linguistic communication can do much more than convey information about 3D shapes and scenes.

At this point we suspect that most of our readers recognize that when language is used to describe and to manipulate concepts outside of the geometry of 3D space, the concept called "symmetry" will be generalized to the concept called "analogy." Analogy refers to the similarity, or identity, of one concept to another. It is used in this way in all aspects of cognition, including decision making memory, creative thinking, emotion, explanation, and problem solving, as well as in the perception of properties other than 3D shape and scenes. Instantiations of analogy include exemplification, comparison, metaphor, simile, allegory, and parable. Analogy is the key to understanding proverbs and the idioms used in ordinary language, but it is also used in science and philosophy when concepts such as association, comparison, and correspondence are employed. What is being said here is that new insights into language communication and its role in cognition may be obtained through formalizing "analogy" by using the tools that have been developed for working with symmetry. Once this is done, we may be able to extend what we accomplished with 3D shapes and 3D scenes, where we explained how human beings form their veridical visual representations to other aspects of cognition, particularly to language, where we hope to be able to show how human beings form their veridical representations of somebody else's thoughts. This will set the stage for generalizing our Turing-type test for shapes and scenes to a Turing-type test for language and thinking.

Acknowledgments

The author thanks Dr. Robert M. Steinman for suggestions that influenced this chapter as well as Dr. Acacio de Barros for very useful discussions and comments. The author is currently supported by a grant from the National Eye Institute (1R01EY024666-01). The theoretical and empirical work of the author and his collaborators, referred to in this chapter, was supported by NSF, AFOSR, DOD, and DOE.

Notes

1. The right half is identical to the left half after a 3D reflection, but this additional reflection is not allowed here because it would lead to the comparison between the transformation MNM and the transformation MN, which does not characterize the symmetry of a natural law.
2. Many other theories of 3D shape perception have been proposed during the long history of research on this important subject. A universal characteristic of these other theories was that they minimized the role of priors, if they included them at all. Symmetry was completely left out, so it is not surprising that these theories could not explain veridical vision. The authors of these theories felt that this is just fine, because all existing empirical data showed that vision was far from veridical. To the best of the present author's knowledge, all of these experiments on 3D shape perception were flawed, because they used impoverished stimuli and degenerate viewing conditions. Furthermore, symmetrical objects, which are found everywhere in our natural environment, were completely excluded in their laboratory experiments. The rest is history.
3. Equation 11.3 is a necessary condition for mirror symmetry. The additional constraint that is needed for a sufficient condition is that the line segment connecting the two symmetrical points is the normal line of the symmetry plane.
4. The human subjects viewed binocularly, and Čapek was fitted with a pair of cameras.

References

Attneave, F. (1954). Some informational aspects of visual perception. *Psychological Review, 61*, 183–193.

Barlow, H. B. (1961). Possible principles underlying the transformations of sensory messages. In W. A. Rosenblith (Ed.), *Sensory communication* (pp. 217–234). Cambridge: The MIT Press.

Chater, N. (1996). Reconciling simplicity and likelihood principles in perceptual organization. *Psychological Review, 103*, 566–581.

Chomsky, N. (1959). A review of B. F. Skinner's verbal behavior. *Language, 35*, 26–58.

Duncker, K., & Lees, L. S. (1945). On problem-solving. *Psychological Monographs, 58*(5), i–113.

Graham, S. M., Joshi, A., & Pizlo, Z. (2000). The traveling salesman problem: A hierarchical model. *Memory & Cognition, 28*, 1191–1204.

Hildebrandt, S., & Tromba, A. (1996). *The parsimonious universe. Shape and form in the natural world.* New York: Springer.

Koffka, K. (1935). *Principles of gestalt psychology.* New York: Harcourt, Brace.

Köhler, W. (1920/1938). Physical gestalten. In W. D. Ellis (Ed.), *A source book of gestalt psychology* (pp. 17–54). New York: Routlege & Kegan.

Kwon, T., Li, Y., Sawada, T. & Pizlo. Z. (2015). Gestalt-like constraints produce veridical (Euclidean) percepts of 3D indoor scenes. Vision Research, Advance online publication. dx.doi.org/10.1016/j.visres.2015.09.011.

Kwon, T. K., Agrawal, K., Li, Y., & Pizlo, Z. (2015). *Spatially-global integration of closed, fragmented contours by means of shortest-path in a log-polar representation* Vision Research, Advance online publication. dx.doi.org/10.1016/j.visres.2015.06.007.

Li, M., & Vitanyi, P. M. (1994). *An introduction to Kolmogorov complexity and its applications.* New York: Springer.

Li, Y., Sawada, T., Shi, Y., Kwon, T., & Pizlo, Z. (2011). A Bayesian model of binocular perception of 3D mirror symmetric polyhedra. *Journal of Vision, 11,* 1–20.

Mach, E. (1886/1959). *The analysis of sensations.* New York: Dover.

Marr, D. (1982). *Vision.* New York: W. H. Freeman.

Narens, L. (2002). *Theories of meaningfulness.* Mahwah, NJ: Lawrence Erlbaum Associates.

Noether, E. (1918). Invariante variations probleme. *Nachrichten von der Gesellschaft der Wissenschaften zu Göttingen, mathematisch-physikalische Klasse, 1918,* 235–257.

Pizlo, Z. (2001). Perception viewed as an inverse problem. *Vision Research, 41,* 3145–3161.

Pizlo, Z. (2008). *3D shape: Its unique place in visual perception.* Cambridge, MA: MIT Press.

Pizlo, Z., Li, Y., Sawada, T., & Steinman, R. M. (2014). *Making a machine that sees like us.* New York: Oxford University Press.

Pizlo, Z., Li, Y., & Steinman, R. M. (2006, August). A new paradigm for 3D shape perception [abstract]. In *Perception* (Vol. 35, p. 182). St. Petersburg, Russia.

Pizlo, Z., & Stefanov, E. (2013). Solving large problems with a small working memory. *Journal of Problem Solving, 6,* 34–43.

Poggio, T., Torre, V., & Koch, C. (1985). Computational vision and regularization theory. *Nature, 317,* 314–319.

Rissanen, J. (1978). A universal prior for integers and estimation by minimum description length. *Annals of Statistics, 11,* 416–431.

Rosen, J. (2008). *Symmetry rules.* Berlin: Springer.

Rosen, J., & Freundlich, Y. (1978). Symmetry and conservation. *American Journal of Physics, 46,* 1030–1041.

Sawada, T., Li, Y., & Pizlo, Z. (2011). Any pair of 2D curves is consistent with a 3D symmetric interpretation. *Symmetry, 3,* 365–388.

Sawada, T., Li, Y., & Pizlo, Z. (2014). Detecting 3-D mirror symmetry in a 2-D camera image for 3-D shape recovery. *Proceedings of IEEE, 102,* 1588–1606.

Sawada, T., Li, Y., & Pizlo, Z. (2015). Shape perception. In J. R. Busemeyer, J. T. Townsend, Z. Wang, & A. Eidels (Eds.), *Oxford handbook of computational and mathematical psychology.* New York: Oxford University Press.

Searle, J. R. (1980). Minds, brains, and programs. *Behavioral and Brain Sciences, 3* (03), 417–424.

Shannon, C. E. (1948). A mathematical theory of communication. *The Bell System Technical Journal, 27,* 379–423, 623–656.

Shepard, R. N. (1981). Psychophysical complementarity. In: M. Kubovy & J. R. Pomerantz (Eds.), (pp. 279–341). *Perceptual Organization,* Hillsdale, NJ: Erlbaum.

Turing, A. M. (1950). Computing machinery and intelligence. *Mind, 59,* 433–460.

Van der Helm, P. A. (2000). Simplicity versus likelihood in visual perception: From surprisals to precisals. *Psychological Bulletin, 126,* 770–800.

Wertheimer, M. (1923/1958). Principles of perceptual organization. In D. C. Beardslee & M. Wertheimer (Eds.), *Readings in perception* (pp. 115–135). New York: D. van Nostrand.

Wertheimer, M. (1945). *Productive thinking.* New York: Harper & Brothers.

Wigner, E. P. (1967). *Symmetries and reflections. Scientific essays.* Bloomington, IN: Indiana University Press.

12 Cognitive Psychometrics

William H. Batchelder

12.1 Introduction

My laboratory at UC Irvine is called the Cognitive Psychometrics Lab. By the term *cognitive psychometrics*, I mean the use of cognitive models as measurement tools, and I believe that most of my research falls under that rubric. In this chapter, I will explain how I came to use the term *cognitive psychometrics* and give some examples of what sort of research I believe falls naturally under this rubric. To cover this ground, the chapter will lay out some of the history and current status of work in the areas of cognitive modeling and psychometric test theory. There are, I believe, major differences in the dominant research strategies in these two areas, differences that have impeded potentially important work combining ideas from both areas. I am quite certain that not all scholars familiar with these two areas will agree with my perspective; however, I hope that by presenting it, some new thoughts and perspectives about these two areas may be generated.

The chapter consists of several sections. The rest of this introduction provides some personal history that led me to become a mathematical psychologist active in creating and applying cognitive models. It describes some early background of the development of mathematical psychology and cognitive modeling at Stanford University in the 1960s. This background involves, among others, Professor James T. Townsend, in whose honor this Festschrift is offered. The second section covers even earlier history by describing the two movements in the psychological sciences where mathematics and statistics have played major roles. In the third section, I discuss similarities between behavioral learning theory and cognitive modeling, while also raising the possibility that cognitive modeling, as it is often conducted, may suffer the same ends as behavioral learning theory. Namely that area once occupied the forefront of psychological theory only to end up playing a relatively minor role in the evolution of psychological thought. The fourth section discusses the similarities and differences in the strategies of researchers in the areas of cognitive modeling and psychometric modeling, and it sheds some light on why there is relatively little collaborative research involving these two areas. This section illustrates the differences by presenting an example of each of these kinds of modeling. In the fifth section, I describe in more detail what I mean by cognitive psychometrics and provide several examples of cognitive psychometric models from others and my own work. Finally, there is a short conclusion.

I decided to become a psychologist in 1960 when I was a junior majoring in chemistry at Indiana University. I was certain that I wanted to have a career applying mathematics of various types in some scientific field, but I was unsettled as to which field to pursue. I was fortunate to be working on two research projects in psychology, one with Professors Arnold Binder and William K. Estes and the other with Professor Frank J. Restle. Both Estes and Restle were among the first generation of scholars developing the new area of mathematical psychology, an area that started as a distinct field in the 1950s (e.g., Batchelder, 2000, 2010). It was through these two projects that I had my first experience with how formal cognitive models could be developed to predict data collected in standard experimental paradigms. This work inspired me to take graduate courses in psychology to finish my undergraduate work at Indiana University, and I was pleased to be accepted into the mathematical psychology Ph.D. program at Stanford University in 1962 as a first-year graduate student.

The Stanford program included perhaps the strongest group of professors in the country developing mathematical psychology at that time. These scholars included Estes, who shifted from Indiana University to Stanford in 1962, as well as Patrick Suppes, Richard C. Atkinson, Gordon H. Bower, Edward Crothers, and, for a period, James G. Greeno. At Stanford with those scholars, cognitive modeling began in earnest and soon thereafter it became a major accepted approach in cognitive psychology. It is important for the main thrust of the chapter to note that the Stanford mathematical psychology program did not include any study of psychometrics, which at that time was the other major subarea of psychology that employed mathematics and statistics.

The graduate students in the Stanford program were also important in advancing cognitive modeling; for example, my first-year cohort included Townsend as well as Robert A. Bjork, Alan Ruskin, John I. Yellott Jr., and Joseph L. Young. In later years, the Stanford graduate program included John R. Anderson, Douglas R. Hintzman, Michael S. Humphreys, Michael Levine, Stephen W. Link, Geoffrey R. Loftus, M. Frank Norman, David E. Rummelhart, Richard M. Shiffrin, and George Wolford to name a few. More generally, the students who went through the Stanford program, as well as others from similar programs in other universities, were hired into major psychology departments, and they and their Ph.D. students contributed greatly to the establishment and growth of mathematical psychology and especially cognitive modeling as a major component of theory in all the areas of cognitive experimental psychology. By now, cognitive modeling has been an active area for over 50 years, and it is the main goal of this chapter to propose one of the ways that it may continue to be important for many more years as a major force in psychological theory and practice.

As will be seen, my proposal is that cognitive modelers link their work more closely with psychometric measurement approaches in order to establish standardized measurement methods to assess latent cognitive processes in special populations. Psychometricians have developed statistically sophisticated measurement models that can assess people's level of knowledge, intelligence, or opinion. However, only rarely are these psychometric models constructed to assess latent cognitive functions, such as memory storage, memory retrieval, insight, selective attention, category or concept formation, the structure and size of semantic memory systems, and the like. These cognitive skills grow at different rates in children; they are at differential risk with the onset of various diseases or changes in mental health, and often they tend to decline with aging and especially with dementia. The ability to measure these latent cognitive variables in standardized settings would contribute greatly in many areas of the psychological sciences. In the next section, I examine the separate origins of the fields of mathematical psychology and psychometrics. The goal is to aid in understanding why there is so little interaction between these two areas.

12.2 Mathematics and Statistics in Psychology

Mathematics and statistics were used in some psychological areas before psychology itself became an accepted academic discipline. Examples of this early work are described in Batchelder (2015). Academic psychology started in the late 1800s, and its roots can be traced to scientific developments in Germany and England. Most historians of psychology accept Wilhelm Wundt and the beginnings of his experimental psychology laboratory at Leipzig, Germany, in 1879 as the start of academic psychology (e.g., Boring, 1950; Hergenhahn, 2001). Before Wundt's laboratory started, the German tradition in psychology was established with the scientific work of Gustav Fechner, Hermann von Helmholtz, Johannes Muller, and Ernst Weber, as well as Wundt and others. Many of these early German researchers were quite strong mathematically, and, in fact, both Fechner and Helmholtz were physicists. The key characteristic of the early work by German researchers was that it was almost entirely concerned with understanding how basic human processes functioned in areas like attention, memory, sensation, perception, and psychophysics. In particular, German experimental psychology produced relatively little research on how humans differed in their capacity to perform in psychological tasks.

The psychological tradition in England started in the late 1800s, and it was quite separate from the German tradition. The English tradition concerned itself with how individuals differed, and its origins can be traced to the theory of evolution developed by Darwin (1859, 1871). Of course Darwin's major concern was with individual differences in physical traits; however, Darwin also showed an interest in psychological traits. For example, his most psychological book was *The Expression of Emotions in Man and Animals* (Darwin, 1872), and this work attempted to understand the differences between and within species on the nature of emotional responses.

The person who is credited with the beginnings of English psychology was Sir Francis Galton, a cousin of Darwin (Boring, 1950; Hergenhahn, 2001). Galton's research mostly centered on measuring individual differences between people on a variety of physical, personality, and cognitive traits. His interests in individual differences led him to study differences in both physical and psychological traits in over nine thousand individuals. This work required the development and use of new statistical measurement tools such as correlation, the quincunx, the bivariate Gaussian, and models for analyzing twin studies.

Galton was a principle figure behind the fact that England became a center for the development of statistical theory as well as the field of psychometrics. Psychometrics as a field developed with close connections to the historical development of the field of statistics. For example, English statisticians who followed Galton included Roland Fisher, William Gosset, Karl Pearson, and Charles Spearman, and Galton and the others each contributed in major ways both to statistics and to psychometrics. For example, Fisher developed the analysis of variants to handle experimental designs in many fields, including experimental psychology; Pearson collaborated with Galton to develop the Pearson product-moment correlation coefficient to measure and compare the degree of association between two psychological traits; Spearman (1904) started the area of factor analysis in an effort to understand the correlational structure between psychological tests; and the Galton-Watson branching process was an early stochastic process designed to study the extinction of family names across generations. Indeed, efforts to solve statistical and experimental design problems that arose within the fields of biology, psychology, and medicine is one of the reasons that the history of the field of statistics from the late 1800s on is so strongly tied to England (e.g., Porter, 1986; Stigler, 1986).

12.3 Behavioral Learning Theory and Cognitive Modeling

Psychometrics started with the work of Galton, so this tradition has been part of psychological theory since the late 1800s. However, cognitive modeling itself came onto the scene much later, in the 1950s, with the origin of the field of mathematical psychology. During the first half of the 20th century, the information sciences developed many concepts that cognitive psychologists could use as the basis for constructing formal models of human cognition. Some of these concepts came from areas such as automata theory, cybernetics, game theory, information theory, signal processing, operations research, and stochastic processes. Starting in the 1950s, a number of experimental psychologists began to develop cognitive models specified in terms of some of these concepts, and some researchers in the information sciences began to do collaborative work with psychologists.

Prior to the start of cognitive modeling, behavioral learning theory had been the dominant theoretical area in psychology since the early 1900s, and this area is definitely one of the forerunners of cognitive modeling. A number of learning theories were developed, for example, Pavlov's theory of classical conditioning, Thorndike's S-R bond theory, Skinner's work with operant responses, Hull's mathematico-deductive theory, and Tolman's purposive behaviorism, just to name a few of the major theories (see Hilgard & Bower, 1966). These learning theorists received many honors for their work, and they were central in shaping the field of experimental and theoretical psychology at that time.

Whereas the particular learning theories differed, the theorists shared a variety of foundational assumptions. Among these were that (1) there are basic laws of learning that apply identically across a wide range of animals and humans; (2) these laws can be discovered by following the hypothetico-deductive approach to science, where experiments are designed with the potential to falsify hypotheses; (3) complex learned acts can be decomposed into smaller units of learned behavior; (4) species-specific behavioral differences are unimportant; (5) little knowledge of the brain is needed; (6) the basic laws of learning can be discovered by conducting experiments with animals placed in contrived experimental situations; and (7) once the basic units of learning along with their laws are discovered, others could use them to understand such complex behaviors as learning to play a sport, learning a language, or learning how to manipulate mathematical quantities.

Many animal learning experiments were conducted in service of establishing one or another of these theories as the scientifically correct theory of the basic learning process. However, none of the major learning theories became accepted as established science, and today none of them play a major role in psychological theory. One reason for this, I think, is that there were never any clear demonstrations that complex behavior could be understood in terms of any of the learning theories. In fact, I venture to claim that no psychological theorist today believes that any of the foundational assumptions shared by the learning theorists are true. Starting around the 1960s, behavioral learning theory began to fade from its central position in psychological theory, while at the same time cognitive psychology and the associated area of cognitive modeling began to rise in importance.

While all the experimental work done in the era of learning theory failed to establish a basic science of learning, it is fair to note that it did provide useful facts that could be used in medicine, clinical psychology, and neuroscience. In particular, psychologists learned in detail from their experiments exactly what a particular type of animal would do in a particular type of experimental situation. These facts continue to be useful in testing the effects of drugs in medical science, as well as the effects of brain manipulations on behavior in neuroscience. Further, several clinical therapies were patterned after some of the experimental results in learning theory, for example, Watson's desensitization therapy and Skinner's token economy. These continue to play a role in clinical psychology today.

Cognitive modeling has been popular for over a half century by now, and in my view it has some elements in common with the rise and eventual fall in the importance of behavioral learning theory. For most of the history of cognitive modeling, researchers have shared several foundational assumptions. Among these are that (1) there are basic theories of human cognition that offer a unified understanding of cognition across a wide range of real-world situations; (2) these theories can be discovered by following the hypothetico-deductive approach to science, where experiments are designed with the potential to falsify specific cognitive models; (3) the basic data for the models are observable behaviors from controlled experiments with college students, each of whom responds to a series of related item-events; (4) many item-events can be administered to a participant in a short period of time, and their responses are independent events; (5) the participants have very similar cognitive abilities, so their data can be pooled rather than analyzed separately; (6) the item-events fall into homogeneous classes that permit pooling the data within each item-event class; and (7) that little knowledge of the brain is needed to discover the scientific theories of cognition.

By now, there are a large number of cognitive models in most areas of cognitive psychology such as memory, categorization, decision making, and choice response time, and the creators of these models have been very influential in shaping the nature of psychological theory. Nevertheless, it appears quite obvious to me that none of this cognitive modeling work has led to the establishment of any generally accepted theory of cognition. Instead, there has been an active and creative process of inventing and refuting various cognitive models, and this process continues to accumulate findings of the sort that model A is better than model B for understanding data C. For example, in the area of episodic memory, there are a very large number of cognitive models, including ACT-R models (e.g., Anderson, Bothell, Lebiere, & Matessa, 1998), global matching models (e.g., Clark & Grondlund, 1996; Humphreys, Pike, Bain, & Tehan, 1989), Hidden Markov models (e.g., Greeno & Bjork, 1973; Wickens, 1982), multinomial processing tree models (e.g., Batchelder & Riefer, 1999), parallel distributed processing models (Rumelhart, McClelland,

& the PDP Research Group, 1986), signal detection models (e.g., MacMillan & Creelman, 2005), and stimulus-sampling models (e.g., Estes, 1960). Further, in the many years since most of these models were first proposed, there have been many more published cognitive models of episodic memory, and most have been presented in the spirit of seeking correct scientific theory. However, none of this very creative work has led to a generally accepted established scientific theory of any facet of episodic memory.

The same story could be told about the profusion of cognitive models in other areas, such as classification, choice response time, and decision making. As is true for episodic memory, many cognitive models have been proposed, and yet it seems we are nowhere near establishing a generally accepted scientific theory of cognition in any of these areas as well. In fact, scientists in the currently popular area of cognitive neuroscience have begun to develop their own neurally based theories for all of these areas, and this new neural modeling work rarely cites any of the large number of existing cognitive models that have been developed for the same experimental phenomena. I think it is a reasonable concern that the area of cognitive modeling viewed as the pursuit of established scientific theory may end up following the same pattern as the historical rise and fall of behavioral learning theory.

From what I have said so far, a reasonable surmise might be that I believe that all the cognitive modeling work that has gone on is worth very little. However, that does not correspond at all to my view. What I do think is that much of the work in cognitive modeling, just as the earlier work in behavioral learning theory, has preceded with the scientific goal of establishing basic scientific theory, and as such, that effort has failed. What has happened instead is that cognitive modelers have learned how to interpret and understand data in selected experimental paradigms in terms of parameters that represent latent cognitive processes. For example, in episodic memory, models have been able to interpret data obtained in specialized experimental paradigms in terms of such latent processes as encoding into short- and long-term memory, semantic organization, source discrimination, forgetting rates, and retrieval. No one model has a generally accepted specification of these processes that holds across a large variety of experimental variations; however, a number of cognitive models exist that can convincingly describe data, in particular, standardized experimental paradigms. The value of such models is not that they contribute to a final scientific theory of episodic memory; instead, their value is that they can be used as measurement models that can assess individual differences in latent cognitive skills. The key, I believe, is that when a model that has worked well in the past fails to handle an experimental variation, it is important not to abandon it as falsified in the spirit of the hypothetico-deductive approach to science. Instead one wants to restrict the experimental conditions for its use. In this way, standard conditions for the use of a cognitive model as a measurement tool can be established.

12.4 Comparing Cognitive Modeling and Psychometric Test Theory

Mathematical psychologists and psychometricians both develop probabilistic models and associated statistical inference procedures. Cognitive models and models in test theory share many characteristics. In particular, they are both developed to assess and understand aspects of cognitive performance in terms of specified statistical parameters. Even more important, as described later in this section, is the fact that the usual data structure for both types of models is exactly the same. Namely it is a participant by item-event random response matrix. For these reasons, it might seem natural that there would be a great deal of collaboration between researchers in these fields. But in fact, in my experience, such collaborations are relatively rare, and researchers working in one of these two areas are relatively unfamiliar with work done in the other area.

I believe that the lack of research collaborations between cognitive modelers and psychometricians can be traced in part to the largely separate German and English approaches to psychology described earlier in Section 12.2 (see also Cronbach 1957, for a similar view). Another reason for the relative disconnect is that formalists in the two areas are often seen to be pursuing quite different research goals. As discussed in Section 12.3, cognitive modelers often seek to develop general scientific theory using the hypothetico-deductive approach to research; whereas, psychometric modelers often seek to develop useful measurement tools that can be used only if very specific conditions are met (e.g., Lord & Novick, 1968). In any scientific field, there is a fundamental distinction between basic and applied science, where the former seeks fundamental scientific laws and the latter seeks to use these to create practical applications. While this difference in goals leads to quite different styles in conducting research, in the physical sciences, these roles have been coordinated productively. However, in my view, the usual relationship between the roles of basic science and its applications found in other sciences so far has been largely lacking in the psychological sciences.

In the rest of this section, I will expand on my views by examining two models, one a cognitive model and the other a psychometric test model. First, it is important to describe the data structure and model specification strategy shared by most cognitive and psychometric test modelers. There are many experimental situations in cognitive modeling where data are collected from several participants, each of whom produce responses to the same (or equivalent) set of item-events. Examples of item-events are old and new items in a recognition memory experiment, studied items in a free recall experiment, pairs of gambles in a choice experiment, trials in a probability learning experiment, or test stimuli in a categorization task. The data for these situations are realizations of one or more random response matrices,

$$\mathbf{X} = (X_{ik})_{N \times M}, \tag{12.1}$$

where there are N participants, M item-events, and X_{ik} is a random variable for the response of the ith participant to the kth item-event. It is of interest to observe that this is exactly the same structure of many data sets in psychometric test theory. In the psychometric case, the N participants are test-takers or graders, and examples of item-events are aptitude test items, items calling for a degree of opinion, or essays to be graded.

In addition to a common data structure, both cognitive modelers and psychometricians often specify parametric probability models for the data structure $\mathbf{X}$. Such models have a parameter $\Theta = (\theta_1, \theta_2, \ldots, \theta_S) \in \Omega_S \subseteq \mathrm{Re}^S$. Both types of modelers invest psychological meaning to the individual components of Θ, and, in addition, usually the parameter is chosen so that conditional independence holds, namely,

$$\Pr(\mathbf{X} = \mathbf{x} \mid \Theta) = \prod_{i=1}^{N} \prod_{k=1}^{M} \Pr(X_{ik} = x_{ik} \mid \Theta) \tag{12.2}$$

for all possible realizations $\mathbf{x}$ of the random matrix $\mathbf{X}$. Despite these similarities, there is a great deal of difference between how the two types of modelers define and interpret their parameters. In order to make this point, it is useful to consider two concrete examples: one a simple psychometric test model from Item Response Theory (IRT; e.g., Embretson & Reise, 2000) and the other a cognitive model of episodic recognition memory. Despite the simplicity of these two examples, I believe that they reveal many of the differences between cognitive and psychometric models as they have been developed over the last half-century.

For the psychometric modeling example, consider the Rasch model (e.g., Fischer & Molenaar, 1995; Rasch, 1960). In this model, the item-events are test items in some area of knowledge, and the responses of the test-takers are scored dichotomously as correct or wrong:

$$X_{ik} = \begin{cases} 1 & i \text{ correct on item } k \\ 0 & i \text{ wrong on item } k \end{cases}.$$

The model specifies an ability parameter for each test-taker, $\mathbf{A} = (\alpha_i)_{1 \times N} \subseteq \mathrm{Re}^N$, and a difficulty parameter for each item, $\mathbf{B} = (\beta_k)_{1 \times M} \subseteq \mathrm{Re}^M$.

Conditional independence in (12.2) is specified in the form

$$P[X_{ik} = x_{ik} \mid \Theta = (\mathbf{A}, \mathbf{B})] = \begin{cases} \dfrac{1}{1 + \exp[-(\alpha_i - \beta_k)]} & \text{if } x_{ik} = 1 \\ \dfrac{\exp[-(\alpha_i - \beta_k)]}{1 + \exp[-(\alpha_i - \beta_k)]} & \text{if } x_{ik} = 0 \end{cases}. \quad (12.3)$$

It should be noticed that the model in Equation 12.3 is not identified because the response probabilities are invariant under the addition of the same constant to all ability and difficulty parameters. Standard tools for statistical inference for the model handle this issue by some restriction, such as fixing the average item difficulty to zero.

One way to describe the model is that it represents the probability of a correct response to an item as a joint function of the test-taker's ability and the item's difficulty and, further, that there is no "interaction" between these two quantities. To see this point, one can compute

$$\text{logit}[\Pr(X_{ik} = 1 \mid \alpha_i, \beta_k)] = \log \frac{\Pr\left(X_{ik} = 1 \mid \alpha_i, \beta_j\right)}{\Pr\left(X_{ik} = 0 \mid \alpha_k, \beta_j\right)} = \log \exp(\alpha_i - \beta_k)$$

$$= \alpha_i - \beta_k. \quad (12.4)$$

In other words, to model heterogeneity in both test-takers and items, the assumption is made that if a particular test-taker has more ability than another one on a particular item, then this ability ordering between the two test-takers remains true for all items. Such a simplifying assumption is plausible if the test has items drawn from some common base, such as geography questions or geometry questions, and in any event the assumption is testable.

For the cognitive model, I selected the double-high threshold (DHT) model of simple episodic recognition memory. There is a large and growing literature concerning the value of threshold models for recognition memory (e.g., Batchelder & Alexander, 2013; Kellen, Klauer, & Bröder, 2013; Pazzaglia, Dube, & Rotello, 2013); however, the choice of the DHT model in this section is in no way an effort to support or disavow the value of this model. Instead, it is intended to serve my purpose to characterize the basic structure of much of cognitive modeling in general. The structure of a simple recognition memory experiment involves a study and a test session. In the study session, each participant is exposed to a list of M_1 words (items), and in the test phase, these words are presented one at a time and intermixed randomly with M_2 unstudied items (foils). So the item-events are the $M = M_1 + M_2$ words.

Usually, in a case where there are two or more classes of items, one represents the data structure by a random matrix for each class of items in the form of Equation 12.1. In this case, the two random matrices are

$$\mathbf{X}_1 = (X_{1ik})_{N \times M_1}, \mathbf{X}_2 = (X_{2ik})_{N \times M_2}, \tag{12.5}$$

where X_1 is for old studied items and X_2 is for new unstudied foils. In the case of the DHT model, the participant makes a Yes/No response to each test item, indicating whether or not they believe that the item was a previously studied item. Thus the responses are scored dichotomously by

$$X_{t,ik} = \begin{cases} 1 & i \text{ says Yes to item } k \\ 0 & i \text{ says No to item } k \end{cases},$$

where $t = 1$ for old items and $t = 2$ for foils.

In its simplest form, the DHT model has only two component parameters. One of the parameters is D, the probability that a participant detects whether or not a test item is an old studied item. The other is g, the probability that if the participant does not detect the status of a test item, she guesses that it is an old studied item. Thus the parameter for the DHT model is $\Theta = (D, g) \in \Omega_\Theta = [0,1]^2$. Conditional independence in Equation 12.2 holds for each matrix in Equation 12.5 as follows:

$$\Pr[\mathbf{X}_t = \mathbf{x} \mid (D, g)] = \prod_{i=1}^{N} \prod_{k=1}^{M_t} \Pr(X_{t,ik} = x_{t,ik} \mid D, g), \tag{12.6}$$

for $t = 1, 2$. Then for the DHT model, the individual components of Equation 12.6 are given by

$$\Pr(X_{1,ik} = 1 \mid D, g) = D + (1 - D)g, \Pr(X_{2,ik} = 1 \mid D, g)$$
$$= (1 - D)g \tag{12.7}$$

and

$$\Pr(X_{1,ik} = 0 \mid D, g) = (1 - D)(1 - g), \Pr(X_{2,ik} = 0 \mid D, g)$$
$$= D + (1 - D)(1 - g). \tag{12.8}$$

The terms of signal detection, the components in Equation 12.7 are known, respectively, as the hit and false alarm probabilities, and the terms in Equation 12.8, respectively, are the miss and correct rejection probabilities. A consequence of 12.6 is that the DHT assumes that the random variables in $\mathbf{X}_1$ and $\mathbf{X}_2$ are stochastically independent and within each item type, identically distributed.

On the surface, the Rasch and DHT models share some similarities. For one, they both deal with dichotomous response data in the form of Equation 12.1. In addition, the Rasch model is applied to items requiring the use of knowledge in semantic memory to generate responses, and the

DHT requires the use of information in episodic memory to generate responses. However, there are several salient differences between the two models. Most salient is that the Rasch model postulates individual differences among both the test-takers and the items, whereas the DHT model (as presented) assumes no individual differences within either participants or items within a particular type. A second difference is that the Rasch model makes no psychological claims about how responses are generated by searching semantic memory; they are either correct or wrong. In contrast, the DHT model has a cognitive story, albeit a very simple one, about how the responses are generated. This assumption is that there are detection thresholds for both types of items and that they are sufficiently high so that old items are never detected as foils and foils are never detected as old items. If participants fail to detect the type of the item, then they guess. The main points for these two relatively simple models also hold in most cases for more complex cognitive and test theory models.

Foremost in the comparison between these two approaches to modeling are issues relating to the assumption of whether or not there is homogeneity in both participants and items. Until relatively recently, most statistical inference for cognitive models was based on the assumption that the response random variables for each class of items are independent and identically distributed (i.i.d.). The participants are often drawn from an undergraduate population, where the instructors routinely give a grade distribution from A to F. That this population might represent homogeneous abilities in a cognitive task is at best a very suspect assumption. Of course, it has become mandatory in experimental journal articles to address the issue of possible participant heterogeneity when advancing a new cognitive model. Indeed, in papers dealing with the competition between two or more models for the same type of experiment, authors sometimes try to show that violations of participant heterogeneity may be behind the apparent success of a rival model (e.g., Ashby, Maddox, & Lee, 1994; Batchelder, 1975; Hintzman, 1980; Hintzman & Hartry, 1990).

In the case of participant-by-item categorical data like those of the recognition memory experiment, J. Smith and Batchelder (2008) provide non-parametric, model-free permutation tests of the hypothesis of participant and/or item homogeneity. In my experience with using these tests, it is almost always the case that a set of categorical data rejects the assumption of participant homogeneity. Fortunately, in the last decade or so, cognitive modelers have learned how to make their models hierarchical so that parameters can vary over participants, because they are drawn from a hierarchical distribution (e.g., Klauer, 2010; Lee & Wagenmakers, 2013; Rouder et al., 2007). These developments are crucial for the development of cognitive psychometric models as tools to measure individual differences in cognitive processes. There are a variety of both classical and Bayesian inference procedures for estimating hierarchical models, and Bayesian approaches based on Markov Chain Monte Carlo samplers are currently very popular because of the availability of easily accessible and free software such as JAGS (Plummer, 2003) and WinBUGS (Nitzoufras, 2009).

The assumption of whether or not to allow heterogeneity on the item-event side is a much more salient difference between the two types of modeling. Psychometric modelers understand that if you want to measure a particular ability, it is useful to provide test items that range from easy to hard. Imagine trying to estimate people's high jumping ability by having them repeatedly try to jump over a four-foot height. Obviously, it is a much better approach to have a few bars at two feet, a few at four feet, and a few at six feet. On the other hand, most cognitive modeling experiments, especially ones in the area of memory, select item-events to be at the same level of difficulty. For example, for an episodic recognition memory study, items within a particular class are almost always selected from tight ranges on concreteness norms, frequency of usage norms, and word length. In addition, the items are often shuffled across participants to avoid the possibility that a particular item in a particular study order position might be more or less memorable than the other items. The tradition in cognitive modeling to select homogeneous item-events not only restricts the precision with which a cognitive process can be measured, but it restricts the type of data that are used to try and establish a scientific theory of cognition.

So far in comparing the two examples of models, we have seen the restrictive effects of the typical assumption of cognitive modelers that the data are identically distributed over participants and classes of similar items. While cognitive modelers have recently learned how to detect and model participant and item heterogeneity, there are strong residual concerns that many of the older published studies using cognitive models are flawed because of unmodeled heterogeneities, especially in the participants.

Next it is useful to consider some of the disadvantages of the example psychometric model. The Rasch model does well in modeling the heterogeneities in test-taker ability and item difficulty; however, it says absolutely nothing about how test-takers engage in cognitive processes to make their responses to test items. When given a test question, presumably the test-takers consult their semantic memory, make cognitive or neural computations, frame a response, etc. Cognitive models, unlike psychometric test models, attempt to model these sorts of cognitive processes. Of course most cognitive models are much more psychologically complex than the DHT model, but as shown earlier, even that model has some cognitive assumptions about how responses are generated. The goal of cognitive psychometrics is to combine the advantages that each modeling style has to offer.

12.5 Examples of Cognitive Psychometric Models

Despite the failure of all the cognitive modeling work to lead to established general scientific theory, there are many cognitive models that have a good track record in interpreting data in specific standardized cognitive paradigms in terms of latent cognitive processes. Any of these models have the potential to be tools to measure cognitive processes if confined to tasks where they are known to work. The research strategy in cognitive psychometrics is to select some of these models and develop their inference under specifications that allow the parameters to vary over participants and sometimes items. Then these models may become useful measurement models for examining both individual participant and group-level differences in cognitive processing in special participant populations.

By now there are a number of articles written by cognitive modelers who have used their models in the spirit of cognitive psychometrics, so it is clear that some cognitive modelers already have seen the value of the cognitive psychometrics approach, even without tying their work explicitly to psychometric measurement theory. In my view, this is likely to be an increasingly popular approach in cognitive modeling, and I expect that more of this work will exhibit increasing statistical sophistication. The rest of this section will describe just a few examples of using cognitive models as measurement tools. I plead guilty of selecting most of these examples from my own work; a number of examples from others' work could also have been selected. Rather than describing each model in the examples in detail, ample references will be provided for additional study.

Example 1. The Elo Chess Rating Model. The psychometrician Louis Thurstone (1927) developed paired-comparison models to understand the structure of choice among pairs of objects in a paired-comparison experimental design. Thurstone's idea was to specify a Gaussian distribution of momentary utility for each choice object. When presented with two objects, one chooses by comparing their momentary utilities that are represented by independent draws from their respective distributions. Then the chosen object is the one with the largest momentary utility. In applications of Thurstone's models, the utility distributions remain fixed over a series of choices.

The engineer Apard Elo (1978) had the idea of using a similar type of model for rating chess players, where the rating of a particular chess player is the mean of his or her corresponding Gaussian. Then the model's predicted result of a chess game (win, loss, or draw) is determined by the difference in the momentary utilities of the players, where the chess game is drawn if the difference is in a parameterized small interval $(-t,t)$, $t > 0$, about zero. Elo's major idea was to allow the underlying abilities of the players, represented by the means of their Gaussians, to be changing rather than fixed. His model can be viewed as an approximation to a dynamic Thurstonian system, and Batchelder and Bershad (1979) developed the appropriate dynamical stochastic system to represent Elo's ideas. Further, in Batchelder, Bershad, and Simpson (1992), the approach was extended to accommodate other paired-comparison models. Further developments of the Elo system by others have led to the system used internationally by the World Chess Federation (F.I.D.E.) to measure dynamically changing chess abilities, and it has proven to be a good predictor of chess results. In addition, versions of the Elo system have been developed as rating tools in other competitive games and sports.

Example 2. Multinomial Processing Tree Models. Perhaps the most extensive example of cognitive psychometric modeling can be seen in the many applications of multinomial processing tree (MPT) models (Batchelder, 2009; Riefer & Batchelder, 1988). These models are for categorical data, where each participant is required to make responses to multiple items, each of which falls into a small number of observable response categories. The class of MPT models is defined by a special way of specifying the category probabilities in terms of latent parameters that are interpretable as measuring cognitive processes that are postulated to combine to generate the responses. Specifically, an MPT model is represented by a rooted tree, where the internal nodes correspond to latent parameters, and the leaves correspond to observable categories. Each branch in the tree corresponds to a sequence of cognitive events that leads to a particular response. The specifics are described in detail in Batchelder and Riefer (1999) and Hu and Batchelder (1994), and an overview is in Batchelder and Alexander (2013).

The MPT class includes cognitive models for standard paradigms in human memory, attention, categorization, choice, and social psychology. Erdfelder et al. (2009), in the lead article in a special issue of *Zeitschrift für Psychologie* on MPT models, list 70 such models and variations. Many of these MPT models have been used to measure latent cognitive processes in various special populations, including normal aging (Riefer & Batchelder, 1991; R. E. Smith & Bayen, 2006), types of schizophrenics (Keefe, Arnold, Bayen, & Harvey, 1999; Riefer, Knapp, Batchelder, Bamber, & Manifold, 2002), types of alcoholics (Riefer et al., 2002), and developmental dyslexia (Chechile, 2007). Batchelder (1998) describes the differences between experimental studies and clinical assessment tests in the context of MPT models, and Batchelder and Riefer (2007) describes many applications of MPT models to clinical assessment. In addition, several papers have extended the statistical inference for MPT models to allow heterogeneity in either participants or items (e.g., Klauer, 2010; Matzke, Dolan, Batchelder, & Wagenmakers, 2015; J. B. Smith & Batchelder, 2010).

Example 3. Choice Response Time Modeling. There are several examples of work that I would classify as cognitive psychometrics that are well outside of my own work. I selected the work of Roger Ratcliff for this example because I find it among the best of these other examples. The experimental design is speeded response time, where participants must quickly decide which of two options satisfies an experimenter-defined criterion, for example, which display has the most dots (numerosity judgments), whether or not a presented word was on a recognition study list (recognition memory), or whether or not a string of letters forms a word (lexical decision). Of course individuals differ in behavioral measures such as choice response times (RTs) and accuracy, and the goal of this example is to show that cognitive models for this paradigm can be used to assess individual differences in special populations concerning the cognitive processes underlying these differences.

There have been many models developed for choice response-time studies, and, as is the case for episodic memory models, none of these models have become generally accepted as the scientifically correct model over a large range of such tasks. One of the most popular models for choice response-time is the diffusion model developed by Roger Ratcliff (e.g., Ratcliff, 1978). The model has several psychologically interpretable latent parameters, e.g., parameters for one's prior expectations that the correct choice is the one presented on the left or the one presented on the right, the rate at which information relevant to a correct decision is processed, the criteria for deciding that enough information has been gathered to initiate a decision, and the time to prepare and make a response.

Ratcliff's diffusion model has been applied many times as a cognitive psychometric model to study individual differences in cognitive processes in special populations. For example, in Ratcliff and Van Dongen (2009) the effects of sleep deprivation were studied. Not surprisingly, sleep deprivation has an effect of slowing down response times; however, with the use of the diffusion model, it was possible to locate the effects of deprivation on specific cognitive processes. The results showed that sleep deprivation affects multiple components of cognitive processing, ranging from stimulus processing to peripheral nondecision processes. Thus sleep deprivation appears to have wide-ranging effects. In particular, reduced attentional arousal and impaired central processing combine to produce an overall decline in cognitive functioning under sleep deprivation.

In another example, Ratcliff, Thapar, and McKoon (2010) examined the effects of aging and IQ in choice response-time studies involving recognition memory and lexical decision. As expected, RTs slowed with increasing age; however, perhaps surprisingly, accuracy did not vary much with age. It was interesting that the model showed that the slowing of RT with age appears to be due to stiffer response criteria rather than slowed processing (drift) rates. In the case of IQ differences, lower IQs were associated both with slower RTs and less accurate responses. Unlike the case of age differences, lower IQs were associated with slower processing rates, but not with stiffer criteria for response selection.

White, Ratcliff, Vasey, and McKoon (2010) described how the diffusion model could be used to understand the cognitive processes involved in patients with different psychopathologies. The authors point out that clinicians often use raw behavioral measures such as RT and accuracy in the study of clinical symptomologies; however, without a model of choice response-time such as the diffusion model, it is difficult to pinpoint the reasons behind differences between participant groups in terms of these behavioral variables. Instead, with the aid of the diffusion model, specific cognitive processes can be separated and used to understand group differences in the behavioral measures. To illustrate their approach to understanding clinical disorders, they applied the diffusion model to study participants with high- and low-trait anxiety. They discovered that those with high-trait anxiety tended to exhibit caution by strengthening their response criteria following an error, whereas those with low-trait anxiety did not.

Example 4. Cultural Consensus Theory (CCT). In the social and behavioral sciences, there are many situations where a group of people may share knowledge or beliefs that are unknown a priori to a researcher. CCT is an established cognitive modeling approach that researchers can employ to discover such consensus views if they exist. CCT was invented in the late 1980s (e.g., Batchelder & Romney, 1986, 1988; Romney, Weller, & Batchelder, 1986). Soon thereafter it became a popular methodology in social and cultural anthropology (e.g., Romney & Batchelder, 1999; Weller, 2007). CCT consists of a collection of formal cognitive response models and statistical inference methods for analyzing the responses of the group members to questions about their shared knowledge. The models are used to determine if there is evidence for a shared consensus and if so, to estimate the consensus answers to the questions as well as other heterogeneous characteristics of the respondents and the questions such as respondent ability, respondent bias, and item difficulty. In this way, CCT models can be viewed as cognitively based response models for information pooling.

Currently published theoretical and applied papers have established cognitive models and appropriate Bayesian hierarchical inference procedures for true/false formats (e.g., Batchelder & Anders, 2012; Oravecz, Anders, & Batchelder, 2015), ordinal (Likert) scales (e.g., Anders & Batchelder, 2015), and continuous, slider scales (e.g., Anders, Oravecz, & Batchelder, 2014). In addition, all these models have been augmented to include the possibility that the group of respondents fall into two or more subgroups, each of which is characterized by a different consensus answer pattern to the questions (e.g., Anders & Batchelder, 2012). Recent applications include determining ties in a social network (Agrawal & Batchelder, 2012), analyzing social survey data (Oravecz, Faust, & Batchelder, 2014), essay grading (France & Batchelder, 2015), combining eyewitness reports (DePulseau, Aßfalg, Erdfelder, and Bernstein 2012), forecasting future events (Anders et al., 2014), pooling grammaticality judgments (Anders & Batchelder, 2015), analyzing online reviews (France & Batchelder, 2014), and determining folk medical beliefs (Weller, 2007).

Example 5. Hidden Markov Chain Models of Free Recall. Many clinical test batteries for dementia include a free recall task, e.g., Alzheimer's Disease Assessment Scale (ADAS-Cog; Chu et al., 2000) and the Consortium to Establish a Registry for Alzheimer's Disease (CERAD; Fillenbaum et al., 2008). This task involves presenting a set list of words one-at-a time for study, followed by a recall test, where patients recall as many of these studied words as possible. In a typical task, the study and test trials are alternated several times and then after a delay there are one or more recall tests. It has been well established that patients with mild cognitive impairment (MCI) or early stages of Alzheimer's disease (AD) perform less well than normal age-controlled, healthy elderly. However, these conclusions are drawn from raw recall scores, and they do not shed any light on what cognitive processes might be at risk with increasing levels of dementia.

In Batchelder, Chosak-Reiter, Shankle, and Dick (1997) and Alexander, Satalich, Shankle, and Batchelder (in press), a Hidden Markov Model (HMM) of free recall is developed for the free recall component of several clinical tests, including the ones in the ADAS-Cog and CERAD batteries. The model is developed from several earlier efforts to model memory paradigms with HMMs (e.g., Greeno & Bjork, 1973; Wickens, 1982). HMM models were popular in memory paradigms from about 1960–1980; however, with the development of more elaborate models, e.g., global matching models (Clark & Grondlund, 1996), they pretty much ceased to be developed. It turns out that the HMM that was developed in Alexander et al. (in press) as a cognitive psychometric model provided strong suggestions about which cognitive processes are at risk with increasing levels of dementia.

The model has three memory states, including a short-term memory (STM) state and a long-term memory (LTM) state; however, unlike most earlier Markov models for memory, the recall probability in the LTM is allowed to decay slowly to handle the performance on the delayed recall trials. The model is able to fit the serial position curve with LTM storage parameters that decline with study list order and STM retrieval parameters that increase with study list order. Estimates of the parameters show that there are steep declines with increasing dementia in some but not all of the parameters of the model. More generally, it is shown that the model is able to provide an interpretation of the recall data in terms of interpretable latent memory parameters that goes well beyond the usual analyses of the clinical assessment data in terms of percent correct.

12.6 Conclusion

This chapter has reviewed two areas of psychology where mathematics and statistics are used extensively, namely, psychometric test theory and cognitive modeling. It is argued that these two areas can be joined in an approach called cognitive psychometrics. Cognitive models attempt to understand the cognitive processes at play in various areas of cognition, and psychometric test models attempt to measure individual differences in standardized knowledge tests. Successful cognitive models have been developed for selective experimental paradigms, but so far there are no generally accepted models for any area of cognition. Psychometric test models have succeeded in measuring individual differences in knowledge in certain areas, but these models do not measure the cognitive processes at play when test-takers access their knowledge structures. Cognitive psychometric models are used to measure individual differences in latent cognitive processes in specific cognitive paradigms. They provide a way to understand the underlying reasons why there are performance differences in special populations that undergo standardized assessment tasks.

References

Agrawal, K., & Batchelder, W. H. (2012). Cultural consensus theory: Aggregating signed graphs under a balance constraint. In S. J. Yang, A. M. Greenberg, & M. Endsley (Eds.), *Social computing, behavioral-cultural modeling and prediction, LNCS 7227* (pp. 53–60). New York: Springer-Verlag.

Alexander, G. E., Satalich, T. A., Shankle, W. R., & Batchelder, W. H. (in press). A cognitive psychometric model for the psychodiagnostic assessment of memory-related deficits. *Psychological Assessment*.

Anders, R., & Batchelder, W. H. (2012). Cultural consensus theory for multiple consensus truths. *Journal of Mathematical Psychology, 56*, 452–469.

Anders, R., & Batchelder, W. H. (2015). Cultural consensus theory for the ordinal data case. *Psychometrika, 80*, 151–195.

Anders, R., Oravecz, Z., & Batchelder, W. H. (2014). Cultural consensus theory for continuous responses: A latent appraisal model for information pooling. *Journal of Mathematical Psychology, 61*, 1–13.

Anderson, J. R., Bothell, D., Lebiere, C., & Matessa, M. (1998). An integrative theory of list memory. *Journal of Memory & Language, 38*, 341–380.

Ashby, F. G., Maddox, W. T., & Lee, W. W. (1994). On the dangers of averaging across subjects when using multidimensional scaling or the similarity-choice model. *Psychological Science, 5*, 144–151.

Batchelder, W. H. (1975). Individual differences in the all or none and incremental learning controversy. *Journal of Mathematical Psychology, 12*, 53–74.

Batchelder, W. H. (1998). Multinomial processing tree models and psychological assessment. *Psychological Assessment, 10*, 331–344.

Batchelder, W. H. (2000). Mathematical psychology. In A. E. Kazdin (Ed.), *Encyclopedia of psychology*. Washington, DC: American Psychological Association and Oxford University Press.

Batchelder, W. H. (2009). Cognitive psychometrics: Using multinomial processing tree models as measurement tools. In S. E. Embretson (Ed.), *Measuring psychological constructs: Advances in model based measurement* (pp. 71–93). Washington DC: American Psychological Association Books.

Batchelder, W. H. (2010). Mathematical psychology. In L. Nadel (Ed.), *Wiley interdisciplinary reviews: Cognitive sciences* (pp. 759–765). New York: Wiley.

Batchelder, W. H. (2015). Mathematical psychology: History. In J. D. Wright (Ed.), *Encyclopedia of social and behavioral sciences* (2nd ed., Vol. 6, pp. 808–815). Oxford: Elsevier.

Batchelder, W. H., & Alexander, G. A. (2013). Discrete-state models: Comments on Pazzaglia, Dube, & Rotello (2013). *Psychological Bulletin, 139*, 1204–1212.

Batchelder, W. H., & Anders, R. (2012). Cultural consensus theory: Comparing different concepts of cultural truth. *Journal of Mathematical Psychology, 56*, 316–332.

Batchelder, W. H., & Bershad, N. J. (1979). The statistical analysis of a Thurstonian model for rating chess players. *Journal of Mathematical Psychology, 19*, 39–60.

Batchelder, W. H., Bershad, N. J., & Simpson, R. S. (1992). Dynamic paired-comparison scaling. *Journal of Mathematical Psychology, 36*, 185–212.

Batchelder, W. H., Chosak-Reiter, J., Shankle, W. R., & Dick, M. B. (1997). A multinomial modeling analysis of memory deficits in Alzheimer's and vascular dementia. *Journal of Gerontology: Psychological Sciences, 52B*, 206–215.

Batchelder, W. H., & Riefer, D. M. (1999). Theoretical and empirical review of multinomial process tree modeling. *Psychonomic Bulletin & Review, 6*, 57–86.

Batchelder, W. H., & Riefer, D. M. (2007). Using multinomial processing tree models to measure cognitive deficits in clinical populations. In R. W. J. Neufeld (Ed.), *Advances in clinical cognitive sciences: Formal models and assessment of processes and symptoms* (pp. 19–50). Washington, DC: APA Books.

Batchelder, W. H., & Romney, A. K. (1986). The statistical analysis of a general Condorcet model for dichotomous choice situations. In B. Grofman & G. Owen (Eds.), *Information pooling and group decision making: Proceedings of the second University of California, Irvine conference on political economy* (p. 103?–111). Greenwich, Conn: JAI Press.

Batchelder, W. H., & Romney, A. K. (1988). Test theory without an answer key. *Psychometrika, 53*, 71–92.

Boring, E. G. (1950). *A history of experimental psychology* (2nd edition). New York: Appleton-Century-Crofts, Inc.

Chechile, R. A. (2007). A model-based storage retrieval analysis of developmental dyslexia. In R. W. J. Neufeld (Ed.), *Advances in clinical cognitive sciences: Formal models and assessment of processes and symptoms* (chap. 2). Washington, DC: APA Books.

Chu, L. W., Chiu, K. C., Hui, S. L., Yu, G. K., Tsui, W. J., & Lee, P. W. (2000). The reliability and validity of the Alzheimer's Disease Assessment Scale Cognitive Subscale (ADAS-Cog) among elderly Chinese in Hong Kong. *Annals of the Academy of Medicine, Singapore, 29*, 474–485.

Clark, S. E., & Grondlund, S. D. (1996). Global matching models of recognition memory: How the models match the data. *Psychonomic Bulletin & Review, 3*, 37–60.

Cronbach, L. J. (1957). The two disciplines of scientific psychology. *American Psychologist, 12*, 671–684.

Darwin, C. (1859). *On the origin of the species by means of natural selection.* London: Muray.

Darwin, C. (1871). *The descent of man.* London: Muray.

Darwin, C. (1872). *The expressions of emotions in man and animals.* New York: Oxford University Press (original work published 1872).

DePulseau, B. W., Aßfalg, A., Erdfelder, E., & Bernstein, D. M. (2012). Extracting the truth from conflicting eyewitness reports: A formal modeling approach. *Journal of Experimental Psychology: Applied, 18*, 390–403.

Elo, A. E. (1978). *The rating of chessplayers, past and present.* New York: Arco.

Embretson, S. E., & Reise, S. P. (2000). *Item response theory for psychologists.* Mahwah, NJ: Lawrence Erlbaum Associates.

Erdfelder, E., Auer, T.-S., Hilbig, B. E., Assalg, A., Moshagen, M., & Nadarevic, L. (2009). Multinomial processing tree models: A review of the literature. *Zeitschrift für Psychologie, 217*, 108–124.

Estes, W. K. (1960). Learning theory and the new mental chemistry. *Psychological Review, 67*, 207–223.

Fillenbaum, G. G., van Belle, G., Morris, J. C., Mohs, R. C., Mirra, S. S., Davis, P. C., ... others (2008). Consortium to establish a registry for Alzheimer's disease (cerad): The first twenty years. *Alzheimer's & Dementia, 4*(2), 96–109.

Fischer, G. H., & Molenaar, I. W. (1995). *Rasch models: Foundations, recent developments and applications*. New York: Springer-Verlag.

France, S. L., & Batchelder, W. H. (2014). Unsupervised consensus analysis for on-line review and questionnaire data. *Information Sciences, 283*, 241–257.

France, S. L., & Batchelder, W. H. (2015). Maximum likelihood item easiness models for test theory without an answer key. *Educational and Psychological Measurement, 75*, 57–77.

Greeno, J. G., & Bjork, R. A. (1973). Mathematical learning theory and the new "mental forestry." *Annual Review of Psychology, 24*, 81–116.

Hergenhahn, B. R. (2001). *An introduction to the history of psychology* (4th ed.). Belmont, CA: Wadsworth/Thomson Learning.

Hilgard, E. R., & Bower, G. H. (1966). *Theories of learning*, 3rd edition. New York: Appleton-Century-Crofts.

Hintzman, D. L. (1980). Simpson's paradox and the analysis of memory retrieval. *Psychological Review, 87*, 398–410.

Hintzman, D. L., & Hartry, A. L. (1990). Item effects in recognition and fragment completion: Contingency relations vary for different subsets of words. *Journal of Experimental Psychology: Learning, Memory, & Cognition, 16*, 955–969.

Hu, X., & Batchelder, W. H. (1994). The statistical analysis of general processing tree models with the EM algorithm. *Psychometrika, 59*, 21–47.

Humphreys, M. S., Pike, R., Bain, J. A., & Tehan, G. (1989). Global matching: A comparison of the SAM, MINERVA II, MATRIX, and TODAM models. *Journal of Mathematical Psychology, 33*, 36–67.

Keefe, R. S. E., Arnold, M. C., Bayen, U. J., & Harvey, P. D. (1999). Source monitoring deficits in patients with schizophrenia: A multinomial modeling analysis. *Psychological Medicine, 29*, 903–914.

Kellen, D., Klauer, K. C., & Bröder, A. (2013). Recognition memory and binary response ROC: A comparison by minimum description length. *Psychological Bulletin & Review, 20*, 693–719.

Klauer, K. C. (2010). Hierarchical multinomial processing tree models: A latent trait approach. *Psychometrika, 75*, 70–98.

Lee, M. D., & Wagenmakers, E.-J. (2013). *Bayesian modeling for cognitive science: A practical course*. Cambridge: Cambridge University Press.

Lord, F. M., & Novick, M. R. (1968). *Statistical theories of mental test scores*. Reading, MA: Addison-Wesley.

MacMillan, N. A., & Creelman, C. D. (2005). *Detection theory: A users guide* (2nd edition). Mahwah, NJ: Lawrence Erlbaum Associates.

Matzke, D., Dolan, C., Batchelder, W. H., & Wagenmakers, E.-J. (2015). Bayesian estimation of multinomial processing tree models with heterogeneity in participants and items. *Psychometrika, 80*, 205–235.

Nitzoufras, I. (2009). *Bayesian modeling using WinBUGS*. Hoboken NJ: Wiley.

Oravecz, Z., Anders, R., & Batchelder, W. H. (2015). Hierarchical bayesian modeling for test theory without and answer key. *Psychometrika, 80*, 341–364.

Oravecz, Z., Faust, K., & Batchelder, W. H. (2014). An extended cultural consensus theory model to account for cognitive processes in decision making in social surveys. *Sociological Methodology, 26*, 185–228.

Pazzaglia, A., Dube, C., & Rotello, C. (2013). A critical comparison of discrete-state and continuous models of recognition memory: Implications for recognition memory and beyond. *Psychological Bulletin, 139*, 1173–1202.

Plummer, M. (2003). JAGS: A program for analysis of Bayesian graphical models using Gibbs sampling. In *Proceedings of the 3rd international workshop on distributed statistical computing (dsc 2003)*. Vienna, Austria.

Porter, T. M. (1986). *The rise of statistical thinking 1820-1900*. Princeton, NJ: Princeton University Press.

Rasch, G. (1960). *Probabilistic models for some intelligence and attainment tests*. Copenhagen: Danmarks Paedagogishe Institut.

Ratcliff, R. (1978). A theory of memory retrieval. *Psychological Review, 85*, 59–108.

Ratcliff, R., Thapar, A., & McKoon, G. (2010). Individual differences and aging, and IQ in two-choice tasks. *Cognitive Psychology, 60*, 127–157.

Ratcliff, R., & Van Dongen, H. P. (2009). Sleep deprivation affects multiple distinct cognitive processes. *Psychonomic Bulletin & Review, 16*, 742–751.

Riefer, D. M., & Batchelder, W. H. (1988). Multinomial modeling and the measurement of cognitive processes. *Psychological Review, 95*, 318–339.

Riefer, D. M., & Batchelder, W. H. (1991). Age differences in storage and retrieval: A multinomial modeling analysis. *Bulletin of the Psychonomic Society, 29*, 415–418.

Riefer, D. M., Knapp, B. R., Batchelder, W. H., Bamber, D., & Manifold, V. (2002). Cognitive psychometrics: Assessing storage and retrieval deficits in special populations with multinomial processing tree models. *Psychological Assessment, 14*, 184–201.

Romney, A. K., & Batchelder, W. H. (1999). Cultural consensus theory. In F. Keil & R. Wilson (Eds.), *The MIT encyclopedia of the cognitive sciences* (pp. 208–209). Cambridge, MA: The MIT Press.

Romney, A. K., Weller, S. C., & Batchelder, W. H. (1986). Culture as consensus: A theory of culture and informant accuracy. *American Anthropologist, 88*, 313–338.

Rouder, J. N., Lu, J., Sun, D., Speckman, P., Morey, R., & Naveh-Benjamin, M. (2007). Signal detection models with random participant and item effects. *Psychometrika, 72*, 621–642.

Rumelhart, D. E., McClelland, J. L., & the PDP Research Group (1986). *Parallel distributed processing: Explorations in the microstructure of cognition. vol 1. foundations*. Cambridge, MA: MIT Press.

Smith, J., & Batchelder, W. H. (2008). Assessing individual differences in categorical data. *Psychonomic Bulletin & Review, 15*, 713–731.

Smith, J. B., & Batchelder, W. H. (2010). Beta-MPT: Multinomial processing tree models for addressing individual differences. *Journal of Mathematical Psychology, 54*, 167–183.

Smith, R. E., & Bayen, U. J. (2006). The source of adult age differences in prospective memory: A multinomial modeling approach. *Journal of Experimental Psychology: Learning, Memory, and Cognition, 32*, 623–635.

Spearman, C. (1904). General intelligence objectively determined and measured. *American Journal of Psychology, 15*, 201–293.

Stigler, S. M. (1986). *The history of statistics: The measurement of uncertainty before 1900*. Cambridge, MA: Harvard University Press.

Thurstone, L. L. (1927). The law of comparative judgment. *Psychological Review, 34*, 273–286.

Weller, S. C. (2007). Cultural consensus theory: Applications and frequently asked questions. *Field Methods, 19*, 339–368.

White, C. N., Ratcliff, R., Vasey, M. W., & McKoon, G. (2010). Using diffusion models to understand clinical disorders. *Journal of Mathematical Psychology, 54*, 39–52.

Wickens, T. D. (1982). *Models for behavior: Stochastic processes in psychology*. San Francisco, CA: Freeman and Company.

Index

Alexandrov Topology 48, 50, 52–3, 55, 63
arborescence 72–4
attention 113, 125, 129–34, 143, 155–7, 159–61, 163–5, 167, 171, 192, 259–60; selective attention 114, 141, 143, 171–90, 197, 202–4, 247
attentional *see* attention
attribute-wise models 154–60, 164–5, 167–8

behavioral learning theory 245, 249–51
binary choice *see* choice
Borel sets 49

capacity 77, 79–80, 86, 100, 114–15, 144; limited capacity 79, 135
categorization 81, 86, 201, 250, 253, 259
choice 141–2, 144, 153, 158, 160, 167, 250, 259–60; intertemporal choice 152–7, 161–5
class 14, 49, 56, 66; parent 14–15, 31
classification 86, 174, 185–6, 200–1, 204, 208, 251
clustering 237; coefficient of variation 132–4
cognitive models 77, 86–7, 100, 245–6, 249–52, 256–62
cognitive psychometrics 245–6, 257–9, 262
collinearity 128–9, 141
comparability graph 70–3
comparable *see* ordered processes
complexity 86, 115, 141, 164, 227, 236–7
conditional independence 16–18, 27, 253–5
configural 63

conservation laws 225, 230, 238–9
context 47, 49, 58, 63, 109, 114, 116, 118, 129, 142, 190
context effects *see* context
context invariance 107, 109, 137, 141
contextual factors *see* context
contrast ratio 134
correspondence 107, 110, 113, 117, 124, 126, 138–9, 191, 231, 242
Cultural Consensus Theory 261
cumulative distribution function *see* distribution

decisional separability 175–82, 188, 199–210
decision bounds 176, 198–9, 202
Decision Field Theory (DFT) 156, 161–6
decision making 87, 108, 130, 242, 250
deduction 21, 24
delay discounting 153–4, 163
depth 120–1, 123, 125–8, 130, 138–9, 174
differential structure 120–1, 125
discrimination 115, 119, 130, 132–4, 138–9, 145, 173, 191, 251
dispersive order 39
distance-based decision process 202–8, 212
distribution 23, 37–45, 99, 111, 135–6, 141, 144, 158–61, 167, 175–7, 197, 200, 206–8, 210–19, 258; beta 43–4; bivariate normal 158, 175–6, 208, 248; Cauchy 41, 43; exponential 41, 99; Kumaraswamy 43–4; logistic 41, 158, 167; log-Normal 160; normal 158, 159–60, 162, 175–6, 208, 258; response time

37, 136, 145, 160, 164, 167, 197, 200, 206–8; Weibull 40–1, 43
divided attention *see* attention
double factorial 83–4, 98
double high threshold model (DHT) 254–7
d-prime (d') 133, 177, 180, 188, 191
dynamic model 152, 163–4

Elo Chess Rating Model 258
entailment 20–1, 23, 25, 30–3
equivalence 26, 49, 50–1, 54, 56, 166, 224
Euclidean 127–8, 140, 145, 199, 203, 231–2, 236
exceptional subclass 14–15, 31, 33–4
extreme order statistic 40–1

field (mathematical) 48, 119, 126
field (visual) 127
filtering 185–6, 188, 200–1, 206; filtering test 200
forced-choice *see* choice
Formal Concept Analysis 48
full-factorial design 85, 90, 92, 95

Garner effects 172–3, 175, 178, 180–1, 184–92, 200
Garner interference *see* Garner effects
Generalizations 13
General Recognition Theory (GRT) 172, 174, 197
Gestalt 63, 226–7, 239, 241
graph 47, 56, 69–74

hazard function 37, 135–6
hazard rate *see* hazard function
Hidden Markov Chain Model 261
hypergraph 47, 57

ideal-observer 14; I 73, 81, 87
identification 114, 137, 143, 144, 173, 176, 179–80, 182, 186, 198–9, 208
image 109–10, 116–17, 119–29, 137–9, 145, 228, 230–6, 241–2
imperfect rules *see* rules
incomparable *see* unordered processes
information 16, 32, 37, 47, 49, 58, 61, 68, 72, 82, 107–45, 166, 171–5, 186, 192–3, 200, 227, 236, 239
information processing 108, 135, 141, 144, 175, 193

inheritance 14–15, 31, 34
interaction contrast 82, 84, 91–2
invariance 107, 117–18, 130, 136–41, 191, 206, 225, 230, 238; context invariance 107, 141–2; marginal response invariance 177, 179–82, 187–8; observational invariance 140
invariance structure *see* invariance
irrelevant variation 179, 185, 188–9, 191

least-action principle 225–7, 230–9
Luce's Choice Theory 144

manifold 2-D 110, 120
mean absolute deviation around median (MAD) 42
mean-shift integrality 180, 207, 210, 214
measurement 107, 117–18, 134, 137, 172, 176–7, 186, 245, 247–8, 251, 258; functional measurement 187–8
memory 65, 79, 81, 86, 88, 94, 114, 134, 144, 242, 247, 250–7, 262; recognition memory 256, 260; short-term memory 78; working memory 114–15
mental architecture 89, 165–6, 197, 219–20; parallel architecture 65, 67, 74, 77–80, 86–7, 89, 90, 92–102, 135, 141, 144, 165–6, 197, 215; serial architecture 65–8, 77–80, 85–6, 92–102, 135, 143, 165–6, 211, 213, 215
mental networks *see* mental architecture
Michelson contrast *see* contrast ratio
mild cognitive impairment 262
model selection 80, 100
motion 109, 114, 119, 125–6, 128–9, 136–9, 237
multinomial processing tree 65–74, 250, 259

Noether's Theorem 230
noise 131, 145, 163, 181, 198, 233
non-parametric model testing 77, 80, 256

observation 37, 107, 112, 117, 177, 203
observational invariance *see* invariance

optimal 204, 237; optimal decision 197, 201, 207, 215, 218; optimal response (*see* optimal decision)
order 37, 41, 47–64, 66, 77, 80, 81, 115, 118, 125, 165, 206, 257; convex order 38; dilation order 38, 40; dispersive order 39; Lorenz order 38; stochastic order 37, 80, 88
ordered processes 67–8, 70

parallel classification 201
parallel process *see* mental architecture
perceptual decision making *see* decision making
perceptual independence 141–2, 171–9, 191, 198, 206, 208
perceptual representation *see* representation
perceptual separability 175–91, 198, 200, 206, 218
perimetric complexity *see* complexity
perturbation 138–9, 145
precision 131
prior knowledge 114, 116, 142, 144
probabilistic models 154–5, 157, 159–66, 168, 252
processing capacity *see* capacity
processing order 77, 84, 87–8, 95, 99
process stretching 87
propositional calculus 18–19
prospective task 155
psychological space *see* mental representations
psychophysics 108, 119, 131, 133–4, 144, 247
pure stretching method 80, 86

quantile function 38–9, 41, 43–4
quantile spread 40, 43; quantile spread order 42

Rasch model 253, 255–7
reaction time *see* response time
reasoning 13–14, 18, 20, 26, 32–3
relational structure *see* structure
relations 26, 37, 47, 49–52, 56, 58–9, 63, 73, 107, 115, 118, 125, 128–30, 136, 140, 225, 237, 241
representation 109–10, 117, 142, 198, 201, 226, 229; mental representation 233

representational theory of measurement 118
resolution 107, 115, 117, 125, 130–4, 138
response selection 212, 260
response time (RT) 78, 82–3, 88, 101, 134–5, 154, 159–60, 164, 166–8, 197–208, 212, 219, 250, 259–60
retinal image 120, 126–9, 137, 138, 228, 230, 232
ring (mathematical) 48
risky choice *see* choice
RT-distance hypothesis 199–201, 211
rules 13–34, 109

same-different judgment 197, 201–8
second-order probability logic 18
selection 173, 175, 179, 181
selective attention *see* attention
selective influence 67, 78, 80
serial architecture *see* mental architecture
serial classification 201
serial-parallel networks 77, 95, 101
set theory 47
shape 107, 110–11, 114, 118, 120–8, 131, 137–9, 142, 171, 178–9, 188, 224, 228, 230–1, 233–8, 241–3; shape of a function 40, 79, 88–9, 93, 95–100, 135, 212, 215; shape parameter 44
short-term memory *see* memory
Signal Detection Theory (SDT) 111, 131, 137, 144, 175, 199–200, 223; multidimensional signal detection theory 197
simple interaction test 90
space 19, 52, 59, 101, 109, 114, 123, 126–9, 137, 139–42, 175–7, 186, 198, 201–3, 218, 224, 232–8, 242
spatiotemporal 107, 109–10, 114, 118–20, 137, 142
spatiotemporal continua 118–19
stimulus complexity *see* complexity
stopping rule 77, 84, 87–8, 92–102, 165–6, 219
Stroop effect 172, 175, 178, 181–92
structure 48–50, 74, 78, 107, 109, 110, 114, 118, 120, 121, 122, 125–45, 167, 179, 183–4, 197, 206, 237, 247, 252–4; relational structures 47,

63, 107, 115–18, 128, 132, 134, 142
subclassification model 201–2, 204, 206–15
subnetworks 93–9, 101
subset system 47–64; chained subset system 62
surface 107, 110–11, 114, 120–7, 131, 138–42, 184, 229, 239
symbol 19–20, 30, 107, 109–10, 141
symbolic representation *see* representation
symmetry 28, 42, 49–50, 125, 136, 210, 225–6, 228–43
Systems Factorial Technology (SFT) 77, 80–102

tolerance relation 49–50, 53, 56–8

Transitive Orientation Algorithm 68–71
tree 65–6, 69, 72–4, 259
Turing test 223

Uncertainty 111, 132, 144, 208
unordered processes 67–8

variability 33, 37, 40, 44, 112, 131, 145, 154, 157–60, 164, 188, 198, 204
veridical perception 236
visual search 81, 87, 114, 134, 144

Weber fraction 133–4, 145
working memory *see* memory
workload capacity *see* capacity